ON THE BARRICADES OF BERLIN

August Heinrich Brass
1818-1876

Every historical account of this revolution is a narrative that will reveal somehow the political position of the historian who offers it. The way in which Weiland challenges the dominant liberal narrative is astonishingly well documented and convincing. His analysis successfully deconstructs the "progressive" self-image of the German liberal bourgeoisie that thought it would profit from a revolution that succeeded in '48 primarily due to the sacrifices made by courageous men and women of the working class.

... [T]he style and the tone of the book are inspiring, and I hope that the inspiration that moved the three authors, August Brass, Peter Light, and Andreas Weiland, can motivate the reader to think in a deeper and harder way about the present necessity to question a status quo that, as such, features many elements that should cause at least as much resistance as the situation in 1848 happened to cause in Berlin. If we remain onlookers today, not unlike so many saturated Germans in '48, would this not be conducive to the disintegration of the social fabric and the ecological devastation of the planet? This question is posed implicitly in the book.

Dr. Magdi Youssef
Professor of Comparative Literature and Culture Studies
University of Bonn

I have read The Barricades of Berlin with great attention, especially as we see again, today, barricades in France: formed by stuff provided by consumer society–burning car tires, smashed things taken from expensive stores at the Champs-Élysées and broken by "left-wing" and "right-wing" folks, by workers, the unemployed, and students, all angry with the neoliberal establishment.

Both the eyewitness report by August Brass, an activist in the March Revolution of 1848 that shook Berlin, Prussia and Germany, and the thoughtful, elaborate commentary on it by Andreas Weiland are well worth reading.

Pavel Branko
film critic and author of *Against the Current*,
and *In the Morning I wake up, surprised at not being dead*

ON THE BARRICADES OF BERLIN

An Account of the 1848 Revolution

August Brass

Translated and edited by
Andreas Weiland with Peter Light

Montréal/Chicago/London

Copyright © 2021 Black Rose Books

Thank you for purchasing this Black Rose Books publication. No part of this book may be reproduced or transmitted in any form, by any means electronic or mechanical including photocopying and recording, or by any information storage or retrieval system–without written permission from the publisher, or, in the case of photocopying or other reprographic copying, a license from the Canadian Copyright Licensing Agency, Access Copyright, with the exception of brief passages quoted by a reviewer in a newspaper or magazine. If you acquired an illicit electronic copy of this book, please consider making a donation to Black Rose Books.

Black Rose Books No. TT404

Library and Archives Canada Cataloguing in Publication

Title: On the barricades of Berlin : an account of the 1848 revolution / August Brass ; translated by Andreas Weiland ; foreword by Peter Light.
Other titles: Berlin's Barrikaden. English
Names: Brass, August, 1818-1876, author. | Weiland, Andreas, 1944- translator. | Light, Peter, 1943- writer of foreword.
Description: Translation of: Berlin's Barrikaden, Ihre Entstehung, ihre Verteidigung und ihre Folgen.
Identifiers: Canadiana (print) 2019008099X | Canadiana (ebook) 20190082437 | ISBN 9781551647081 (hardcover) | ISBN 9781551647104 (softcover) | ISBN 9781551647128 (PDF)
Subjects: LCSH: Brass, August, 1818-1876. | LCSH: Berlin (Germany)—History—Revolution, 1848-1849. | LCSH: Berlin (Germany)—History—Revolution, 1848-1849—Personal narratives.
Classification: LCC DD876 .B7313 2019 | DDC 943/.155074—dc23

C.P.35788 Succ. Léo-Pariseau
Montréal, QC, H2X 0A4
Canada

Explore our books and subscribe to our newsletter:
www.blackrosebooks.com

Ordering Information

USA/INTERNATIONAL	CANADA	UK/IRELAND
University of Chicago Press Chicago Distribution Center 11030 South Langley Avenue Chicago, IL 60628	University of Toronto Press 5201 Dufferin Street Toronto, ON M3H 5T8	Central Books 50 Freshwater Road Chadwell Heath, London RM8 1RX
(800) 621-2736 (USA) (773) 702-7000 (International) orders@press.uchicago.edu	1-800-565-9523 utpbooks@utpress.utoronto.ca	+44 (0) 20 8525 8800 contactus@centralbooks.com

CONTENTS

Acknowledgements 6
Foreword by Peter Light 7
Introduction by Andreas Weiland 9

The Barricades of Berlin by August Brass

    Preface 29
    Part I: Start of 1848 to March 11: Thunderclouds on the Horizon 32
    Part II: March 12-17: The Course is Set 52
    Part III: Friday, March 17: The Turning Point 76
    Interlude: A Personal Moment of Memory and Emotion 81
    Part IV: Afternoon, March 18: To the Barricades! 83
    Part V: Evening, March 18th: The Second Phase of the Fighting 108
    Part VI: Night, March 18-19: The Third Phase of the Fighting 111
    Part VII: Morning, March 19: The Red Dawn of Freedom 116
    Part VIII: March 19: Peace! Peace! 120
    Part IX: Morning, March 20: Liberation of the Polish Prisoners 127
    Part X: March 21: The King Rides the Streets 131
    Part XI: March 22: The Funeral 134
    Part XII: March 22: Closing Words of Wisdom and Inspiration 139

The March Revolution: A Botched Revolution? by Andreas Weiland 143
Epilogue by Andreas Weiland 332
Last Words by Peter Light 344
August Heinrich Brass 352

ACKNOWLEDGEMENTS

I wish to thank my old classmate and life-long friend Angelo (Fred) Evelyn for introducing me to the translator of this book, Andreas Weiland; and, of course, Andreas himself, from the bottom of my heart, who has persevered with this work through many delays and tribulations, and who has done such a wonderful job of revealing what had been hidden from me and my family lineage of nineteen living Brass descendants, bringing to life so well this voice from another time and place.

- Peter Light

FOREWORD

by PETER LIGHT

I first heard of August Brass while growing up in Vancouver, Canada, in the 1940s and 50s. I later learned that he died in 1876 at the age of fifty-eight when his daughter Gertrude—my father's mother—was but nine years old. This notwithstanding, my father, born in Berlin, Germany in 1903, remembers his mother saying, "Ach, Gunter, you are so much like your Grandpa Brass."

From my father I had learned that this great-grandfather of mine, August Heinrich Brass, had "fought behind the barricades" during the "failed" 1848 German Revolution; had held off the King's army for two days; was forced to flee to Switzerland; was pardoned by the Kaiser, Otto von Bismarck, who became his "personal friend;" had founded a daily newspaper which he put at the service of the Kaiser's government; and then, disillusioned with the Kaiser's policies, resigned and started his own, independent newspaper.

I subsequently verified that all this information was a more or less accurate oral transmission in accord with the historical record.

I first discovered, with growing wonder and excitement as I began to explore my genealogy in 1999, that there actually was a historical record. I learned that Brass was a well-known literary figure of his time; that he was also a personal friend of Karl Marx; that he hadn't just *fought* behind the barricades, but had *led* part of the fight; that he and a fellow revolutionary have had a monument erected in their honor—in 1999, in Alexanderplatz (Alexander Square)—for fighting the soldiers under the command of general Johann Karl von Möllendorff to a stand-still there; and that—wonder of wonders—he had actually written a book about it entitled "Berlin's Barrikaden, Ihre Entstehung, ihre Vertheidigung und ihre Folgen. Eine Geschichte der Märzrevolution." I learned later from a scholar of German history—my translator and editor, Andreas Weiland—that this book is most likely the earliest extensive first-person account of the March Revolution known to exist—completed and to the publisher just twelve days after one hundred and eighty-three dead "fighters of the people" were put into the ground.

Increasingly gripped by the manuscript as it emerged in English for the first time, and as the vivid story I was reading unfolded and built to its climax, there was no greater moment for me than when my own personal history, my family lore, the written word before me, and visual imagery came together and to life as I found myself reading the personal accounts by my great-grandfather of the battle in Alexander—and of the funeral which followed—while viewing, at the same time, dramatic paintings realistically depicting the very scenes being described. These moments set the stage for the shiver of wonder I experienced as I first read—one hundred and sixty-four years after they were written—the words chosen by August Brass to end his memoir:

"May our offspring never forget how dearly we paid for our and their freedom; may they know how to preserve this good dearly paid for!"

Perhaps obtaining this book, having it translated into English, and having it published is part of my preservation of that good.

Peter Light
Roberts Creek, B.C. Canada
June 2012

INTRODUCTION

by ANDREAS WEILAND

The German Revolution of 1848–49 was a key event in German and perhaps European history. That it failed is a fact. That it had to fail is by no means certain. It was a potential turning point in history, with perhaps great prospects. Certainly, its failure made it a turning point of sorts in a negative sense. Without its defeat, there would have been no prolongation of the reactionary role of Prussia, of Prussian kings, and other kings and princes in German lands; the stifling political climate following the defeat of Napoleonic France would have ended in Central Europe; Polish independence might have become possible; and without the continued dominance of a militaristic aristocratic stratum—above all, in Prussia—there would probably have been no basis for the Franco-German War of 1870-71 and perhaps, for that very reason, also no readiness to go to war in 1914. Of course, these are dreams, for history took a different course. It is all the more interesting to study why the revolution in March 1848, seemingly successful, according to August Brass' account, failed—and failed at the decisive moment in the capital of the economically and politically, as well as militarily, dominant Prussia, whose army went on to finish off the revolution in the rest of Germany, after having vanquished it in Berlin.

There is, however, another reason why we should study the events of the March Revolution, and, especially, look closely at the account of August Brass, an idealistic democrat, valiant and full of hopes, who certainly desired a freer Prussia and Germany and who, though no radical or even, really, a socialist, certainly was full of empathetic solidarity towards "the people"—the sons and perhaps sometimes also the daughters of the *subaltern classes* (to use an expression preferred by Gramsci in his prison writings), men who defended the barricades against the Prussian army and brave women who aided insurgent fighters. This reason for studying the events that took place in March is no longer purely academic or a matter of a perhaps nostalgic or grieving look at a now seemingly distant past. It concerns the present and it concerns the future, for many strategies and many treacherous tricks of the dominant classes, of the military and political leaders, have not changed as much as we might be inclined to believe. And the class structure of society, despite its apparent changes and modifications, persists as a class structure. The population today is divided, as it was then, and it is so, in this or that way, regardless of whether we direct our attention to the situation in Germany, the U.S., Spain, Greece, Brazil, or Egypt.

Peter Light, an activist within the Canadian peace movement many years ago,[1] and a committed theorist and practitioner of permaculture as well as an amateur genealogist today, is the one who rediscovered—in an attempt to throw more light on the sociocultural roots of his free-thinking, out-spoken, anti-war, -church and -Queen, and democratically committed father—the book written by his great-grandfather, August Brass. This initially was certainly for his own benefit and inspiration, but he soon decided that it might also be an inspiration to others.

Peter Light, permaculture homesteader

It is he who alerted me to the existence of this book—something I am deeply thankful for. It is, no doubt, a valuable book, both in view of what Brass, not just a fighter on the barricades, but a participant observer, described and recognized; and in terms of what the book reveals that is more than Brass himself was able to see and comprehend.

But if we read the book in a way that lets us take many things that Brass says at face value, and this despite the awareness that 1848 and 1849 became known later on as years of a *failed* revolution, we will not be able to draw the proper conclusions from the lessons that this short period of German history, this short period of a seemingly *successful* revolution, might offer to us. One thing is quite certain: the reader should not remain unaware of accounts by other key actors in these events, accounts and statements written in part in 1848-1850, but not always published then and not known to Brass when he wrote his book. As they are available today to historians, they must be consulted in order to get a clearer idea of the contradictions that continued to exist in those days of revolution, persisting to a huge degree in spite of it, glossed over only by talk about reconciliation, and overshadowed by illusions about a 'good' king and an undivided population enflamed by a spirit of brotherhood.

But even a careful reading of Brass's book provides enough hints, and alludes to such facts, that should make the reader shy away from the final euphoric feelings that Brass expressed at the very moment when his account celebrates "peace," the withdrawal of the army, the "concessions" of the king, and a supposed "arming of the people," in the aftermath of a revolutionary struggle after many hours of intense street fighting.

Something else is essential for an evaluation of the events recounted and interpreted by Brass. Just as much as we should study the period described by our author, we must be aware of the days and months that *followed* the period covered by Brass. Focusing on the situation in Berlin (and the Prussian context), I am thinking of such days as March 20, March 23, March 25, March 26, March 27, March 30 and March 31, of the days of April and early May, and certainly of the days of June that found a climax on June 14, 1848. It is in these days that the polarization existing in the city—that had been briefly noticed by August Brass occasionally in his account, only to be glossed over by him and by others, and shoved aside, in a spirit of reconciliation—became sharply apparent, as things happened that might have preannounced a potential "second revolution" in Berlin and Prussia, and a possible victory of the "people's cause."

But perhaps the chance that this might have happened was a slim one, and we must ask ourselves, "'why?" History at least proceeded in another way; mistake after mistake was committed, defeat after defeat occurred. Despite large demonstrations and important popular assemblies held in those days, despite correct demands uttered, and skirmishes and armed confrontations, the relations of forces remained undecided; finally, the scales were tipped in favor of the "reaction," and the predictable—but not immediately possible—counterrevolution finally happened on November 8, 1848 in the capital of Prussia, Berlin, and thus in the rest of Prussia. In many ways, the victory of the reaction in this important German state made it very difficult, if not almost impossible, to avoid the final defeat of the revolution in southwestern Germany in the following year, a defeat due to the resurfaced military might of the Prussian monarchy.

As this is not the occasion for a detailed exposition of these matters, I will provide only this sketchy outline of my thoughts and reservations with regard to an optimistic reading of the eventful days of the March Revolution in Berlin that are presented in the book offered here (a book that has now been translated for the first time into English) *as a time of great triumph of the revolutionaries* while in fact, unnoticed by idealistic men like August Brass, the seeds of defeat were planted at a decisive moment in the period Brass describes. We may ask ourselves whether men like Brass, a courageous fighter, a liberal democrat, and writer of "red songs" that revealed his sympathies for the working poor, were not blind to this, and whether such blindness and the readiness to forgive, to seek reconciliation and compromise, and to protect the monarch and the monarchy that had just been battled and defeated, did not contribute to this as well.

In a letter to Peter Light, I tried to put what had happened in those days in context, certainly a contemporary context. It was an attempt to reflect on the difficult, material and politico-economical and socio-cultural—and thus also ideological—conditions that characterized and still characterize the dangers and chances of attempts to effect radical political and social change. Having mentioned the October Revolution and the difficulties the revolutionaries in Russia had to cope with, and having also sketched the sequence of successes and failures of an initially revolutionary society coveted by those who aimed at equality and democracy, I wrote:

> Come to think of it, I see no country on earth that is emancipated or where citizens are in charge, rather than being 'led' in this or that way. I see attempts to walk in a direction that might lead to more civil rights, more social and economic freedom, thus equality, not just so-called "(formally equal) chances to succeed." It hurts when you see these attempts squashed, stifled, aborted—in various ways. What have they done to the Soviet Union when they encircled it during the civil war—the French, British, Japanese—with their expedition corps, their armies in Russia (and America looked on approvingly)? What did they do to Spain in the 1930s, to Greece since 1945, to Brazil when João Goulart was president, to Chile under Allende? To Nicaragua, Guatemala, El Salvador? How many interventions were there in Mexico during the 20th century? Why was Lumumba murdered—and by whom?—and Thomas Sankara? Why was the first Algerian president ousted (Ben Bella)?

> And did not China desire peace after the civil war ended in 1949, and still had to send her soldiers to Korea?[2] It was the South Korean dictatorship that professed an officially declared policy of attacking the North (when the moment would be ripe)—much like Chiang Kai-shek reiterated his readiness to 'reconquer' the mainland.[3] And then it is also interesting to note that the bloody repression on Cheju Island and in quite a few cities in the Southwesterly part of Korea's mainland predated the outbreak of the civil war only by days and months. The North did attack the bloodily repressive South Korean dictatorship, it is true, and it was a regime that I would call Stalinist today, but its president had been a fighter in the anti-Japanese resistance, and the effort of ordinary North Koreans—in the context of the Korean civil war—seems to have been due in large measure to their support of a regime they saw as patriotic, rather than consisting largely of former collaborators of colonialist Japan, installed by the U.S. occupation force.

> Koreans saw themselves not as aggressors in World War II, but as victims, and were right in this. They desired unity, a majority did so, probably, and still do, probably, in the North and the South. If the regime in the North was deficient (in my view) in various ways, it still was the only

regime that could genuinely claim to be patriotic rather than a puppet regime. Stalin, aware of Korean nationalism, had withdrawn the Soviet Russian occupation force from the North (something he did not dare to do in East Germany), although the American units were stationed in the South, and propped up the dictatorship of Syngman Rhee. Was it understandable that the North came to aid the uprising in the South, despite being wrong, perhaps, because it entailed the cost they had to pay for taking on the American army?[4] At any rate, the quest for justice, democracy, an end to American occupation, and structures of mutual help was suppressed in the South. Another failed revolution…Why?

As far as China is concerned, the repercussions were also considerable. Did it damage the idea that the common people had of their revolution? Did it damage the revolution when they intervened? In 1949, before the withdrawal of the last troops of the Guomindang, even daughters of rich rural landlords had heard that 'the people reported only good things about the 8th Route Army.' I know—I heard it from a woman whose mother, the daughter of such a rich landlord in Shandong, had told her daughter exactly that, in Taiwan during the 1960s. It is true, China did not want to get involved—neither the government nor the people desired to do so. Mao resisted when Stalin demanded that he must intervene,[5] but then gave in: they did not want American troops stationed right on the Chinese border. The initial flaw or 'sin' was the partition of innocent Korea—a result of a Great Power poker 'deal' that drew up a map with spheres of interest. Damn it! But that was the reality, after all. Had to be taken into account. The Greeks, when they fought Greek collaborators of Nazi occupiers in their homeland, also did not take the spheres of interest into account. They, too, suffered badly when the West intervened in the civil war.

Ah, Peter—is there no way to escape from what is never free of constraints, needs to be pragmatic, to a certain extent, when big powers play with the fate of people? Yes, with Cuba's people, too. A free and good beginning did not stay so good. Still, better in many ways than much else in Latin America. But when I see the new generation of non-elected leaders (or are they - *elected*, I mean—in Cuba's own, for me, strange way?), when I see them in their business suits, I ask whether I should let go of a lot of hopes still harbored against (perhaps) all reason. How obvious it is that economic constraints can enforce so much that runs counter to the ideals of equality and democracy!

Is that also why I want to return to the book written by August Brass? No—not in order to idealize him, or this revolution, but in order to point out the constraints, the facts, limitations inscribed in the class structure, the material interests, the ideological limitations of this insurgent citizenry, divided at the outset, largely united for a brief moment, and soon again conscious of divergent status, unequal status (in some cases connected with 'privilege'), of divergent interests. But even those who were democratic revolutionaries (without hesitation) were divided—was it because of unforgivable illusions about Frederick William? Was it because constitutional monarchists assessed the *rapport des forces* more accurately, thus more correctly, than the radical LIBERAL republicans (or even those few communist workers in Berlin who were members of the Bund der Kommunisten / Federation of Communists, a secret international organization of workers and craftsmen and intellectuals)?[6]

The army, the Prussian army, was beaten, or at least momentarily on the defensive, in *one* city, Berlin, but how many units were there in Prussia? And a killed or captive King would have been easily replaced by the King's brother, the Prince of Prussia, whom the revolutionaries unforgivably let flee and relocate to Potsdam, the other Royal residence besides Berlin, and then, via Hamburg, to Britain.[7] Still, it is clear that even with the most combative brother of the King taken hostage, there would have been others next in line. Still, it is clear that the King and the monarchy were on the defensive, tremendously weakened, and that the situation was ripe for perhaps radical, democratic change.[8]

…

What made the army switch sides from the King to the populace in France during the course of events in 1789? And why did the peasantry rise up in revolt, why did they set the *chateaus* of the aristocracy aflame and side with the petty-bourgeois and working-class insurgents in the capital, Paris? And why wasn't an attempt made by the Berlin revolutionaries—those in the streets, and those elected to the Prussian National Assembly—to successfully mobilize the bitterly suffering and undoubtedly angry peasantry in Prussia and all of Germany that was increasingly exposed to the cruel 'logic of the market' and still not completely freed from the load of all feudal burdens?[9] They could have done it, even as delegates who formed only a minority, by calling out loudly and openly in the assembly that the peasants should rise, by declaring them free of the shackles that tied them, still, against all reason, to anachronistic duties—some of them even to bonds of servitude.

In Prussia, it was the law passed *after the defeat* of the revolution, in the context of reestablished conservative hegemony, that 'completed' the half-hearted piecemeal step-by-step liberation of peasants by way of the law passed on March 2, 1850. The reaction did it—recognizing the dangers that this unsolved problem had posed for them in the days of upheaval. It was an insufficient—in fact—a *bad* law that burdened a large number of poor peasants with monetary payments to their former feudal overlords in order to be completely free of unpaid labor they owed them. Because the peasants obtained no credit from the government and paid in installments, many remained obliged to deliver feudal dues, while being additionally burdened with a debt load too big for them.

The failure of the revolutionaries (who had fought in the streets!) to act decisively in the immediate aftermath of armed struggle in the days and weeks *when, for a very brief period, they could almost dictate things to a frightened but resentful king and then, in April and May, perhaps also to a supposedly 'liberal' cabinet in close contact and basic agreement with the king*, is obvious but hard to explain. They failed where it mattered most; they failed—in March—to arm the people in the cities. They left the initiative to men like von Arnim[10] and Minutoli and Nobiling.[11] They disarmed the revolution—or rather, they looked on when it was disarmed. But a similar critique can be leveled against the elected delegates who professed democratic aims. Of course, a decisive turn of events had occurred[12] when the struggle for direct elections was lost, resulting in an inadequate representation of the subaltern classes and of their spokespersons in the Prussian National Assembly. Still, one must critique the hesitation of the more democratic ones of the liberal 'constitutional monarchist' delegates in the assembly, and of the republican petty-bourgeois faction of the democrats, to form the necessary tactical coalition in this essential period that saw the reaction still on the defensive in May, for it was exactly such a temporary coalition that was required in order to proceed determinedly with the full liberation of the peasants from all feudal burdens by way of a radical law that would foresee no compensation to their aristocratic overlords. These supposedly democratic delegates elected to the Assembly let a moment of opportunity quickly pass. They, too, missed a chance to disempower the 'old reactionary forces' in Prussia once and for all. It was a moment when the revolution could still have succeeded, and not only temporarily in Berlin (and a few other cities), for a law liberating the peasantry and addressing the hunger of rural day laborers for land by partitioning the large aristocratic estates might have mobilized the peasantry quite generally. It could have turned a number of small local and regional 'prairie fires' into a larger revolutionary storm in the countryside. This failure, it seems, was decisive in a country that was still largely agrarian. And it was, in fact, unforgivable.[13]

…

But many courageous fighters on the barricades—among them people like Brass, an educated son of the upper middle class (or, in other words, a man belonging to a highly educated segment of Berlin's enfranchised petty-bourgeoisie)—clearly rejected republicanism as adventurism; and also ignored the need to 'revolutionize' the countryside. They were careful people, many of them cunctatory and law-and-order-loving, and often avowed 'constitutional monarchist,' perhaps having the British model in mind, which still barred the large and growing working class of that country from participation in the political process and which outlawed strikes and social agitation.

The question clearly is whether these men—liberals, but also democrats without doubt, and like Brass, perhaps for no small reason, full of sympathy for the liberal yet monarchist chief of police in Berlin (the head of a vast network of ever-present informers, who asked the army to act on March 17, 1848[14])—or, on the other hand, the republicans, and above all their left-wing section (represented by the views voiced in the *Rhenanian Gazette* in 1842-43 and the *New Rhenanian Gazette* during the revolution), assessed the relations of forces more realistically.

But then, *toute révolution est un coup de dés* – there is no revolution without risks; THOSE WHO DO NOT DARE ANYTHING, CANNOT WIN. And the vast majority of Berlin's leading revolutionaries wanted peace quickly, and desired to harvest the fruits of the victory peacefully, like anxious petty-bourgeois souls, while the truly conservative of their class brethren conspired with the court, and the King and his camarilla were already preparing the counter-revolution.

...

A local victory, though, in the capital of Prussia, and a king and his family, who were in fact briefly hostages of the revolutionaries—like the French king and his wife in 1789—provided a chance that was not recognized, a moment of opportunity that lasted only briefly, and that evaporated when the decisive men of the moment, leaders of the struggle, failed to act and let themselves be influenced by their childlike belief in the goodness of those in Prussia who would so soon brutally defeat the German revolution in a merciless, extremely violent manner.

I think that this revolution warrants comparisons with other failed revolutions, most notably the 'Arab spring' in Cairo,[15] in order to ponder which objective factors and which strategic mistakes contributed in both cases to defeat and the triumph of the 'reaction': was it the impermanence of momentary unity of mutually distrustful and unreconciled social forces and their respective positions? Was it miscalculation, false evaluation of 'players' who proved to be, at the end of the day, counterrevolutionaries?

In the case of Egypt, the Cairo revolutionaries, during a certain phase, greeted army soldiers as sons of the people, feeling protected by them, accepting their wholesale (as it turned out, 'steered,' largely tactical) support, rather than convincing recruits to change sides. Mubarak became the culprit, the target, not the general staff and the generals as such, as the backbone of the military dictatorship. Illusions—in Prussia, about the king, about men like Nobiling and Minutoli and von Arnim; in Cairo, about the army, about the generals who seemed ready (tactically, it turned out) to jail the dictator and allow a free, democratic development of the country!

...

Then, in both historic situations, you have the antagonistic composition of the revolutionary bloc: in Egypt, anti-secular Muslim Brothers [Brotherhood], long persecuted under Nasser and then, by subsequent governments (Sadat; Mubarak); pro-Western, pro-Capitalist liberals; and anti-capitalist trade-unionists and diverse leftist groups and intellectuals—a minority, no doubt, but representing objectively the social and democratic interests of a majority unable to grasp and formulate real needs in accordance with vaguely harbored aspirations: bread, jobs, housing, dignity. In Berlin: a significant section of the bourgeoisie and the upper segments of the petty-bourgeoisie (all of them consisting of men who feared losing modest privileges to the proletarian 'mob'); then, the educated, liberal petty-bourgeoisie, including the students: desirous of modest reform. Craving a constitution, juries, religious freedom, and political rights for all (save the workers?). Among the bourgeoisie of the capital, only a few Jewish bankers joined this second, democratic spectrum, deserting their arch-conservative, anti-revolutionary class brethren. But mind you, dear friend: industrial entrepreneurs like Borsig were upstarts. They had little in common with owners of chinaware factories, or other manufacturers of luxury goods endowed with royal patents, monopolies and other privileges (e.g. as purveyors to the Court). Borsig clearly was a liberal.

Yes, and then you have the third spectrum; then you get the subaltern, proletarian masses, the vast majority of the inhabitants of Berlin: they are not presenting a leader for the revolution, even though Stefan Born has all the qualities of a leader; but he is a Communist, a radical, viewed with suspicion by the Woenigers, Brass, Wache, by a banker Mendheim, and most certainly by the superbly informed spymaster, von Minutoli. It is the proletarian part of the population, the workers of companies (like that run by Borsig), and even more and especially, and in very large numbers, the journeymen, it's these people who form the broad mass of the fighters on the barricade, just like their class brethren form the majority of the fighters everywhere in that year, in insurgent Europe, from Paris to Milano, to Vienna, and Dresden. But the leaders are from the ranks of the petty-bourgeoisie, humanists like Brass: careful, weighing the situation, certainly personally courageous, but politically moderate, hesitant.

When the demonstration is organized that presents the slain bodies of revolutionary fighters to the king, forcing him to take off his hat, this is organized not by men like Woeniger and Brass and highly educated liberal Jewish democrats: it is organized by the proletarian sons of the people, who remain anonymous. It is a provocation, a test of one's own force or power, and of the power of the other, royal side at this moment: the question of power is posed; now the next step should be taken: the king and his brothers, his wife, his entire family should be taken prisoner—just as it had happened in France exactly 60 years before. The revolution should now *dictate* the next step to the King, taken hostage. But it doesn't happen. A civil guard, a 'citizens guard,' is formed, following the reactionary example of France during the 1830s and 40s. It is formed almost exclusively by *citizens*, property-owning, enfranchised people, a tiny minority of Berlin's population. Its aim is to defend bourgeois property against the 'mob,' the proletariat; its self-proclaimed duty is to defend and protect the king—against the 'mob,' the proletariat, the majority of Berlin's inhabitants.

With few exceptions—in the course of events in 1848–1849, up to the army's renewed act of entering Berlin, and occupying it, and dispersing the assembly of elected representatives—journeymen and industrial workers are kept out of this 'citizens' guard,' though one or two detachments of mechanics are formed. These units of 'Maschinenbau' workers are not properly integrated; and they form only a small fragment of the 'guard.' On June 14, 1848, the guard shoots at them, kills some, and wounds others; this occurred when the mechanics placed them themselves—unarmed—as peacemakers between these 'protectors of law and order' and workers who were just leaving the arsenal that had been stormed. Workers—not only the hungry construction workers who had armed themselves with shovels and other tools, ready to march to the palace, the city's center, in an act of protest—were attacked by this *arm of the armed victorious 'people'* more than once. But the 'people,' in this case, were once more the bourgeoisie and petty-bourgeoisie, the anti-constitutional, anti-revolutionary monarchists, the constitutional, briefly revolutionary, monarchists, and the radical liberal petty-bourgeois republicans who, too, are sidelined in the account of Brass, just like the communist Stefan Born.

Stephan Born, 1824-1898, founder of the Allgemeine Arbeiterverbrüderung (General Fraternity of Workers), the first nationwide trade union formed by the incipient German workers' movement. After his involvement in the ultimately failed revolution of 1848–49, he went into exile in Switzerland, just like August Brass and many other German revolutionaries. In 1860 he became honorary professor in Basel.

Introduction

If one thing is truly revealing in the account of August Brass, it is how he interprets, very positively and empathically, the reaction of the king when Frederick William takes off his helmet, unable to speak, 'too deeply moved to utter a single word,' as Brass sees it in his highly interesting and certainly revealing historical account of the events in front of the palace on March 19, 1848. There exist, however, written accounts by aristocratic persons close to the king which leave us in no doubt that in this situation the king felt deeply humiliated and full of ire, which in turn filled him with a spirit of resentment which propelled his readiness to plot and prepare the decisive counter-revolutionary blow in Berlin that was to hasten the defeat of other regional revolutions in Germany, defeated by the Prussian army that had recovered from the shock of suffering defeat at the hands of an insurgent population in March '48 in house to house urban combat. *[translator: I have reversed the order of words.]*

It is true that Brass, like so many others, was personally courageous. Like Frederick Engels, he took part in the 'campaign in Baden,' the final struggle of resistance of Germany's radical democrats against a superior Prussian army. It was in the fortified city of Rastatt that a large number of revolutionaries held out in 1849, engaging the Prussian troops, keeping them from quickly pursuing the bulk of the revolutionary army, which thus gained time and managed to cross the Swiss border, finding a sanctuary in neutral Switzerland. The defenders of Rastatt, with the exception of those few who managed to escape through the sewers and find boats of fisherman at the river bank that made it possible to escape across the Rhine to France, were sentenced to long jail terms, and some were executed by the Prussians, like my grandma's cousin who she talked about occasionally when I was a child. Cousin Schiele, who was a fighter in the red army of revolutionary workers in central Germany, vanquished by a Freikorps unit of right-wing university students, was, like many other workers who surrendered, executed on the spot in Hettstett in 1921 or '23.

Yes, a personal letter. Even though a few inaccuracies have now been corrected, it reveals in an uncensored way why, for me—a resident of this tormented, often rotten country, Germany—the account by August Brass is still intriguing. History did not end in 1848 with a brief revolutionary victory, or with the defeat of that German democratic revolution of 1848–49; it did not end with Noske's cunning cooperation with the Kaiser's generals, when the November Revolution of 1918 was "tamed"; it did not end with aborted revolutionary attempts in Germany in 1921 and 1923; and it did not end when a deficient democracy in Germany was scrapped by Nazis who won when their party received nearly 44 per cent of the popular vote in the election of March 5, 1933—the last formally free election until August 14, 1949, even though Social Democrats and Communists were already being severely harassed—as the election *did* in fact take place after the Nazi seizure of power and after they, in all likelihood, had put the parliament building, the Reichstag, aflame, blaming it on the Communists. Nazism was brought down, at the end. Let us be confident: even today, with the triumph of neoliberalism and the end of history declared by prominent authors like Francis Fukuyama, history *will* go on. And in view of the widening gap between the 0.1 percent and the rest (or should I say, those 6 or 8 men—or families—who own as much as one half of mankind, combined), the reasons for studying the successes and mistakes of bygone revolutions and thus of their protagonists may be all too apparent to those who prefer not to close their eyes and choose apathy, resignation, conformist adaptation to so-called "facts that can't be changed," or careerism and, in the last analysis, servile opportunism.

- Andreas Weiland

Introduction

Endnotes

[1] Regarding Peter Light as a peace activist, see online information on the Comox Project which says this, among other things: "The Comox Project was the only peace project that included both study of the area involved and direct action.... It was also the first in the province of British Columbia, the second in Canada, after the La Macaza Project a year earlier, in Quebec, that Light helped organize, along with Dimitri Roussopoulos, Dan Daniels, and Andre Cardinal, to engage in mass non-violent civil disobedience. In May 1965, Voodoo interceptors armed with Genie unguided air-to-air rockets at Comox Air Base were given nuclear war heads. Vancouver Peace Centre activists decided some action was needed, not just by outsiders, but involving the community. The person most responsible for getting this action off the ground was Peter Light, 22, who had already engaged in a number of non-violent protests and marches...." (The Comox Project File. URL http://vcmtalk.com/the_comox_project; accessed 23 May 2018, 10:12 PM - Copyright 2009 red lion publishing.) See also: Larry Gambone, *The Comox Project: Civil Disobedience at the Comox Air Base, Summer 1965*. Nanaimo, B.C.: Red Lion Press, 2007. – Regarding Peter Light's commitment to ecological issues and especially to permaculture, see for instance: Peter Light, "No Challenge", in: *Permaculture Design Magazine*, Nov. 2016, and also such information on his permaculture workshops as the following 12 photographs on flicker: https://www. flickr.com/photos/harry/268082655.

[2] Perhaps the very fact that the Chinese leadership saw itself compelled by outside factors to intervene in the Korean War at a time when a long period of anti-Japanese military resistance and civil war had just ended the year previous, while the population was now deeply desirous of peace, had a very negative influence on the further development of China. There exists a deep difference between voluntary discipline and imposed discipline, and it must have affected relations between the "top," or more generally, "higher echelons" and "the people" in the long run.

[3] At least propagandistically Chiang Kai-shek turned the island of Taiwan into "an anti-communist bastion dedicated to re-conquering the mainland." This widely known fact is confirmed once more in an article published in the Taiwan News. See Annie Huang (Associated Press), "Chiang Kai-shek's Legacy Attracts Respectful Chinese Tourists to Taiwanese Park", in: Taiwan News, March 17, 2007. Online edition. URL https://www.taiwannews.com.tw/en/news/409881, accessed May 28, 2018, 9:45 PM. – The fact that the Syngman Rhee regime embraced an agenda of attacking and conquering the North is mentioned by Bruce Cumings.

[4] See Bruce Cumings, *The Origins of the Korean War; 1: Liberation and the Emergence of Separate Regimes*, Princeton, NJ: Princeton Univ. Press, 1981. Also: Bruce Cumings, *The Origins of the Korean War Part 2: The Roaring of the Cataract 1947 – 1950*. Princeton, NJ : Princeton Univ. Press, 1990, XVIII, 957 pp. ISBN 0-691-07843-2. Also see Bruce Cumings, *The Korean War: A History*, New York NY: Modern Library / Random House Publishing Group, 2010. The U.S. government has published intercepted communication between Stalin and Mao in this regard, and the available documents show that Mao hesitated and actually resisted requests to intervene in the war before finally giving in to Stalin's prodding, in all likelihood also because the American advance was fast and they soon reached the Yalu river frontier.

⁵ The polarizing existence of two main tendencies that existed in the "revolutionary camp" (that is to say, on their side of the barricades) on March 18 and 19 was not very obvious during these days of armed resistance. People fought side by side. Nonetheless, the division was expressed visually on the barricades. The horizontally-striped and the vertically-striped German tricoloured flags flown on the barricades attest to the presence of considerable numbers of both constitutional monarchists (of either a conservative liberal, "moderate liberal," or decidedly "democratic" liberal persuasion) and, on the other hand, of anti-socialist liberal republicans and "red" republicans among the fighters who resisted the King, the reactionary "Old Powers," and, concretely, the soldiers. The vertically-striped tricoloured flag was used by the republicans. It is interesting that these republicans are only referred to as something marginal in the account provided by August Brass; there is the lone voice in the Palace Square shouting "A Republic!" And this although their flags are clearly as present on the barricades as those of the liberal monarchists who demanded, mainly, a progressive "constitution," but no republic and no thorough solutions of the "social question." It is true that in the book written by Brass there is the dark, threateningly silent throng of those who suddenly appear in the Palace Square, where they confront the King and Queen with the dead bodies of those revolutionaries who were killed in action. But these anonymous masses of the subaltern classes who are aware of their grief and their misery—and who, later on, went on to voice immediate demands—appear without leaders and without a "face"; they evoke emotions of sympathy in protagonists like Brass, but they are also seen as posing a danger, to property, law and order, to the king and his family. It is this mass that prompts the monarchist Liberals to form a "Civil Guard" with the support of men close to the king, a bourgeois force soon used against workers that never became a people's militia.

⁶ See W. B. [= Wilhelm Blos], "Die Flucht des Prinzen von Preußen, nachmaligen Kaisers Wilhelm I. Nach den Aufzeichnungen des Majors O. im Stabe des Prinzen von Preußen [The Flight of the Prince of Prussia, later on Emperor William I. According to the Notes of Major O. in the Staff of the Prince of Prussia]. Stuttgart, Greiner & Pfeiffer" [book review], in: Die Neue Zeit : Wochenschrift der deutschen Sozialdemokratie [The New Era: Weekly of German Social Democracy]. – 32nd Year (1913-1914), Vol. 1 (1914), No. 24, pp. 916 -918. – electronic version: URL http://library.fes.de/cgi-bin/neuzeit.pl?id=07.09080&dok=1913-14a&f=191314a_0916&l=191314a_0918&c=191314a_0916; accessed May 12, 2018, 8 PM).

⁷ As David Barclay writes, "For the most part, Prussia's traditional ruling elites responded to these movements [the revolution in Berlin and such insurrections in the countryside as occurred in Silesia during 1848] not with decisive actions, but with fear that bordered on paralysis." Barclay also quotes Gerd Heinrich as saying, in the introduction to the memoirs of General von Prittwitz, the top military commander in Berlin during the March Revolution, that there existed a generalized crisis in Prussia's "primary leadership stratum" in the spring of 1848. Barclay adds, "As Frederick William later put it to [...] Leopold von Ranke, 'In those days we were all lying on our bellies.' [...]" (David E. Barclay, "Revolution and counter-revolution in Prussia, 1840-50", in: Philip G. Dwyer (ed.), *Modern Prussian History: 1830-1947*. London and New York: Routledge, 2013, pp. 66-84, here: p. 73. – The words of Frederick William IV that they were all laying on their bellies were uttered in the presence of the aristocrat Leopold von Ranke, a major Prussian historian in the 19th century and at the same time a member of the circle close to the king, and they were quoted by him in his biographical entry on the

Introduction

king, published in ADB. See Leopold von Ranke, "Friedrich Wilhelm IV., König von Preußen", in: *Allgemeine Deutsche Biographie* [General German Biography (= ADB)], Vol. 7, Leipzig: Duncker & Humblot, 1877, pp. 729–776.

8   In fact, uprisings in the countryside occurred. Dipper speaks of "a European peasant revolution within the 'bourgeois' revolution'," adding that "all peasant movements had rural origins and [...] were violent"; he also attempts a class analysis with regard to the population in the countryside. According to him, the large number of (Prussian) day laborers and of poor peasant families with very small plots who also engaged in cottage industry or other forms of attaining supplementary income was substantial. They needed monetary income in order to buy food because they weren't self-sufficient agricultural producers. [See Christof Dipper, "Rural Revolutionary Movements: Germany, France, Italy", in: Dieter Dowe, Heinz-Gerhard Haupt, Dieter Langewiesche, and Jonathan Sperber (eds.), *Europe in 1848: Revolution and Reform*. New York and Oxford UK: Berghahn Books, 2000, reprinted in 2008; here especially pp.416-421.] In view of significant crop failures and steeply rising food prices in the late 1840s, many part-time peasants and especially the day laborers who could not afford to buy sufficient food on the market were threatened by starvation. In Prussia about half the potato harvest was lost [in 1846]. The problems thus caused were exacerbated by the loss in 1846 of almost half of the rye harvest [in Northwestern Europe], while the wheat harvest was considerably below normal. This was disastrous, with bread from rye or wheat being even more important than potatoes in continental European diets. It bears emphasis that the failure of the Dutch, Belgium and Prussian rye harvest of 40-50% in 1846 was extreme by nineteenth century standards [...]" (See Eric Vanhaute, Richard Paping and Cormac Ó Gráda, "The European Subsistence Crisis of 1845–1850: A Comparative Perspective", in: Cormac Ó Gráda, Richard Paping and Eric Vanhoute (eds.), *When the Potato Failed: Causes and Effects of the Last European Subsistence Crisis*. Turnhout: Brepols, 2007, p. 11.) As Vanhoute et al. noted, careful analysis of the spontaneous violent protests that resulted shows that "strong group formation and 'horizontal' communication (on market supply and prices)" mattered greatly. (Ibidem, p. 17) The effect that the food question was having on the readiness of the subaltern classes both in the cities and the countryside to actually rise up against the established order is also noted by Robert Gildea. (See Robert Gildea, *Barricades and Borders: Europe 1800-1914*, Oxford UK: Oxford University Press, 2003. The "liberal" Camphausen-Hansemann government and the other "liberal" governments of 1848 (Auerswald; von Pfuel) that represented the desire of the bourgeoisie to abide by a "pact" with the king never made the slightest attempt to mobilize the masses in the countryside against the old reactionary political and social forces that were to triumph, jointly with their king, in November 1848. It must be noted, however, that Stefan Born—a member of the Federation of Communists—was soon active in Silesia where the most noteworthy of all rural insurgencies in the countryside occurred.

9   Count Adolf Heinrich von Armin-Boitzenburg, a member of the liberal faction of the Prussian aristocracy, had been named head of government by the King on March 19, 1848, at a moment when the Queen, terrified by the exceedingly big and undoubtedly both somber and threatening cortege of revolutionaries who placed their comrades killed in action in the palace yard, had exclaimed: "Now the guillotine is the only thing that's still missing!" This exclamation was reported by Major O., the officer who aided and accompanied the widely hated Prince of Prussia, William, during his flight to Hamburg, the seaport where William

boarded a ship that took him to England and thus into temporary exile (see W. B. [i.e., Wilhelm Blos], "Die Flucht des Prinzen von Preußen [...]", ibidem.); the statement was also confirmed more recently by others who discovered that it was recorded in preserved Prussian government files. – Von Arnim stepped back as head of government on March 29, 1848, vacating his post in favor of a big Rhenish financial capitalist picked by the king as von Arnim's successor, Gottfried Ludolf Camphausen. But let me repeat here that, on the very day when he had been named head of government, on March 19, von Arnim had been standing on the balcony with the King and the Queen when the latter exclaimed the words just quoted. Count von Arnim was certainly a loyalist, and his concern regarding the safety of the king and the royal family prompted him in all likelihood to take the steps, jointly with von Minutoli and Nobiling, that led to the formation of a trustworthy military force that could replace the army which had left Berlin completely, due to perhaps misunderstood royal orders. Those who could obviously not be trusted by von Arnim, von Minutoli or the king were the darkly threatening masses that challenged royal power in those days of its utter weakness and that humiliated the king by compelling him to take off his helmet in front of the slain revolutionaries.

10 It was the alderman (Stadtrat) Nobiling who had been assigned by the chief of police, von Minutoli, with the organization of the "citizens militia" or civil guard, according to the author Werner von Westhafen [a pseudonym?]. (See Werner von Westhafen, „Die Naunynstraße", in: *Kreuzberger Chronik*, No. 159, June 2014. http://www.kreuzberger-chronik.de/chroniken/2014/juni/strasse.html .) Nobiling was a conservative master craftsman (dyer by profession) and formerly a major in active service in the Prussian army, but after the revolutionary struggle in Berlin he was obviously posing as a liberal and it might be said that he was actually just as liberal, in a conservative way, as von Minutoli, Count A.H. von Arnim-Boitzenburg, or Lieutenant General von Pfuel, none of them really old-fashioned reactionaries, but all very loyal to a reactionary, constitution-hating king, who knew only two images of "his Prussian people": the subjects who loved him and did not desire social and political change, the things he abhorred; and the devilish and subversive forces of disorder, seduced by "foreigners"—strange messengers of evil from the West, especially France. Westhafen's account that refers to Nobiling's important initial role when the Citizens' Guard was formed reiterates what Lieutenant General von Prittwitz, the reactionary commanding general of the royal army in Berlin during the days of armed revolution, wrote shortly after the March Revolution in his memoirs that were published much later. Prittwitz was inside the palace in those days, a participant observer with keen insights regarding the things that went on, and von Prittwitz notes very exactly the coordinated steps taken by the newly named "liberal" head of the government, Count von Arnim, by the chief of police, and by the monarchist alderman. The information on Nobiling used by me here is largely owed to Gerd Heinrich, "Einleitung" (Introduction), in: Karl Ludwig von Prittwitz, *Berlin 1848: Das Erinnerungswerk des Generalleutnant Karl Ludwig von Prittwitz und andere Quellen zur Berliner Märzrevolution und zur Geschichte Preussens um die Mitte des 19. Jahrhunderts* (The memoirs of lieutenant general Karl Ludwig von Prittwitz and other sources concerning the Berlin March Revolution and the history of Prussia in the mid-19th century), edited and with an introduction by Gerd Heinrich. Berlin and New York: de Gruyter, 1985, p. XVIII – ISBN 978-3-11-008326-2). These memoirs were written shortly after the revolutionary events but published only in 1985.

Introduction

11   This turn of events in April and early May 1848 was due to steps taken by the alliance that the Camphausen government formed with the king, steps that at the time were met with an inadequate response from the internally divided democratic "camp." Further developments resulted from them, but by no means inescapably so. Among these steps, the most unacceptable, from the point of view of democrats, was the bill concerning the election process drafted by the government; the next step was the second and in fact final convocation of the United Diet (a basically nonrepresentative, structurally still almost feudal, at any rate pre-revolutionary "parliament") that was decreed by the king; this was followed by the vote of this undemocratic body in favor of indirect elections prior to the United Diet's final dissolution, and by the adamant refusal of the "liberal" bourgeois government to give way to pressure from below in favor of direct elections. Obviously, the liberal advocates of a far more genuine democracy than Camphausen was ready to accept, and the democratic Left preferred not to unite; both democratic factions feared the same thing, viz., to consequently ask the "masses" to take to the streets: the liberal petty-bourgeois democrats because they seem to have believed in deliberations rather than mass action, the Left—except for a few people like Schlöffel and those workers he spoke for—because they seem to have feared that in acting alone they would only invite defeat. It was non-action that meant defeat and, in violation of the newly gained freedom of the press, Schlöffel was charged with publishing seditious content and condemned to military "fortress imprisonment" in the first political trial after the revolution. A mass demonstration of those workers who took to the street despite the advice of Leftists like Born and others was confronted with armed might: bayonets against peaceful workers, the new language of Camphausen, Hansemann, & Co. There were simply too few in the streets that confronted a "citizens' guard" or "civil guard" of conservative burghers that would have been powerless against tens of thousands, but that clearly was not with regard to the limited numbers of those who had decided to protest, hoping to voice their demands in front of the palace in order to exercise some kind of pressure on the government. Of course, people like Camphausen and von Minutoli were deeply convinced that pressure exercised by "the crowd" must not be brought to bear on a government or the king. For them it was a poker game, a test of forces, a question of power, and power had to rest solely with the government, the cabinet appointed by the king. The Camphausens of that time understood that everything was a question of power: the radicals who wanted a more genuine democracy rather than a democratic façade, saw it; the procrastinating democrats who believed in deliberations did not.

12   In fact, there were revolutionary actions in the countryside. But democrats in favor of a "reconciliation" and an "agreement" with the king, thus supportive of a "constitutional monarchy," like Brass and like all the moderate liberal delegates who formed the majority in the Prussian National Assembly together with the conservative Liberals (backing, of course, the new Camphausen/Hansemann government!), never made an attempt to pass a law that would have genuinely freed the Prussian peasants from remaining feudal burdens. In other words, they missed the chance to change the social relations in the countryside and to win an important ally, i.e. the peasantry. And this in order not to alienate those who would nonetheless be the decisive social force behind the counterrevolution: the "Old Powers" in Prussia—the landed aristocracy (big estate owners clinging to antiquated "feudal" rights and, last but not least, the perverse system of manorial

administration of justice), and their "cousins," the aristocrats who filled the decisive posts in the bureaucracy and the army.

13 See Hans Herzfeld, „Erstes Kapitel: Allgemeine Entwicklung und politische Geschichte" [First Chapter: General Development and Political History], in: Hans Herzfeld and Gerd Heinrich (eds.), *Berlin und die Provinz Brandenburg im 19. und 20. Jahrhundert* [Berlin and the Province of Brandenburg during the 18th and 19th century]. Berlin: de Gruyter, 1968, p.57.

14 The plausibility of an attempt to relate the Arab Spring to historical situations like the March Revolution of 1848 is also recognized by Duncan Kelly. Kelly writes in his passages on "Conditions of possibility" that "one might explore the 'conditions of possibility' [of change] by recalling the ways in which the relatively recent 'Arab Spring was refined and revised into an update of the 'original' springtime of the peoples in revolutionary Europe across 1848. Democracy was possible ...." But what he fails to add is that it was neither attained in the German March Revolution and its sequels nor in the revolutionary attempt made in Egypt; it was briefly attained in France in 1848, grossly deformed in late June, 1849, and abolished in that country in 1852. And it is still an open question what the future will bring in Tunisia—the country where the Arab Spring began in 2011. See Duncan Kelly, "Intellectual History and the History of Political Thought", in: Richard Whatmore and Brian Young (eds.), *A Companion to Intellectual History*. Wiley Blackwell 2015, pp.141-154. – In his abstract to said article, Duncan Kelly pointed out that in writing his article he was intending to "examine [...] the tense relationship between the history of political thought and intellectual history, arguing that a modern history of political thought first took shape as intellectual history in response to the 1848 revolutions in Europe, and that it did so in order to make claims about contemporary politics." In others words, "Let's learn from history, especially from past mistakes!" Kelly's obvious concern is to "set in motion a central dilemma for the discipline of the history of political thought, namely, whether or not there is a necessary rather than a contingent relationship between the need to study political thought and practice historically, in order to speak meaningfully about political ideas and activity in the present." Perhaps the reader, by turning to the book written by August Brass, will also start to relate past "political thought and practice" to "the present."

On the Barricades of Berlin

An Account of the 1848 Revolution

August Brass

PREFACE

Looking, during a moment of leisure in the midst of these days of work and activity, at the overall result of the eventful period which is of so much significance for the history of Germany and the history of the world, the events of the short time of a single month still appear in our mind in colourful confusion. It is as if we had dreamt one of those wondrous fairy tales which leave us breathless, in view of terrors and fright. One of those that confront us with night. A dark night indeed, full of thunder and lightning, which only occasionally gives way to the warm glow of sunlight that fills the faint spirit with new hope. But finally, all is going to be well again, the bad spell disappears, and the sun shines brightly and gloriously in the blue dome of the sky. Such is the history of this single month.

On the twenty-second of February, this struggle for freedom and rights began on the banks of the Seine, and on the twenty-second of the subsequent month we buried, in Berlin, the corpses of those who fell in this sacred struggle.

Peace be with them—but peace with us, too; let them be the last ones! I don't say this to all those of you who rush keenly ahead and keep pushing forward faster than the thoughtful person among you is prepared to follow, or the weak chap, not yet used to the light, is capable of following. You are obeying this first, primordial commandment of the deity: Forward! But you are not going to bring us any harm; you are going to prepare for us the path and you will level that path which we are going to take and which we must take when the time has come. I rather address you who, by stubbornly holding on to old, rotten institutions, take your own interests to be endangered by freedom. Freedom endangers no one—it only endangers injustice. To you I turn who are still unable and unwilling to comprehend what has happened. And to all of you who assume that freedom is not so securely based that it can induce you to give up the attempt to jolt it with impudent hands.

For otherwise you have been pious and god-fearing enough, attending church every Sunday and learning nearly all of the Bible by heart. Have you never thought about the meaning of the word written in this book of books with iron, eternal letters, "And when the time was fulfilled..."?

When the time was fulfilled, the altars and columns of the old deities fell down from their pedestals; far and wide across all lands of the globe the cross was glowing in the early morning light of a better time, and the peoples, singing hymns, went on a pilgrimage to the grave of the saviour.

And when the time was fulfilled, Luther posted a written paper on the palace church in Wittenberg—and in Rome, in his mighty palatial castle, the ruler of Christendom was trembling.

And when the time was fulfilled, Mirabeau, facing the bayonets of the tyrant, proclaimed on June 23 of the year 1789, in the name of the populace oppressed for so long, its rights and its freedom.

Here, in Germany, too, the time has been fulfilled.

Just as the cross, the symbol of the saviour, was glowing far and wide across the lands in *that* time, today the three-coloured flag, the symbol of freedom, flies proudly above all countries and peoples—above all, above all! And just like Martin Luther once posted that piece of paper on the church in Wittenberg, we, too, attach a tiny sheet of paper to the temple of despotism, and this sheet is the Constitution. For the time has been fulfilled.

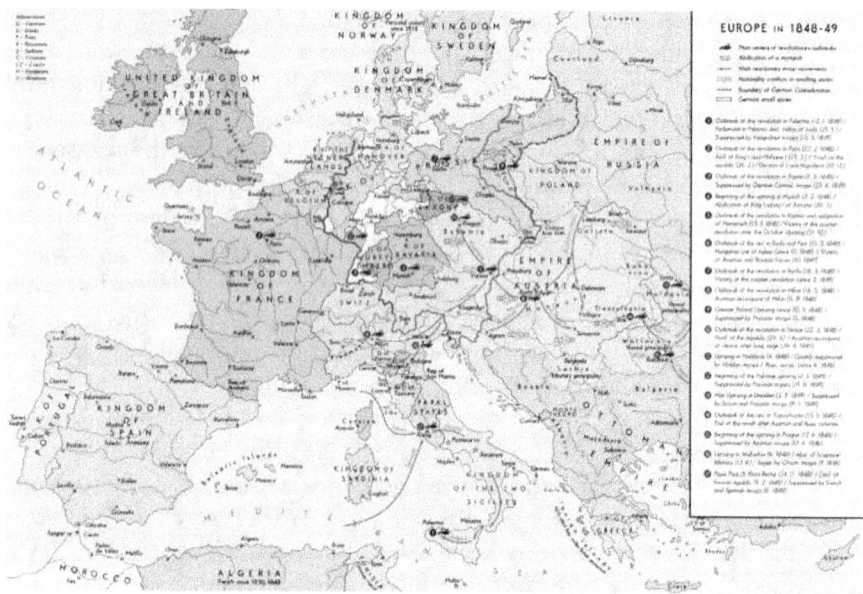

Map of Europe in 1848–1849 depicting the main revolutionary centres, important counter-revolutionary troop movements and states with abdications.

Who will dare to infringe upon this time and its good right? But now I am, entirely against my will, in the process of giving a fine speech in favor of this great movement which splashed across all of Europe. And yet, it was merely my intention to declare that, on the contrary, I have wanted to make it my most immediate concern to narrate, *in a language devoid of all passion*, the events which are so close to all of us. I wanted to say that I have made it my task to correctly appreciate both parties, as much as this is possible. – Well, this is going to be nice indeed if even at the very beginning, a surging emotion overtakes calm consideration!

At any rate, in all these matters I will make it my duty to remain faithful to the truth, only reporting what happened and what is confirmed by trustworthy witnesses. And in the interest of truth and the right of everyone, I shall give account of the sources I rely on.

At the same time I take this occasion to thank all those who supported me in my work by way of their generous contributions. Despite the considerable plenitude of the material obtained, it may well be possible to discover some lacunae in this short description of this eventful time. But in this short stretch of time between the events themselves and the publication of these lines, it was not, regardless of all the good will and sober intention, possible to offer you, the reader, a more complete work. Perhaps a more skillful pen will be able, later on, to fuse the multifaceted materials published here into a more complete and coherent whole. And thus the generous reader may forgive the shortcomings of this small publication by taking it merely as what it attempts to be: a contribution to the history of our days.

Berlin, April 3, 1848
August Brass

PART I

Start of 1848 to March 11: Thunderclouds on the Horizon

If it's the work of God, it will be permanent.
If it's the work of man, it will be transient.

But it will last, this large work, this revolution of the year 1848, for it is the work of God. Neither the barricades in Paris, in Vienna, in Berlin, nor the heroic sacrifice of their defenders or the abundantly spilled blood of a people that had become defenseless—no, nothing of this sort has made this revolution. It was the time, it was God himself, who called the people to arms. For the time is God, and woe to him who in stubborn arrogance dares to oppose the commandment of this God!

Dark, ill-boding thunderclouds had appeared on the political horizon at the beginning of 1848.

The Sonderbund War was a civil war fought against seceding cantons in 1847. Swiss citizens fought against Swiss citizens in the Battle of Geltwil.

The civil war in Switzerland had come to an unexpectedly quick end and, above all, one that was welcomed by all those of good will. And this despite the threatening position taken by the conservative big powers, especially Prussia

Start of 1848 to March 11: Thunderclouds on the Horizon

and Austria, vis-à-vis the liberal party. After Austria had amassed troops near the border, a party in Neuenburg, at the instigation of the Prussian cabinet, made the weak attempt to claim a neutral status for the canton in order to supply Prussia, if necessary, with a pretext for armed meddling in Swiss affairs, in response to a supposed violation of a neutral area. The position of France was in conformity with the degraded policy of Louis Philippe and his faithful companion, Guizot.

Louis Philippe, the "bourgeois monarch" (shown in a painting by Winterhalter, left). And the extremely unpopular François Guizot (1787-1874), foreign minister in 1840-1846, prime minister since 1847 until the February Revolution of 1848, and a close friend of the bankers Jacques Lafitte (a property speculator) and Charles Perrier, who also befriended the King.

Without declaring itself in favor of one party or the other, the French government clandestinely sent weapons and ammunition to the Sonderbund. And their ambassador, the Count Bois le Comte, with his secretaries at the embassy, assumed the erstwhile task of spying in support of the Sonderbund, as he believed himself to be protected from being hung by his sanctified diplomatic status. England alone declared, in accordance with the open and honest policy of Palmerston, that it desired a peaceful solution for the Swiss troubles and that it regarded any armed intervention by foreign powers as absolutely unjustified.

During these diplomatic interventions, the federation of twelve cantons had already quickly and forcefully put an end to the affair. While the Austrians were still bringing troops to the frontier, Freiburg and Luzern had been taken. The French ambassador had been sent home: and when Prussia decidedly argued in favor of the neutrality of Neuenburg and threatened to defend it with armed might if necessary, the Tagsatzung [as the Swiss parliament meeting in session was called at the time] supplied the forceful answer that it did not know of any King of Prussia entitled to meddle in Neuenburgian affairs, and in so far as Neuenburg was merely a rebellious canton, it would be compelled with armed force to fulfil its obligations. Neuenburg, too, ended up paying the imposed contributions. And those who had, with such proud expectations observed every step of the Prussian cabinet, were quite surprised that it responded with merely a deep silence to such a manful challenge.

Session of the Swiss parliament in 1847. Meetings of this parliament were referred to as Tagsatzung meetings.

Whereas the inner conflicts of Switzerland led to a welcome reorganization in this way, and in fact much quicker than expected, soon enough the eyes of Europe turned to another country where a populace, long assumed to have sunk into lamentable apathy, was taking up arms in order to fight for its freedom and rights. We refer to the revolt in Naples and Sicily and the related movements triggered by it in the other Italian states.

For the first time since it had been put in place with iron consistency, the political system established [in Europe] by Metternich began to become shaky.

Jean de Noailles (left) and Metternich (right) in Vienna (1815). Metternich was Austrian foreign minister since 1809 and Chancellor of Austria from 1821 until the revolution in Vienna caused him to flee the country in 1848.

France, which had put itself so irrevocably into the hands of this absolute prince of Absolutism since the [so-called] Affair of the Spanish Marriages was indeed to restrict itself to being a calm onlooker in this affair. But the attitude of the opposition in Paris had become such a threatening one since the Chamber had been summoned again that many believed they had to fear the worst. And on top of this, England declared at the time that it would regard any interference in these Italian affairs as a declaration of war. And therefore, the Viennese cabinet had to be content for the moment with amassing considerable military forces in Lombardy. This was done partly in order to be prepared for all eventualities, partly in order to immediately quell, by armed force, any revolt of its Italian provinces.

While the course pursued by Metternich's politics for so many years was indeed despicable, it will nonetheless appear to all statesmen as a rare example of admirable consequence, characterized by sharp-sighted deduction and calculation of future states of affair as well as an unparalleled adroitness in the exploitation of present conditions. The way he managed to control France from his office in Vienna is unsurpassable. Only someone like him could dare to oppose himself to the immense pressures of his time. His fall was the decisive moment of the European revolutions, and all of you who have not yet been able to accustom yourselves to the thought of forgetting these dreams of the ancient régime out of which you were shaken so roughly—leave all those hopes behind! Those who up to now felt his iron grip have finally thrown off the degrading yoke; they have nailed his insignia on the gallows.

"'The constitution requires movement.' (Metternich on the run.)"–This is the first political caricature created in Vienna. It was published in 1848.

Beware, beware, therefore: for your fate would be the same. But no one would be able to add to your memorial of shame what we have to say about him: that he was a great man. There was no event in European politics, none at all, that would have surprised Metternich. He was prepared for them all—except one thing that he was unprepared for. He had not believed that we would have a Pope who would join the quest for freedom as energetically as Pius IX.

Pope Pius IX (original name: Giovanni Maria Mastai-Ferretti) as cardinal, shortly

Since this man had occupied the papal position, it could be observed that Metternich's politics began to waver a bit. And for the first time, the enthusiastic call "Evviva Pio novo" [long live Pope Pius the ninth] was chasing sleep away from the bed of this feared oppressor of free thought who, during the days of July [the July Revolution of 1830], had heard the thunder of guns and the chant of La Parisienne [a revolutionary song], and who had yet remained cold.

Freedom leading the people (La liberté guidant le people), painted in 1830 by Eugène Delacroix.

Soon he had, to his satisfaction, seen the "bourgeois monarch" [the new French king] dependent on him. And now, in this critical moment, he believed that he could count on an even stronger support than that indifferent one which the ministry of Guizot adhered to, with regard to all steps taken by the Viennese cabinet. But could such a step be risked?

It had been expected that the French government would speak up with determination when, in breach of international law, Kraków had been incorporated into the Austrian monarchy. Instead, France had been content to issue a miserable note of protest. The role played by Guizot during the war in Switzerland as well as the ambiguous position taken by him during the Italian events could not but make every unbiased person recognize the aims pursued by Louis Philippe in his system of government. Any open support of Austrian interests regarding the Italian events quite naturally had to lead to a break between Louis Philippe and the French people. In that case, a two-fold war had to be expected. And thus it was necessary to end one in order to be able to start the other. It seemed that this was possible without risk. The military preparation against the poor, betrayed people had been completed. The fortifications of Paris had seen cannons put in place and the troops that manned them had received ammunition and provisions. Secretly, large quantities of supplies had been brought to Paris. And if Louis Philippe may have vacillated for a moment, the most determined directives of Metternich drove him forward on that course which in the end was to cost him and his family both kingdom and crown.

The royal address of the "Citizen King" delivered before both chambers of parliament, convened in joint session on December 28, 1847, was a declaration of war against the people, the same people who seventeen years ago had lifted him onto the throne, who had welcomed him unanimously and in jubilant manner, and whom he had wretchedly betrayed all these years.

The events that occurred in Paris are well-known. The opposition closed ranks; many comprehended that the decisive moment had arrived. But in both chambers of parliament a majority, formed by officials and bought persons, carried the vote. Their motion responding to the royal address was adopted, in exactly the manner in which this servile party had drafted it. And thus the opposition could only appeal to the people who were being deceived. The decision was reached that the "reform banquet" (a gathering of the reformers) was to take place by any means, as a resolute demonstration against the system of government—nobody believed that weapons would really be used in order to suppress it. But Louis Philippe wanted war; the directives of Metternich insisted on it even more determinedly because in Italy the popular movements had assumed the most serious quality; the insurrection in Palermo had already spread to all of Sicily while the other Italian states were obviously joining the movement to a greater or lesser extent. In Milano, too, in Pavia and many places of Lombardy, demonstrations had occurred that gave enough reason to anticipate the serious participation of the entire population. In the Hungarian Diet, the stance of the opposition was cause for concern. And in view of the bad financial situation of the Austrian monarchy, it was clear that maintaining the army units stationed in Northern Italy in a state of military preparedness occasioned expenditures which could hardly be shouldered indefinitely. Lombardy certainly expected French support for its movement. An insurrection in Paris, violently suppressed, would be tantamount to an Austrian victory at the banks of the River Po; it would mean a defeat of the inhabitants of Palermo, a fall of the Estates convened in Pressburg. This single coup, executed by the hand of Metternich in Paris, was to decide the fate of the entire world and provide a new, permanent support for his destabilizing principle.

On the evening of February 21, the French prime minister declared that the "reform banquet" meeting that was to take place the next day would be impeded, if necessary, by military force. The opposition turned to the people for support. And the next day, the fight began.

Barricades in rue Royale, Paris, 1848.

Horace Vernet, The Barricade at Rue Soufflot, Paris 1848.–
The painting was completed in the same year.

But the populace was victorious; Louis Philippe abdicated in favor of the Count of Paris, but even this move came too late. The Republic was proclaimed, and as a wretched, miserable refugee, the "Citizen King" left the country which had called him seventeen years ago in order to bring it happiness. As he left, there was not a single tear shed over that, in all of France. A deplorable man! King for seventeen years, and no friend, not a single one who would grieve for him, who would see him in exile and comfort him.

The French king mocked by the caricature Charles Philipon had drawn during his trial in 1831 (left), and by the lithography "Les Poires" that Honoré Daumier (right), published in Philipon's satirical journal in 1831. Graffiti depicting the king as a pear soon appeared on the walls of Paris and other French cities. The fat "bourgeois pear" allied to the grande bourgeoisie was widely loathed by the populace that finally toppled him in February 1848.

When the news of the flight of Louis Philippe reached Berlin, a member of the royal family is said to have shrugged his shoulders derisively, saying, "Born on the barricades—slain on the barricades!" Whosoever said so did not foresee that barricades are always a real option against the power of every despot, even if this power claims to be derived, not from barricades, but from the grace of god.

In the meantime, the news arriving from Paris had caused an immense excitement in Berlin. People looked forward to the latest newspapers with an urgency that pushed aside every other interest. And even in those locations which lacked a climate of lively political debate, those newspapers which contained the latest news from the West were read aloud in front of the public and, very much to the displeasure of a small section of those who saw such a movement as ill-fated, all of these incoming news reports were explained and discussed. At the same time, the notion spread that the time had arrived to finally make known the wishes of the people directly in front of the throne which up to then had surrounded itself with ministers which were enemies of every kind of freedom movement of both the people and the affairs of the state. And all of this received a further boost thanks to the movements which sprang up, one after the other, at first in the Rhenish provinces and then in the South German states.

Petitions that begged signatures began to circulate among the citizenry, thanks to a number of more freely thinking men. These petitions asked for freedom of the press, a stronger representation of the middle class in the provincial parliament, a certain, periodic reelection of the same, and a more intimate union of [the states that made up] Germany. Among a large part of the property-owning citizens, however, such petitions found only a small positive echo or none at all. The propertied class, known for its stable quietism—a class of people who immersed themselves in the life of the populace only in those rare cases when the opportunity arose to be thanked profusely in the papers for having given, from their full purse, a few coins for the famine-stricken in Upper Silesia or elsewhere—this part of the citizenry kept their distance from this movement, and thus the petitions in question found no positive resonance.[1]

The Silesian Weavers (painting by Huebner, 1846). The "merchant-manufacturer" is scrutinizing the products offered by hand-loom weavers working at home, searching for real or imagined flaws, in order to cut the price.

---

[1] Hand-loom weavers queuing up in the office of a wealthy "manufacturer" who would buy their cottage-industrial goods at a ridiculously low price, condemning them thereby to starvation. In Huebner's *The Silesian Weavers*, done in 1846, the merchant-"manufacturer" is scrutinizing the products of their works, searching for real or imagined flaws, in order to cut the price. A despairing woman apparently has just been told that the bale of cloth she offered is either completely rejected or nearly worthless! Two years earlier, in 1844, a spontaneous insurrection of hand-loom weavers had resulted in smashed offices, sacked mansions, burned factories, and destroyed machines that were putting handloom weavers out of work.

Start of 1848 to March 11: Thunderclouds on the Horizon

The German text reads: "Misery in Silesia. Hunger and despair. Official remedy."
The Prussian military was taking care of the despairing weavers.
(From the journal Fliegende Blätter, vol. 1848.)

A somewhat more courageous attitude could be observed when reports arrived, day after day, concerning the uprising of the people in Southern Germany, when the fickle attitude of the [new] German Federal Diet or Bundestag was noted, and when people began to admire the men of Hanau, Mannheim, Frankfurt and other places. There were those who would have loved to harvest the fruits of revolution but did not want the revolution. This attitude was prevalent throughout, in the aforementioned class of Berlin's inhabitants.

A more successful step seemed to have been taken, however, when at the same time a number of young men, mostly students of the academy of architectural studies, the so-called Bau-Akademie, assembled in a coffee-house on Leipzig Street in order to debate a petition they wanted to present to the king [King Wilhelm the 1V]

King Frederick William IV of Prussia, photo taken in 1847 (left). And a caricature by an unknown artist (right) portraying him in 1848 with champagne, while he is quite obviously wondering whether he should not accept the crown of a united Germany.

as an expression of "the wishes of the young generation." This young generation had truly a better right to formulate and sign such petitions than the representatives of our city in their pettiness were ready to concede. For one thing, the news of the secession of Neuenburg had reached Berlin in the meantime. In the face of the situation prevailing at the time, such an event could well lead to war. And who else but these bright and sturdy youngsters would have been sent into battle instantly, whereas those others would remain comfortably at home, hoping to divide the fruits of victory which the young generation would have won. And this generation should be denied the right to present its wishes to the throne for the defense of which they were ready to shed their best lifeblood? But we will come back to this later on and shall continue now with our narration in chronological manner.

This assembly of young men in Leipzig Street decided first of all to meet in larger numbers in a more suitable inn, in order to proceed with the deliberation of the petition and the next steps that should be taken. The so-called "Zelten" near Berlin, a place that had previously served for other, similar meetings, especially in the case of "movements" [revolutionary activities] initiated by the party known as the "Friends of Light," was again chosen as a meeting place. And thus, on Monday, March 6th, a small number of people had been meeting there, and though there was no other result of this meeting than the decision to meet again the next day, this assembly must still be seen as the first 'sign of life' of the great deeds that have happened since then.

Drawing of a "popular assembly" (Volksversammlung) in the Thiergarten park. This shows one of the many meetings of discontent Berliners that took place at the Zelten since mid-March, 1848.

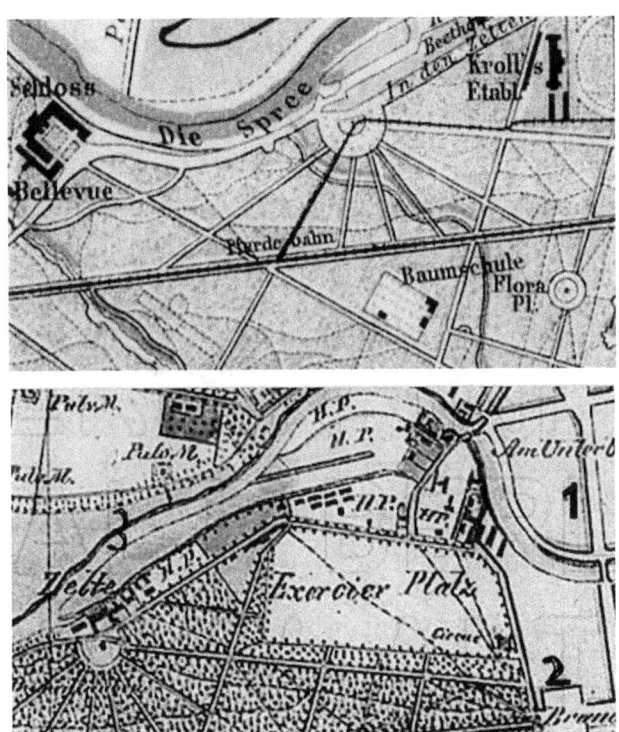

(Above:) This is a close-up of the Zelten area. (Below:) The Zelten (also: Zelte) location is located near the River Spree in the Northeastern part of the Tiergarten. The plan also shows the connection between the Zelten and the Brandenburg Gate that those attending popular assemblies at the Zelten would use.
(1 = William St.; 2 = Brandenburg Gate; 3 = River Spree. William Street = Wilhelm Str. is the Westernmost North-South axis of Berlin South of the river in 1848.)

The assembly that was convened the next day cannot be described as having been attended by a large number of people either. At most, there were five or six hundred men, for no means of communication other than word of mouth had been available in order to extend invitations. The character of this assembly was completely different from that observed in the case of the earlier ones, however. People from all walks of life—artisans, merchants, artists, scholars—had come. And when the petition formulated the day before had been deliberated and discussed in various respects and had also been partially rejected, it finally assumed a more definite form. And the decision was reached to exhibit the following version of it, in lithographed form in various public locations, in order to collect signatures.

The text of the petition was as follows:

Most serene highness, Our King, most merciful King and Lord!

The serious events which move Europe make a steadfast "sticking together" of the German princes and subjects an irrefutable necessity. Your Majesty himself has asked the German people of Prussia to gather around their king, like an iron wall, so that the course of intellectual and material progress, which the peoples of Europe have embarked upon in such upright manner, will not be interrupted by the tempests of the time.

We are therefore securely confident that Your Majesty will present us with a gracious prayer.

But the power of enthusiasm which makes a people gather round its king, the power of love for the fatherland, is not produced as mightily by the accident of being born on a given part of the earth, or by a shared language and shared customs, or by the external fact of a given state, as it is produced by securely granted, free institutions, which arm every one among the people with the same free, manly pride to which other people owe their national grandeur.

The definite need to have greater political freedom has entered the consciousness of the people, and it is the certain measuring stick that allows one to ascertain the maturity of a nation.

Such a need exists now.

But, being level-headed, we push back all those wishes which only further development of intellectual and material progress will bring to light in the people, and instead, we concur with the wishes of the other German peoples which have been made known already to the German princes and have been granted by a few of them. These wishes are

1) Unconditional freedom of the press.
2) Complete freedom of speech.
3) Immediate and complete amnesty for all those who have been condemned and persecuted because of political offenses or offenses relating to matters connected with the press.
4) Freedom of assembly and of association.
5) Equal political rights for all, regardless of religion and property.
6) Jury-based trials and independence of judges.
7) Diminution of the standing army, and the arming of the people [i.e. a people's militia], with free choice of leaders.
8) A general German representative body representing the people.
9) Rapid convening of the United Diet of the [Prussian] Provinces.

> Only if these wishes are granted, will it be possible to secure the concord between King and People on which the power of the Nation depends, both in internal and external respect. We remain in profound subservience vis-à-vis Your Majesty, etc.

It had been resolved to have this petition presented directly to the king by a delegation of ten chosen members. But the police authorities had already received a report of the steps that had been taken. The members selected to present the petition had been named. And as this delegation had agreed on the Berlin Newspaper Hall as their meeting-place (where a lithographed copy of the petition was exhibited, as well, for the purpose of collecting signatures), the Chief of Police, Mr. von Minuteli, came on the following day, on Wednesday noon, to the Newspaper Hall where he told the assembled members of the delegation that the presentation of this petition by a delegation could not occur. He would counter such a delegation in the most forceful manner, relying on all means at his disposal. On the other hand, there were no objections if they would have the petition delivered by mail. And he would give his word, guaranteeing that the King would really receive it.

In answer to this open and well-meaning explanation. the men of this delegation said however, in the same frank manner, that they had been selected by the signatories of the petition to present the same in person. In order to depart from the process decided upon, they had no other way but to obtain a general decision in that sense. Therefore, it would be necessary to convene another assembly in order to inform it about the information obtained from the Chief of Police and to discuss another way of presenting the petition to His Majesty the King.

It reveals a particular and characteristic behavioral trait of the Chief of Police that he approved this step. In his position as chief of the police authority he was obliged to impede such an assembly; on the other hand, as a man of honor he understood that these men he was facing had incurred an obligation which they could only get out of in this way if they were to act honorably.

Julius von Minutoli (1804-1860), Chief of police in Berlin and supreme spymaster of the Prussian monarchy until he resigned shortly after the Storming of the Arsenal (Zeughaus Sturm) in the summer of 1848. He had a close and friendly rapport with the king.

Thus, the third assembly took place in the "Zelten," and this on Thursday, March 9th. The attendance was significantly better than in the first two instances. Some three thousand people had come together. And as the space available was not sufficient, the speakers stood in the doorway of the assembly hall, in order to be understood by the listeners already inside and by those assembled outside. The vote, subsequent to the debates, took place outside, and for this purpose a platform used by musicians on the days when concerts were given was being used. A few speakers had suggested that the petition should be handed over by mediators such as Mr. von Bodelschwingh who was a member of the cabinet, or Alexander von Humboldt. These suggestions as well as the other one, by Mr. von Minutoli, to send the petition by mail, were rejected almost unanimously. And finally, among several proposals with considerable support, one was accepted. It boiled down to the following: that the petition should be handed to the city council, and that this "corporation" should be requested, in the names of the undersigned, to make sure that it would reach the King. That no one thought as yet of making a more forceful demonstration is best revealed by the fact that, during this deliberation, the question was posed whether the assembled were inclined to hand this petition to the city council members in corpore. As it turned out, a vast majority declared themselves against this.

Honoring this peaceful character of the assembly, the Chief of Police had also abstained from any further interference. Only a few policemen were patrolling through the Thiergarten, even though the guards had been reinforced, troops consigned to the barracks, and policemen and soldiers positioned in some parts of town.

Start of 1848 to March 11: Thunderclouds on the Horizon

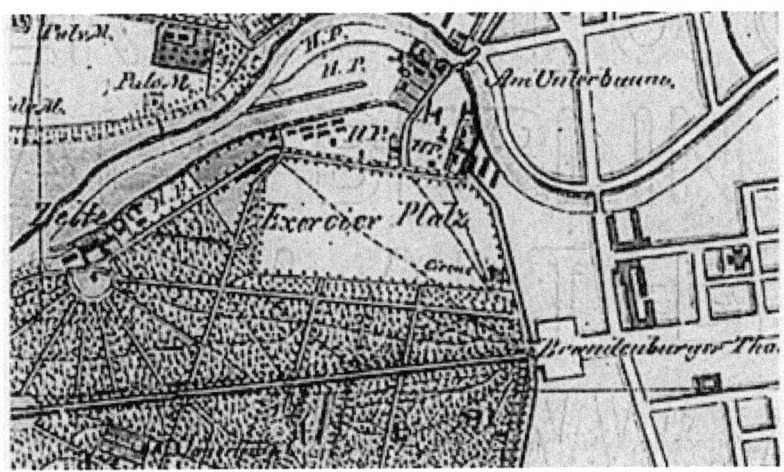

This section of the 1836 Berlin town plans shows a considerable portion of the Thiergarten park. The part designed by Lenné that is shown on his 1835 plan of the Thiergarten is farther to the West. The main East-West axis of the park–a continuation of the Under the Linden Blvd. (Unter den Linden)–is clearly visible West of the Brandenburg Gate (Brandenburger Thor).

Western parts of the capital including the area at William St. (up to the bridge) and the continuation of this street North of the bridge–locations that saw barricades and fierce fighting on Match 18-19–are also visible, as is the Lowertree Bridge (Unterbaum-Brücke) and the area called Am Unterbaum. The army crossed this bridge and attacked from the rear when they could not take the barricade at the William St. bridge.

On Thursday afternoon, while said assembly was under way, a meeting of the city councilors had simultaneously taken place. Amongst other things, they engaged in a deliberation of a petition that was signed by burghers possessing the right to vote which had been forwarded to their elected representatives. The councilors had elected a deputation that was to assess this petition and they had also agreed that in three days, on Saturday, March 11, they would deliberate on this matter in public session, after having heard the expert advice of the deputation.

An enormous audience had assembled when this session took place. Another motion was to be debated as well. Prompted by a petition of burghers during the preceding council meeting, it had also been passed on to a deputation for further consideration. According to this motion, a protection committee consisting of armed citizens was to be established which was to maintain law and order in the city. This petition as well as the one received on Thursday, in addition to others that had been adopted in the "Zelten," were the items on the agenda.

By then, the deputation elected in order to assess the citizens' petition that had been received had decided it was about time that such a petition was handed to the king. And, adopting it as [essentially] their own, the members of the deputation had drafted the previous day the following petition, which the city council was now to vote on:

> Your majesty, the King, our most merciful Lord, Most serene highness, Most powerful King, Most merciful King and Lord!
>
> The serious and fateful events of the last few days which are spreading from one country to the next have filled the hearts and minds with a tension we have never before experienced! With an expectation of the imminent rebirth of the German fatherland! By such a rebirth, the present generation—for 33 years a mere spectator of events—will regain again its unused and, for this very reason, dwindling energies. The German people deeply and strongly feel that it has become mature, and worthy of sitting in council with its Princes, in order to give testimony with regard to its intellectual and material needs.
>
> It has been the supreme desire and intention of Your Majesty that such a time should not see the Prussian people unprepared. Ever since ascending to the throne, Your Majesty has, in wise anticipation, added stone to stone, and just a few days ago, by Your supreme Pronouncement of the 3rd of this month, taken an important step in the direction of the evolution of the Constitutional rights of the Prussian people. This Cabinet Order informs us furthermore of the joyous news that Your Majesty has taken away the obstacles which have stood in the way of freedom of the press that had been guaranteed to the German people a generation ago. We look forward to the promised law concerning the press, full of confidence that it will limit itself to punishing the cases of real abuse of the press.
>
> But the moment is pressing. Each day brings further news of new events. The political horizon may suddenly darken and engender intoxicated activism before the fatherland has reached agreement in council. The most diverse desires, questions and hopes are thwarting each other. And all traffic [i.e., business] is paralyzed by distrust, in the face of a present that has become questionable, while an uncertain future is eyed fearfully. Trade and industry are coming to a halt, work is at risk; a sense of the approaching economic crisis can only accelerate this crisis, the consequences of which human wisdom cannot fathom.
>
> Under these circumstances, the desires of all unite in asking Your Majesty to command the rapid convocation of the United Provincial Parliaments. In the name of our fellow citizens, in the name of their most holy and dearest interests, we entrust this request to Your Majesty while beseeching our most merciful King and Lord with deeply moved souls to fulfill it. The certainty that Your Majesty will surround Himself in such difficult times with those men who have gained the respect of the well-meaning in view of their deliberations that took place last year, and thus with men who have

begun to indissolubly link the Prussian with the German fatherland, will instill again serenity and trust in the mind as well as security and reason in the circumstances of bourgeois life.

There exist times when new [social] conditions have matured underneath the shell of the old ones and when it necessary to recognize these irrefutable facts—even though everything should proceed strongly and soberly, in the form of a law-governed development. Ours is such a time, and we therefore take it to be our sacred duty to directly present to Your Majesty the desires and convictions that have already been voiced by municipalities and estates for many years.

The corporation of burghers is in complete agreement in this regard: they consider the completion of the Prussian effort to bring about a Constitution an indispensable precondition for a flourishing future, especially in so far as the [rather] gradual headway made in this regard [up to now] is contributing more to an excited atmosphere than it helps to calm it in the present situation. But we can consider the [parliament of] estates as a faithful mirror of popular opinion and of the sentiment of the people only on the condition that they are truly the result of popular representation and that they can reach a decision by simple majority.

Ever since Your Majesty has caused a revamping of the judicial system by introducing publicly held trials—at first in this city—the wish has become stronger day by day to see this innovation strengthened as soon as possible by the introduction of a jury.

The complete equality of all religious denominations, without preference accorded by the State to the one at the expense of the other, and the realization of equal civil rights of their respective members has become the custom of the day as a consequence of today's more mild and conciliatory notions. And therefore, certainly, the time has arrived that our jurisdiction, on its part, abandon all restrictions that members of certain denominations are subject to.

If the Prussian monarch, who is watched attentively at this moment by all of Germany, proceeds in this direction in full agreement with His "United Provincial Estates," then Germany will be based on the foundation of shared political institutions. Then, the glorious heritage of the deceased king, the [German] Customs Union [or Zollverein], will pose a mighty challenge. And then, the same will also be true of the high-minded intentions regarding the foundation of a German Law which Your Majesty has revealed when Prussia suggested a Law Relating to Bills of Exchange and a Postal Treaty. Germans will take the position among the peoples which they deserve. And if Germany, up to now, has not known how to occupy this position, as the Proclamation of the Federal Diet admits, we must hold the shortcomings of the Federal Constitution in part responsible and may well trust in the proven German conviction of Your Majesty that this Constitution will be strengthened in the near future, in order to fully represent the interests of the nation.

It is only in discord with the rest of Germany that we see cause for serious concern. Once the profound and heartfelt fraternization of the German tribes has been achieved, or is at least openly and forcefully sought, there no longer exists any reason to see Germany's princes and peoples endangered in case of war. At least, if war is not due to diplomatic schemes but to a violation of German soil.

In deepest reverence, Your royal majesty's most subservient, faithfully obedient Lord Mayor, Mayor, City Councillors, and Aldermen of Berlin

Berlin, March 13, 1848

In order to enable a better understanding of this petition and the debates it caused, it is necessary to add that on the preceding evening the State Gazette [i.e., "Staatszeitung"] had published the well-known decree of the King, directed to the government [i.e. the cabinet], concerning a Law Pertaining to the Press that was to be passed in all of Germany regarding freedom of the press that would be based on it. A rumor had spread in Berlin for a few days already that in the next few days the hated censorship would be lifted by a Cabinet Order. And thus, the decree of March 8 that has just been mentioned could only cause ill feelings because now the freedom of the press that one had assumed to be so near at hand appeared to be postponed indefinitely again. There were only a few men in the assembly of city councilors, however, who shared this view, and the words of the councilman Nauwerk were almost received with indignation by this rigidly conservative corporation when he said that, rather than expressing joy on account of this message by the king, regret should have been articulated. Because, in place of the expected freedom of the press, all that had happened was that things were put off indefinitely once again. Only one or two others rose in support of this motion, and thus the above petition was adopted in the version fully presented here. The other petition, however, which was introduced by the assembly that had taken place in the "Zelten," was rejected with the added remark that the city councilors, on their part, did not feel inclined to comment on individual points raised there. And that, on the other hand, they could not degrade themselves so far as to become the postmen for a crowd which, for the most part, did not consist of enfranchised citizens but merely of "protected clients" [i.e., inhabitants of the city without the voting and other rights of a burgher (an enfranchised citizen) of Berlin].

Start of 1848 to March 11: Thunderclouds on the Horizon

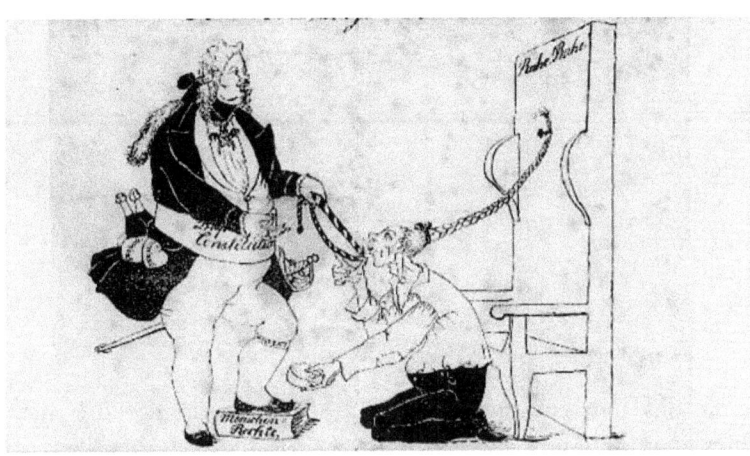

A caricature from the year 1848. The King is wearing a sash with the word Constitution displayed on it but he is putting his left foot on "human rights" and demands "Ruhe Ruhe" – the silence of his subjects. The subject kneeling before him like a shoeshine boy is about to be fastened to what may be a kind of dog leash. Or is he in danger of being hanged?

We cannot say exactly whether it was on this occasion or during the subsequent debate on "protection committees" that the city councilor Seidel, a man who got rich by leasing a "privilege" which weighs heavily both on burghers and protected clients, used the word "mob." Signs of disapproval were noted on this occasion, coming both from the tribune seating the audience and from city councilors holding better views. Thereafter, the orator attempted to make clear, in rather gauche fashion, that he had not used the word in such a spiteful sense. But it was impossible to erase the impression it had made. And as the assembly of city councilors refused to forward a petition that allegedly had been largely adopted by non-citizens, so-called protected clients, no one could fail to ignore anymore the narrow-minded conservatism which dominated this assembly.

PART II

March 12–17: The Course is Set

It was at this moment, no matter how little importance one may have attributed to it up to now—at this very moment, indeed—that the course was set that would lead to the revolution fought on the barricades. For the first time, four times one hundred thousand *"protected clients"* of Berlin arrived at the definite conviction that they were exposed—without protection, without representation—to every kind of despotism, so that nobody existed who would have their concerns at heart. And this, in fact, included the conviction that the so-called representatives of the town did not see themselves as the representatives of its entire population; that these people were convinced, instead, that they were merely obliged to preserve the interests of their corporation [the "citizenry," the property-owning, enfranchised minority] which consists of hardly a tenth of our population, and which has bought this privileged right by nothing else than a small sum of money.

But it was not enough that these people had been informed about their helpless situation in artificial, posh condescension; it was also necessary to abuse and insult them. If the first constituted an injustice, we must appeal to the sensitivity of each of our readers when it's a question of characterizing the second practice. But this "mob" has secured for itself the most splendid satisfaction which was available. Fighting for twenty-four hours on the barricades, the hand reddened by the blood of the comrades who fell next to him, there wasn't a single man among this plebeian crowd who acted in such a way that one could dare to refer to him by this term.

But we must repeat this once again: it was the decision of the city councilors, reached on March 11, that decided the bloody character of the revolution. For the [disenfranchised] "protected clients," the option of sending a delegation had already been barred by the Chief of Police. And when it was attempted to proceed in this way nonetheless, asking the Secret Counselor of the Cabinet, Mr. Illaire, to obtain for the delegates an audience with the king, the answer received was this: The delegation should refrain from it; the king would not love such demonstrations; on the other hand, they were free to rely on the city mail service that would forward their petition.

King Frederick William IV closing the door to the citizens who want to present a petition. The Prince of Prussia is "backing" him fiercely. This caricature was circulated in Germany during the March Revolution.

But they did not choose the mail service; they chose the *barricades*.

We don't believe in the least degree that it would have been possible to obtain *the sovereign rights of the people* by way of a peaceful delegation, dressed in black tail coat and white gloves.

No, no, if we intend to be honest with ourselves, we must not deceive ourselves in this regard. One does not receive such rights as a gift; one has to fight for them. The king could not—and was not even allowed to—give them to us any sooner. Only a populace that has risked, in open struggle, both possessions and blood for its sake, only such a population is worthy of attaining this great bequest [freedom] of the human mind. Therefore we can and must discern in these bloody days of March nothing but the natural course of an illness of our State which could lead to a recovery again only by way of this bloody crisis. There had been enough petitions, submitted pleas, and delegations to enlighten the king with respect to the wishes of his people. Whether the latter was worthy of attaining the fulfillment of these wishes and capable of truly using these considerable rights could only be decided on the barricades.

Therefore, it would fully contradict this view—a view that every thinking person must agree with—if we were to maintain that by a more forceful involvement with our civil authorities, especially the assembly of city councilors, this bloody collision of royal rights and popular rights could have been avoided. But nonetheless, a different attitude, especially of the assembly of city-councilors, would have been desirable—and we refer not only to their attitude *before* but also to that assumed *after* the revolution.

It was a sad indication of lack of character in many of these men when we saw them on the day of the revolution and in its aftermath hiding in their houses, rather than assembling in the place where, for better or worse, they have been deciding the matters of the city for so long. And they should have been assembling on that day in that place, in order to stay there, meeting in permanence, bringing some measure of order into the chaotic events which of necessity must follow in the wake of such scenes. It is true that we have seen also a few of these men—men from which we, frankly speaking, have not expected such behavior—with their rapier drawn, leading the people on the barricades. But there, too, wasn't their proper place. They should have been in the city hall, as pointed out already. If, however, at the very moment when we write this, we can read posters stuck up near street corners which demand the erection of a memorial for those who died on the barricades in that *glorious* struggle, and if this is undersigned by the man who, hardly two weeks ago, called these same people the "mob" in a public assembly, then we must confess to ourselves that we can only look forward to a bleak future if it is such men who want to place themselves again at the top of our representative body.

This meeting of [Berlin city] councilors that took place on March 11, and that was of such importance in the history of the revolution, had to be adjourned abruptly due to tumultuous scenes that occurred on the tribune especially Mssrs. Berends (Julius Berends), Nauwerk (Carl Nauwerck) and Mertens. Then they dispersed and those who had elected the signatories of the petition adopted in the "Zelten" as their representatives went first of all to the Newspaper Reading Hall and, in the evening, to the "Zelten" in order to discuss the measures that had to be taken now. As mentioned already, the result was the request that an audience be granted by the king; a request transmitted via the Secret Counselor of the Cabinet, Mr. Illaire, that was rejected. The next Sunday passed in sullen silence and anxious expectation of the things to come.

On Monday [March 13], finally, after having taken all possible steps (as we have seen) in order to convince the civil authorities that they should side with the people, the leaders of the revolution started with a more decisive and splendid demonstration than before. It was—and we believe indeed to be informed in a fairly precise manner about the course of the revolution—the initial intention of those men who had placed themselves at the head of the movement, to organize now *one*—just one!—instance of more serious resistance of the masses by assembling a large crowd, made up of members of all classes. The people had to be told that this was not an ordinary concourse but a serious and, if necessary, bloody struggle in the holiest interest of man. It had been agreed upon that this struggle was to break out everywhere in town on Thursday [March 16]. Until then, one was to refrain from all resistance, partly in order to organize and arm in a better way, partly in order to encourage those who did not reckon with a general rising of the people, being still inclined to mistake these movements for merely an ordinary concourse in the street.

Indeed, a considerable crowd had assembled on Monday, the 13th, in the empty square in front of the "Zelten." Including those who left briefly and then came back, there may well have been more than ten thousand. Everything still looked rather peaceful. One could see men who had brought their wives and children, as if this was an outing. People were singing songs, drinking beer; and occasionally speakers would rise to address the people, finding attentive listeners among the folks that surrounded them. In addition, thousands of copies of the following petition were distributed and were read quite eagerly:

> Most serene highness! At a time so heavily distressing and pressing for years already, the workers of all ranks dare to direct a request at Your Majesty. This request asks for rapid remedy of the present, great poverty and joblessness of all workers and for safeguarding their future. The State flourishes and prospers only where, by way of work, the people can satisfy their vital needs and where everyone can make his claims, as a paying individual. We are oppressed, however, by Capitalists and Usurers; the presently existing laws are not able to protect us against them. We therefore dare to suggest to Your Majesty most devotedly that a [new] department be created, a Department for Workers which must be composed exclusively by employers and workers, and whose members must be elected by the same out of their midst. Only such a department would be able to recognize the true reason for the pressing situation of the people, to improve the lot of workers, to protect the State against threatening danger, and to protect both property and life from all imminent devastations. Awaiting your answer in deep devotedness etc.

Rumors concerning this people's assembly had, however, occasioned cautionary measures on the part of the government. The cavalry had been ordered to be ready by 6 o'clock. In the evening, as it got dark, these troops—joined by masses of infantrymen—left the barracks and occupied parts of the Thiergarten, of Linden [Street] and especially the Royal Palace [area], as well as yet other parts of town.

Prior to this, the Chief of Police, Mr. von Minutoli, had appeared in the Thiergarten in order to register, with his own eyes and ears, the atmosphere of this people's assembly.

He addressed the assembled people in a friendly manner, and we must not leave unmentioned on this occasion that we had already had the opportunity, on this same day, to admire and respect the dignified manners of this gentleman who, among all of our authorities, occupied the most difficult position during the revolution and who, nonetheless, at every moment behaved with such honorableness that [neither] of the two opposing parties is denying him the fullest measure of respect and appreciation. But we would become guilty of an injustice vis-à-vis the public if we should fail to add that in addition to this respect and to this appreciation, which is finally the reward of every gentleman who is doing his duty, Mr. von Minuteli also knew how to earn the love of the entire population of Berlin; a sentiment that will not remain limited to the narrow [confines enclosed by the] city walls of Berlin but will extend itself to all provinces of Prussia and all states of Germany.

Surrounded by a raging crowd which seemed immediately ready to make the threats come true that were uttered against him, this brave man, finding it impossible to advance through the masses that were streaming towards the

"Zelten," called for a buggy. He sat down in it and, instead of returning to town, as many others would have done in order to seek help and the protection of the army, he rode to the location of the assembly, alone and unprotected, trusting solely in his good cause. And here, he tried to move the assembled crowd by his amicable persuasion.

Perhaps this people's assembly would have dispersed, just as on previous evenings, without further disruption if there hadn't been the sight of the military, present in large numbers, that provoked and embittered the crowd. In several places, an intervention of the troops was believed to be necessary; in several locations, the cavalrymen directed their horses into the masses in order to disperse them. And they succeeded to do so without any resistance. By eleven o'clock, all the streets had already been cleared.

On the following day, at two o'clock, the petition of the city councilors which we have included further above, was presented to the king by a deputation of the aldermen and the councilmen.

The king replied to it more or less as follows, according to reports by the press:

> His Majesty is aware of the significance of the moment; this was the first petition he accepted in person in this turbulent time, and it has occasioned in his Highness a pleasant feeling that it is coming from His beloved native city which has preserved itself, in this time of commotion, in such a gratifying manner. When things have heated up all around, it is not possible indeed to expect that only here the mood would be below the freezing point. And all this considered, it had to be appreciated that in a city of this size which certainly did not lack elements tempted to spread disorder, the order was not significantly disturbed. Even yesterday night could not mar this appreciation in a significant manner. In the case of all those in whose behavior His Majesty greatly trusts, the most sober and level-headed attitude could be ascertained. And His Majesty has been pleased by the attitude of the citizens.
>
> As far as the petition itself was concerned, His Majesty was unable to answer it in a highly stylized speech, as was the custom in other countries –only in a conversational tone. He would renew some works. First of all, He was glad to reply, regarding the main request, that it had already been granted. That the United Provincial Parliaments should meet in session had been decided several days ago. And the Royal Patent that would allow them to meet had been already signed. Full of confidence, the King was looking forward to this session, as a genuinely Prussian conviction would not be lacking. Least of all in days of danger.
>
> With great openness and great trust, His Majesty would face the Parliament. His watchword was, '...free peoples, free princes': only if both were free, general welfare could flourish. The other requests could

only find a solution through Parliament; it was not necessary therefore to comment on them in detail.

One expression, however, that had been included in the petition, His Majesty [feels] compelled to mention: an expression that was directed against the gradual development of the Constitution: this he could not at all agree with. There are certain things which one cannot hasten if the danger is to be avoided that they are turned upside down. This was also the lesson of the neighboring country where, in a life-time, 15 constitutions sworn upon had followed one another and where, only recently, the self-created edifice had collapsed. One must not build a house in six weeks which demands that it should take one and a half years to build; neither may it be constructed on sandy ground if it is to endure! – "Valiant and thoughtful," these are the watchwords of a good commander. Without penalty, they may not be separated, forgetting the one while the other is emphasized! This is what His Majesty keeps in mind. The worthy and venerable German order may not be disregarded; the distinction of estates is indeed German, too. Whoever strives against this, is exposing himself to dangers. In this respect as well, negative examples are not lacking! And likewise, property as the historical base of the status occupied by the different estates has to be taken into account. All of this is something that only the [Prussian] Diet can deal with.

Just as His Majesty trusts in the Diet, the people should trust it and "thus make possible an intimate union of government, estates and the people." This concord should be the highest aim inscribed in all efforts until the convocation of the Diet, and when the Diet is meeting in session. Only by being steadfastly united, can they avert the misfortune from the German fatherland which a revolutionary war would cause it to suffer! His Majesty does not want to be responsible for discord. As far as Germany is concerned, its fortune is not placed in His hand. Whatever His power can attain [in this respect], His Majesty is going to honestly and seriously attempt, so that this time of crisis may turn the scales in favor of its unity, power and greatness.

It is as dear to His heart as that of Prussia.

An answer of this kind to such a petition had been foreseeable indeed. A more determined manner on the part of that authority of the town which was so close to the throne might have produced a deeper impression on the king. But being so falsely informed as to the mood of the people, by those he had to see as its representatives, it could appear [to him] as a satisfying concession that on that day, in addition to the already known order concerning the abolition of censorship, the following royal patent concerning the convocation of the United Provincial Parliaments had been published:

Conjointly with the Imperial Austrian Government, We, Frederick William, by the Grace of God King of Prussia etc. etc., have invited our German allies to unite immediately in common deliberation regarding those measures which are necessary, in the present difficult and dangerous situation, for the good of the German fatherland. And we are determined to seek with all Our power a result from the deliberations that will lead to a real regeneration of the German Confederation, so that the German people will be truly united by it—strengthened by free institutions, however no less protected against the dangers of revolt and anarchy—thus regaining its old greatness, so that Germany may find its deserved position in Europe. But whatever the success of these Our efforts may be, measures will be conditioned by them which require the cooperation of Our faithful Estates, for the sake of their implementation. For this reason and because, in such great and decisive epochs as the present one, we feel strong only in union with our Estates, we have decided to convene the United Provincial Estates on Thursday, April 27, of this year, in Our Capital and Residence, the city of Berlin, and advise the chief minister to effect the convocation of the same by the Minister of the Interior, while taking all the necessary preparatory steps.

Berlin, March 14, 1848 Frederick William
[Friedrich Wilhelm]

In this way, Tuesday morning passed, but an anxious tension had affected every mind, and looking into the future in a grave manner, people felt full well that the next few days would bring something decisive.

Irritating minds even more, there appeared, in the afternoon, the following announcement of the aldermen and the police in the form of [two] posters:

> The unsettled mood in the neighboring countries has caused a stir in our State as well and it has fomented desires among the citizenry. In joint action with the city councilors of this town, we have deposited these desires at the throne of His Majesty the King.
>
> Fellow citizens and inhabitants of Berlin! All of us know the heart and will of the King. Both have been unceasingly directed towards the welfare and political development of the fatherland.
>
> And just a few days ago, we could see the most beautiful signs of His trust in His people. Let us not stray from the path of law and order; let us refrain from all steps that are liable to be misinterpreted and which could lead to increased agitation and disturbance of the [established] order.
>
> Together with all good citizens and inhabitants of our town, we regret the nonsense of yesterday night which made necessary the co-involvement of the armed forces for the sake of the preservation of lawful order. We are

compelled to desire, therefore, that each and every one of us keep himself and those under his supervision away from any agitated assembly, as such assembly is neither necessary nor conducive to the attainment of our desires while exposing our families to great danger.

Berlin, March 14, 1848
Lord Mayor, Mayor and aldermen of this Royal Residence

A popular assembly that was taking place yesterday evening in the Thiergarten at the "Zelten" has set in motion such an important number of people that the deployment of army units became necessary as a preventive measure. This measure fulfilled the intended purpose and it was only necessary in a few locations to disperse the crowd. As popular assemblies are not allowed, the urgent demand is herewith made known to the public that they must not take part in such gatherings. For it is not only the leading agitators and participants involved, but also people present out of curiosity, who will expose themselves to those consequences which result from violating the provisions of the law. Furthermore, we find it necessary to remind everyone of the following ordinances:

As soon as, in the case of a concourse, the crowd has been required by the commanding officer to disperse, or when this has been expressed by beating the drums three times or by sounding the trumpet, those who do not immediately act according to this demand shall, simply on this count, be sentenced to 6 months in prison—or forced labor; paragraph 8 of the ordinance of December 30, 1798; paragraph 7 of the ordinance of August 17, 1835.

At the same time, the house wardens are reminded [that they are obliged] to lock the doors of their houses in the case of a concourse. Parents, school teachers, and persons of high standing are required to keep back their children, pupils and servants. They must see to it that the latter do not increase the crowd by joining it, under whatever pretext. The owners of factories and master craftsmen are obliged to take such measures as would hinder their workers, journeymen and apprentices to leave the workshops and apartments. Naughty boys who cause restlessness and commit only acts of nonsense on the occasion of a concourse in the streets and in public places (agitation caused by shouting and whistling being counted among these acts), are punished according to § 183 Section 20 Part II of the *General Law of the Land [Allgemeine Landrecht]*.

Berlin, March 14, 1848
Royal Governor - von Pinek
Royal Chief of Police - von Minuteli

On the other hand, posters were glued to walls at night time, especially to the walls of barracks, asking the soldiers not to shoot at the people if unrest should develop, but to make the people's cause their own cause. These attempts, however, did not only fail utterly to obtain the intended effect; on the contrary, the military authorities saw in this only another reason to admonish the troops to stick more closely together and to remain faithful to their sworn oath. On the whole, the mood of the ordinary recruit gradually began to be rather irritated. Kept in the barracks, ready at every moment to begin a fight against a large mass of people whose acts had been described to him as lawless, their purpose reportedly being the toppling of all existing order, it could only be bitterness that befell the ordinary recruit in the end. A bitterness that would later on give occasion to such horrible scenes, and which became noticeable already on this day.

Regardless of all warnings, a large crowd assembled again on this day in the Palace Square and in the streets leading towards it.

The Royal Palace in Berlin, painted in 1838 by Klose . The long façade of the Palace faces the Palace Square (Schloss Platz). The façade we see is the South side of the Palace. The gap between the houses to the left and the palace leads to the street called "Palace Freedom." It is from this position that the army attacked the demonstrators assembled in the Palace Square, on one occasion.

It was especially in the square just mentioned that a tightly packed crowd had formed attempting to ridicule the soldiers positioned there with loud screaming and shouting. Out of the midst of this crowd that had just been required to disperse, an impudent hand was raised, holding a pistol and firing a shot into the air. A deep silence, punctuated by not a single sound from the ranks of the military or from the citizens, followed upon this shot. It had signaled, in a sense, the bloody fighting that was to take place only a few days later. But even the large number of curious onlookers that had come here were deeply and gravely impressed by this event.

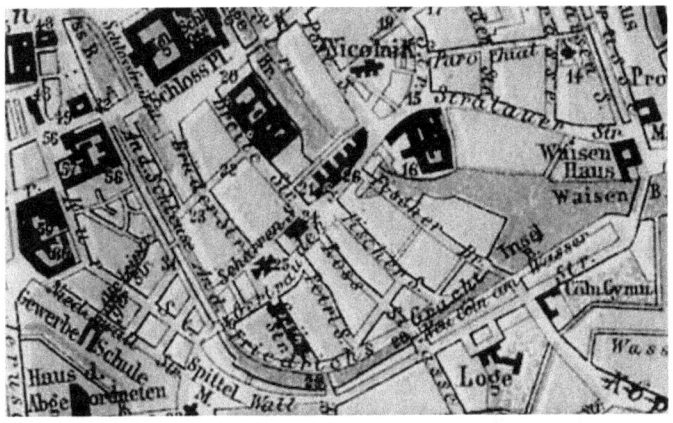

The Palace and the streets, squares and bridges to the South of it. From a plan of 1875. The part of capital situated just South of the Palace, enclosed by the canal and the River Spree, is the civilian (non-Royal) portion of the borough known as Coelln. With its Palace Square, and such streets as Broadway (Breite Str.) and Brothers Street (Brüder Str.), it was the earliest major scene of the army's brutal action against demonstrators and pedestrians accidentally near these places. "Schloss Pl." (Schloss Platz) means Palace Square. "Breite Str." = Broadway; "Brüder Str." = Brothers' St.

Soon after this pause (a quietness that was indeed deeply moving), the screaming and shouting set in again and the troops moved forward against the crowd which, being unarmed, did not stand firm but dispersed, instead, in all directions. It was now that, in some places of the town, the most pitiful scenes occurred. The cavalry, charging through densely packed crowds that could not resist in the slightest way, struck mercilessly with their sabres. This happened especially at the location known as the *Werderian Mills*, just where, to the right of it—before one reaches the *Canal Locks Bridge*—the street called *By the River Locks* ends as a kind of dead-end alley.

Pedestrians are standing next to the railing of the Canal Locks Bridge, looking down to the water and the barges. Section of a painting is by Albert Kiekebusch (done in 1892).

It was here that a large number of quiet citizens had sought refuge while the cavalry, having broken into a gallop, was chasing the fleeing. Some cavalrymen directed their horses into the closely packed crowd and ruthlessly hit out with the sabres in all directions until finally, fearing death, those farthest away from them broke through a gate leading down to the river, where they saved their skin by boarding the ships that anchored here.

Similar things happened in Green Street though not in entirely the same horrible manner, because the escape route was closed to no one here. Some weak attempts were made here as well to build a barricade with the boards of a fence that was enclosing the construction site of [St.] Peter's Church. But it was abandoned without a defense effort when the troops approached.

Occurrences that were no less frightful happened in Brothers Street, but in order to avoid a repetition of the story with all the details, the declaration of a number of respected citizens of Berlin shall be presented here in place of our own narration of the events. These citizens convened the following day in order to take down the minutes concerning the behavior of the troops, register a complaint with the appropriate authorities, and demand satisfaction in the name of the citizenry.

On the same day when the above poster appeared in the streets, General von Pfuel (speaking for the royal government) and von Minutoli (the Berlin chief of police) issued a "Notification" or public announcement, again in the form of a poster, complaining about "excesses in the street" (Strassenexcesse) that civilians had caused on the preceeding day, deploring that "troublemakers" evaded, and regretting that "peaceful citizens" present on the scene were wounded. They promised a "strict investigation" and asserted that the severity of the law would be applied. (Also against soldiers?) The text ended by demanding that the citizens should be quiet. Honorable citizens should help to maintain order.

The text on record reads as follows:

> The undersigned inhabitants of Brothers Street, as eyewitnesses, testify that the following is true:
>
> Yesterday evening at 9 o'clock, a horn of the cavalry was sounded in the area of Brothers Street close to Newman Street (but this was not the signal given in intervals that asks a crowd to disperse). Immediately afterwards a tumult broke out in this area, and sparks lit up in the street, as if a detachment of the cavalry was engaged in battle.
>
> Immediately afterwards, a detachment of cuirassiers—more or less an *escadron* [squadron]—approached at a rapid gallop from said area towards the Palace Square in irregular formation and with terrible shouting. But they did not drive a single person coming from that area [i.e. the Brothers St./Newman St. junction] in front of them.
>
> The cuirassiers were extremely nervous; they spurred their horses so much that several fell; they rode on the sidewalks and beat against the closed doors of the houses with their *palaches*. And generally speaking, they acted as if they were confronting a superior enemy, whereas not a single one of the troublemakers chased away from Newman alley was in front of them.
>
> Apparently left entirely to themselves, the cuirassiers had engaged quite a while in shouting and mad behavior, in front of the houses 1 to 4 and 40 to 45 of Brothers Street, when individual persons approached in intervals from the side of the Palace Square that was occupied by the military. They were perhaps six, at most ten and they went their way quietly, keeping close to the walls of the houses. These persons cannot possibly have been involved in what may or may not have been excessive actions in Newman alley. After all, they came from the opposite direction. But nonetheless they became the target of an unbelievable rage of the cuirassiers. Every single person was attacked, sometimes from two or three cuirassiers simultaneously, and they were beaten down with the *palaches* in the most merciless manner. And every time one of them escaped his pursuers, he was attacked, again and again, by the entire line of cuirassiers and at times hit by two or three *palaches* at once.
>
> It has been noted repeatedly that no obstreperous behavior of an individual and no refusal of a group of people to disperse had occurred; nor had there been an attack by a crowd on the armed forces. It was rather the brute force of hundreds of armed cuirassiers which was directed against individual defenseless and quiet wanderers. It seems that only one officer accompanied the troops, for it was only after considerable time

had elapsed that the voice of a commanding officer attempted to stop the atrocity. Due to the shouts of the cuirassiers this produced no effect for some time, until finally the commander turned his weapon against a cuirassier engaged in the maltreatment of a human being.

It must not go unmentioned that ahead of this occurrence no patrol had passed through Brothers Street even though there was sufficient reason to do so because, since 8 o'clock, the troops that had taken up positions on the Palace Square had been mocked by a small crowd of about 50 persons that assembled time and again at the corner of Brothers Street and the Palace Square and then ran away in the direction of Peter's Square. But before and after each such event, it had been unproblematic to pass through Brothers Street.

The infantry troops positioned in the Palace Square at the Palace Square/ Brothers Street junction, who let the wanderers enter Brothers Street, must have been witnesses of the occurrences described further above.

About forty citizens living in Brothers Street who had been eyewitnesses of these occurrences signed this complaint in the house of the Judicial Councilor Bergling, at No.2 Brothers Street. Among their midst, they chose a delegation, comprised of the Judicial Councilor Bergling, the author Dr. Woeniger, the mechanic Lewert, the banker Mendheim and the dyer Schwendy. Only a minor excitement would have sufficed, when this statement was drafted on the morning of the fifteenth, to have started the revolt. Thousands of people, workers as well as citizens, milled through Brothers Street in order to see the traces of the fight that had occurred in the previous evening. A general indignation due to the way in which the troops had proceeded was voiced. And there would have been a serious explosion of anger if Dr. Woeniger had not addressed the masses which, as has already been noted, included men of all walks of life. He informed them of the steps that were to be taken in order to give the citizenry satisfaction and thus precluded every excessive reaction.

Then, the *judicial councilor*, Mr. Bergling, went to see the commander of the troops, von Ditfurth, and the Minister of the Interior, von Bodelschwingh, whereas the other delegates went to see the Lord Mayor.

It reveals a lot with regard to the attitude of the latter that the delegation met him at 11 o'clock, still in his dressing gown, and, as it seemed, rather inclined to deal with the affair quite nonchalantly. Addressed by Dr. Woeniger, he said that one should not address him so "formally." They should rather sit down and calmly discuss the matter. This triggered an excited debate on the part of Dr. Woeniger and the banker Mendheim, whereupon the Lord Mayor changed his behavior and promised to do everything in his power in order to obtain satisfaction for the citizens. The delegates do not seem to have completely trusted these promises, however, and immediately went to see the chief-of-police. Being

March 12-17: The Course is Set

The Commander's House (Kommandantenhaus) at Under the Linden Blvd., opposite the main arsenal or 'Zeughaus' (left), and the commander of the Berlin garrison and governor of the Prussian capital, general Wilhelm von Ditfurth (right).

Ernst von Bodelschwingh (left image) was Prussian minister of the interior since 1845. He was soon disagreeing with the king's position, being convinced of the necessity of a constitution, but stayed in office nonetheless during the period of fruitless debate between the government and the United Diet regarding this matter. But on March 12, 1848, he asked the king for permission to step back from office because he saw troubles ahead. He was replaced by Arnim von Boitzenburh on March 19. Wilhelm Krausnick (right), the royalist Lord Mayor of Berlin since 1834, was compelled by popular pressure to resign immediately after the March Revolution but was reinstated by the counterrevolution in 1851 and remained Lord Mayor till 1861.

told that he was present at a session of the city councilors, they went there and informed him of their grievances. The chief-of-police encountered them in a very friendly manner and expressed his deep regret regarding the entire occurrence, something the Lord Mayor had not done. Even though the police had not been responsible for the excesses of the military, he declared that he nonetheless would seek to prevent a repetition of such deplorable events, and that he had already offered to resign from office if troops would continue to be employed without asking him. Then, the delegation turned also to the assembly of city councilors that was meeting in secret session. They asked the president of the assembly, Mr. Fournier, to come out and meet them. When the delegates representing Brothers Street encountered him, they met another delegation consisting of the clothier Mueller and the *demesne* official Deutsch. These delegations merged and having jointly voiced their protest against the military, they confronted the president of the assembly of city councilors with the following demands: (1) Withdrawal of the troops, until a real attack of the people on persons and property has occurred; (2) permission that in such a case "commissions of citizens" may be organized for the purpose of calming down the people. These requests are remarkable in so far as they must be seen as the immediate, certain point of origin of the citizen commissions that were formed later on.

Immediately, the assembly of city councilors began deliberations regarding this matter and a turbulent session ensued. It was above all the councilor Mertens who insisted, with much passion, on the citizens commissions.

After several hours, the president of the assembly informed the waiting delegations as follows: the assembly of city councilors has immediately chosen some of its members as delegates who are to see the governor, the Lord Mayor and the chief-of-police, in order to voice complaints. In addition, posters intended to calm the situation shall be put up at all street corners. The assembly also intended to see to it that the borough presidents would be empowered to ask citizens to exert a pacifying influence on the crowd. And last but not least, the government was to be induced to *withdraw* the military completely. Or, if that would not seem appropriate, to let it figure in the mildest possible way. The members of the delegations weren't particularly satisfied because their request concerning the establishment of proper citizen commissions was hardly being fulfilled. But they departed.

The Brothers Street delegation now returned to Brothers Street where the crowd had swelled even more ominously and was waiting impatiently for a response. The judicial councilor, Bergling, had returned as well, and had obtained a calming document from the commander [of the troops], von Ditfurth and from the Minister of the Interior, von Bodelschwingh.

Dr. Woeniger communicated its content to the people by way of a speech which gave information on the endeavors of the delegation and which admonished them to refrain from further excesses. This speech that was received with general, lively applause, quite obviously had a calming effect. And it was due to it that, particularly among the citizens, a more satisfied attitude prevailed. An especially calming effect can be attributed to the fact that Dr. Woeniger mentioned the possibility that the troops would be withdrawn completely.

Positive consequences can also be ascribed to the printed text of the statements made by the commander [of the troops] and the Minister [of the Interior] that was distributed by the Brother Street delegation, accompanied by a calming introduction. The document said:

Fellow citizens! This morning, several inhabitants of Brothers Street convened as a consequence of the regrettable events that occurred yesterday evening in this same street. They entrusted the undersigned delegation with the task of immediately registering a complaint. We have set out to accomplish this task at once and, specifically, filed the following requests:

1) that the troops shall remain completely withdrawn, except in the event that attacks on persons or property should occur; and

2) that until then, it shall be left to the citizens to preserve quietness.

We have good reason to believe that these requests will be granted and have already received the rescript added further below in response to our complaint, which we herewith make known to everyone.

Fellow-citizen! We direct to you the urgent request to avoid everything that can only lead to new misfortune. Let us trust the assurances of the authorities and let us show them that we are strong enough to maintain law and order.

Berlin, March 15, 1848
Bergling, Judicial Councilor; Lewert, mechanic; Mendheim, banker; Schwendy, dyer; Dr. Woeniger, writer

----

In response to the report filed with the Minister of the Interior by several inhabitants of Brothers Street, concerning the maltreatment of peaceful inhabitants by a detachment of the regiment of cuirassiers belonging to the [Royal] Guard, we have at once appointed a joint commission entrusted with an investigation to find out exact details of this regrettable event, so that those which might be found guilty can received the appropriate punishment.

In return, we expect that the inhabitants of Brothers Street, just as other citizens of the town, will participate in quieting the excited minds as much as they can, thus preventing vaster misfortune.

The judicial councilor Bergling is requested to make this disclosure known to his neighbors.

Berlin, March 15, 1848
The Governor. The Minister of the Interior,
On behalf of him: v. Bodelschwingh,
v. Ditfurth, Commander.

What is remarkable is the fact that the Prince of Prussia [the brother of the King] was rather annoyed when this official decree became known in the palace in the late evening. He saw it as an insult to the troops and protested against their withdrawal. At the same time, Berlin's top censor, the normal censor and Secret Councilor at the Court, Dr. John, found himself compelled to start a censorship investigation because Dr. Woeniger got said address printed without the necessary *imprimatur*, obviously because it had been necessary to act quickly. The fact that he dared to do this and that he found a print shop (Moeser's printery) willing to go along shows how weak, antiquated and rotten certain institutions were considered to be at the time.

A second public announcement which was posted at street corners that afternoon, and which likewise left a calming impression in the minds of the citizenry, read as follows:

> Regardless of the warning words of our announcement published yesterday, several excesses taking place in the streets in the evening have necessitated the deployment and, in some locations, the action of the troops. It is regrettable that on this occasion, in addition to the troublemakers—among them several who could flee, thus escaping arrest—several peaceful citizens, present by mere chance, have been wounded. *In order to clarify these occurrences, an investigative procedure has been initiated in order to make sure the severity of the law can be applied everywhere* [* the authorities refrained from saying in a more direct manner: "regardless of rank"! A "vertical" concept, referring to higher and lower rank, was purposefully replaced by a "horizontal" concept: "Wherever, in society injustice must be punished, we will do it; we will at least investigate the case." In other words, they shied away from talking openly about rank, because they knew that the people thought: Oh well, aristocratic officers can act with impunity. Which was pretty much the case, probably.].* We can only add to this the exhortation that on the part of the inhabitants everything should be done to prevent further action of the military by assuming a quiet attitude, and we put our trust in the often tested, good public spiritedness of the Berliners, because we believe that an association of honorable citizens can contribute a great deal to the maintenance of law and order.
>
> Berlin, March 15, 1848
> The Royal Government. (signed) v. Pfuel.
> Royal Chief-of-Police. (signed) v. Minutoli.

The hinted wish expressed herewith, though only in rather general terms, that the citizens should step in, of course did not hinder the masses which had milled through the streets all day long, to swell and to crowd especially the Palace Square. It seems that the two announcements mentioned further above contributed to the rumor that the military would not step in. And indeed, one could see several citizens with white armbands among the people who were talking to them in a friendly manner and sought to convince them that they should disperse peacefully. It seemed indeed that there would be a renewed occurrence of the scenes witnessed on the previous evenings; but as a precautionary measure the guards stationed in the Coelln City Hall had been withdrawn; it was apparently feared that they could be easily overpowered by a surprise attack.

The Coelln Fish Market and Coelln City Hall, the central bldg. in the background (to the right of St. Peter's Church, further away).
The corner of Broadway (Breite Str.) and Gertrude St. (Gertrauden Str.) is on the right side of the Fish Market square, next to the city hall bldg. This was the site of one of the most contested barricades during the March Revolution. On March 18, revolutionary fighters under the command of the machine-builder Karl Siegrist (also spelled Sigerist) defended the barricade against several attacks of the infantry and the artillery. After abandonment of the barricade, ten revolutionaries captured in Coelln City Hall were executed on the spot by soldiers. Siegrist was held responsible for the storming of the arsenal later and sentenced to 7 years in a military "fortress prison" in June 14, 1848. This sentence was commuted by the court of appeals to one year in a military prison on Oct. 7, 1848. (See Neue Rheinische Zeitung (New Rhenanian Gazette), No. 48, July 18, 1848.)
A historical marker praising democracy and revolution and commemorating Siegrist's valiant role and the death of those executed existed here. It was later removed.

After the departure of the men, the populace broke into the guard-house and demolished it; they also sought to break into a gun store.

Regardless of the lack of serious success attributable to these events, the military authorities now believed that they had to step in with even greater severity than before. And at 7 o'clock, beating the attack drums, a detachment of the infantry left the palace in order to clear the square. The people sought to protect themselves by erecting a few barricades. But these were defended as insufficiently as they were built, and when the infantry fired a salvo, they all fled in every direction. At the Virginsbridge, which had been pulled up in order to close it to the cavalry, a fight with handguns ensued, and in other parts of the town, in Gertrude Street, in Green Street and at Doenhof's Square, barricades had been erected. But all of them were poorly defended and they were abandoned to the military.

That the military authorities assessed these riots as serious can be deduced from the fact that loaded cannons were positioned in the palace yard.

But on the other hand, as far as the people were concerned, the character of the *emeute* [insurrection] began to change, as well. The news of the revolution in Vienna had already arrived, and it had a wondrous effect on everybody's mind. Groups of people formed at every street corner and there, orators informed the people about it and asked them to imitate it and to stay on. Above and beyond this, a general indignation prevailed because the soldiers had fired shots.

It was already midnight when the crowds dispersed. Everyone seriously prepared for the struggle of the coming day.

Early in the morning, on Thursday, March 16, the streets that had been the scene of fighting on the previous evening were visited by a large crowd of curious people. During the night, there had been efforts to clear as many barricades as possible. But the nervousness of the citizenry had been considerably increased due to the occurrences of the past evening. They had indeed believed that the military would refrain from stepping in, and yet this had happened in a more serious way than before. The news of the great revolution in Vienna had been confirmed that morning in such a way that no one could have any doubts about this. And after an intimate union of citizens and workers had been impeded on the previous day by the above-mentioned proclamation of the Minister [of the Interior], Bodelschwingh, and the Commander, Ditfurth, such a union was even more inevitable on Thursday, as the political aims of the *emeute* took shape more clearly.

By noon the center of action had moved from Brothers Street and the Palace Square to the square in front of the Opera. We cannot give concise reasons for this. It seems to have been mainly due to the rumor that the university students, starting from the university, wanted to embark on a serious demonstration. It is not really credible that an attack on the arsenal or on the palace of the Prince of Prussia was intended. But this much is certain: in the latter location, the deepest consternation prevailed; suitcases were packed, and the prince was intent on leaving his domicile via its backdoor at Behren Street if there should be the slightest indication of an attack.

In the meantime, everyone prepared for a more serious fight in the evening. The citizens had closed the doors of their houses the previous evenings in accordance with the decrees of the police; they were now advised to leave their doors open in order to offer a sanctuary to fleeing persons. The populace began to arm itself, and in the afternoon, a small party, consisting of citizens, met in the *Hofjaeger* [Inn], in order to deliberate how a forceful resistance of the people could be organized in the best way. Everyone was prepared for the decisive blow.

It was then that the following announcement was put up at street corners:

> For three days already the property and security of the citizens of Berlin has been in the greatest of dangers. The voice of the corporation of burghers has declared itself with resolution against such a scheme and is prepared to help. It has been decided therefore to form in every borough of the town a Commission of Protection which shall consist of all citizens who are civil servants. They will in turn select, among the co-citizens of their borough, the most appropriate and best-known men and especially the senior master craftsmen and guild presidents.
>
> The badge of these protective officers shall be a black and white armband worn on the left arm, with the printed words: "protective officer" ["Schutz-Beamter"] on it, as well as a white baton.
>
> Resistance against these protective officers shall be punished in the same manner as resistance against [regular] representatives of the authorities or against the guards.
>
> Whosoever shall wear the armband and baton of a protective officer without authorization shall be punished in such a way as if he had arrogated the exercise of the duties and powers of the authorities, and he must reckon with immediate arrest.
>
> We place our trust in our co-citizens and in the entire population of the city that they will give their full approval and support to this institution [the Commission of Protection] which has been devised in the interest of public law and order.
>
> Berlin, March 16, 1848
> The Lord Mayor, Mayor and City Council of the Royal Residence.

The impression which this announcement left on the public was indeed anything but satisfactory. On the one hand, it was felt to be a very arrogant measure of the city government that it endowed these protective officers with a legal status when facing the people, so that resistance against them was to be punished in the same way as resistance against officials representing the authorities; in this way, every person would be subject to the capriciousness of people whose moral character and ability to perform such an office remained untested due to any lack of a chance to do so. On the other hand, the protective officers, in view of their difficult and at the same time dangerous position, found it entirely inappropriate that they had been given no other weapon than a baton hardly two feet in length which the [cutting] humor of the Berlin populace at once mockingly referred to as "a ball paddle."

That the announcement had mentioned a *danger* to *property* had also caused a generally felt indignation among all classes. There had indeed been attempts to break into a few gun stores. But this attempt of a defenseless crowd to obtain guns hardly deserved such a spiteful term. And we would wish indeed that we could say about the military which had engaged in fighting that it had respected the property it was supposed to protect as much as these people had done.

Nonetheless the Commissions of Protection began to fulfill their function in the evening, and thanks to them, at first no outbreak of a bigger movement occurred that evening. It was necessary for the moment to see on which side these citizens would be. The university students had in part joined the Commissions of Protection, as well. And about one hundred and fifty of them, equipped with the aforementioned baton and the armband, appeared among the people. Addressing them with persuasive words, they attempted to disperse them. They did not succeed, however. As the masses were displaying a more and more threatening attitude, a platoon of infantrymen which had been positioned in the back of the New Guard House, marched into the street, then turned around, in order to face Linden Street, and after the horn had been sounded three times in intervals that were much too short to give the crowd enough time to disperse, regardless of how serious an attempt to do so they might have made, the first row of soldiers fired into the assembled masses. Two people were killed and many were wounded more or less seriously by this salvo.

In the other parts of town everything seemed to be quiet. As mentioned already, it was necessary to wait and see how the Commissions of Protection would act. It was only in Hunter Street and Upper Wall Street that tumultuous scenes could be observed which are described in a report to General von Pfuel, signed by many visitors of the newspaper reading hall, including some military officers. This report provides a sad account of the way the military dealt with the citizens.

> Your Excellency! After the untimely and provocative intervention of the military had turned ordinary noise-making in the street into a ruckus, and after the blood of innocent citizens, even women, had been spilled on March 13, 14 and 15, while the citizenry had not even been asked to do, somehow, its duty and partake in time in the preservation of order, finally the city government's announcement appeared on the 16th. It provided the information that Commissions of Protection would be formed in all boroughs of the town which should be responsible for the preservation of order. The task of these Commissions of Protection was to limit the intervention of the military to cases of an extreme emergency. And this, it was assumed, would be the case only if the protective officers would not succeed to preserve the peace and if they asked the military for help. This hurriedly decided measure was put in effect too late—and incompletely, at that. It was already 6:30, as the letter addressed to you today by Mr.

Nicol. von Beguelin points out, when the army fired into a mass of people who were present in the Opera Square, trusting in the new measure and moving about in a location which up to that time had not been dangerous. As a consequence, it is said, several persons were killed.

The horror caused by these shots spread rapidly in the neighborhood, and repeatedly a deafening noise heard in Upper Wall Street and Hunter Street put everybody in a flurry and a state of fright.

About an hour after this incident, a torrent of people, emitting cries of fear, came from the so-called "Flying Buttress" and rushed down Upper Wall Street in the direction of Hunter Street. There were shouts, some of them to the effect that the military was pursuing them, others to the effect that the soldiers were firing down the street. Some even shouted, They are firing *cartouches*! In the Berlin newspaper reading hall, many members of the most educated classes were present at the time, either reading quietly or engaging in a conversation in the club rooms, and among them the Undersigned named in the enclosure. When the shouting started, they dashed to the windows. The multitude got stuck at the junction of Upper Wall Street and Hunter Street. They all shouted out at once. Somebody cried, "Erect a barricade!"—an absurd suggestion, as there was no material present that would have been sufficient to block a very wide street, especially when the intrusion of the troops was fearfully anticipated at any moment.

Nevertheless some brought wooden beams from nearby streets and alleys and placed them in the middle of the street. There were also those calls for "Weapons, weapons" that had already been heard during the last few evenings. And somebody sped to the basement of Mr. Miquet in Hunter Street and brought back an axe which was used to break into the shop at the other side of the Hunter [Jaeger] Street junction, because people hoped they would find weapons. All of these actions seemed to be inspirations of a fear of death and occurred in utmost haste and confusion, while none of those thus involved thought of finishing what he had begun.

The announcement of the Government and Chief-of-Police of this town, made public on March 14, had among other things reminded house owners of their obligation to close their doors whenever an unlawful assembly was forming. In view of the brutality of the military which, during these days, chased innocent people through the streets, beating them down [with sabres], it is impossible for every house owner who has a heart and possesses reason to fulfill the letter of this instruction quite literally. The owner of the houses number 12 and 13 at Upper Wall Street, van Hasebrouk, personally went to the door with the key in his hand, and saw to it that the door was closed but opened it immediately for everybody who sought refuge in the house. The owner of the Berlin Newspaper Hall, G. Julius, placed the chief servant of the place, the former corporal Korthe, at the door in support of the house owner. Then he went inside the hall and asked those standing by the windows to step back. Everyone, without exception, responded to this request, even though many of the present and most highly esteemed guests were extremely excited in view of what happened. The windows were closed one after the other and, in some cases, the blinds were also lowered. Inside the building, the light of the gas lamps was turned down low. The purpose of this measure was to avoid the possibility that a large crowd would be attracted by the bright light.

In the meantime, Mr. Miquet had run to the infantrymen positioned in the bank building, and had asked for help. A detachment under the command of a lieutenant appeared in front of the house and at the moment when the door had just been opened to let a few persons enter who were subscribers of the newspaper hall and came to visit it, some infantrymen, with attached bayonets, attempted to enter, as well. The houseowner and the chief servant Korthe called out to them that those entering belonged to the house and that they were about to close the door again. Nonetheless, those up front in the group of infantrymen violently entered the door and placed the point of the bayonets on the chest of the houseowner and of chief servant Korthe. One of the infantrymen shouted, "*Sacre nom de Dieu*, I'll stab you, *canaille!*" The other one seemed to be ready indeed to stab Mr. van Hasebrouk, when the Lieutenant stopped him, shouting, "Wait, 'till I give the command!"

As the lieutenant pointed out, the reason for this violent intrusion into a peaceful house was that somebody had allegedly thrown a stone at his men.

Because the houseowner disputed it, he shouted, "The house must be cleared!" In order to achieve the execution of this inane order, he commanded the bugler to sound the horn three times. This happened three times, almost without interval. Of course, no person in the house understood this signal. The anxious ones rushed to and fro, hurried up staircases, crowded in the salons. Suddenly the errand boy of the institute ascended the stairs in a hurry and, entering the office, he shouted, "They're shooting into the house!" The confusion produced by this shout was indescribable. The *premier-lieutenant* Zimmermann who was present in the establishment of the newspaper hall, shouted: "Gentlemen, just remain calm. They will hardly shoot here into the windows!" But the following facts prove that it was indeed intended to do so.

Six infantrymen, placed in the corridor at both sides of the entrance door, were commanded to load their rifles and this they did. On the other side of the house, a part of the detachment had been positioned, and they were loading their rifles, too. One of the Undersigned, the architect Mr. Franke, who had just arrived in the street and who asked the commanding officer whether he could cross the street without danger, received the answer, "No, don't go. We're about to shoot into the windows." The same Mr. Franke, as well as Mr. Kuscheit, who was about to leave his house accompanied by his wife, in fact, all of these three persons heard that one of the Messieurs protective officers who had joined the infantrymen, was shouting, "That hornets' nest has to be smoked out."

When one of the servants who had observed the loading of the guns dashed into the establishment, exclaiming, "They're loading already, soon they'll shoot," the two lieutenants in the establishment, Zimmermann and Siemens, and with them the owner of the newspaper hall, rushed down to the corridor in order to talk to the officer in charge. The captain of the detachment had by now entered the corridor as well. It was then that lieutenant Zimmermann observed that the signal had been entirely incomprehensible even to the well-informed because it signified, in case of an unlawful assembly in the street, that the people should disperse. It could hardly serve to lure the people of a house into the street so that they would in fact form an unlawful assembly. The captain did not know what to say in answer to this remark. Turning to the house owner, he claimed that a stone had been thrown at his men from this house. G. Julius retorted, "From my establishment, on the first floor?" "That has not been claimed," the captain retorted. "No one has said so; the stone came from the second floor."—"I would bet my own head," the owner of the newspaper hall retorted, "that no stone has been thrown from the flat of the merchant Friedhelm." "Nor from the attic, the door of which I closed myself ten minutes ago," the house owner added.

A stone had indeed been thrown at the soldiers, according to the statement of the merchant S. Simon who is among the Undersigned. But it came from the corner of Hunter Street and landed in front of the house, in Upper Wall Street.

The owner of the newspaper reading hall was just beginning to ask the captain what gave him the right to act in the way he had acted, observing that he had intended to shoot into a peaceful house from which allegedly a single stone had fallen or had allegedly been thrown—rather than taking the step of informing the houseowner—when an infantryman approached and gave a report, whereupon the captain and his men departed without a single word.

The Undersigned, owner of the newspaper hall, is informing Your Excellency in detail about the event described above, based on his own observation and the statements of those who signed as well, and asks you to take the steps that are necessary to investigate this matter and to punish this intentional, entirely unjustified, senseless and baseless, hitherto unheard of violation of the peace of the house by military force. G. Julius.

PART III

Friday, March 17: The Turning Point

We now arrive at the real turning point of the Berlin March Revolution. When that party which had concentrated initially on the task of enlightening the populace with respect to its general interest that it should fight for—and which had at the same time sought to organize more forceful resistance—had achieved its goals in part, the most necessary factor that was needed for the success of the entire endeavor was still lacking: the intimate union [or alliance] of the citizens and the workers. This intimate union occurred on Friday, the seventeenth.

Relatively small political meetings of the citizenry that took place separately [unconnected with those of the common people: artisans, factory workers, servants, etc.] had already constituted themselves during the morning of this Friday, in order to present petitions to the King. All of them aimed at freedom of the press, the right to freely assemble, the withdrawal of the troops, and the arming the people. But they also insisted that these measures had to be taken *at once*. One of these meetings—a continuation of a meeting held on the previous day—took place in an *établissment* known as the "Kemperhof" [Inn].

It was telling that the participants did not glance fearfully at other persons that took part in these meetings but instead, talked freely and without inhibitions. Thus, a comic incidence happened during the meeting just mentioned, exactly when those present were about to vote on the question whether to send another petition to the king or begin immediately—each one of them, as best he could—to bring about the arming of the people. It was then that a man in civilian clothes stepped between the two parties and declared that it was superfluous to take a vote, that he was the police *commissarius* of the borough, and that he was compelled to dissolve the meeting. The chairperson, Dr. Woeniger, however, declared in the name of those assembled that the participants were convinced they were acting entirely legally and that they would only cede to force. Apart from that, they asked the *commissaire* to remain present during the meeting as they would justify everything that would be discussed and that would happen, in front of the highest authority. The result of this meeting was yet another very forceful protest to the king and the agreement to assemble again in the evening in another *établissement* in order to deliberate about further steps to be taken.

Friday, March 17: The Turning Point

In the meantime, during the course of the day, the Commissions of Protection had been organized in accordance with a printed diagram that had been distributed to the diverse boroughs. At noon, quiet seemed to have fully returned. Business experienced a new upturn. But the conviction increased just as much that the blood spilled so far should not have been shed in vain and that, in so far as Vienna had already marched on, it was necessary to think of the political re-birth of Prussia. That a great demonstration should take place in this regard, was an opinion that people agreed on; but how it should be organized was a question that could not be answered easily. It turned out that the solution was to be found by a citizen assembly that took place on Friday afternoon, March 17, in a pub at No. 108, Koepenick Street. *Here, in this assembly, the immediate starting point of the revolution is to be found.*

Due to suggestions from several parties, this assembly convened in the afternoon at about 3 o'clock. It consisted of citizens and [ordinary] inhabitants, representing thirteen different [protection] precincts. After lengthy and serious debates, they finally agreed on this: that a large, peaceful demonstration expressing the wishes of the people should take place, in order to compel the government to respond to them. They decided that a petition should be addressed to the King which would express the main demands and which should be handed over on the next day, in the afternoon at 2 o'clock, by several thousand citizens wearing the baton and armband of protective officers, via a deputation. While the petition was handed over and until an answer was received, the citizens should remain in silence on the Palace Square. Concerning the envisioned demands, the following list was drawn up: 1. Freedom of the press; 2. Speedy convocation of the United Diet; 4. The arming of the *citizens*; 5. resignation of the cabinet; 6. Paying attention to the working classes. Insofar as objections were voiced to item 5 while item 6 could not be phrased clearly, and because above and beyond this the opinion prevailed that these two items should anyway be dealt with by the Diet and that now it was preeminent to attain the unity of the [various] parties, item 5 and 6 were dropped from the list and they limited themselves to the first four items. [Translator's note: The author, A. Brass, does not mention the third item.] Dr. Woeniger was appointed to immediately draw up a draft of the petition. He agreed to do so on the spot, and the following petition was approved at once by said assembly:

Most serene highness, most powerful King, most merciful King and Lord!

Deeply moved by the events of the last few days, we, the submissively Undersigned, appointed protective officers of this city thanks to the trust of our fellow citizens, approach the throne of Your Majesty. We have accepted the serious obligation to protect the peace of this city; furthermore, to ward off useless bloodshed. We would, however, after careful consideration, fulfill our task only partially if we would deem it sufficient to pacify the crowd by soothing words. For, indeed, regardless of the influence which our strong will may hope to exert, we would strive to attain something that is impossible.

Most merciful King! The inner lack of peace of our city is not that of today and yesterday. It is rooted deeply in the history of our generation. The desire of greater political freedom has shown itself for a long time by a thousand and yet another thousand symptoms. It has not been awakened by the events in the West; it has merely taken more conscious form. If this desire is not satisfied, any attempt to preserve the full peace, the full concord between prince and people would prove a vain effort.

Most merciful King! It is not our intention to strive for something that is unattainable. We limit ourselves to the most necessary, preparing by this the path for further development. This, the most necessary, includes:

1) Withdrawal of the armed forces;
2) Organization of a citizens' guard [or militia composed of armed citizens];
3) Granting unlimited freedom of the press that has been assured to us for the period of a lifetime already;
4) Convocation of the United Diet.

If this is granted, if this is granted immediately, we guarantee the true peace of our city; for we are far from believing what has just been said—that "the property and security of the citizens of Berlin is exposed to the greatest of dangers." We have deep trust in the forceful, law-abiding attitude of our inhabitants.

Yes, Your Majesty, our entire people is filled with a deep and strong sense that it is mature and capable enough to sit in council with its princes. If you grant this, the entire people will be protective officers—protecting the liberty of the fatherland, the security of the throne, and the welfare of all.

Your Royal Majesty! With a deeply moved heart we beg you—let your Serene Highness grant what we request; preserve this glory, which it is in danger of losing, for Prussia: that is spearheading the cultural development of Germany.

We remain Your Royal Majesty's most submissive protective officers, elected by the citizens and inhabitants of this city.

Berlin, March 17, 1848.

When this [petition] had been adopted [by the assembly], they left, in the evening, to inform the commissions of protection all over the city of this decision and to

Friday, March 17: The Turning Point

invite them to take part, the following day at two o'clock, [in the demonstration] on the Palace Square. This happened partly by way of urgent calls for support directed at the protection commissions patrolling in the streets but especially by making the petition known in one of the main meeting points of the protection commissions, the Coelln City Hall.

Here, several hundred citizens entrusted with the task of protection had assembled in the debating hall of the Coelln City Hall when, at 8 o'clock [in the evening], Dr. Woeniger appeared at the head of all the protective citizens of the Brothers' Street precinct, and asked for permission to speak. Having climbed the rostrum, he explained to the assembly the importance of the moment, pointing out how Prussia would be disgraced if it should lag behind Austria. He demanded that the protective citizenry should not be content to curb the unrest in the streets, but they should remind the government of its duty, as well. Finally, he read the petition to them, and asked the assembly to join the procession that would be heading towards the palace on the next day. There was thunderous applause. Turning against it, the alderman Gaertner rose and affirmed that all of this would only produce excitements. He suggested that the commissions should not take part *in corpore* but by way of deputations. As far as the petition was concerned, he and everyone present could only approve of it. The city councilor Mueller went further than that; he admonished everyone to keep calm, and in place of these deliberations, he advocated patrolling the streets. At this point, the director of the Coeln high school, Dr. August, rose. With a mighty and solemn voice he argued polemically against the entire motion: One should not cause new excitements. The government would certainly grant everything. Prussia had always found its own way. In this case, too, one should not ape foreign countries and bring petitions simply because Munich, Leipzig, Karlsruhe etc. had done so. He would demand peace and quiet and wanted to warn against new movements. He would ask and implore Dr. Woeniger to desist and to do everything in his power in order to effect a change of opinion of the assembly in Koepenick Street.

There issued an unspeakable commotion. One half [of those assembled] jubilated in joyous applause; the other half raged and thumped; a private quarrel, unleashed by someone who was slightly drunk, added to the noise. Dr. Woeniger declared: "Gentlemen, it's too late. Our demands are already being distributed in the city. Let everybody query his conscience what it is that he owes the fatherland. If you reject the demonstration, you will get the revolution." Hereafter, the larger part of those assembled left the room because somebody just in had reported that all the commissions of protection were absent in the Palace Square where a large multitude was milling around.

The news of this occurrence spread with lightning speed, and it soon arrived at another main meeting point of the commissions of protection, the auditorium of the Friedrich-Werdersche high school, and from here, it reached the nearby apartment of Lord Mayor Krausnick, where mayor Naunyn and several aldermen were present. Here the news caused great consternation, and Naunyn took it on himself to hurry immediately to the apartment of Dr. Woeniger in order to make him desist from his intention. He did not meet him at home. And at any rate, Dr. Woeniger could not be found all through the evening, the night, and the next morning—a fact that worried his friends not a little. He had disappeared for good cause. It was planned to arrest him that night. And he had preferred to lodge *incognito* in an inn.

INTERLUDE

A Personal Moment of Memory and Emotion

Perhaps I have succeeded up to this point to place the words nicely, in a well-ordered and reasonable way, and to narrate the facts one after the other, as soberly as befits a historian. But here, when I turn to this day, everything is getting colorful and confused in my memory. –I see myself again behind the defiant barricade and around me I see these wild and at the same time serious faces, men with inadequate weapons in their hands—sabres, axes, iron rods— but with an expression on their dark angry faces that was worth more than the loaded guns of a *peloton* of pale soldiers that were, finally, so merciless vis-à-vis the unarmed enemy. I hear the thunder of the artillery, the salvos that were fired by the infantry, the splintering of wooden beams that formed the barricade. I hear the cheering shouts, the cries of hooray by which these unarmed men who did not fear death greeted the cracking sound of my good rifle.

But there is also another cry that mixes with all this, a cry which even now rings occasionally in my dreams, waking me from my sleep. It is the mortal cry of this poor lad with long blond hair and bold blue eyes, his fresh face reddened by fight. But two of his comrades carry him to the door of the next house where merciful hands of some women attempt to staunch the flow of blood and to cool his hot forehead and the thirsty lips. Water—Water! –My mother! It is the final sigh of the poor fellow. He died without seeing her again, without pressing her hand, without her tears. But the touch of the hands of these women who silently lift the head of the dying youth and place it in their lap is not less gentle, their tears are not less hot than the tears of a mother. Is it not their own son who in this very minute is out in the street, too? Perhaps someone is carrying him now as well, pale and bleeding, from the barricade into a home where a stranger is moved to pity, just as they are moved to pity by this poor boy. For it is not a motley crowd that is fighting here for freedom; it's the sons of a single large family, and cursed be those who due to their wretched egotism have been alienated from this family.

But out in the street the bitter fight continues, this fight between the old age and the new. Still, the tri-coloured flag is proudly flying on the barricade; the compact columns of the infantry have attacked two times; two times they have been beaten back. Then the colonel of the regiment himself takes the position at the head of the discouraged troops. Forward! But the bullet of a rifle throws the brave one, who would have been worthy to die for a better cause, from his horse. The soldiers, welcomed by a hail of stones, don't want to proceed anymore. –A loud hooray of the people, announcing ill fortune, reaches the columns further away, and from behind the barricades, the defenders of the same appear, to shake hands in reconciliation with soldiers who only a few minutes ago shot at them.

But the bloody work is not over. From afar, from other quarters of the town, the rolling thunder of small arms is heard, mixed with the cracking of rifles. There, too, the people still hold their positions. –Hooray!

By word of mouth the rumor spreads that fresh troops are to replace the tired ones. These hours are used to prepare new means of defense. The barricades are reinforced, stones are carried to the rooftops, the riflemen obtain new ammunition, the tired gain strength through rest. But what kind of rest? I don't know whether you can call it rest when one is standing on the roof of a house, holding one's rifle, with beating heart, awaiting at any moment the new attack.

It was a painful feeling that overcame me in those moments, and which probably overcame most of those who brought a warm heart with them to the place of battle in the horrors of this terrible night. It wasn't a feeling of discouragement, but it was the terrible pain felt when seeing the sons of the fatherland turn against each other, up in arms. For the victory we win over them is not the fresh, laurel-crowned victory over the mercenaries of a foreign tyrant. No—this victory is a defeat. That was the first thought which befell me up there, on the roof of the house, and then many other thoughts, and also the thought of you, my loved ones, and you, you poor crying child—how I last saw you, and also this thought, whether I would see your friendly eyes again.

But there erupts, all of a sudden, a loud hooray all across the densely packed roofs. A dark red glow of fire flames up at the horizon, then another one. –Fire, fire! Out of the pale moonlight, the red flames are licking. Now and then there is the lightning flash of cannons; then again the salvo of rifles. The fresh evening breeze blows the warm smoke of gunpowder towards us, and a faint shudder runs through our bodies. But listen! The sound of drums. Down there, in the streets, from the windows, from everywhere, a shout resounds: Everyone to his position! The muffled whimper of the warning bell is heard in between; the soldiers approach. Now there is no time anymore to think and to feel; it proudly swells the chest that you are a man, that you are called to fight for freedom. Bursts of rifle shots set in, tiles struck by bullets are splintering; a cry of death—aim well, comrades—revenge!—and such a shout is not lost. Here, there are only men who know how to handle their guns, and so the fight erupts more intensely and more furiously, until mutual fatigue separates the fighters.

So here you have it, the fight in the night between the eighteenth and nineteenth of March.

PART IV

Afternoon, March 18: To the Barricades!

If I am to narrate the events of this fateful day one after the other, I have to start by saying how, in the morning of this day, a rumor had spread like wildfire which was to be confirmed soon after, by posters put up by the city government, that the King had granted the long-promised freedom of the press and that, at the same time, he had decreed a new message concerning the accelerated convocation of the Diet.

In the meantime, however, and in all likelihood as a consequence of the suggestion made by Dr. Woeniger on the previous day, an extremely well attended assembly had convened at 47 New Frederick's Street, in the room usInterludeually used for religious service by the Lutheran congregation. At ten o'clock, the alderman Dr. Koblanck, the town syndicus, Moewes, and the junior barrister of the Supreme Court, Wache, appeared, the latter then being entrusted with chairing the assembly. The syndicus implored the assembly emphatically and almost in tears to abstain from the march to the palace. The alderman Koblanck supported him in said matter. The Secret Commercial Councilor [Geheime Kommerzienrath, cf. Geheimrat] Karl had appeared as well and he reported that by now, much had been accorded by the King, especially freedom from censorship. One should show patience until the evening. The assembly objected to the demand that one should show patience by pointing out that the events [in Vienna, Hanau and elsewhere] demanded that the [urgent] questions of the day be resolved rapidly whereas the chair[person], junior barrister Wache, alerted them to the fact that, as a good means to achieve clarity, he would later on expound his proposals concerning a resolution [of the assembly] directed at the city councilors. The city councilor Holbein who was present supported him in this regard by declaring that the city councilors were just now meeting in session, that they were deliberating in order to make all the requests that this assembly might adopt, and which it might be concerned about, known to His Majesty the King. And this in a very detailed way and before noon, by a deputation they would send off. Furthermore, the meeting of the city councilors would certainly be continued in order to take note of the resolutions adopted by the citizenry in about an hour, and in order to add to these their own resolutions. Now the ex-alderman D.A. Benda demanded the right to speak. And in a fairly long speech, delivered with much enthusiasm, he set out that what mattered now weren't ordinary questions such as freedom of the press and convening the [united] provincial estates but the removal of those persons from the council of the King who had sown distrust and discord between the King and the people. He would therefore propose a motion for dismissal of the present Cabinet. This speech was met with general applause by the assembly. Hereafter still further motions were proposed: a free constitution of the estates; withdrawal of the army; arming of the citizenry; establishment of juries; finally, legal equality of all religious denominations. Those present believed that it would be possible to make these motions known to the King around noon by way of a deputation, something that seemed the more urgent because word had spread that the King intended to move the next day to Potsdam. And in the following week, the [annual] *fair* would take place at the Palace Square which could easily suffer from the presence of an assembling crowd of people.

Now, still more speeches of different sentiment were heard, the book dealer Simion, Dr. Friedlaender, Dr. Weyl and others advocating in part an immediate procession to the Palace. Meanwhile, there appeared again two other members of the city government, alderman Duncker and town syndicus Hedemann. They informed the assembly that the city government had already delivered to the throne a request based on the most liberal foundation and could expect that it would be granted in the shortest of times. In the evening of the present day, the official gazettes would also announce complete freedom from censorship and an even faster convocation of the provincial estates for the 4th day of the next month. This announcement had a slightly calming effect on the assembly which the chair, using all of his energy and the most penetrating voice, had been hardly able to control in order to refrain it from more far-reaching motions and resolutions. Finally the same junior barrister Wache proposed the motion—already laid down in writing by him and brought with him—that was directed to the meeting of city councillors: that they should, above all, aim at the arming of the protective officers. And that, in order to better guarantee and safeguard this institution, they should demand a law which would define them as public officials, declaring every attack on them an attack on government personnel. And that soldiers and army officers, on pain of having to face the legally foreseen penalties in case of contravention, would have to avoid any attack on the inhabitants of a precinct as long as protective officers were still on duty in the streets. The motion was applauded. But it was at any rate insisted on, as well, that the other, aforementioned demands of the people should also be transmitted to the city councilors. And it was decided to proceed together to their meeting room in the Coeln city hall, in order to make these resolutions known orally. For this purpose, several delegates were elected, among them, in addition to the chairperson [of the assembly], messieurs D.A. Benda, Dr. Friedlaender and Dr. Weyl.

Around twelve o'clock, the entirety of those assembled departed [for the Coelln City Hall]. In the meantime, the meeting of city councilors had been dissolved because their deputation had been sent to the palace. But the arriving citizens were invited to the tribune of the meeting room, and their delegates to the meeting room itself, where they should wait for the return of the deputation and the other city councilors.

This [return] occurred at about one o'clock. The members of the deputation, the city councillors Seidel, Schaeffer, v. Raumer, Dr. Veit, Behrends reported the highly satisfying welcome received from His Majesty the King. Finally, the chairperson of the assembly of city councilors, Fournier, appeared himself, and he too reported that all requests submitted by the city councilors, viz. change of the present cabinet, freedom from censorship, rapid convocation of the provincial estates, a free constitution of the estates with estates permitted to pass acts and thus take effective decisions, arming of citizens, and withdrawal of the army, had been received by the King with the most favorable indications of being granted very soon: indeed, they had in part been fully granted already. A roaring applause followed on the tribune during this session of city councilors which suddenly turned into a public session. The delegates of the citizenry were invited to sit down on the seats usually reserved for commissions of the city government, and the junior barrister Wache thanked the city councilors in the name of the entire citizenry: the resolutions they had adopted and that had just been heard were meeting the expectations of the citizenry; but, he added, an irrefutable demand of the people, not only within these city walls, but of the population of the entire country, was equal treatment of all religious denominations based on a liberal foundation. But, he added, in so far as a petition aiming thereat had not been heard among the requests of the city councilors presented before the throne, he had to discharge himself of his obligation by asking that the meeting of city councilors should make this wish of the entire people known to the king in the most rapid manner. At the same time, the orator added that he was feeling the entire weight and responsibility inscribed in this moment; it was only in them, the city councilors, the true representatives of the citizens in view of their public sessions and their character as guarantors, that people did trust completely, in these restless and difficult times. They had been the only authority which one had wanted to entrust motions of such importance with, instead of turning immediately to the King. They should therefore regard the extraordinary character of the step taken by the citizenry on this day as a prophylactic means against further excited steps and take care of the citizenry with the usual warmth. A general and long applause of the city councilors and the audience followed when he had ended his speech. But when, in reply, the chairperson, Fournier, declared that this last motion of the citizenry, concerning equality of all religions, had again, on this occasion, just as on earlier occasions, been presented by the urban authorities to His Majesty the King, and that this request, too, had received a very satisfying answer by the King, there issued a truly long storm of applause which finally receded when the session was dissolved while the delegates of the citizenry were joyfully embraced by the city councilors.

It was decided immediately to festively illuminate the city in the evening of that day.

While those taking part in this assembly thought of festivities, a crowd of a size that was not insignificant had formed in front of the palace. They belonged, it may be concluded in view of the way they were dressed, mostly to the upper stratum of the citizenry.

Dr. Woeniger had appeared too, around two o'clock. And because it was impossible in view of the densely packed crowd to get to the gate of the palace, it was proposed to lift him on the shoulders and thus carry him through the crush, so that he could hand the aforementioned petition from the Koepenick Street meeting to the officer on guard for further delivery. Woeniger, however, and many other members of the deputation were of the opinion that it was better to restrain oneself in this regard and to await further developments because one half of the items mentioned in the petition had already been granted.

Among those assembled one could also notice many of the aforementioned protective officers, wearing a short black coat and the armband, but without batons. At any rate, nobody was armed, for all had come to bring the King a joyous hooray to thank him for the granted concessions. Everybody was only the more steadfastly convinced that the King as well would only ascribe this intention to the assembly when the latter appeared on the balcony of the palace. He seemed visibly moved; I saw him, how he placed one hand on his heart while raising the other towards heaven. He could not speak: the roaring crowd, the thundering shouts of hooray, made it impossible for him to make

The "Palace Freedom"–the location "behind the palace" from which attacking troops emerged–is the street immediately in front of the Southwestern façade of the palace that we see here. It runs parallel to this visible side of the palace that is seen by the painter from the Canal Locks Bridge (Schleusenbruecke).

himself heard. But one was convinced that this inability to speak was the joyous expression of the mighty feelings of a King who, for the first time, sees a free people surrounding the steps of his throne, ready to shed their best heart-blood for him and his crown. May God forgive those who, at this moment, stood at his side and who were able to deceive him regarding the intentions of this people.

As there was loud jubilation due to the fact that the King had appeared in person; as some city councilors, lifted on the shoulders of bystanders, were reading to the crowd the Royal messages concerning the convocation of the Diet and concerning the press; and as people were embracing each other, congratulating each other on these attainments, cheering a grand future, suddenly a detachment of dragoons, [coming] from the side known as the *Schlossfreiheit* [or 'Palace Freedom'], appeared in the Palace Square, facing the assembled people.

Everybody thought there was a misunderstanding, an untimely sense of duty of a subaltern commander. An old man with gray hair, waving a hat in one hand, a white piece of cloth in the other, ran up to the soldiers, shouting, "Long live the King!"—"Turn back, withdraw the soldiers!"

It was believed that the mere appearance of the troops would intimidate the crowd after the bloody scenes of the past few days, it was intended to disperse the people non-violently, and when the dragoons turned around, it was generally thought that the moment of peace was near at hand. There was probably no one who really feared danger; there wasn't the slightest thought present in those assembled that the usual signal asking the crowd to disperse would be given; there was no one present who, at this moment, harboured a hostile intention in his heart.

Indeed, that signal was *not* given; but the dragoons turned around again and, at a gallop and with drawn sabres, attacked the defenseless crowd, hitting at them from all directions. At the same time, the infantry burst from the palace, and the crowd ran away in all directions. Shots were fired; by which side, God may know.

And through the streets, the shout of the betrayed citizens reverberated: Hurry to the arms! To the arms!

These were the events at the Palace Square, on Saturday, March 18th, in the early afternoon, between two and three o'clock.

Referring to these occurrences, the proclamation of the King, written in the bloody night between the eighteenth and nineteenth of March, says that the cavalry cleaned up the Palace Square *at a modest pace* and *with sheathed weapons*, and two rifles of the infantry went off by chance.

My Lord and King! May such men never again approach the throne of Your Majesty who could dare to pronounce, even in such a moment, such lies in front of the holy face of Your Majesty. If so, then the throne of Your Majesty will rest on a steadfast and secure foundation in the tempest of this time, for the love and trust of the people will form the firm cornerstones of the same. I

The Gate at the Southwestern side of the Palace that opens onto the street called "Palace Freedom" (from a painting by H. Ziller). When Ziller painted this, the houses at the Palace Freedom had already been razed. The troops attacking the crowd in the Palace Square may have left the palace through its large West Gate that we see here very clearly. In the background, hemmed in between the palace and other buildings, the Southern part of the empty square can be seen. The houses in the background are situated at the Canal Locks St. (right side), and those even further away are located at the Palace Square.

protest in the name of thousands who were present during these events, I protest in the name of world history against the untruths that have filled Your Majesty's Royal ear: *at a gallop and with unsheathed weapons, the cavalrymen went, in this hour, at Your Majesty's subjects.*

A single shout of horror swept through Berlin. In all directions, the news of what had happened was spread by the fleeing, and with lightning speed the barricades went up *in all the streets; in all, without exception.* And these were not the poorly constructed obstacles of earlier days that would fall apart all by themselves, behind which pale, starved faces had sought protection from the sabres of pursuing cavalrymen. No, these were barricades founded on the civic spirit of a free people, and defended by the same.

The lethargy which on other occasions usually keeps the inhabitants of this royal seat and capital from acting rashly, had made way to an activity which surprised everyone. From all sides, material for the construction of barricades was brought; women and children were actively helping to erect them.

And if the troops had not returned so quickly to their assembly point, the Palace, the battalions, each in isolation, would have been involved in individual fights, and the ending of this bloody drama would perhaps have been even more terrible for both sides. But as it were, the troops hurried back to the Palace Square as quickly as possible, which then, in combination with Linden Street, formed the base for military operations. From here, the diverse attacks on individual town quarters were directed later on. But meanwhile the attempt was still made to forestall the imminent bloodbath, inasmuch as the city councilor Heymann who had fled with some of his colleagues to Brothers

Street, foresaw the danger of the moment and suggested to these gentlemen that they should once more see the King in order to request the immediate withdrawal of the military. But this proposal was not successful. Risking their lives, these brave men crossed the lines of the troops which were blocking the way to the Palace. There they encountered at first the secretary of war, who was later joined by [two other members of the cabinet], the ministers von Arnim and von Bodelschwingh.

Supported by several other citizens and the town syndicus Moewes, Heymann implored these gentlemen with tears in his eyes to withdraw the military, to lead them to the King, or to make the latter at least appear on the balcony. He got the reply, however, that no one could shoulder such a responsibility. The King had shown himself twice to the people and uttered the wish that the crowd should disperse; the Prussian soldier was never and under no circumstances allowed to about-turn. The gentlemen directed the same requests at the royal princes which by now had descended to the Palace Yard, and indeed Prince Carl went away after having promised to see the King and attempt a renewed mediation. The Prince of Prussia, however, replied to the supplicants—and these are his **own** words—*"I shall not withdraw the military a single inch; I would rather shed my princely blood."* Alderman Nobiling had by now appeared in the Palace Square, as well, in order to direct his pleas to the generals who were there. But everything remained in vain, and so this gentleman asked the citizens that were present to try and see whether well-meaning words directed to the people could not still be helpful. For this purpose, the syndicus Moewes climbed a cart that had been stopped at the Long Bridge, in order to read aloud the Royal proclamations yet another time.

The Long Bridge (Lange Brücke) and the Palace in the background. This bridge across the River Spree is adjacent to the South Eastern corner of the Palace and connects the Palace Square and King's Street (Koenigs Strasse), a major scene of battle during the revolution.

Because his voice was so weak, Moewes and Mr. Curtius, the editor of the *Spenersche Zeitung* [a newspaper], took turns and perhaps at *this* moment the soothing of the excited minds might still have been possible. People had seen that the chief-of-police had entered the Palace; they did not know, however, that the Prince of Prussia wanted to bar him entry to the King, that this prince was determined to risk by all means a decision brought about by the bayonets.

A large crowd had accompanied the chief-of-police to the Palace Square. This location was thus filled again by people of all ranks who informed each other about the regrettable occurrence. And they expected everything from the mediation of Mr. von Minutoli.

The dragoons who had previously attacked had left by now; a squad of ulans had replaced them and the infantry had withdrawn to the palace yard. As I have said already, at this moment it was still *possible* to quiet things down, even though it was not likely. The following event made this possibility vanish, too.

A citizen who had witnessed the attack of the dragoons and who still believed in a "misunderstanding," an old, venerable-looking man with white hair, stepped forward to the officer of the ulans, saying to him, in a partly indignant, partly mediating way, that indeed one had harboured no hostile intentions against the Palace or the troops, that the behavior of the dragoons had been irresponsible etc. The officer listened to these complaints with seeming indifference and the speaker, being excited, placed his hand while talking, as inadvertently as this might easily happen to somebody engaged in a passionate conversation, on the leg of the officer that was hanging down from the saddle. It was impossible that the latter could interpret such a movement as an attack. But nevertheless, he tore back his horse in the same instance and unsheathed his sabre. His men did the same. The blades lighted up; it remains unknown whether somebody was wounded; but the shout: *So it's war; so it's combat—not reconciliation!* rose from among the masses. In no time at all, the Palace Square was cleared of people, and the stillness of death was only interrupted at times by the neighing of the horses and the commands of the officers.

Thus the last attempt to attain reconciliation had been aborted. The barricades rose with lightning speed in the streets; everybody, whatever his social rank, lent a hand. To the troops that had been put up in the villages surrounding the city, orders were sent that they should approach speedily; in fact, measures had been taken in advance to *more than double* the strength of the Berlin garrison. But the citizens, too, were ready for the fight, although they were not well-equipped. The merchants opened their stores; they handed out gun powder, bullets, and percussion caps free of charge. The merchants dealing in goods made of iron distributed axes and hatchets voluntarily among the people. The fight began.

Already, soon after three o'clock, when in other, more distant locations people were still busy building barricades, the firing of rifles set in, in the area closest to the palace. And it was left to the sorely afflicted inhabitants of Brothers Street to see the first victim of this unfortunate day. Four soldiers carried away one of their mortally wounded comrades on a stretcher. This was probably the soldier who had stood on guard at the bank and who had been shot when a struggle for his gun had erupted. When these men had reached Peter's Square, they were stopped by the construction workers who were there. They deserted the wounded man and tried to save their skins by fleeing. They would probably have become victims of the embittered people if some well-meaning citizens hadn't stepped in and liberated them from the hands of those who surrounded them.

At first, the people began this memorable fight at the corner of Upper Wall Street and Hunter Street. It was there that people had erected a barricade formed by three carts that had been wedged together, as well as various gutter bridges, and the sentry box of the bank. A second barricade followed at the corner of Werder Street and Wall Street. A detachment of dragoons attacked the first barricade but it was welcomed by a hail of stones and had to turn around. The citizens who were there had very few rifles, however. And when an infantry battalion approached from the other side and fired heavily at the roofs, this barricade was taken and the defenders luckily saved themselves for the most part by fleeing to the roofs of neighboring houses.

Confrontation between citizens and soldiers during the March Revolution. From a "Pictorial Journal" (Bilderzeitung) published in 1848. The flags shown here are those of republican revolutionaries; they imitate the design of the tricolored flag that the French Republic used. Fighters using horizontally striped black, red, and yellow flags in 1848 accepted clear social hierarchies, thus a certain role of the aristocracy, and they were merely asking the king to convert the late absolutist state into a constitutional monarchy.

But before we go on to describe these bloody scenes, we must first of all speak of the position which the chief-of-police, Mr. von Minutoli, had taken throughout the course of this entire week. His position under the given circumstances was surely the most difficult. It turned even more difficult because he, the only one among the authorities, saw the situation with unprejudiced eyes. He did not rely exclusively on reports by his underlings—people who, on the one hand, due to the magnifying glass of fear and on the other hand because of blind trust in the status quo, raised insignificant things to the status of important ones, whereas they did not recognize the importance of other things. And so he had been active everywhere himself. And everywhere he had informed himself about the true situation thanks to his own experience as an eye-witness. He was the only one among all those surrounding the person of the King who had probably recognized the political significance of the moment. And being always averse to forms that rigidly hold on to that which exists, he had never been able to counter free movements and progress with such iron force as others would have done in his place. Thanks to several changes in the administration [of the police] which were bearing witness to his efforts and which affected the smallest details, he had known how to gain the love and trust of the inhabitants of Berlin even in years gone by. The way he behaved in these critical times secured these gains for him to the greatest extent.

It has been said that Mr. von Minutoli persistently and with all his energy struggled against military measures and that he attempted to avert their application to the extent that this was within his powers. We can say nothing with any certainty in this regard; only so much is certain: that the police officers undertook almost no—or at most, very few—actions of their own from the moment when, on March 13th, considerable troops were used in order to disperse the populace. Ever since, the activity of the chief-of-police confined itself to the already mentioned, traditional instructions and ordinances intended to quiet the tumult. Above and beyond this, he abstained from any further interference in the matter itself. The discussed assemblies of citizens in the "Hofjaeger" [Inn], the "Kemperhof" [Inn], and also in Koepenick Street were known to Mr. von Minutoli and it would have been easy for him to hinder or dissolve them. But he did not do this, as he had to recognize, in addition to their well-meaning intentions, the honorable principles of these assemblies, as well. It was only on Saturday, the 18th, at a time when Mr. von Minutoli had the sad satisfaction to see how his prophecies were fulfilled in the most horrible manner, that he could be seen again in person. And while people were still working to reinforce the barricades, he came along from the Palace, wearing his uniform, and entering the streets of the Fredericktown quarter. It required considerable courage indeed to step between the excited and embittered crowds of people whose passions were extremely hot. The horrible death of an officer of the *gendarmerie* at Doenhof's Square who became a victim of the ire of the people at about the same time, is a sad proof of this. The intention of the chief-of-police concerning this walk taken through the streets [of revolting Berlin] seemed to be at first to find out in person whether the citizens harboured indeed the intention to offer general and resolute resistance to the troops. Of course a large crowd surrounded him [pretty soon]. Threats were heard, as well. But without paying attention to them, he continued on his way down Margrave Street, then along Zimmer Street and Frederick's Street, and from there to Riflemen's Street where he entered the house of a police *commissaire* who was living there, briefly addressing the people from one of its windows. He said that in the interest of the people he had begged the King almost on his knees to withdraw the troops but this was refused. And now, having convinced himself that the citizens were disposed to engage in struggle by all means, he wanted to urge all those present to arm themselves; he wanted to lead them to the Palace in order to prove to the King, who was surrounded by evil advisers, that the entire population was rising, that this was not a [mere] street disturbance, that it was a revolution. He, the chief-of-police, wanted to place himself at the head of this crowd. He would be the first to present his chest to the bullets of the soldiers, so no one would take him for a traitor; the cause of the citizens was now his cause too; it had always been his.

Indeed a procession rather significant in numbers formed, with several members of the riflemen's guild, who were wearing their uniforms, marching at its front. Mr. v. Minutoli stepped up to them and with him at their head this procession went along Charlotte Street up to Crown Street. In this moment of excitement and distrust a few voices were raised, however, exclaiming that one should not follow him; he just wanted to deliver the citizens to the soldiers. Indeed, this shout had such a powerful effect that the procession dissolved whereas only a few citizens, among them also members of the riflemen's association, remained assembled around Mr. von Minutoli. Indeed, they went to the palace, but they returned after half an hour and, climbing onto diverse barricades, they announced to the assembled people that the King had absolutely refused to withdraw the troops; they should arm, in order to take up the fight.

At this moment, fighting broke out in the Fredericktown [district]. There had already been—almost simultaneously with the attack on the barricades at the Newspaper Reading Hall—at first a cavalry attack and then an infantry attack on the barricade at the corner of Moor Street and Margrave Street while the infantry which had taken the barricade at the Newspaper Reading Hall, advanced up to the corner of Upper Wall Street and Bailiff Square. But the people that had assembled here were already armed. They had broken into a gun store at Moor Street. Sellers of ironware had voluntarily opened their storage rooms. And when the infantry wanted to march across Bailiff Square, it was welcomed by such heavy fire that their further advance was obstructed even though the barricade at Bailiff Square and Upper Wall Street was soon given up as indefensible. –

While the barricades were still being erected, the people had already attempted to force their way into "Bailiff House." But they had been beaten back by the guards in this building. An attempt to set the house on fire had been aborted as well, even though they had advanced so far that smoke came from the windows to the right of the entrance. It was here that an exchange of bursts of [rifle] fire continued, while the troops did not dare to advance any further. From the windows of "Bailiff House," the troops stationed there were firing as well; and it was especially the citizens on the roof of the house at the corner of Moor Street and Jerusalem Street who vigorously returned the fire. In view of the comprehended importance of this position, an attempt was made to advance to Bailiff Square from Moor Street, in order to be able to fire on the citizens from two sides. The barricades erected there were defended at this moment by not a single gun. A company of the [Royal] Guards, a unit which quite generally was involved in action in the area, attacked at this spot; they directed several salvos at the roofs but were greeted from up there by a horrible hail of stones. This was especially true in the case of the flat roof above the colonnades. But the bullets did little harm, as the men were protected by the balustrades. And before the troops reached the barricade, they turned around and withdrew again as quickly as possible to Constable Market.

Constable Market (Gendarmen-Markt), section of an old photography.
The Theater is on the right and the New Church (also known as the German Dome) is seen in the background, on the South Side of the square. The French Dome of French Church, originally built for the French community of Huguenot immigrants in Berlin, is located on the North Side, facing the German Dome of the Lutherans.

Thus, the fighting took place here when evening arrived. The troops had not yet advanced beyond Bailiff Square. But they kept firing uninterruptedly at the citizens who registered many wounded and killed in this area. In a house at Jerusalem Street which harbours a rather well-known dance floor for the common people, a kind of hospital had been set up. There were physicians and women who looked after the suffering, comforting them and giving them every possible care. By ten o'clock in the evening, this hospital had one dead and six severely wounded men, as those who had only received a slight contusion came only to be bandaged and immediately hurried back to the place of battle.

At the time of the attack at Bailiff Square, the 2nd (Stettin-based) infantry regiment, coming from Linden Street, pushed into Big Frederick's Street [the wider, and more recently constructed part of this street]. Here, too, the first barricade was taken without much resistance. It was only at the corner of Dove Street that the barricade, which had been reinforced as much as possible, was defended with such energy that the infantry could not advance any further.

This lithography created in 1848 by Theodor Hosemann shows Heinrich Glasewaldt, a 20-year-old metal-worker and Ernst Zinna, a 17-year-old apprenticed metal worker, who gave their life while courageously defending the barricade at the corner of Hunter Street and Frederick Street.

As the long and straight avenue [of Frederick's St.] made it possible to use the artillery, two cannons were moved into position, unlimbered at the corner of French Street, and then raked the area, first with cannon balls and then with cartouches. But this cannonade had only a small impact because the defenders of the barricades had immediately withdrawn behind the houses at the corners of the many streets that intersect Frederick's Street. The impact that the cannon balls had on the barricades turned out to be insufficient because it would have required prolonged firing to cause them to collapse. The cartouches fired had the result, however, that finally the barricade at Dove Street was taken. Its defenders withdrew in part to streets branching off, and in part to the next barricade at the corner of Moor Street. This one was given up, however, after brief resistance. On the other hand, a furious fight ensued at the barricade situated at the corner of Crown Street and Frederick's Street.

Barricade at the corner of Crown St. (Kronen St.) and Frederick St. (Friedrich Str.)

There, a lot of citizens equipped with rifles stood on the flat roof of one of the houses. From behind the barricade and from the windows of the other houses, guns were fired, too. And in the course of this attack one of the general staff officers—we don't know whether it was the colonel himself or one of the battalion commanders—was shot down from his horse when he attacked at the head of the columns.

The repeated charges against these barricades were beaten back by the citizens with such energy that it instilled respect and admiration in the brave troops. And we think there will be no one among our readers who will not be glad that we also pay respect to the battalion that was fighting here. These troops had battled all through the afternoon, they had lost many men, and the evening had arrived quite a while earlier when they undertook their last attack against the barricade at Crown Street. But here, too, they had to retreat after having faced the bullets and the stones that were thrown with glorious dedication. They did so in the way that is proper for a Prussian soldier. They retreated as far as Moor Street, stopped and took off their rifles.

Was the reason for this that these men had spent all their bullets in the course of fighting that had lasted almost seven hours? Or was there another reason? At any rate, the rumor spread among the citizens that this regiment did not want to fire any more on them. People now emerged from behind

Afternoon, March 18: To the Barricades!

the barricades; they spoke in a very friendly manner with the officers and the soldiers. The fighters from the barricades shared spirits and food with those men who had confronted them as enemies a few moments ago. In short, this was a scene that probably could be witnessed in very few other places of battle—a scene of genuine soldierly spirit. Both parties had learned to respect one another. Several citizens were shouting, though, that the battalion should hand over its weapons. An old captain with a mustache and a tanned face responded brusquely, however, "Kids, we cannot give you our weapons, we are Prussian soldiers. But I give you my word as an officer that we will not shoot anymore at citizens!" Loud, tumultuous jubilation followed. People were shouting, Long live the second regiment! Long live the citizens! In short, it was a moment of joyous satisfaction after such a bloody fight. And yet exactly this location was to become the theater of horrific scenes a few hours later, scenes which must cause pain in every honest soldier's heart, when the 9th company of the 2nd regiment of the [Royal] Guards carried out a surprise attack on the houses at the corner of Crown Street and murdered most of the defenders—who had not expected such an attack—with their bayonets. And this, although they encountered no resistance. Showing no mercy, they used bullets only for those who attempted to save their skin through flight. We shall return later on to these, and similar, events.

In order to support the attack of the troops in Frederick's Street, an attack occurred from Constable Market, through Charlotte Street, against [the barricades along] Leipzig Street. There, at said market, was at any rate the assembly point for the troops engaged in action in the Fredericktown [district], for considerable detachments of the cavalry had appeared there—at first, in order to take charge of prisoners and take them away; but also in order to secure the connection to the palace. The first attack on the barricade in this area—a barricade reinforced by many broken pieces of glass heaped up on the side of Constable Market because an attack by the cavalry was feared—only happened when it was already past 8 o'clock in the evening. Here, too, fierce gun fire and a heavy hail of stones welcomed the troops. They had to retreat; and a second attack that took place about two hours later was also beaten back by the brave defenders. On this occasion the source whose kindness we owe these notes included in said notes the information that the officers, noting that the fiercest rifle fire was directed exactly against them, had put on simple soldiers' coats, in order to thus deceive the citizens. I myself did not have the opportunity to note whether this happened in other locations as well.

This last attack coincided more or less with the arrival of the twelfth (Frankfort) regiment. Like the other outside troops, it had been quartered in locations close to Berlin. The resistance which the regiment encountered at first in Leipzig Street was a very slight one because this area features many government buildings, as everyone knows. As well, it is inhabited by the aristocracy, which of course remained neutral in such fights. A furious battle ensued at the corner of Wall Street where, right at the beginning of the fight, the small sentry at the corner of Crown Street and Wall Street had been taken. This had quite generally been the case at all locations of the town, especially in the case of the more remote guards stationed at the city gates which were overwhelmed sooner or later by the people.

Thus, at half past four, the relatively numerous guards at the New Market were also attacked. A brave journeyman, a metal worker, lead a valiant bunch of men against them, brandishing a flag. The attacked attempted to save their skin by fleeing but the persecutors caught up with them in Rose Street where their rifles and other weapons were taken. But they were let go without being hurt any further. The taking of this guard building was of particular importance because a significant supply of weapons was found in the upper storeys of the same, especially sabres of the territorial army [or "Landwehr"] which were immediately distributed among the people.

The storming of the military prison at Linden Street also furnished the people with many sabres and pistols that were found in the rooms inhabited by the teaching squad and the officers. And, additionally, they got the rifles of the men on guard. Right away, it was proposed to set the building on fire and this was already carried out in part. But thanks to the influence of some sane and thoughtful people, this useless arson did not happen.

The main Arsenal (Zeughaus) of Berlin, situated at the avenue known as Under the Linden Trees (Unter den Linden).

The arsenal at No. 4 Linden Street that belonged to the Royal Guard regiment formed by men of the territorial army was only attacked late at night. People expected to find relatively large quantities of arms here but they did not anticipate the forceful resistance that they encountered. It turned out that the riflemen of the Royal Guard regiment of the cuirassiers had remained there [as a garrison]. The attackers encountered heavy and well-aimed fire. As a consequence, the attempt was made to set the building on fire, after a number of fighters—between ten and twelve wounded and dead—had been lost here already. But as this failed as well, and because it was obvious that it wasn't possible to storm the building without the most horrible bloodshed, they refrained from it for the moment. Towards the morning, another attack was prepared because it was believed that it was possible to surprise the tired troops more easily and that they would not insist any longer on rendering such stubborn resistance. This assumption was confirmed to an even higher degree than had been expected, for it became clear that the troops had completely departed in the darkness of night. About one thousand rifles were found here and distributed. They lacked the *pistons* and bayonets, however, as the latter had been brought a few days ago to the large arsenal. All the metal workers in Fredericktown were busy at once making the lacking *pistons*. And in an unbelievably short time, a large number of rifles were ready for use.

The arsenal of the territorial army at the road to Potsdam, the Potsdam Communication [road], was not attacked. It was garrisoned by the eleventh company of the thirty-first regiment, and in addition by the "regulars" of the third battalion of the twentieth territorial army regiment. In addition, the guards stationed at the Anhaltian Gate were present, having taken refuge here. And also a number of territorial army officers, who had voluntarily taken upon themselves the obligation to shoot at their fellow citizens even though they were citizens and inhabitants of Berlin: a sentiment that bears witness to a very honorable clinging to the principles of the *ancien régime,* if we attempt to explain this to ourselves at all, trying to reconcile it with the fact that several of these same gentlemen were already pinning the tri-colored *cocarde* to their chest the very next day, as if they had attained victory on the side of the people.

But now we continue with our report.

It was after the battle in the Fredericktown [district] had already started that gunfire broke out in King's Street. We are compelled to digress now, in order to point out that we have absolutely no way to ascertain the exact time when the different battles began because almost nobody in these horrible hours measured the time with certainty and because we have received reports from trustworthy men which nonetheless contain references to the time that differ to the extent of almost an hour. It may have been at about five o'clock [in the afternoon] when the fusilier battalion of the first regiment of the Royal Guard advanced in attack across the Long Bridge, into this street [i.e., King's Street]

Bursts of gun fire and a hail of stones from windows and roofs welcomed the attackers. Even though they had already heard the noise of firing that resounded in other quarters of the city, these troops seemed to be of the opinion that they were dealing with a defenseless people, just as during the evenings before, and that they would be able to quite easily disperse the folks, without endangering themselves, for they fell back in terror when the bullets fired by the citizens struck their rows and when the wounded collapsed.

General Neumann, who was present in the Palace Square, shouted at the wavering troops, "How is that? The [Royal] Guard retreats?" So the column advanced again and targeted the former post office, to the right of the Long Bridge.

Because the regiments were fully equipped for regular battle, the men carried with them the tools needed for trench work that belong to every company. And so they started to force the door of said building open at the spot where the entrance for the ticket office of the Kingstown Theater is located. As they failed in their endeavour, the grenadiers smashed a window, opened a door from the inside and now pushed into the house. Simultaneously, other detachments advanced down King's Street towards the barricade at Post [Office] Street. This barricade had not yet been completed and so it was given up quite soon. The soldiers advanced, directing heavy fire at the windows. And because the first shots fired at them had come from the windows of a restaurant, these windows served the troops as their principal target.

It is on this occasion that the event happened which is narrated in such diverse versions and which is connected with major von Preuss.

A trustworthy lad told us about it as follows: After the barricade at Post Street had been taken and while the soldiers who had taken up positions on both sides of the street, opposite the house at the street corner, were shooting at the windows of this building, a man stepped up to the commanding officer. And pointing at the windows of the restaurant, he indicated to the officer that it was from there that shots had been fired and that those who had fired them would still be found inside. This man was a Mr. von Preuss, a retired major. Having received this information, the commanding officer, together with a number of soldiers, went into the house of major von Preuss and they shot from the windows of his apartment into those of the restaurant on the opposite side of the street. This was all our witness had seen. But this incident became the cause for an act of popular justice which was directed against major von Preuss and which took place on the following day. For it was on Sunday around noon that a crowd of people led by a well-dressed man approached via King's Street and surrounded the house of the major who, fearing no ill, according to the later testimony of one of his tenants, was just having lunch. Shouting "Just look, this is where the traitor is living who betrayed the people," the leader of the crowd threw a stone into the window of the major. At the same time, a number of shots were heard and many stones smashed the window panes while the people were intruding into the house. The major is said to have barely made an escape, together with his folks, through a door that opens toward King's Street, for it took only a few minutes for the intruders to enter his apartment. Now a terrible scene of destruction began. All the furniture, beds, precious things, a coffer—in short, all the belongings chanced upon, including bed linen and clothes—were thrown into the street and burned in a fire that had been quickly ignited for this purpose. The people had brought two fire hoses as a precaution, so that the fire might not cause damage to an adjacent house. Those who dared to appropriate any of the items thrown into the street were compelled to come back. They had to give up the stolen goods and were summarily punished for their lack of honesty by having a few fire department buckets full of cold water poured on their heads. A gloomy silence, a scary kind of order, prevailed during this act of popular justice. We have to add that the maid of the major was calmly allowed to get her belongings and carry them safely away. And that all the other dwellers inhabiting the house were not hurt or molested at all.

Even though this incidence can hardly be justified, the facts mentioned show that it did not spring from a private thirst for revenge, as has been asserted by a number of ill-disposed persons. It rather finds its complete grounds in the terrible scene that had occurred in the coffee house where the soldiers, with their bayonets, had mercilessly proceeded against the defenseless who had wanted to surrender without further resistance. For in this location, as well as elsewhere, it occurred that the grenadiers stabbed people who found themselves in a situation of helplessness, killing them with their bayonets while they were hiding under a table.

As the other barricades in King's Street heroically resisted the attacks of the infantry, the artillery was now called in. Initially grenades were fired, and then cartouches, from a position at the Long Bridge. And thanks to artillery cover thus provided, the infantry had finally reached the King's Bridge in the evening, by seven o'clock. The barricades at New King's Street, however, and at several locations at Alexander Square, put a stop to their further advance.

Now, heavy *tirailleur* fire started on both sides which lasted throughout the entire night, being only briefly interrupted a number of times.

Attacking the barricade at Alexander Square, Berlin, in the afternoon of March 18, 1848.

Soldiers had taken up a position behind the barricade at the King's Bridge that was made of bags of flour. Later on, taking advantage of the darkness of night, a platoon had reached the Kingstown Theater. But it was driven back by the people and had to recede into King's Street.

This was the battle situation in this area.

Struggle on the barricades at Alexander Square. August Brass, with Friedrich Urban, led the successful defense of this position on March 18 and 19 against the troops commanded by General Moellendorff. Brass was elected captain of the revolutionaries defending the barricade situated at the point where the New King's Road opens into Alexander Square. This barricade is depicted by the painting reproduced here. Urban commanded the fighters of the barricade immediately East of it, at Landsberg Street (Landsberger Str.). Today a historical marker commemorates their role in this struggle.

While the fire of rifles and the thunder of cannons in the King's Street area and Fredericktown was heard, no attack had yet taken place on Broadway. Here a tremendous barricade rose that extended from Coelln City Hall to the other side of the street which narrows at this location. This barricade was defended by a rather significant number of riflemen, some of whom had taken up positions inside Coelln City Hall while others had chosen the two street corner houses of the old Horse Road at its intersection with Broadway. One of these houses was the property of the cake shop owner d'Heureuse; in the other one, the Café de l'Europe is located. The balcony of the latter was surrounded by thick boards and holes had been cut in these boards through which it was possible to fire. Behind the barricade in front of which a big fire had been ignited, there were men with rifles, as well. Stones had been brought to the rooftops and people impatiently awaited the attack. Here, the citizens again began the battle by shooting at the troops amassed in the Palace Square. In view of the big distance, their firing did not cause significant damage.

In the meantime, another attempt was made at this time to avert the shedding of blood, knowledge of which we owe to the report of Dr. Minding: The bookseller Dr. J.L. Gumbinner, the medical practitioner Dr. Loewe, the two borough presidents Lademann and Ring, and the city councilor Remin, all of them inhabitants of the old Horse Road [Horse Street], met together in order to do their duty based on their insight. They asked some neighbors, addressing even those living as far away as Coelln City Hall, to join them. But in vain. Through the armed and raging crowd they advanced until they reached the dwelling of Bishop Neander in Brothers Street, who joined them with courageous determination, wearing his official clerical robe. These men, crossing the lines of the troops, went with solemn bearing, bareheaded, accompanied by the cheers of citizens, to the Palace. Bravo, you peacemakers, the people cried, bring us peace. After some difficulties they were able to see the king. They who had come to the palace declared that the people were prepared to fight, streets and roofs ready for resistance, the consequences hard to assess. The military should be withdrawn to the barracks. Only in this way could [further] bloodshed be prevented.

His Majesty answered in the most merciful and friendly form and in the same sense that was later on spelled out in the proclamation published in the night between the eighteenth and nineteenth of March: that the people should first give up their positions before the King could withdraw the troops. Leading the deputation to the window, the King pointed to King's Street that was full of blinking weapons, uttering, "You see, this road is mine." He promised to readily grant everything but only upon being asked, while ceding nothing to force. The deputies accompanied the bishop back to his house. And subsequent to this, they attempted in vain to make the people declare their consent to this treaty guaranteed by the word of the King. As they encountered indignant rejection at the barricades, this could only bolster their conviction that no other measure except the immediate withdrawal of the troops would have been able to transform the glorious night of the eighteenth and nineteenth of March into a night of jubilation and brotherhood of all parties.

Only by six p.m. did the infantry advance on Broadway. But the heavy rifle fire and a shower of stones thrown at the soldiers from all sides drove them back repeatedly. Here, too, the cannons were the deciding force. And after heavy cartouche and grenade fire, the barricade was finally attacked once more and this time it was finally taken. At the same time the troops pushed into Coelln City Hall and here, too, there followed a scene of terrible murder.

Desperate cries of fright resounded from the windows, followed by the silence of death. The soldiers positioned themselves in and next to the city hall and kept firing intensely at the two street corner houses of the new Horse Road for more than an hour, until the citizens in the house that belonged to d'Heureuse had spent their ammunition. Now this house was stormed as well, but those inside were treated more mildly and only taken prisoner. The other house, however, was not attacked; instead, the soldiers withdrew to the city hall and to Broadway in order to continue the exchange of fire for some time.

Meanwhile the fight in Louisatown and Dorothytown [districts] had begun and it had been continued in a manner that was just as stubborn and bloody. It would require a separate book if we wanted to describe in a ponderous way every detail of these street fights which basically always show the same traits. A very stubborn resistance was put up in Charlotte Street in the area of Middle Street where citizens fired on the soldiers from the windows of the hotel that is known as the "Suisse Inn" (or "Schweizerhof"). On this occasion, a number of out-of-town people lodging in the hotel are said to have taken an active part in the fight as well. In all these streets, the battle raged, sometimes earlier, sometimes later. The Marshall's Bridge which connects the new William's Street and Louisa Street had been drawn up. People had managed to get a barge stuck at this spot, making it impossible to lower the bridge. And the attack of the soldiers who advanced from Linden Street was repelled several times. Another attack undertaken against the barricade from the direction of the Lower-Barrier Bridge had more success. The citizens had to withdraw and some of them, seeing their escape route cut off, jumped into the river Spree and saved themselves by swimming. But new barricades in Louisatown made a further advance impossible and in order not to be completely cut off, the troops had to stop there.

In the suburb outside the Oranienburg Gate, the workers in the factories of that area had armed themselves as quickly as possible, too. The workers of the Borsig factory had dug up the cobble stones of the road because there was a

The Borsig Iron Works at the northern periphery of Berlin shown by a painting done in 1847.

rumor that the cavalry stationed in the villages wanted to advance into the city. A bit later, a young man on horseback appeared, probably a student, who briefly addressed the people and then led them past the barricade to an attack on the nearby barracks of the *"mounted artillery."* This young man threw himself on the officer who led his people against them, fired his pistol at him without hitting him and then attacked him with his unsheathed sabre. The Borsig folks followed his example and even though they were only armed with stones, they drove back the artillerymen into the barracks, without being able to penetrate into the latter, however. At the same time, an ammunition depot at the Oranienburg Gate was broken into and the weapons which were found there quickly distributed. But then, an artilleryman who had left the barracks through another exit, approached at top speed from the [road known as the] Communication, turned into Fredericks Street and fired a shot. The shot was heard, the workers retreated, but it turned out that the gun had been loaded with a dud. Probably the cannonball had been left in the barrel in the preceding days. This circumstance encouraged the workers anew. They had wanted to close the gate when the cannon was being put in position. But they had not succeeded to close *one of the main doors* of the gate. And through this opening a second shot was fired, a cartouche which threw five workers to the ground, two of them being dead at once. Of the wounded, two died soon after. The people now dispersed, trying to reach the city along other routes. But the gun was withdrawn as well, because attacks with unsheathed weapons from the side-streets, but especially from the Communication, were feared. Instead, a detachment of the infantry of the second regiment of the Royal Guards advanced against the gate. It occupied the same without encountering any resistance, but it did not dare to proceed any further.

It has proved impossible for us, despite all our efforts, to obtain any detailed information about the military strategy that the movements of the troops were based on. But it appears to have been the goal of the commanding general to send his troops from the Palace Square, Constable Market and Linden Street into the individual quarters of town while avoiding by all means the isolation of individual units. This general attack was to be supported by another attack, carried out by troops stationed outside the city. And after both forces were united, they apparently were to proceed jointly against those boroughs which still put up active resistance. General von Moellendorf, commander of the infantry brigade of the Royal Guards, is said to have directed the operations in the beginning.

The troops available for this purpose, which were present at the locations mentioned that served to provide the soldiers with weapons and fresh ammunition, consisted of four Royal Guards regiments, viz. the *first* and the *second* regiment, the Emperor-Alexander-regiment and the Franz-grenadier-regiment. In addition, three regiments of the cavalry were present: one cuirassier regiment, one regiment of dragoons and a regiment of ulans. Furthermore, two [cavalry] squadrons of the Royal Guards corps. These cavalry units were to see action only a few times, however, and this in the early phase of the fighting. Later on they were used to transport and guard prisoners. The rifleman battalion of the [Royal] Guards, known as the Neufchatel bataillon, was not engaged in the fighting at all, as far as I know. It was only used for the occupation of public buildings and for some patrols. But simultaneously with the outbreak of the fighting, the 2nd (Royal) Regiment of Regulars (Garrison of Stettin), which was stationed in Charlottenburg, appeared on the scene. And later on, so did the 31st (Erfurt-based) regiment. Which meant that immediately six infantry regiments could be sent into battle. This impressive mass of infantry must have amounted to 18,000 men without the cavalry, as the regiments had been put in a state of alert. They were supported by the twelfth and eighth infantry regiment (based at Frankfurt-on-Oder), the King's personal guard. These two regiments, put on a state of alert as well, numbered 6,000 men, and if we subtract those commanded to serve elsewhere, and the sick, there still remain about 20,000 battle-proven infantrymen which for the most part were to see action, though some units did not really get involved in the fighting but were used to occupy individual strategic locations. In addition, several cavalry regiments—dragoons, ulans and hussars—were stationed in Pankow, in Reinickendorf and other villages. They were also ready to attack the gates of the city, which means that the total number of the troops stationed in and around Berlin may well have attained 30,000 men. It would of course be desirable to obtain more precise information on this matter from the authorities. But in that case, the information [already] provided would be less questionable than the official reports which up to now have reached us with regard to the number of casualties suffered on the part of the troops. We have attempted everything possible to obtain dependable reports from the side of the General Staff, but unfortunately, every mouth remained shut with regard to this point.

After the troops that had been amassed in the city had taken the barricades within the mentioned parameter, the center point of which must be assumed to have been the Palace Square, they paused for a while, only to push forward again simultaneously with the attack on the gates.

We think that by the above account we have given the reader an approximate idea of the position of the troops on the evening of the 18th. They had advanced no further than Moor Street in the Fredericktown quarter, up to Gertrude Street in the old part of Coelln, and in King's Street as far as Alexander Square. In the Louisatown quarter, they had managed to occupy the Oranienburg Gate. But all the side-streets which led to Louisa Street, as well as this latter street, were in the hands of the people. As mentioned already, it had been attempted several times [by the armed forces] to take the Marshall's Bridge, but in vain. This was accomplished later on, however, due to an attack carried out from the Lower-Barrier area.

Thus, only a small part of Berlin had been seized by the troops when the attack of the 8th regiment against the Frankfurt Gate occurred, as evening was approaching. And a little later, the attack of the 12th regiment on the Potsdam Gate.

The Potsdam Gate, after 1824.

PART V

Evening, March 18th: The Second Phase of the Fighting

We now come to this—the second phase of the fighting.

After its guard building had been stormed [by the people] in the afternoon, the Frankfurt Gate had been heavily barricaded.

It is said that it required the consent of people living there if one wanted to open the gate. And many people dwelling in the area had accused a police *commissarius* of the local police station of having opened a small entry next to the main gate for the troops. These accusations are based merely on assumptions, even though the temporary flight of the officer during that night lends some credibility to them. Thus we can say nothing that is certain about this incident. We can say only this much for sure: The soldiers really entered the town through the small entry in the Gate. And that it did not cost them much of an effort to take the first barricade at Fruit Street. The second barricade at Cabbage Lane was defended more fiercely, however. Without taking the trouble to remove it, the soldiers one by one climbed across it and by eleven o'clock reached Alexander Square via Kaiser Street.

It was a critical moment for the barricades in the Kingstown quarter. From King's Bridge, an attack by the Guards was possible at the same time as another attack from the flank. The barricades at Landsberg Street and at New King's Street, even though constructed in a way that made them very sturdy, would probably have been taken even though the troops could have taken possession of these positions only by incurring heavy losses. But had they been taken, it would have been possible to use artillery at this point in these fairly straight streets. And at least, this would have brought about a moment of crisis in the fight, with doubtful results. But the brave defenders of these barricades had prepared for such a case soon after the news of the attack on their rear had arrived. Easily ignited material had been brought to the large stall at the side of the square. And as soon as the first troops appeared, the stall was set aflame. Of course, the surging sea of flames hindered the 8th regiment to proceed any further. And as, on top of this, the soldiers stood in the light of the flames whereas the citizens were engulfed by darkness, the troops were welcomed by such well-aimed rifle fire that they had to retreat in order to avoid bigger losses.

Evening, March 18th: The Second Phase of the Fighting

For the same reason, the Guards that had taken up positions at the King's Bridge suffered heavy losses while the fire was burning. And they were kept back from every further attempt to continue the attack.

Later, however, and almost simultaneously with the appearance of these troops at Alexander Square, the 12th regiment attacked the Potsdam Gate and the [barricades at] Leipzig Street. They were supported by the advance of a part of the 2nd Guards Regiment, which had replaced the [exhausted] 2nd regiment in Frederick's Street. Here, the barricade at Crown Street that previously had been defended so bravely, was taken as most of its defenders had already departed, in order to intervene in other locations where rifles were more urgently needed. The approaching troops had scarcely been noted. Having fired repeated salvoes into the upper storeys of the houses resulting in the death of even several women, the soldiers then stormed first into a street-corner house with a tobacco shop on the ground floor. They met with almost no resistance. But nonetheless they went ahead in the cruelest manner, just as it had been the case in King's Street and the Coelln City Hall, either shooting all those begging for their lives or stabbing them with their bayonets. From here, the troops advanced up to Leipzig Street where the 12th regiment, coming from the Potsdam Gate, had in the meantime taken the barricades. The first of these barricades had been given up without much resistance. At the corner of Wall Street the fighting was fiercer, however. But it came to an end when the citizens received the news that the barricades at Crown Street and Leipzig Street had been taken.

The other barricades in Leipzig Street, situated further down the road, towards Doenhof's Square, still remained in the hands of the people, however. And now, a heavy *tirailleur* fight ensued with the troops positioned in Leipzig Street and Frederick's Street. But neither of the two sides started an offensive. While the eighth and twelfth infantry regiment advanced, the cavalry had undertaken an attack on the suburbs outside the Rosenthal Gate, the Schoenhausen Gate, Hamburg Gate, Oranienburg Gate and New Gate. But the brave inhabitants of the suburbs had found sufficient time to barricade their streets. And waiting behind their barricades, they repelled every attack of the cavalrymen with determined courage. Because weapons were lacking in this area, especially in the Louisatown quarter, the iron fence at the square next to the New Gate had been laid down [and dismantled], so that people could arm themselves with iron rods. At the same time, the arsenals of the artillery outside the Oranienburg Gate had been set on fire. Probably this was mainly because it was necessary to obstruct the advance of cavalry units not usually stationed in Berlin. A large number of them had stopped at the Wedding Square behind the second Pank Bridge. The Royal Iron Foundry had also been set aflame and we hope that it occurred for no other reason. The fire in the Guard House at the New Gate is said to have been caused by carelessness.

While the glow of these fires, burning simultaneously with the fire at Alexander Square, reddened the horizon, another interruption of the fighting occurred. Apparently, the effect on the morale of the commanders of the troops at this moment was not without consequences. On the one hand, the news of the partially aborted attack carried out by the troops that had been stationed outside the city made further strategic decisions necessary. At the same time, the commanders grasped that the citizens were determined to use all attainable means in the defense of their just cause.

PART VI

Night, March 18–19: The Third Phase of the Fighting

The attack that was unleashed again after a pause which lasted almost two hours constitutes the *third* phase of the fighting. It began in King's Street in the form of another *tirailleur* attack on the barricades found there. But here the barricade at New King's Street had been reinforced by three small cannons taken from the Riflemen's House. These cannons were now loaded with rifle bullets, pieces of iron and so-called "marbles." The street corner house of Mr. Richter, at the corner of New King's Street, was occupied on all storeys by riflemen of the people. And the quick and securely aimed fire of these men obstructed every *debouchement* of the troops across the bridge. At any rate, this building [of Mr. Richter], consisting of seven houses with intermittent large courtyards, offered a curious sight. While a lively rifle fire was kept up from every window, the doors opening towards Alexander Square had been barricaded. But in the section of the house situated behind the street barricade, the doors opening towards New King's Street and the old William Street allowed unhindered and safe communication. In the courtyard space, the most intense activity prevailed. Metal workers repaired rifles. A tin caster provided riflemen with bullets. And from two ransacked powder kegs, the necessary ammunition was distributed with such care and while such order prevailed that the two fire hoses and water buckets placed in the courtyard—which had been brought as a precaution, in order to be used in case of a fire—were actually superfluous. Here the frontline remained the same, from evening until morning.

The advance of the troops in Fredericktown was more successful. The barricades were insufficiently manned because no attack had been feared for the time being. Many defenders had departed in order to find some rest. And when, at about 4 o'clock in the morning, the troops pushed simultaneously into Moor Street, Crown Street, and Leipzig Street, and then thrust all their force against Krausen Street, they were not met with energetic resistance. It was only at the corner of Riflemen's Street and Frederick's Street that they encountered fierce rifle fire from the people who had rapidly run to the barricade. They retreated again to Leipzig Street which they controlled in its entirety, up to Doenhof's Square.

The individual houses adjacent to the barricades that had been taken were now cordoned off. The soldiers entered, and encountering almost no resistance, they took the defenders prisoner. On this occasion, scenes occurred which picture the behavior of the troops in a regrettable way. The house No. 17 Upper Wall Street was assaulted at 6 a.m. A deep silence prevailed in the house, as most inhabitants were still in their beds, when suddenly they were frightened to death. A servant maid had left the house to fetch bread for the breakfast; she had been unable to close the door again because the key was turned the wrong way, and so the house had remained open. Now, inside the house, shots were heard. Every one opened the door of his room or apartment, to see what was going on. Soldiers were shouting, pursuing a man who had taken refuge in the house and who had run up to the uppermost storey. They called out, "Slay him, kill him!" Not content that they could safely apprehend the prisoner who had run away, and was trapped inside the house, they shot and stabbed him. Two soldiers took the man, who was still breathing, and threw him down the stairs. As he fell, his head was beating against every step of the stairs. Completely dead, the maltreated man landed on the floor below and was handed over to four other prisoners who were to carry him away.

In another house, at No. 28 Jerusalem Street, the door was broken open and soldiers intruded into the house. They asked for the owner of the house. The man, paralyzed by an attack of gout, could not leave the bed; his male servant had run away, and thus the maid was forced to light the way for two soldiers who were to search the attic. The attic, however, had been occupied by several citizens who had taken flight across the roofs, except for two men who had not dared to do so because of the danger involved. The soldiers found these two unlucky ones, without weapons, cowering in a corner. One of the soldiers shot the first of these two people down, and when the maid shrieked and trembled, close to dropping the light, the grenadier placed it again in her hand, saying, "Stand firmly, like Bluecher." [A Prussian field marshal, who commanded the Prussian army against Napoleon at Waterloo (1815)]. The second man now fell on his knees and begged for his life but the other soldier, in cold blood, aimed his gun at him and shot the unlucky one in the head. Indeed, not a glorious deed which would increase the glory of Prussian soldiers. Similar scenes occurred everywhere, but while they are to be written into the account books of individuals and find [deleted] meagre excuse in the excitement of the hot battle, we have to mention still another occurrence which took place in the coffee house of Mr. Fluegge, at No. 30 Leipzig Street.

Now it is indeed likely that this book will be accused by one side of being partial. And it is easily possible that this reproach is really justified even though we have attempted to accord each party the proper acknowledgement. But in a time like ours, under the forceful impression of the days that lie behind us, such an impartial enumeration of individual occurrences, presented without passion, is probably an impossibility. As already mentioned in the preface, we have, however, strictly stuck to the rule that nothing but facts confirmed by trustworthy witnesses must be presented. The following fact is communicated by us mainly because we want to give the brave and honorable corps of officers of the entire army the opportunity to either disprove these accusations, which have been leveled against their comrades; or to correctly judge the actions of the same, and these men as well.

"It was around four in the morning," Mr. Fluegge narrates, "when soldiers of the twelfth regiment broke the door of my house and burst into my premises. Inside, there were twelve of my daily customers who had not dared to go home, and in addition, some strangers. (We have to admit, for truth's sake, that from this place shots had been fired at the troops.) All those present, who were in one of the backrooms, and which included no person that resisted, were arrested in the cruelest manner. One was shot in the billiard room and the others pushed down the staircase and taken away. I don't know what happened on the way [to the prison] but one of them (W. Braun) was killed and the others, except for one, severely wounded. In the meantime, the soldiers in my living room did not only break my cabinets open, they also searched small sewing baskets, supposedly searching for weapons. Having intruded into my living room, they even searched my clothes, and I had just entered when a soldier held a parcel with valuable papers in his hand, bills of exchange, promissory notes, receipts and transfer orders worth 359 Thalers. He had not yet seen the cash—it had been put inside a receipt book. I took the parcel from him, saying that these papers (being issued in my name) were of value to me only, not to him. When the soldiers finally had left the house, I found a piece of paper near the door of the living room which had been in my briefcase. The latter was gone and so were about 40 Thalers, mostly foreign transfer orders which had been kept separately inside it. After having smashed many chairs, tables and glasses on purpose, the soldiers also took six bottles of Madeira, a bottle of champagne, arrack, cognac, absinthe. And they had broken open two valuable boxes of cigars and emptied them. The officer who let the men do as they pleased deserves to be named. I asked for his protection but he refused to even reply. One of the arrested men, the one who was not wounded, heard another officer ask in front of the door of my house, 'Who is in charge in this house?' The reply he received was, 'Lieutenant von Wedell.'"

We abstain here from any comment on this occurrence and merely add that we are keeping the handwritten testimony of Mr. Fluegge ready for whoever wants to see it and desires to be informed in this way.

In order to give the reader an idea of the way the prisoners were treated, we now add a report by one of those men who had the sad luck to be caught on Sunday morning in the house of Mr. Schwerdtmann, at the corner of Charlotte Street and Leipzig Street.

"They found me," the man in question narrates, "when the soldiers intruded into the house at about 5:30. I was in a room of the uppermost storey of the Schwerdtmann house. Quietly and without talking back, I gave myself up to the intruding soldiers. But I was thrown down while they shouted, 'You dog, you have fired shots [at us]!' They kicked me and maltreated me with their rifle butts. Then I was dragged down the stairs by my hair. On each half-landing of the staircase I was repeatedly kicked and beaten with rifle butts again, until I found myself finally in the street. I was searched in the most shameless manner and then I was bound in the most outrageous and cruel way, which caused the skin to, quite literally, come off of both my arms. It happened in a way that made the blood stop running in my veins. The soldiers seemed already well-prepared for all this: Some had pretty strong cord with them. It was hanging around their necks; in other cases, it was fastened to their coats. In answer to every plea for milder treatment, I got the hardly consoling reply, 'Dog! You'll still have to kick the bucket today.' Finally we moved on. Having arrived at the theater, we were handed over to the third squadron of the ulans in order to be transported further. During the process of being handed over, I received a kick from an ulan who was standing behind me, so that I fell down. And the involuntary cry that this treatment caused was accompanied by loud laughter from the soldiers who seemed to take this for a good joke. When we had been turned over to the ulans, they wanted to take it out on us as well. All the time, they were tearing at the reins of their horses so that the animals reared and kicked us with their hooves, something that provided ample opportunity for laughter. Finally, thank goodness, we were in the palace. In a room at the ground floor we were questioned by three gentlemen in civilian clothes who were drinking red wine quite comfortably. And then we were led away to the basement of the palace. In front of the entrance to the basement, soldiers of the Emperor Franz grenadier regiment had formed what amounted to a narrow lane. And uttering rough jokes, they pushed us around and finally down the cellar staircase, where I met several hundred co-sufferers, who for the greatest part were wounded, and by and large, had received these wounds while they were being transported."

Here ends the narration of this poor sufferer. We complete the report by adding that during that night, when the basement of the palace was already full of prisoners, a part of them, I think 283, were led to Spandau by a bataillon of the 2nd Guards regiment and a squadron of hussars under the command of major von Clausewitz. The treatment of the prisoners during this transport is said to have been very rough, too. But the other side claims that this was the consequence of a violent attempt to escape. At any rate, so much is certain: that according to all the reports we received, hardly seventy-five citizens died on the barricades and in real battle. The others were taken prisoner and then, during the transport, they were—there is no other word for it—murdered without mercy. During the last attack in Frederick's Street, about fifty men were taken prisoner, none of them wounded. Hardly half of them reached the basement of the palace; the others were cut down on the way, especially by the cavalry. And they, the cavalrymen who had not even taken part in the battle, do not even have the flimsy excuse of agitation caused by the fighting. And we must still add that most officers of this branch of the armed forces belong to those noble families of the country which, due to the age of their lineage, and in view of their wealth, should present a positive example to the entire population. May these men, should they ever encounter armed and equally equipped enemies, and should ill fortune deliver them into their hands, be spared this experience that they would have to tell themselves that it is only God's will if they receive the same cruel treatment in retribution, in view of the brutalities they committed against the people during that fatal night. Nobody among them, however, is permitted to take refugee in the excuse heard already, that not they, but common soldiers, committed these deeds. Is the situation of our army, which costs the country such vast sums, really so bad that the events of a single night can tear the first and most necessary bond of a soldier's life apart so completely: the bond which is discipline? By the way: the following anecdote that we heard from a trustworthy mouth is quite characteristic of the mood of the common man. Prince Carl, standing in the garden of the palace, noted the bad treatment of the prisoners. And quite outraged, he commanded the grenadiers to refrain from it. "If you desire to be brave soldiers," he said, "you must not maltreat the captive enemy. You should rather respect him." An old corporal who stood nearby looked at the prince with surprise for several moments, and then he murmured, turning away dissatisfied, "Hm, hm! First we shall let them shoot at us—and afterwards we must not even give them a blow with the rifle butt!"

In honor of the people, we must say that they manifested no such signs of barbarity—as we must, unfortunately, mention herewith—in regards to the troops. The only incident that we heard about is the occurrence that involved the soldiers on guard in front of the bank, who were shot during the jostle that took place over their gun. In other words, they resisted. In the case of the gendarmerie officer who was shot at Doenhof's Square, this happened when he attempted to escape. And the other incidents which concerned some officers, especially when the military arrest building was stormed, do show the roughness of some individuals. But they did not have a bloody ending.

We have not heard of further cases of roughness against individual soldiers. On the contrary, we must mention with respect that in many locations soldiers were released quietly and left unharmed after they had been compelled to give up their gun and ammunition. Or they even found a safe haven in the homes of citizens. And yet, especially when the many small guard houses had been stormed, there had existed the opportunity to treat many soldiers badly, using repression to make them pay for the roughness of their comrades.

PART VII

Morning, March 19: The Red Dawn of Freedom

With these bloody scenes just over, the morning of the nineteenth of March had broken. But with it also the bright red dawn of freedom.

It is true that due to their last attack the troops had gained ground in Frederick's Street. But their situation was unfortunate. The men had not eaten anything, or very little, since the preceding day, when they had had an opportunity to do so at noon. They were extremely tired and exhausted. The same was true of the horses of the cavalry which had however been fed at the Palace Square or next to the barracks in George Street but which nonetheless would not have endured the strain of the next day.

The mood of the people was different. At Alexander Square only the citizens kept up the rifle fire. There, the troops had spent their ammunition and scarcely returned the fire. Finally, they ceased to do so at all. On the other hand, at the Constable Market, an area that so far had not seen any fighting, both sides prepared for a decisive fight.

Stones and boiling water were kept ready; even the large granite plates of the sidewalk had been brought to the roofs of the houses in order to smash the attacking soldiers. And in some places, even sulphuric acid is said to have been kept ready, in order to be filled into the fire hoses which were to welcome the troops. A terrible day of struggle and destruction was imminent.

The news of the cruelty with which the soldiers had treated entirely innocent prisoners, the narrations of terrible massacres of those who, though at first engaged in battle, had begged for their lives—all of this had embittered the fighters of the people to a degree that had been foreign to them the day before. It was said that the soldiers were merciless. And the citizens, being not for a moment discouraged by this, prepared to sell their life as dearly as possible, and to pay back like with like. People prepared for the destruction of the staircases of the houses in which they were expecting to fight and for the defense of every single storey. They communicated with the town quarters which had been occupied by the troops and they received the good news that the barricades would be erected again behind the back of the soldiers as soon as they departed. In addition, the largest part of the rifles captured at the arsenal had been fitted with pistons. Powder and bullets were lacking nowhere: the merchants had given their entire supplies. In addition, some powder kegs of the military had been captured at the city wall and at St. George's Church. The tin founders had made thousands of bullets during the night. To put it briefly, they were more ready for the fight than they had been on the preceding day. Most of the fighters of the people had also been able to sleep for a couple of hours, and neither food nor drink had been lacking. Everyone had taken up his position courageously, invigorated, while the church bells with their hollow sound were calling the tardy.

The mood of the troops was completely different. They were mentally and physically exhausted and yet they were about to be led into a fight that was to require their entire strength. It was not difficult to predict the outcome of this struggle. The fight would be more terrible, more bloody than the preceding one, but the troops would be destroyed!

But the government saw its sad situation—they began to give in. With this in mind, they began to negotiate with the people. The barricades should be taken away; if this was done, they would withdraw the military. But everywhere, the answer was heard that the barricades would remain in place. They would be defended to the utmost. Not until the troops had left the city would the barricades disappear. An accident that happened at the time may have contributed to a faster way of resolving the tangled situation. General von Moellendorf appeared in Alexander Square as a negotiator. But the armed citizens did not want to recognize him as such. They surrounded him in order to declare him a prisoner. Led to the House of the Riflemen's Association, the general, giving in to the threats of the crowd, is said to have signed an order to the troops commanded by him that they should stop their rifle fire. In the early hours, at about seven o'clock, the following proclamation was posted at the street corners:

To my dear Berliners!

With the decree concerning the convocation [of the Estates] issued today you have received the pledge of faithful sentiments of Your King, felt both for you and for the entire German fatherland. The jubilation of innumerable faithful hearts that were greeting me had hardly ebbed when a small group of troublemakers added rebellious and impudent demands and grew in numbers, while the more well-meaning disappeared. As their advance to the door of the palace justly raised fears of evil intention and because insults against my brave and faithful soldiers were uttered, the square had to be cleansed by the cavalry at walking speed and with sheathed weapon. And two rifles of the infantry went off all by themselves; thanks to God, nobody was hit. A pack of evildoers, largely consisting of strangers, which had known how to remain in hiding for seven days even though they were being looked for, have distorted this occurrence according to their evil plans by taking refuge in an apparent lie. And they filled the heated minds of many of my faithful and dear Berliners with thoughts of revenge, in view of the blood that supposedly had been spilled. Thus they became the terrible originators of the bloodshed. My troops, your brothers and countrymen, have only made use of their weapons when they were forced to do so, in view of the many shots that were fired from the King's Street area. The victorious advance of the troops was the necessary consequence thereof. It is now up to you, inhabitants of my beloved hometown, to prevent bigger damage. By all that you hold sacred: recognize, Your King and most faithful friend implores you, the ill-fated error! Return to peace. Take the remaining barricades away. And send to me men, full of the genuine Berlin spirit, with words appropriate vis-à-vis Your King. And I give you my Royal word that all streets and squares are to be at once cleared of all troops. And the military occupation will be limited to the necessary buildings—the Palace, the arsenal and a few others, and even there it will last for only a short time. Hear the fatherly voice of Your King, inhabitants of my faithful and beautiful Berlin, and forget what happened, as I want to forget it and will forget it, for the sake of the grand future which will begin, under God's blessed peace, for Prussia. And through Prussia, for Germany.

My lovely Queen and truly faithful mother and friend, ailing now and lying in bed, unites her heartfelt, tearful plea with mine.

Written in the night of 18th–19th March, 1848.
Frederick William
[Friedrich Wilhem]

But this proclamation did not accomplish its goal. The complete withdrawal of the military was insisted on, as well as the immediate arming of the people. And people continued arming themselves, in order to be prepared for every eventuality.

In the meantime, deputations had been dispatched to the King from various sides. And for the first time it seems to have dawned on this monarch that he had surrounded himself with advisers who had betrayed him and the people. This King, who had said and expressed in writing on so many occasions that he, a father of his people, wanted to care for their well-being as best he could, had been left in the dark, up to this very moment, about the fact that it was not an assorted mob led by foreign emissaries but the entire people that had fought for their rights, every man among them, with weapons in their hands.

"Gentlemen," he, the King, said to members of one of those deputations which asked for the liberation of the prisoners, "just look at these people, who have been brought here during the night—they are nothing but the sputum of hell."

He meant to say by this that it was only the mob which was fighting now, as he had been informed, and afterwards they would undertake an attack on property.

But the time of lies was over. Every moment, with all the news that arrived, the conviction of the monarch grew that there had been an attempt to rob him of the love of his people. He had expressed the wish to receive deputations of the people who would tell him the truth, honestly and without fear. And when the Lord Mayor, Krausnick, appeared at the head of a deputation of city councilors and municipal public servants, the King declare indignantly that he wanted to talk to men who had fought on the barricades that night.

Then, finally, the truth was heard. Immediate withdrawal of the troops, the liberation of the prisoners, general amnesty, the arming of the people, were accorded by the King; and through all the streets, citizens were running who had taken part in diverse deputations, while the staff officers transmitted the [Royal] order to the regiments to depart.

PART VIII

March 19: Peace! Peace!

It was around ten in the morning when the King uttered this word:
Peace! Peace!
Just as the call "To the arms!" had spread with lightning speed in the streets the day before, this shout reached even the most distant quarters of town with the speed of a wildfire.

Jubilant revolutionaries on a barricade erected on Broadway (Breite Str.) when PEACE was announced on March 19th, 1848.

It was a moment of infinite jubilation, a moment no one who lived through the terror of that terrible night will forget. Peace! Peace! From all the windows, white sheets were flowing. With tears in their eyes, people embraced each other. They shook hands, the young and the old, the rich and the poor, people who had not known each other before but who had formed closer ties of friendship between each other behind the barricades than long years of being acquainted can produce.

March 19: Peace! Peace!

Peace! Peace! In all the streets shots that expressed joy were heard. These men, with their serious faces blackened by gun powder the night before, now showed a completely different expression, an expression of pride and joy; but not that raw, unintelligent jubilation; no, there was not a single person who did not sense the deep and serious significance of this moment. When a battalion of the Guard, with pipes and drums, marched down Broadway, it was surrounded by the people and they demanded that instead of the joyous march, a church hymn should be played. The musicians respected this request, and to the sound of serious and solemn music, the troops marched on.

Meanwhile the Royal Palace had remained occupied by troops for the time being, whereas the Guard returned to its barracks. An immense crowd of people assembled at this time in the Palace Square. And now a drama began which left such a deep impression that the writer can hardly describe it.

From the *Schlossfreiheit* [or "Palace Freedom"], a *cortège* of men of the people were slowly approaching. They carried several corpses of men who had been killed in action during the overnight battle. The dead had been placed on stretchers, their wounds had been uncovered, flowers had been strewn over them. A deep, profound silence greeted this frightful *cortège*; every person present bared his or her head. And through the quickly opening gap in the crowd the solemn pall-bearers moved to the door of the palace and stopped there. Suddenly, from among the people, the shout resounded: the King! the King!

Without the slightest inkling of the sight that was awaiting him, the sorely tried King, accompanied by his spouse and two of his ministers, Count Arnim and Count Schwerin, stepped onto the balcony. They, as well as the King, bared their heads—instinctively and deeply moved. The Queen shed tears but her Royal spouse was too deeply moved to utter a single word.

At this moment, among the earnest, still crowd, a deep voice was suddenly raised, and began the hymn *Jesus, my faith and trust!* And all those thousands of people who had assembled here, deeply moved by the great and serious significance of the moment, joined in. Like thunder, the hymn rose up to the sky—like a terrible, horrendous accusation against those who were guilty of the bloodshed. From all sides more *cortèges* with corpses appeared. These corpses were carried into the courtyard of the Palace. And then, they were laid down, one by one, in a row, in a chamber that had been indicated. It was a pale, bloody assemblage that was lying there, next to each other, in groups of four.

At this moment the monarchy and the throne would have been the toy of he who would have dared to put himself at the head of this deeply moved crowd!

But this moment went by; it was the most fatal of the entire revolution. And the King as well as the people were given the glad hope to move, hand in hand, into a joyous future, so that mutual love would let everyone forget the bloody scenes.

During this moving drama, and a brief pause owing to exhaustion which was noticeable around noon, scenes happened in other parts of the town which were only natural in view of the excited mood of the people. One of them was the already mentioned act of popular justice against major von Preuss. Something similar occurred in the street called *Under the Linden Trees*. Here, the shop of a glove maker who lived there was stormed by the people and all his property was burned in the street. On Saturday afternoon, this man, called Wernicke, had denounced persons who had distributed money among the people, asking them to resist.

All of this happened without any avaricious attack on the property.

Such scenes were to occur the next day in the house of that police *commissaire* who, as mentioned above, was suspected of having opened the Frankfurt Gate for the troops. And also at the Rhenanian Inn, at the corner of Frederick's Street and Leipzig Street, where refreshments had been given to the troops. But here, citizens easily managed to calm the raging crowd with amicable and pacifying words.

The same was the case at the Palace of the Prince of Prussia who was perceived, more than everyone else, as the person who had given the advice to his Royal brother that it was necessary to proceed against the people with utmost severity. At this location, the excitement was enormous. People wanted to burn the palace down. And the fact that the building was preserved is owed entirely to the assiduous efforts of Mr. von Minutoli, who had hurried there and given a speech to the people. A black, red and golden flag had already been placed on the gabled roof of the building, and people said that this had been done by the writer Dr. Eichler. Now the words "Property of the Nation" were written on the walls. And profiting from the illumination of the evening, the same words, written on a banner, were attached to the balcony. Furthermore, these demonstrations against the Prince went as far this: all the merchants who had been licensed by a patent to be privileged suppliers of the Prince, and who had included his coat of arms and the coveted words *Purveyor to the Court of the Prince of Prussia* in their advertisements and on their business stationary, saw themselves compelled to drop that title.

We must come back to more important matters that occurred on this Sunday, however. Among these, the fact that all the ministers resigned in the morning and that a new Cabinet was formed is the most important. The announcement appeared in printed form on the same afternoon, after it had been pronounced orally in the morning. The respective document is the following one:

> I have already accepted yesterday, in the morning, the resignation of the ministers who served up to now, and I have asked Count Arnim to form a new Cabinet.
>
> The latter will preside over the Cabinet and he is also going to temporarily serve as minister of foreign affairs and as minister concerned with matters regarding the Constitution.

I have entrusted Count Schwerin with the Ministry of Religious Affairs.

Provided that he is willing to accept this nomination, the Provincial *Conseilleur Général*, Mr. von Auerbach, who is still absent, is to head the Ministry of the Interior, with the exception of those parts of the *ressort* that Count Arnim has been entrusted with.

For the time being, the Minister of Justice, as well as the two Ministers Count Stolberg and von Rohr, will continue in office until further decisions have been reached on how to fill these positions.

Until a definite decision has been reached, the Directeur Général of the Tax Collection Office, Mr. Kuehne, will be interim Minister of Finance.

Berlin, March 19, 1848.
Frederick William [Friedrich Wilhelm]

Almost at the same time—at any rate, before noon—the Lord Mayor, Krausnick, resigned or was compelled to resign.

The incident that brought about this resignation is of a rather comical nature. The Lord Mayor, who had never gained the love and trust of the citizens to any considerable degree, had practically become a hated person on account of the events of the past few days. And when, on that morning, he came down King's Street, he was recognized by several persons. When he saw himself surrounded by a threatening crowd who wanted him to account for the occurrences that had taken place, Mr. Krausnick deemed it not advisable to engage in a discussion about this matter, but fled to his house, in order to save himself from this truly considerable physical badgering. But the crowd did not disperse. Instead, it grew in a threatening way and the shout "Resign, resign, he must resign!" resounded loud and ever louder. A deputation that was quickly formed went to his house at the same time and asked him to declare immediately, for his own sake, that he would request his dismissal. Thereupon he appeared at the window, giving a speech which was frequently interrupted by the people, however. He said that he had just come from the King, who was disposed to fulfill all the requests of the people, and that he, Krausnick, had been entrusted with the task to recommend men to the King who possessed the confidence of the people, etc. He was hindered in continuing, however, and without finishing his speech, he returned to the palace, protected by a few citizens, in order to find a safe haven. In the evening, he was pestered by caterwauling. And on the following day, posters glued to walls announced that he really had resigned.

Another event on this significant morning, which was very positive, however, was the release of the prisoners in the palace basement and the return of those who had been brought to Spandau.

It is hard to describe the joy when the unexpected news of their imminent liberation reached these men. The treatment they had received was the harshest that can be imagined. In general, it seems that we cannot reproach the authorities with regard to this. In the first place, nobody had been prepared for such an event. As well, there had been no time afterwards to occupy one's self with the desolate condition in which the poor souls found themselves. It was only due to the humane efforts of the police superintendent Hofrichter that the prisoners in the palace basement received some bread and warm soup. Otherwise, they probably would have been entirely forgotten. Other administrative officers whose higher education should let us expect from them a more humane treatment than can be expected from the roughness of common soldiers, amused themselves, however, by making the sad situation of the poor folks even more terrible. This is a distressing symptom of the state of mind of the administrative officers who had been running our administration up to now. In this case, it was above all the *commissaire* of the criminal investigation department, Simon, who had the arms of a man who had been especially active during the people's assemblies cruelly tied, or who had even tied them himself, during the transport of the prisoners to Spandau. And in addition, he instructed a corporal to guard him with extraordinary vigilance because this was a very dangerous person.

We now leave those sad scenes behind us, just like the prisoners felt these gloomy impressions wane under the influence of the immense jubilation that greeted them. Indeed, this moment of liberation must have been a compensation for all they suffered. Being without any news from the theater of battle, in all likelihood even deceived on purpose by wrong information, this moment, in addition to freedom, brought them the news of the victory of their co-citizens.

If we continue now with our narration of all that happened, the most important among them was the *arming of the people* that happened on Sunday afternoon. It was the last of the *articles* of that petition adopted in the Koepenick Street people's assembly which we now have to recognize finally as the innermost foundation of this [revolutionary, democratic] movement. A deputation of protective officers and citizens assembled in front of the Palace a bit after one p.m. in order to thank the King for having finally granted the requests of the people. This was the next cause for the formation of a still very excited crowd which moved once more to the palace door, demanding to see the King. The resignation of the Prince of Prussia was demanded. Some people even shouted: *A Republic!* But they received no attention. Still, this was a moment of dangerous excitement.

Finally, the question of the arming of the people was raised, and on this all those present agreed. Some attempted to steer the debate away from the subject, but in vain. Notably Dr. Gutzkow. He suggested to the crowd, after having delivered a pompous speech in favor of the arming of the people, that they should go to the Parade Ground at 4 o'clock and consider this question thoroughly in a debate, and prepare a legal solution. But people noted the trap and rejected the proposal by way of wild shouting. Indeed, nothing could have been more desirable for a certain party than leading thirty thousand of these people in front of the city gate, in order to see them assembled defenselessly on an empty field.

But this was no longer the time for discussions and deliberation, it was time to act. Finally, the Chief of Police, Mr. von Minutoli, appeared on the terrace of the Palace. He was received with loud jubilation and it was demanded that he should be at the head of the Citizens' Militia. The Chief of Police gave thanks for this show of confidence in him. But he declared that he was incompetent in this respect. Then the crowd demanded that he and some others should immediately see the King and present this request of the people to him. The City Councilor Holbein was the only one present, from among the city councilors. And with a few other citizens he followed the Chief of Police. The King agreed that the arming of the people should take place. Initially, he let Count Schwerin make an oral declaration to this effect in front of the crowd. Later on, he himself appeared and gave the people the desired assurance: "From this moment, I give myself, full of faith and confidence, into the hands of my people," he said. Immense jubilation filled the yard of the palace. Hereupon, Mr. Minutoli appeared and was greeted with new jubilation.

"Gentlemen," he said, "I shall proceed at once with this task and shall ask for the necessary participants in this important work." Soon, the City Councillors Holbein, Haack and Glaue; the factory owner Devaranne; Dr. Woeniger; and the merchant Krug, later on joined by the junior barrister Wache, went to the police headquarters with the Chief of Police, von Minutoli. Thousands followed them. White sheets were hanging from the windows, hats were thrown jubilantly into the air, people shouted, "Long live the Chief of Police." It was again a moment of vast excitement.

At the Police Headquarters, the Chief of Police met immediately with the Committee that had been formed [by the men named above]. And within a short span of time, one of the most important laws in the more recent history of the State [i.e. of Prussia] had been put down on paper. It said:

Announcement.

His Majesty the King, responding to the desire of the inhabitants of Berlin, has deigned to permit the arming of the people. With regard to the latter, the following provisional regulation has been decided by the Undersigned that have been delegated for this purpose:

§1 An arming of the people will be organized.
§2 The citizens ["burghers"] and relatives [sic!] under their legal protection [Schutz*verwandte*] will take part in it.

§3 The cost of arming them will be borne by the State.
§4 The riflemen's guild will be called up immediately and an adequate number of citizens will be armed at once.
§5 More detailed regulations concerning this organization will be issued as quickly as possible in the next few days.

Berlin, March 19, 1848.
von Minutoli. Holbein. Glaue. Haack. Woeniger.
Davaranne. Krug

About an hour later, Dr. Woeniger appeared again in the Palace Yard, holding a copy of the provisional Act in his hand. Thunderous jubilation arose. The crowd moved from the Palace Yard to the Palace Square, and here Dr. Woeniger was lifted onto a low brick wall. Here he pronounced, in front of thousands of people, the first *basic law* of citizen freedom. In the meantime, the City Councilor Holbein had hurried to the House of the Riflemen's Association, because as a first measure, members of the Riflemen's Guild were to stand guard in the Palace. This happened in a very short time. Simultaneously the Law Concerning the Arming of the People appeared in print and was glued to the walls of houses and at street corners. Weapons were distributed to the people from the Arsenal. And it must be stressed that this quick decision, the issuing of the law and the arming of the people that was undertaken at once, saved the monarchy on this day. The crowd recognized in this the most effective guarantee of the future, and at the same time, the honest confidence that the government had [in the people]. From now on, the red-hot, extraordinarily heated atmosphere vanished, and friendlier aspects returned. Joyously fired shots, partly from captured and partly from distributed guns, were heard in the streets. All of the houses were voluntarily illuminated in the evening. The Chief of Police was honored by a torchlight procession and Lord-Mayor Krausnick by a *charivari* [a mock parade to express disapprobation towards someone].

In this way, the fateful day ended. The lights in the windows slowly went out and only the gloomy, blood-red disk of the darkening moon hung in the sky as if it wanted to remind us of the many blood-soaked victims that, stiff and mute as they were, could not take part in the jubilant celebration of this day which they had fought for, paid for with their blood.

A general exhaustion had followed upon the excitement of the day that had passed, and the nightly rest of the sleepers was not disturbed by the slightest incident.

PART IX

Morning, March 20: Liberation of the Polish Prisoners

On Monday morning, the twentieth of March, the tumultuous incidents in front of the Palace of the Prince of Prussia and at the Rhenanian Inn, that have been mentioned already further above, fortunately came to an end, without any further, serious consequences, thanks to the efforts of the Chief of Police and of the citizens. At the same time, people [i.e. *the group of men who had formed around Minutoli, Holbein, etc. while relying on the Riflemen's Association*] continued busily to arm the citizens and did everything possible to organize this procedure at least to some degree.

But the politically most significant moment of this day is the liberation of the Poles arrested because of the revolution of 1846 who still languished in prison.

We report about this the following details:

In the early hours of the morning, the Commissioner of Justice Deyks, the tireless defense lawyer who was mentioned in the press so often at the time of the hearings of the big trial of the Polish [revolutionaries], went to the Chief of Police, von Minutoli, and asked him to obtain for him an audience with the King in order to obtain an amnesty for the Poles whose trials were still pending, and for all those who had been sentenced because of a political offense or because of a violation of the law governing the press. Mr. von Minutoli rejected this request, however, remarking that by this the seething populace could be excited anew, and that he must suggest that it was better to wait for the sentences that were to be pronounced by the Court of Appeals. The Commissioner of Justice Deyks was not at all discouraged by this. He teamed up with Dr. Woeniger, who drew up a letter to Count Arnim, the Chief Minister [or "State Minister"], applying for said audience and also naming its purpose. Mr. von Arnim decidedly refused such a request, calling it not appropriate at the moment, and [also] referred him to the Court of Appeals. But the two gentlemen, Deyks and Woeniger, did not depart. In part, they were backing up their argument by pointing to the respective desires of the people, several thousands of which had assembled in the Palace Square and its neighborhood where they made themselves heard with increasing loudness. In part, they stressed that after an amnesty had been granted for [those who took part in] the revolution, lesser political offences could not be punished any longer. This was decisive. Within a short time, the amnesty decree had been deliberated, drawn up by the attorney of state—the Secret Judicial Councilor Wenzel—and immediately applied.

When the two gentlemen Deyks and Heufelder informed the crowd, which by now numbered many thousands and which spilled over into the adjacent streets, about the truly Royal act of mercy, this was accompanied by immeasurable jubilation. Then they made haste and as quickly as possible they hurried to the State Prison outside the New Gate. It was a moving moment when the door of the prison was opened and Poland's brave sons, crying and speechless, fell upon the breast of the harbingers of their good luck. They had not thought that the end of their suffering was so close at hand.

Soon after, the attorney of state, Wenzel, appeared. Deeply moved by visible joy and sympathy, he carried out the formal part of this act and almost succumbed to the manifestations of joy of the freed Poles, who showed the greatest reverence to this dutiful man. The director of the prison, Captain von Grabowski, was blessed with similar signs of respect.

Surrounded by the other Poles, all of them bareheaded and on foot, L. von Mieroslawski, clasping the hand of Mr. Deyks, as well as Dr. Libelt, hand in hand with Mr. Heufelder, proceeded through a section of Louisa Street and of Frederick's Street, followed by Linden Street, and stopped at the university, accompanied by at least one hundred thousand men. From all the windows of the streets named, white sheets were flowing, and flowers as well as floral wreaths were thrown from them. The students received their Polish brothers well-armed; the citizen's guard of the Main Guard House presented arms; Mieroslawski and Libelt expressed their gratitude and their sympathies for their German brothers; and out of overflowing joy, they were almost crushed by those standing next to them. From among the citizens that had been armed

Karol Libelt, 1807-1875, Polish philosopher.

since yesterday, a guard of honor had been formed under the leadership of the *banquier* Caspar Hirschfeld. And as this guard marched ahead, the column of people reached the Palace Square where his Majesty, the King himself received the mute thanks of the Poles, accompanied by loud jubilation of the people.

Hereupon the procession again headed for the university. The big auditorium was filled with the Poles, the students and a part of the crowd. Dr. Li[e]belt, von Mieroslawski, and Dr. Heufelder, recognized by those present as a courageous fighter in the last few days, as well as the Commissioner of Justice, Deyks, were asked to give a speech, a request articulated by shouts from the assembled. They uttered meaningful words which found considerable approval. And after a man of the people, a worker, had also given a very reasonable speech, the entire assembly once more thanked Mr. Deyks, and Dr. Woeniger, who was absent, for their courageous and successful intervention by way of a loud vivat.

In the afternoon, the following expression of gratitude from the Poles directed to the inhabitants of Berlin appeared at the street corners:

Citizens of Berlin! We owe our liberation after more than two years of imprisonment, first, to the illustrious amnesty decree of His Majesty the King. Still, we owe it to you, citizens of Berlin, that you undertook it to direct a free word in favor of us to the King. You have obtained freedom for us from His Majesty the King. You have led us in a train of triumph to the palace of His Majesty the King, in order to show him the joy felt by his people that has been caused by this Royal act of mercy which is at the same time an act of justice.

Yes! It has been an act of justice that happened after the wind changed in such a wonderful way in European politics. In so far as Germany let the call for national unity of a grand, free and powerful fatherland rise to the sky in all German regions, and after Prussia's ruler himself had promised his people to work for unity, the urge felt by the condemned Poles to work for a united, independent and free fatherland could no longer be considered as high treason.

Citizens of Berlin. The healthy sense of the people is perceiving these facts and judging them better than the wisdom of politics.

Led by this sense, you have greeted, conjointly with our liberation, the future Polish liberty and independence. You feel that not only has the time arrived when the fatal act of the partition of Poland must be expiated again, but that our time also commands that for the safeguarding of a free Germany, an independent Poland must be erected as a bulwark against the forward thrust of the Asians.

O! may this conviction which today is already deeply rooted in the German people also take root in German governments. May especially Prussia's newly constituted liberal government take the initiative in this regard, too—and the hearts of all Poles would fly to it. Just as it has happened here, everywhere Germans and Poles would [cut] fall as brothers against each other's breast. Peace in Europe would be forever secure after the reconstitution of Poland.

If this hope is fulfilled, and God willing it will be fulfilled, for it is the mighty finger of God that has visibly intervened in the fate of the peoples today—you, generous citizens of Berlin, and you, academic citizens of the university of this Capital and Royal Residence, shall live eternally in the love and respect of all Poles. For you were the first to comprehend your and our political national interest. And you were the first to freely express your thoughts and feelings. Long live Germany! Long live Prussia! Long live Berlin! (*There followed the signatures.*)

At the same time, in order to express their gratitude to the citizenry, the liberated desired to take part in those measures which had been decided on, to guard the city. And this conjointly with their countrymen living in Berlin. They wanted to take responsibility for the occupation of the Palace, something that could not be accorded to them for good reason. The sense of honor of the citizenry did not permit it to leave this task to someone else. Instead, as a sign of gratitude for their honorable cast of mind, the Poles were entrusted with the occupation of the post office building.

In the evening, the city was again festively illuminated.

Jubilating, the citizens milled through the streets. And in the late evening, accompanied by armed citizens, those regiments which had still been inside the barracks left the liberated city quietly and without causing any noise.

But around 10 o'clock, a rumor that subsequently proved entirely unfounded, frightened the inhabitants of Berlin. It was alleged that the Prince of Prussia was advancing with all the troops against the city. The call to arms was heard; the citizens that were in their houses hurriedly rushed into the street; in several places, barricades were erected, till finally the patrols that had been dispatched came back with the news that this rumor had no factual foundation. It had been caused by the fact that a stagecoach driver of the overland mail had arrived with the news that he had heard the sound of the "*Mount!*" signal of the cavalry at a distance—sounded by horns which were blown in the outlying villages where the troops were temporarily bivouacking. This was true in so far as the troops had departed from there that night, in order to attain quarters further away.

PART X

March 21: The King Rides the Streets

On Tuesday, March 21st, first of all, the amnesty decree concerning all political and press offenses appeared in print. And then, in addition to this, the following address of the King was delivered, which left a deep and stirring impression on the population of Berlin.

To my people and the German nation.

Full of confidence the King addressed his people thirty-five years ago, in the days of extreme danger. And his confidence was not disappointed: the King, united with his people, saved Prussia and Germany from disgrace and humiliation.

Full of confidence I address today, at a moment when the fatherland is exposed to the greatest of dangers, the German nation, among the most noble tribes of which my people may proudly count itself. Germany has been affected by some inner ferment. And it can be endangered from more than one side by external threats. Salvation from this double, very imminent threat is only possible through the intimate union of the German sovereigns and peoples, under one direction.

Today, I assume this leadership for [the duration of] these days of danger. My people, who do not fear danger, will not desert me, and Germany will follow me full of trust. I have adopted today the old German colors and I have thus placed myself and my people under the banner of the German Empire. Prussia from now on is an intrinsic part of Germany.

The [united provincial] *diet* [of Prussia] that has already been convened and that is to meet [in session] on the second of April appears to be a means, and lawful institution, to tackle, together with My people, the salvation and calming of Germany. In a way yet to be considered, and this immediately, I intend to create the opportunity for the princes and the estates of Germany to meet together with the bodies of this *diet*, in united assembly.

The assembly of German estates that is to be constituted temporarily in this way, shall immediately determine, in joint, free deliberation, all the precautionary measures that are necessary to ward off the interior and external danger that we all face.

What is necessary above all today is
    (1) the formation of a general German popular federal army,
    (2) an armed declaration of neutrality.

Such a patriotic force and such a declaration will cause Europe to respect the sanctity and inviolability of the territory where German is spoken and which is known by German names. Only through unity and strength can peace be safeguarded today in all of our beautiful fatherland that blossoms thanks to trade and industry.

Simultaneously with measures destined to ward off the present danger, the German assembly of the Estates will deliberate on the rebirth and founding of a new Germany, of a united though not uniform Germany, a unity within diversity, a unity coupled with liberty.

General introduction of Constitutions befitting genuine constitutional monarchies in all the member states, with ministers responsible to parliament; public and oral court proceedings with juries in the case of criminal proceedings; equal political and civil rights for members of all religious denominations; and a truly popular, liberal administration are the means which alone can bring about and strengthen such a higher and intrinsic unity.

Berlin, March 21, 1848.
Frederick William. [Friedrich Wilhelm]
Count Arnim. von Rohr. Count Schwerin. Bornemann.
von Arnim. Kuehne.

The fact that on the same day, at midday, eleven o'clock, the King mounted his horse and rode through the city, led by the citizens' guards and wearing a ribbon with the colors of the [German] *tri-color* on his arm, left an impression that was no less joyful and that re-enforced mutual trust.
    A small number of generals and ministers were following him, and thusly the King, on his horse, passed through Linden Street, then Behren Street, King's Street, and Broadway. Everywhere he was received by loud shouts of vivat!—a sign of the steadfast and unshakable love of his people who had only fought against those who had deceived his ears with false reports.
    In several places, the King addressed his people. One should not misunderstand him, he said in one of these talks. If today he had the German tri-color carried forward, at the head of his train, it did not mean that he

intended to usurp a crown. He did not desire to be an usurper and he did not want to push princes from their thrones. But the urgency of the moment demanded that he should place himself at the head of the movements in Germany. Suddenly, in some parts of Germany, unfaithfulness had revealed itself, not with regard to him—for he was not talking about himself in this case—but with regard to Germany. German unity and liberty were threatened; thus it was necessary to protect both, through German faithfulness. If Germany should not be lost at this very moment, he as the most powerful prince in Germany, had to place himself at the front of the entire German movement. All Germans should rally around him; he'd swear that he desired nothing but a constitutionally united Germany.

Speaking at the university, the King also alerted his listeners to the fact that, on various occasions in the course of German history, it had happened that a mighty prince had seized the flag of the empire in order to save the empire. The King thanked the students for their wonderful spirit, which had proved itself during the days of unrest. And he declared that he was proud that Germany had such sons.

The hooray was especially loud when the King ended his speech at the Coeln city hall with the words, "Citizens, I know it well that I'm not strong thanks to the weapons of my certainly strong and brave army, that I am not strong thanks to my filled coffers, but thanks only to the hearts and the faithfulness of my people. And, isn't it so? These hearts, this faithfulness, you are going to give me as a gift! I swear, I only want that which is good for you and for Germany." The King rode up to all the citizens' guards and thanked them for the arduous service that they rendered to him and the city.

PART XI

March 22: The Funeral

In the meantime, people were busy in the course of this day to prepare for the funeral of those who had died on the 18th and 19th of March for the freedom of the people.

Their bodies had at first been placed in the houses of citizens in the neighborhoods of the various scenes of battle. Then they had been brought to the churches of the various boroughs, with the exception of those who had already been deposited in the Royal Palace on Sunday. Washed and in clean clothes and placed in coffins, all of them were carried on Monday night from their various locations to the so-called New Church at the Constable Market. It had not been possible to obtain coffins for about forty of them in this short span of time. And so they were placed, in their original clothes [that they had worn during the fighting], on a pallet made of straw in the empty space in front of the altar. On Tuesday, to the number of these dead fighters all those were added who had died in the meantime in the houses of their relatives.

It was a terrible, deeply moving sight. But in the morning, it assumed a heart-rending character when the next-of-kin—mothers who had looked in vain for their sons and wives who had not seen their husbands since the eve of the battle—being unable to find them, stepped into the church. With staring, wide-open eyes they hurried past the rows of corpses, searching, in the pale twilight, for the sight of those they knew so well and who were so dear to them. A loud, heart-breaking cry would then announce that their last small hope which had filled them when they had entered the eerie site, had vanished. The cry announced that they had found him whom they searched for—with the mute, rigid expression of death on his face, a mortal wound wide open in his chest.

While these moving scenes recurred all day long *inside* the church, workers in front of it were busy constructing a gigantic funeral catafalque next to its grand flight of steps, right in front of the mighty Columned Hall During the night, working by the light of torches, they were still busy completing the work, and on Wednesday morning the scaffolding was finished, and covered by black crêpe and flowers. One hundred and eighty-three coffins had been lined up, side by side.

Thirty-three corpses had not been identified. But on their coffins that wreath of fresh flowers was not lacking, which bereaved families would place on the coffin of the person that had been so dear to them in life. If these lonely

March 22: The Funeral

Adolf Menzel, "Laying out of the Dead Fighters of the March Revolution" (Aufbahrung der Maerzgefallenen). The painting (oil on canvas) was done in 1848. It shows the 183 coffins in front of the "New Church" on a hastily built "catafalque." This was the Brass family's church. The badly conserved painting shows cracks in the oil paint.

and forlorn ones had known no one when alive who had loved them, who had shared grief and joy with them; if they had died on the barricade with the grim solace that there would be no one who would cry for them, who would close their dead eyes; now at least there existed, for the first time in those days, the emotion and the consciousness in the hearts of so many hundreds of thousands that all belonged to one single large family: the family of man. And if this great consciousness which arose from those bloody graves came alive in you, too, who had sunk in the putrid mire of selfishness, and who did not see these people as your brothers but as creatures of some underclass, if this consciousness, I say, remains alive in *you*, if it never departs from you, and if it will be passed on by you to future generations, *then and only then* will the golden morn of *true* freedom dawn: a freedom not attained through the blood shed by men—no, a freedom attained by a basic *ethos*.

Finally, on Wednesday morning, when all the preparations for this grand spectacle had been completed, the solemn funeral ceremony took place.

From every window tri-coloured flags were flying, some of them entangled in black crêpe. The bells of every spire were ringing, and a deep and complete silence prevailed among the various deputations that had arrived in the appointed square from all sides. One could note among them many delegates from other cities who had already arrived on Sunday and Monday, initially with the honorable intention of lending their arm and good rifle to the attacked, hard-pressed inhabitants of Berlin if the fighting should still have continued.

But then, they had stayed on in order to pay respect to their fellow-citizens killed in action.

A certain [Mr.] Urban, who had appeared on Sunday morning at the barricade in the New King's Road after the shooting had ceased and who had attempted several years ago to put himself at the head of a pietist movement, now assumed the pose of a speaker of the people. He proposed that the bodies of the soldiers killed in action should be buried on the same day [as the fighters of the people], and that the regiments [that had just left Berlin] should be called back for this purpose. His proposition was unanimously rejected and the respective posters [that informed the citizenry about his proposition] were ripped from the corners with bitter vehemence.

The ceremony began with ringing bells and the hymn *Jesus, my hope and trust* that was played by a trombone band. A complete silence prevailed on the wide square where the public as well as those who belonged to the funeral procession were crowded together, densely packed, one next to the other. When the hymn ended, the Protestant pastor Sydow stepped up to the altar of the catafalque and gave a deeply moving speech directed to the entire audience. When he had finished, a second, just as powerful speech was given by a Catholic padre, the chaplain Rulandt, and then there followed a Jewish clergyman, the rabbi Sachs. A German-Catholic clergyman was present as well, and stood next to the altar. It was a beneficial indication that as a result of the glorious accomplishment that so many men had died for, the walls which hitherto had separated the different denominations had been torn down as well.

Indeed, this moment was a historical event of deep significance.

After several speeches had been given, the funeral procession started. A band playing a funeral march was at the head of the procession. Then came the Berlin riflemen's guild, followed by the delegates of other riflemen's guilds, notably those from [the cities of] Magdeburg, Halle, Potsdam and Luckenwalde. And then, a member of the funeral committee, the junior barrister Wache, in his position as coordinator of the procession. He was followed by the borough-president Drewitz who carried with him a satin cushion with the inscription: "Dedicated to the heroes of March 18th and 19th, 1848, killed in action: By the women and girls of the New Market borough." Then there followed fifteen young girls of the Association of Families of Jacob's Street. Each one of them carried with her a white cushion with a wreath.

Following these girls, there came one hundred and eighty-three coffins, each one of them carried by six men. Between the coffins ahead of them and those following them, members of trade associations marched with their [trade-union] flags, each association walking in front of the dead that had been its members.

The city councilor Gleich completed this section of the procession. Then came the entire clergy—at the head of them, the two men who would preach at the grave, Bishop Neander and pastor Sydow. And, among the clergymen, there walked the bereaved so that they might be able to receive solace from them. Then followed the members of the university, in official dress. And then, the public servants of all offices of the State. Then the members of the [Art] Academy, together with the societies of artists [and their members]. Then the aldermen, the city councilors, the public servants of the municipality, the deputations of the local citizenry. Then several other deputations. And finally, endless rows of the *citizen soldiers* with their [elected] officers and captains. Dr. Woeniger, as a member of the funeral committee, concluded the [entire] procession.

It is not possible to mention in detail all the deputations that had joined the procession. The daily papers have already reported extensively on the entire ceremony. We want to emphasize here only the following details: at the head of that section of the procession which the students of the university, following their professors clad in official dress, had formed, one could also note Alexander von Humboldt next to the President of the university.

Alexander von Humboldt (1769-1859).

And among the factory workers, lined up behind their bosses, one could see one worker in his blue worker's overall who was richly crowned with laurel wreaths. This was Gus Hesse, a native of Halle [on the Saale] who had been an especially valiant fighter in the night between March 18th and 19th. The Berlin territorial army regiment took part as well, represented by a small delegation. They had lost, among other soldiers, the "wing man" of the tenth company who had been fighting on the barricades [against the Royal Army]. They had been forbidden, however, by orders of the secretary of war, Mr. von Rohr, to appear in uniform. A deputation of Poles had joined the procession, as well. And next to the German flag, in sisterly fashion, there fluttered the colors of Poland which hopefully would soon be reborn again. An especially impressive sight was offered by formations of the artisans' association. And the diverse high schools and other educational institutions had also joined the funeral train, as separate formations.

This procession lasted almost four hours, its head having already reached the distant gate [of the city wall] when those at its end had hardly left the initial gathering place. The procession first proceeded through Charlotte Street to Linden Street and from there, past the Palace, moved along King's Road and Landsberg Street to the gate bearing the same name (Here a large grave had been dug in the so-called Frederick's Grove which was to receive the bodies of the fighters who had given their lives for the sake of freedom.)

As the procession passed by the Opera, the Cathedral's Choir, positioned on the stairs of the Opera House, greeted the train once more with the sounds of the hymn *Jesus, My Hope and Trust*.

It was a serious, deeply significant moment when the head of the train reached the Palace. As it approached, the King, surrounded by his ministers and *aides*, appeared on the balcony. And the two black funeral flags as well as the tri-coloured flag in the middle were lowered in order to greet the procession.

The King himself honored the dead by taking off his helmet (he had appeared in uniform). And with bared head he remained standing there until the coffins had passed. Because this happened in intervals, due to the separate sections of the train mentioned already, he stepped out onto the balcony each time another section [with still more coffins] approached.

Finally, the procession reached the spot of the Frederick's Grove where the immense grave had been dug. Probably no one had anticipated that this location, which had been meant to be a dear place of remembrance of our severely tested King Frederick William III, would ever serve such a purpose.

On the highest point there was the grave. It formed an elongated rectangle, *into which* the coffins where placed in lines—so that an empty spot remained in the middle which was meant for the monument that was still to be erected.

Pastor Sydow again gave a brief funeral sermon and Bishop Neander blessed the dead. Then, three salvos from the guns of the riflemen's association resounded above the grave.

PART XII

March 22: Closing Words of Wisdom and Inspiration

Thereafter, the junior barrister Jung gave the following speech which will appear to our readers as a very interesting addition:

Georg Gottlob Jung (born Jan., 1814, in Rotterdam The Netherlands, d. Oct. 8, 1886 in Berlin), writer, barrister, democratic activist in 1848, and later, a politician.

You have heard words of reconciliation, words of peace—that we should forgive, that we should forget. Well then, brothers! Thoughts of revenge may fade—that coarse revenge which demands blood for blood. But let us atone for the blood of these dead by adopting, as a holy heritage, all that which they died for. And by fighting for it. Let us forgive but not forget.

We want peace but not quietude. Shame on us if we, in sluggish fatigue or gripped by fear of excitement, should recline on these fresh graves, agreeing to a shameful peace which would steal the fruits [of victory] from the victor and rob the atonement from those who are buried here.

Well then, let bloody revenge be silent. But, in place of it, let a spirit that remembers and reminds spring from this blood, a spirit of intellectual watchfulness that will forever shield us against that engrossment, against that indolence, which made the German populace a toy of native and foreign politics.

Well then, gentlemen, like Anthony read the will of murdered Caesar, I read to you the will of the murdered people. Not the will of a tyrant who wanted to buy the favor of the people with gold. But the will of plain, yet free men of the people and for the people who gave more than all treasures. Who gave their lifeblood:

'Be vigilant, it says in this sacred book: be vigilant, O brothers, that the freedom we died for may not wither. That it may not be robbed, nor snatched away by cunning trickery. Be vigilant, o brothers, that Prussia's star may no longer glow merely on brutal battlefields, nor in the venal breast of the courtier. But that it may glow instead in that peaceful sky where the signs of all free and educated nations unite to form a single constellation.

'Be vigilant, brothers—thus resounds the venerable voice from out of the grave— so that the fright of fearful souls, or the interest of those who want to rule at the expense of others, may not inflame the torch of discord among you. If, united, you could die on the barricades, you should be able to live together, united. If the rich one, without suspicion, could share the dangers of battle next to the one who wore a torn jacket, how should he be able to push him back from any institution, any right which was gained in battle?

'Away, forever into the night of oblivion! Away! with all the walls that separate men! Tear them down, the barricades of your heart, now that you have torn down the barricades of the battle. There exists no longer the mob, the coarse crowd, the riff-raff. For it is true that we—thus speak the dead—have sealed, with our blood, your charter of civil rights and letter of liberty.

And thus we leave as heritage to all—thus says the will—equal rights, equality before the law, equality in courts, equal participation in lawmaking.

Freely you may speak and write, freely associate. Woe to him who shall declare any man not denounced by a popular court unable to exercise, or unworthy of enjoying, any one of these rights. The populace itself shall elect its legislators from whatever rank it may choose. And protectively it will guard the institutions which it has given itself. —Woe to him who would diminish, for the most lowly below him, that right which we have willed to him here, with our blood. For we have shown how the common man can speak for the fatherland, speaking

March 22: Closing Words of Wisdom and Inspiration

with the death rattle of his mortally wounded chest. —*Woe to him who wants to declare anyone who could die for his fatherland, to be unworthy, to be incapable, of knowing what is good for him, and of electing his legislator(s) accordingly.*'

Here they all rest together, men of the arts, of literature, of the trades, of physical labor, the latter forming the biggest group. Shall a living person dare to divide what death united?

But you divide when you say, Up to this point extends the ability to vote, to carry arms, to associate, and no further. —Who draws these boundaries? It is your fright. Your unfounded fear of a terrifying mirage which your continuing distrust could turn into something real in the end.

But fright is the most certain arsenal of power, where it finds the weapons needed for the suppression of every one. Fright is the secure harbour where despotism is anchored.

Fright beckons the power which, laughing derisively, then places itself between he who is fearful and he who is feared. Erecting thus, with the help of both, its secure tyranny. Only fearless men are free!

What caused those soldiers turned into fanatics to attack their brothers so wildly? What, if not their separation from the fatherland and its rights? They knew only a dark power which, from unattainable heights, issues its irrevocable commands. Instead of law, they had obedience. Instead of duties, service—blind, unalterable service. They did not fight for the fatherland; they slaughtered for the idol of their superstition. Delivering, as they thought, justified sacrifice.

You have armed against the return of this enemy. You trust in the strength of your courage and of your weapons. But don't trust too much. The hour of rest and fatigue will come. And the enemy sneaks in again among you. And thus, servitude or battle begins anew. You must therefore not only arm against the enemy. Rather, you must disarm him [the soldier, the mercenary, at the service of tyranny,] for ever and ever, by leading him to the altar of the fatherland and giving him, as a brother, equal rights, equal duties. Showing him how that dark legislator [the ruler, the absolute monarch, and his power to command and to decree] is but a mirage which vanishes under the look of free men when the voice of the fatherland is no longer merely the bugle call announcing a battle. When the State no longer speaks to him through drums. When, instead, the election day reminds him of his freedom, and the ballot box of his rights, as an independent human being. When he reads that man is too noble to shed his blood, doing a brutal strangler's work for the sake of another's interests. When he hears in a free popular assembly that the will of the people is the most sacred law which drowns out every commanding voice.

'*Come on, then—let the rose of freedom and fraternity, rather than a wild spirit of revenge, grow from our blood! O care for it well, this noble flower, and pay attention that it will not be taken from you. It is still sprouting and longingly we await its bloom. Still, you have not been granted yet the most important rights, such as the general right to vote, security of every person in the face of the power of the police, freedom of association, freedom of assembly. Still, people are your lawful representatives who were not placed in this position by your will but by privilege, the accidental circumstances of their birth, their property and their activity. We could only will to you the right to these great goods and open up the way.*

O be vigilant; and strive; and think of the blood-drenched, admonishing shadow of your brothers who, verily, did not intend to die for a trifling matter.

When the orator had ended with these words, which left a mighty and moving impression on those thousands of listeners, dusk had fallen and the sun had sunk for the first time on these graves above which the sun of freedom may rise gloriously and radiantly for the survivors.

* * *

These are the events that happened in Berlin in the days of the eighteenth and nineteenth of March of the year one thousand eight hundred and forty-eight. May our offspring never forget how dearly we paid for our and their freedom; may they know how to preserve this good dearly paid for!

COMMENTARY

The March Revolution: A Botched Revolution?

by ANDREAS WEILAND

"Wherever there is oppression, repression, and intensified exploitation, there is resistance, too." (B. F.)[1]

I.

The book by August Brass shows how a movement that leads to armed insurrection can unfold, and how revolutionaries feel when they win "in the streets"—no matter whether these are street protests, as in Spain during the "Democracy, Yes!" movement or in Cairo during the Arab Spring, or, as in Berlin in 1848, during days of bloody fighting and in their immediate aftermath. But revolutions are not only won in the streets—or rather, it seems that the subaltern classes, usually the main force in such conflicts, can lose them in the aftermath of the struggle. This is why it matters to look closely at what happens next, when the fight seems to be won.

August Brass was extremely fast in writing his account of the March Revolution in Berlin. His book that appeared in the year of revolutionary upheaval provided more than an eyewitness account of a courageous participant in the armed struggle for democratic rights. It included, again and again, reflections on the general situation in Prussia and in Germany, and it provided a clear justification for the actions undertaken by the revolutionaries and of the necessity to take up arms. It praised the people, it justified them and it ended by uttering ominous words of warning that the fruits of this struggle for liberty should be carefully preserved. On the whole it was, however, strangely optimistic, later readers in favor of popular emancipation must have thought. They, of course, were aware of the defeat of the long revolution of 1848–1849 and thus knew that the events of March 1848 in Berlin were only an act, though a decisive one, in a much longer and much more bitter drama. Still, it is not only our interest in things long past that prompts questions regarding the way Brass and many of his fellow revolutionaries trusted a king's promise to guarantee constitutional rule and liberal civil rights. This is something that should cause careful analysis. Are there lessons to be drawn from it for today's and tomorrow's contests, for further struggles to achieve a greater measure of human emancipation in many countries of Europe, the Americas, and, quite generally, around the world, thus on a global scale? What can we learn from the book written by Brass about the March Revolution of 1848 if we read it in the context of the entire revolutionary period in Berlin up to the coup d'état of November that pronounced the victory of the counterrevolution not only in the Prussian capital, but in Prussia as a whole, and that prefigured the outcomes of revolutionary struggles in Germany in 1849?

If it is true that the book written by Brass about the heydays of the revolution in March offers valuable insights if read in such an overarching context, it would then be more than a book about thrilling events and enthusiastic hopes; it would be more than a book about Berlin's revolutionaries of 1848, a book merely about the past and about a single country, Germany, a single state, that of Prussia, then governed by King Frederick William IV. It would assume a certain, though perhaps limited, paradigmatic significance. It would allow us to gain insight into the unfolding of a revolutionary process, and thus knowledge of the factors leading to a significant mobilization of the masses, as well as an understanding of the (typical?) mistakes and wavering strategies of those in power at a moment of popular upsurge and systemic weakness, and of the answers found by them—including, perhaps, clever scheming and psychologically motivated ruses. Most significantly, it might help us to see the ability or inability of the revolutionaries to cope with such challenges.

Undoubtedly it is worthwhile to analyze the different positions that surfaced in the revolutionary camp. Do we have to reckon with perhaps understandable illusions and with evaluations of the *rapport des forces* that made intellectuals and "middle class" spokespersons ready to seek compromise? And how conscious of their power, how aware of their social and political interests, how "mature"—on the whole—were the popular masses who bore the brunt of the battle in the struggle against the brutal and repressive assault of the Prussian army during the days of street fighting in the capital, Berlin? Were they, on the whole, unable to articulate their position, and thus dependent on compromising leaders? Can we decipher an avantgarde of radical workers among them? Could they have won the revolution by more conscious and determined action during the decisive days—for instance, by putting an end to monarchic rule and establishing a republic? All of these are hypothetical questions, asked in hindsight, based on what the archives revealed and what the events of spring and summer, 1848, let us surmise. To ask these questions will not change the course of past history anymore, and it is pointless to blame those who are long dead and who did what they were capable of doing, remaining true, in their own best way, to their convictions and seeking to attain a betterment of an unbearable situation. Still, it is worthwhile to widen the perspective and ask questions that many fighters could not apparently ask during the days of battle in Berlin. The value of this book could consist exactly in this—that we learn not only from the courage and dedication of the revolutionaries of 1848, but even more from an analysis of the consequences of their flaws and limitations, their blindness, their illusions, and the ways they missed opportunities. Even with this purpose in mind we should however keep in mind the words of Marx that no psychological approach that seeks to blame the failure of the revolution on the personal shortcomings of this or that leading revolutionary figure will be adequate, because the key question in Berlin during these decisive days and month was the question of the maturity of the urban working class.

Germany is a country that experienced a belated development of *modern industrial capitalism* and *the modern form of the state*,[2] at least in comparison with England, France, and Belgium.[3] Of course, "modern society," as we know it—which presupposes the development of these two related phenomenon—can also be said to have developed fairly early in German lands if we do not compare it with Western Europe but think of a neighboring country like Poland that had been the victim of three partitions and, with the last one, had become a de facto colony of three big powers which annexed parts of it (in 1772, 1793, and 1795) with the effect that no independent Poland remained. Incidentally, all of these rapacious powers can be described as *late absolutist regimes*, in contrast to Britain and also to France where the monarchy had been replaced by a short-lived republic in the wake of the revolution of 1789 and—after a temporary triumph of the reaction—by a constitutional monarchy in 1830.

Persistent late absolutism in Austria (respectively Austria-Hungary, as it would later be referred to), Prussia, and Czarist Russia no doubt braked social progress, both in the countries of the "colonizers" and in the lands of the "colonized" (Poland, the Czech and Slovak lands, Hungary, Croatia, and so on). In Germany, belated development entailed the formation of a German republic 126 years after it had been formed briefly (in 1792) in France. Late absolutism survived in Prussia until 1848, when it appeared to everyone that finally a liberal constitution was "granted"—or rather enforced, as there can be no doubt that it was "promised" reluctantly by Frederick Wilhelm IV, and this in a situation of extreme weakness of the monarchy and of the "old powers" in Prussia that were its decisive pillars of support: the military, the bureaucracy, and the land-owning aristocracy that still kept defending important privileges and other vestiges of a bygone feudal era.

That the promise of constitutional rule was extorted on March 19 by the sheer facticity of the situation and the presence of a victorious population in front of, and soon also inside, the palace—even though only in small numbers and soon functioning as a protecting "civil guard"—cannot be put in doubt.[4] It was a promise made under extreme pressure, in view of urgent demands for "Volksbewaffnung" (*"arming of the people"*) or a "Bürgergarde" (*burgher guard; civil guard*)[5] and it was made in the *immediate* aftermath of an armed revolution.[6] It is clear that a sense of defeat had gripped the King on this day, as

Ranke has written,[7] and if Ranke is not mistaken this sense of defeat overtook the monarch at the moment when he was "stepping on the balcony of his palace" (Ranke) because the masses crowding the Palace Square had demanded so determinedly that he should appear.[8] The crowd had seen only Count Arnim and Count Schwerin[9] on the balcony of the Palace,[10] while he had tried to remain in the background. When he actually stepped on the balcony to face the bodies of Berliners killed by his soldiers, the angry calls that he should take off his helmet had forced him to do it.[11]

It was then that the queen had been overheard exclaiming, "The only thing that is missing for us now is the guillotine!"[12]

August Brass reports that at the same time, "the resignation of the Prince of Prussia was demanded" and that "some people shouted [...] *A Republic!*" As August Brass saw it, it "was a moment of dangerous excitement" and he adds, a little later, that "[t]he monarchy and the throne would have been the toy of him who would have dared to put himself at the head of this deeply moved crowd!"

Obviously, none of the democratic intellectuals who had been so actively involved as speakers during the popular assemblies of the recent pre-revolutionary period had the guts to take steps in this direction. In the case of August Brass, it is plausible to assume that this was so because he may have been in favor of a constitutional monarchy in March, 1848.[13] He undoubtedly desired political change, but it seems that he wanted no radical change, perhaps because he assessed the situation as "not ripe" for it. In this he was typical of many "middle class" intellectuals at the time, including many Young Hegelians, although some of these leaned towards a bourgeois republic. Though speeches were made, addressing the crowd, only one worker is mentioned by Brass. Apparently, this working man was not one of those radicals—mostly politicized journeymen—who had placed republican flags on the houses and barricades they had defended against the army. We may conclude this from the fact that, according to Brass, the man made a "very reasonable speech" when addressing the assembly. But the makeshift rostrum, if there was any, was obviously dominated by men who did not hail from the working class. The men and women who had borne the brunt of the fighting—employed journeymen, workers—in short, the hard working, badly nourished, disenfranchised subaltern classes which made up the majority of the population of Berlin—did not play a major role when it came to things like making speeches.

And still, despite this ambivalence that lets us recognize revolutionary ire and sparks of voiced radicalism (mainly in the form of shouts that demand a republic) side by side with an ominous muteness of the city's common folks, who seem to have waited for well-known democrats, agitators, journalists, and writers like Brass to point the way, it was recognizable even to the author of the book *The Barricades of Berlin* that Berlin witnessed, on March 19, a historic moment, a moment when the scales could have been tipped in at least two opposing directions.

In other words, on this 19th of March a definite window of opportunity had been opened by the events that culminated on that day, a day that appears in hindsight as both triumphantly illustrious and ominous. The army was withdrawing; the morale of a formerly largely intransigent king had been weakened during the preceding weeks and days. And now, with a commander of the troops in charge in Berlin who said that the troops were exhausted and could no longer fight, the king's (and queen's) morale was shattered. If Louis XVI had been in a weak position in Paris in the summer of 1789, this was even more true now of Frederick William IV. Of course, every real revolution implies risks, it implies the dangers of defeat and of the death of its leaders and foremost supporters. But when was the chance of a real success better than now? In view of the erstwhile outcome of the struggle for control of the capital, the immediate measures that might have been taken hypothetically are:

1. election of a provisional revolutionary government on March 19 by the revolutionary population of Berlin, represented by all those present in the palace square;
2. election of official captains of the detachments of those who fought for democratic rights during the events of March 16–19 by the fighters of the detachments themselves, thus formal organization of all the revolutionary fighters as a people's militia of Berlin, and immediate occupation and control of all armories (Zeughäuser) of Berlin;
3. measures to effectively bar all members of the royal household, especially the king, the queen, and most importantly, the brother of the king, William, Prince of Prussia, from leaving the capital;
4. obtaining a royal order demanding the Prussian army (its officers and common soldiers) to swear allegiance to the new government, to be followed by subsequent replacement of its aristocratic officers by commoners;
5. dispatchment of secret emissaries to democrats in Magdeburg, Cologne, and all other Prussian cities of some importance, in order to trigger the revolutionary takeover of these cities, to be followed by;
6. the set-up of revolutionary borough committees and revolutionary city governments in the provinces; and concomitant preparation and holding of free and equal municipal elections in the capital, i.e. election of revolutionary delegates by all inhabitants of Berlin except known counter-revolutionaries—this implied the scrapping of the old legal frame of reference that disenfranchised as many as 440,000 inhabitants of Berlin in March 1848;
7. dispatchment of emissaries to the countryside in an effort to link up effectually with peasant rebellions (in Silesia and also outside Prussia, in Southern Germany).

Let us note that such measures were not taken, and that we have no evidence that they were considered.

But something else happened on March 19, 1848: the crowd pushed for one thing above all, in view of their recent struggle and, even more, in view of their recent experience with the king's army. It was the unequivocally expressed demand that the monarch must consent to the arming of the people.[14] This demand was very understandable in view of the actions of the Prussian army that had resulted in the large number of men being killed in action, the murder of fighters who had been taken prisoner during the struggle, and the death of several women and children who had also been killed in the days of armed revolution. But in addition to this, almost everybody remembered the death of people attacked during the week preceding the bloody combat that had just been waged.[15] Perhaps something else let the masses assembled in the Palace Square on that day attribute great significance to this foremost of their demands. It was the fact that their "request" reflected a widespread notion among democrats—a democratic demand that we encounter in other cities and other parts of Germany, too.[16] It may well have been a consequence of the recognition that only an armed people can assert its will vis-à-vis a ruler or a class that rules. But how strange that this demand should be made known to a defeated king by a victorious populace in the form of a deferential "petition!"

At any rate, Brass, the eyewitness, reports that the demand was uttered, and apparently the king had no choice but to express his consent. Initially it was Count Schwerin who made "an oral declaration to this effect in front of the crowd. Later on, [...] [the king] himself appeared and gave the people the desired assurance: *'From this moment, I give myself, full of faith and confidence, into the hands of my people,'* he said." In fact, with no army or even the usual Royal Guard units at his disposal, for they had been ordered to leave the capital and most of them were already departing, leaving him behind, alone and vulnerable in his palace, he had no other choice. He recognized the momentary factually existing *rapport des forces* for what it was; that is to say, the genuine appearance of an unfavorable situation that, due to the course of events and in view of his own blunders and those of his generals, made him the de facto hostage of Berlin's insurgent population.

But did the revolutionaries recognize this as well? Did Berlin's population recognize it, or at least a part of it—and if so, which part? Was the population united in its aims and sentiments? August Brass notes, that upon hearing the words of surrender from a king who had so stubbornly rejected so many democratic requests before March 19, "[i]mmense jubilation filled the yard of the palace." His statement reveals at least one thing beyond the apparent fact of jubilation: it tells us once more and unequivocally, confirmed by the eyewitness, August Brass, that the crowd did not only fill the Palace Square; they were also inside the Palace, even in its interior yard.

Whether the jubilation hailed an accomplished popular victory or the king himself is a question that Brass does not ask, for he seems to assume the latter. He also does not ask who or which group among those assembled in front and inside the palace put this demand squarely on the table at this moment, leaving Count Arnim, Count Schwerin and the King no choice but to signal Royal consent. A lot seems to speak, however, for the hypothesis that both interpretations with regard to the first question raised are valid: there must have been those who hailed the victorious populace, and there were also those who trusted the king and who were ready to hail him so soon after a bloody fight.

What happened next, at least as Brass reports it, were initial steps immediately undertaken in fulfilment of the consented request that the people shall be armed. The account given by him in his book mentions an announcement of March 19, signed by the Chief of Police, von Minutoli, and by Holbein, Glaue, Haack and Dr. Woeniger.

In its § 2, the announcement mentions who will be armed: "The citizens and 'Schutzverwandte'" (*protected clients*). This amounted to a declaration that all able-bodied, male Berliners, except those under age and the old ones, would be armed—albeit by the authorities. Thus the fact was ignored that many Berliners were already armed, and in view of this fact they were able to seize the armories in Berlin, as the army was already departing or had already largely departed. It will be necessary to remember § 2 in view of the fact that, not much later, the revolutionary fighters who had manned the barricades were required to hand in their weapons.

§ 4 was extremely dubious. It mentioned who will be armed immediately: "The riflemen's guild" and "an adequate number of citizens!" Citizens—not "protected clients!" And "adequate"—in fact, well-chosen—citizens to boot. As other sources have pointed out, the Riflemen's Guild was formed by people who could afford to buy both a rifle and the expensive uniform and hat worn by members of this guild. It is true that many if not most of its members had taken part in the struggle during the last two days, but nevertheless is was very clear that the Riflemen's Guild was a club of rather well-off enfranchised citizens. The phrase "an adequate number of citizens" should, indeed, have made people with genuine democratic convictions, like August Brass, think twice. Obviously, trustworthy citizens were singled out, and as we know, the term "citizen" (*burgher*; in German, "*Bürger*") unmistakably referred to those enfranchised under the old pre-revolutionary regulations, thus to no more than roughly 40,000 out of 440,000 inhabitants of Berlin. The term "adequate" can indeed be interpreted as implying that it was intended to pick the "adequate" candidates among the 40,000 enfranchised citizens; in other words, it may point to a wish to exercise *control* over the composition of the new "militia" that the announcement seemed to promise. As it soon turned out, this militia never became a people's militia; it became, with few exceptions, a "Burgher Guard" or "Citizens' Guard,"[17] an exclusive instrument of propertied, or at least moderately well-off inhabitants of the city—and thus an instrument of law and order.

Other sources point out that Count Schwerin was not the only one involved in the quick action taken already on March 19th in order to abort the wish to arm the populace in defense of the revolution. The clear aim that can be deciphered is rather different: a force of law and order that would recruit trustworthy enfranchised citizens of Berlin was desired—both by the King's ministers, by the King, and by quite a few among the privileged and enfranchised commoners, members of the bourgeoisie, and the well-off parts of the intermediate strata (the "middle class" or petty-bourgeoisie). The key agents in instituting this new force of order—a force that was to act, as it were, temporarily, as a substitute of the army in a situation of revolutionary uncertainty and subverted royal power—were Count von Arnim, Mr. Nobiling,[18] and the "liberal"[19] chief of police, Julius von Minutoli, a key official in charge of a notorious spy network and a sober man in close contact with the king who had wanted very early on to avoid the steps taken by officers of the army and by the king that lead to the revolutionary outbreak, and who would have preferred a soft transition to a less absolutist monarchy.

As further developments would soon show, the Citizens' Guard that was created embryonically on the day of popular revolutionary victory in Berlin never became an armed popular militia. It never amounted to a real fulfillment of the demand that the people should be armed. As Rüdiger Hachtmann notes,

> the citizens guard included, up to the moment of its dissolution by mid-November (1848), only those Berliners that were enfranchised, and who therefore possessed a house or disposed of a certain income. Members of the subaltern classes were excluded from this quite literally bourgeois guard. Moreover, in contrast to the summer and fall of 1848, this burgher militia was still strongly conservative in outlook in early April.[20]

As it were, a large part of the "victorious" population in Berlin, including August Brass, saw the concession that the people should be armed as a triumph and as a guarantee of the other democratic conquests that seemed to be implied when the monarch gave in to unequivocal popular demands uttered in the Palace Square by the assembled crowd. The presence of the masses in the square and in the palace yard (and soon in the palace) made these petitions in fact popular demands that dictated what must be "accorded" if more drastic ways of enforcing democratic progress were to be avoided. And so the King did not only take off his cap on March 19, honoring the revolutionaries killed in action, quite against his most deeply felt convictions; he also decided to ride on his horse through Berlin on March 21 wearing the black, red and golden tricolor of the revolution.

The March Revolution: A Botched Revolution?

The King rides through Berlin on March 21, 1848, "wearing a ribbon with the colors of the [German] tricolore - the colors of the revolution – on his arm. Screenshot of an old wood engraving. Obviously, a caricature.

But the consent given to the arming of the people, and even more the promise of a constitution that Frederick William IV made on March 19, ran counter to many of the most cherished views held by the monarch. As Baumgart noted, "A characteristic feature of the personality of the King is this: that his nature was like Hamlet's and that he was aware of this; that he was overly emotional and full of dreaminess, but that he could only pretend to this effusive enthusiasm; and that behind it there was also a concealment of reason and calculation." In this respect, Ranke's characterization misses something when he said of the King's policy that it sprang "from no kind of calculation."(31) We have rather to agree with the Austrian diplomat George Esterhazy who wrote to his colleague Rechberg in February 1856, "It is remarkable that there are people who [...] are still deceived by the so-called 'piety' of King Frederick William IV, the most accomplished comedian of the present, and basically our most poisonous adversary."[21]

As to the promise of a constitution made on March 19, 1848 by Frederick William, it is questionable whether he intended to remain faithful to the spirit of a democratic spring that his words seemed to embody. And the symbolic act of wearing the colors of the revolution on March 21 may have been nothing but a calculated farce, enacted to survive as monarch in a situation of momentary defeat and intended to foster illusions among the population of Berlin. In a note or letter that Frederick William IV secretly wrote to his brother William, Prince of Prussia, he said on March 22, 1848, "Yesterday I had to wear the colors of the empire voluntarily, in order to save everything. If this game succeeds [...], I will take them off again!"[22]

The words written by King Frederick William IV to William, Prince of Prussia, reveal both a comprehension of his momentary situation, an endangered position as ruler, tremendously weakened by the suddenly created new relations of forces that resulted due to the events of March 16–19, and a will to regain initiative. It was his factual situation and his instinctive as well as conscious response to it that apparently let him appoint "liberal conservatives" like Count Arnim and Count Schwerin,[23] not unlike Frederick William III had appointed the liberal-conservative Baron von Stein in a similar situation of weakness when the survival of the Prussian monarchy was threatened by Napoleon. It is obvious that, quite clearly in contradiction to his former intransigence when faced with liberal calls for a constitution, he now opted for a more flexible, searching strategy that reflected his will and desire to maintain or recoup a certain measure of control.

Put so suddenly on the defensive, Frederick William IV instinctively comprehended that he had to appear to the population of Berlin as a king who was ready to be committed to change, and thus he grasped his chance to pose as a Saulus converted to a Paulus; in other words, as a good king who had been simply disinformed and let astray by a conservative "camarilla"—a view soon shared by many among the crowd he addressed.[24] Using this chance, he indeed regained a surprising measure of new freedom of action, whereas, on the other hand, the democratic chance of the revolutionaries to change things profoundly in Prussia and Germany that existed on March 19, 1848 (and perhaps also to a lesser extent in the next few days), by pressing more clearly forward and taking decisive steps, was obviously missed to a large extent and the circumstances under which they could act became more difficult. The King and the people who were now advising him continued to regain the initiative, opting—as we will soon see—for an ostentatiously liberal course.[25]

In so far as we can say that the days of March 19–22 are the beginning of a transitional period of open horizons, possibilities continued to exist—if only up to a point, perhaps—for the "old" and the "new." It is a period of uncertain relations of forces and certainly also of instability that would persist in the spring and summer of 1848.

As we will see, the "victory" attained on the barricades, and confirmed or "consented" by a king because he knew that he was on the defensive, was soon put in question. Things believed to be attained, like the arming of the people, were reinterpreted and purposefully obstructed; the very idea of free and equal elections was misconstrued as meaning "indirect" (and in view of the practical consequences, unequal) elections, and the promised constitution never materialized during the critical period of class struggle between March 29 and September 8, 1848 (or November 1)—a period that saw the King appoint legalist, decidedly anti-revolutionary prime-ministers, all of them described by historians as "moderate" liberals in charge of governments that pursued basically anti-popular policies, guided by distrust of the "plebeian elements" of the capital, the so-called *mob*, the unruly masses, until even the modest gains that consisted in the mere existence of bourgeois governments and the endless continuation of controversial, but largely ineffective, debates in the Constituent Assembly[26] proved to be too much to bear for the reactionary royalist camp, thus ending a situation of dual power that saw, among other things, the unresolved questions regarding the loyalty of the army (was it to be sworn in to the government or to remain bound by its oath to the king?) ineffectively debated. But any uncertainty about such loyalty, and any democratic gains, were wiped out by a military coup d'état of the King.

The military coup d'état of the King in November, 1848 (thus the appointment of General von Brandenburg as prime minister (on November 2) and the military occupation of Berlin by 40,000 troops under the command of General von Wrangel on November 10, 1848)[27] amounted to a complete counter-revolution that was soon confirmed or "institutionalized" by the royally imposed constitution of December 1848 and even more fundamentally by the constitution of 1850, which was again royally imposed. Written by conservative social forces, this constitution enacted once and for all unequal suffrage in Prussia in the way that was to be practiced here until the revolution of November 1918. The loss of even the flawed democratic rights that the people attained thanks to the briefly successful March Revolution in Berlin had thus been sealed by determined acts of the Prussian reactionaries, and Frederick William IV was again in full control of his kingdom and capital in the only way that counts, for indeed, the successful strategy of reactionary "Realpolitik" proved that under certain conditions, "power comes out of a barrel of a gun." A preparatory and directly, as well as indirectly, relevant factor contributing to this result can be clearly identified, for it is apparent that driven by fear of the "masses" and hostile to the idea and goal of a republic that could empower these "unruly" masses that longed to be heard, to make grievances known and to assert their needs, the "moderate" bourgeois governments named by the king (rather than put in place by the revolutionary population of Berlin and other cities) obstructed not only attempts to democratize the election process, but just as significantly all measures that could lead to a genuine arming of the people. They clearly feared the "rabble" or "mob" more than the victory of the "Old Powers" of Prussia. It is for this reason that Walter Schmidt, the doyen of historical research on the March Revolution, speaks of "the treason of the bourgeoisie."[28]

II.

Was this defeat of democracy inescapable? Was everything depending on the ability to act (rather than talk) of the Young Hegelians (among them a few proponents of a republican Germany, a German republic) and on democratic middle-class writers and intellectuals, perhaps even on the relatively progressive elements among the kingdom's commercial middle class and perhaps also on figures like Borsig, "liberal" entrepreneurs typical of an emerging industrial bourgeoisie?

As it turned out, this German bourgeoisie was largely a timid, anxious class, utterly egotistical, too. It is true that, as Boch notes, the "*Question of a Constitution*" that had been briefly raised since 1815 even in Prussia but that then "had been put aside since 1820, was posed anew"[29] in the 1840s, and this especially in South West Germany, in Prussia's Rhine Province, and thanks to Jacoby, in Königsberg.

> And within just a few years, there grew a decidedly politically offensive liberal movement directed at the entire Prussian state [apparatus] that was able to coalesce the [*haute*] *bourgeois* circles of the [Rhine] province which had been previously indifferent quite often with regard to questions of "great politics," and that could even exert an influence on the "small" bourgeoisie and the rather conservative [...] economic middle-class milieu [...].[30]

But as it turned out, the February Revolution in France changed things greatly, and the rebellious mood of the subaltern classes that could be witnessed since the early days of March in more and more of the bigger cities and in the countryside, as well, added to fears among the propertied classes. And thus it turned out that in 1848, most of the "Camphausens and Hansemanns" that had excelled as leaders of the liberal opposition in the press, in Provincial Diets of the Monarchy and, when it was convened in 1847, in Prussia's United Diet—and with them, perhaps the bourgeoisie as a whole—turned out to be absent during the revolutionary days of March and ready for compromise and an alliance with exactly the social forces that the revolutionaries had combated. Quite obviously, the bourgeoisie was a class that not only chose to desert, but that even *opposed* its own goals and gave up its hopes and ideals of full bourgeois emancipation, and this very early on, in 1848. This the *haute bourgeoisie* did out of fear of the "mob." And one must add that it was a fear that was shared in Berlin also by another class faction of the bourgeoisie, that is to say, most of the comparatively numerous better-off parts of the intermediate strata, the "middle classes," or to put it more precisely, the well-off. We must count among them wealthy merely locally active merchants and merely locally notable bankers, but also the better-paid or at least modestly well-paid middle-ranking public servants of the Prussian administrative bureaucracy, judges and public prosecutors, university professors and perhaps also high school "professors" (many boasting a Ph.D., known as a doctoral degree in Germany). Then, of course, this "middle class" included the well-off "intermediate" bracket excelling among the city's many, and often impoverished, independent master artisans; it included "rentiers" and all the others with at least modest incomes. And of course, we must not forget the industrialists. In view of their deficient capital structure and likely dependence on bank loans, most probably belonged to this so-called "middle class," that is to say, the *core* or central class faction of the "Bürgertum" or bourgeoisie in Berlin. The term "Bürgertum" (*burgher stratum*) is of course a treacherous one; the very fact that one is using it is revealing; it has ideological implications—for the term "burgher" (*Bürger*) was a premodern one. The old rank-based (*ständisch*) pseudo-parliament of the Prussian monarchy differentiated between aristocrats, burghers, and free, well-off rural dwellers, represented unequally. And thus, in terms of its semantic history, the term "Bürgertum" continues to emphasize the notion of status, as it originally alluded to a *ständisch*, rank-based, pre-modern conception of this class faction. This "middle class" or Bürgertum (bourgeoisie proper, bourgeoisie in the narrow sense) was best represented at the time by the Königliche Privilegirte Berlinische Zeitung, more commonly known as Voss Zeitung and Voss'sche Zeitung. On the whole, it had supported the change of March 19 that made Count Arnim prime minister and went on to support the subsequent Camphausen government since early April even more wholeheartedly. It is often described as Berlin's "liberal bourgeoisie" because it wanted the promises of a constitution it had received without having, in its entirety, fought for it during the days of armed struggle, the men of the Rifleman Association that joined the struggle, notwithstanding. Many among this class would have been content with the assurances the King had given on the morning of March 18, when the fighting broke out. When later in March (or was it April?), a law or decree that had already been promised by the King in his declaration of March 22[31] announced the right of Prussians to freely form associations, most of them—if they did not refrain from political activism at all, and did not stay away from associations—tended towards the Constitutional Club. This club or political association would support, on the whole a man like Camphausen, even though on some occasions it criticized him and his government, for instance in an article on the Camphausen government's draft of a constitution that the Voss'sche Zeitung would publish on May 25.[32] Clearly, the club—like a considerable segment of the bourgeois "middle class" of Berlin—was a bit more "democratic" than the "big bourgeois" *wannabe aristocrats* Camphausens or Hansemanns: a little bit to the Left of them, if the term "Left" can be used at all when speaking of these political tendencies. At any rate, the number of those middle class people who tended towards the Patriotic Club (Patriotischer Club)—that was somewhat to the Right of the Constitutional Club—was probably smaller, and the Prussia Association (Preussen Verein) was an arch-reactionary association dear to certain senior bureaucratic officials, agrarian landowners, and the most backward elements of the petty-bourgeoisie.

Clearly, the Berlin 'middle class' wanted political reform, but not too much; in this they shared the political line of the big bourgeoisie, of men like Camphausen and Hansemann, unaware of the fact that such men wanted more political rights for themselves and their peers than they were, at first and originally, ready to concede to the "middle class." The points of view of both class factions converged in so far as both wanted to exclude the subaltern classes, the *vast majority* of the Berliners and of Prussia, from a say in "public affairs" (*the res publica*), deeming them too unfit, too dumb and dull, and too radical, *or dangerous* because of a propensity and spontaneous tendency to revolt, with or without involvement of petty-bourgeois agitators and the educated among the workers.

Undoubtedly this "liberal bourgeoisie" of Berlin—and of Prussia, of Germany as a whole—was socially conservative and politically reactionary when it came to denying rights to the workers. The Constitutional Club would support the election law that the Camphausen government was to introduce in April, something that the petty-bourgeois liberal radicals (known as Democrats) and the republicans and republican socialists would not do; because it hurt the subaltern classes, it materially violated the concept of fair and equal political representation of all.

As for the "haute bourgeoisie"—the "big bourgeoisie," as the term is sometimes rendered in English—it was not a very visible class faction in Berlin during the 1840s. It was clearly more present in financial centers like Frankfurt and Cologne, and it was less significant, both quantitatively and qualitatively, in Berlin than in various other major urban centers in Germany.[33] Its "liberalism" is highlighted by many statements of Hansemann, but it included also outright conservatives.

The *Kleinbürgertum* or petty-bourgeoisie presented a different and more complicated pictures. It comprised hawkers and small shopkeepers, who were often house owners and enfranchised burghers, but who could otherwise hardly make ends meet. The same was true of another segment of the city's petty-bourgeoisie: the bulk of the independent artisans (Handwerker)—master craftsmen (Meister) who often owned a house with a workshop, but hardly could afford to pay a wage worker. Many had only one apprentice, others employed a journeyman and an apprentice. Still others had no helper at all. The economic crisis, but also the effect that modern industrial production abroad and in new Prussian factories increasingly had on handicrafts, contributed to their tendential proletarization. Another segment consisted of the poorer and often insecurely situated persons among the educated. It is fashionable to refer to them as "proletarianized intellectuals" but the term "intellectual" is, by and large, a term that would bestow undeserved recognition. Many are mediocre or lousy writers of novels that often borrow a lot from commercially successful trivial, thus popular works published in France; others are journalists, "Lohnschreiber," who sell their wares to the owner of a paper, and with it, sometimes, their political conscience; all of them are knights of the pen who have a hard time surviving in a phase of a prolonged economic "recession" and sagging demand, even for "intellectual" products. But with the revolution and the debates and controversies stimulates, their services are suddenly met with increasing demand. Then, we have the majority of the elementary school teachers, and all the other lowly and ill-paid employees of the city and the state administration, all those who had secure incomes and who, despite their economic dependence as wage laborers had achieved some "status" and respect. If they did not own a house and did not pay direct taxes as well, they were not enfranchised in Berlin; if they did, they were. Who, among them, belonged to the petty-bourgeoisie? All of them? In the strict sense, those who were self-employed did. In another, more status-focused, thus conventional sense, those with an acknowledged non-proletarian occupation were counted among the petty-bourgeoisie. As in the 20th century, the petty-bourgeoisie of Berlin in the 1840s was an unpredictable, volatile class faction. It included in its ranks astonishingly progressive and democratic individuals, and also very backward if not outright reactionary ones, and of course many who were, like many workers, deprived of access to knowledge and culture due to their poverty and the constraints imposed on them by their daily economic struggle to make ends meet.

All of these class factions in Berlin, the *haute bourgeoisie* or big bourgeoisie, the classical Bürgertum or "middle class," and the petty-bourgeoisie (to the extent that the category was referring to genuinely petty-bourgeois persons, thus direct tax-paying houseowners and the small group of non-house-owners who had paid the "Bürgergeld" (literally: *burgher money* or *citizen money*) and who had thus bought the right to vote in municipal elections) formed the group of "enfranchised" Berliners. According to August Brass, this privileged group amounted to about 40,000 persons[34] which is a rough guess, presumably; Rüdiger Hachtmann provides the figure of 36,000, based on careful study of the archived material and other historical evidence. Another trustworthy historian gives a lower figure with respect to those who were permitted to vote in the municipal election of a new city council in April 1848, thus after the revolutionary combat of March 18–19. The divergence between the two figures, 36,000 and 25,000, may result in part from the fact that the previous election of the city council may have taken place, and in all likelihood did take place, under better economic conditions. The economic crisis of 1846–48 reduced intake of small and medium businesses, and many who paid direct taxes in earlier years may have ceased to do so and thus dropped out of the group of registered voters. In addition, the revolution as such also hurt business and aggravated the situation, thus reducing the numbers of voters even more.

The interesting thing about these figures (whether 36,000 or 25,000, does not matter so much here) certainly is that this gives us a first, very vague idea of the numerical strength of the city's combined big, middle, and small bourgeoisie; and that it also gives us, by implication, a good sense of the huge size of Berlin's subaltern classes. But this impression has to be modified, because the figure that gives us the size of Berlin's enfranchised group indicates only the number of the *male* members of the "propertied classes!" In other words, the total of *disenfranchised* persons in Berlin included also women and children still underage, and thus even those of Berlin's enfranchised, economically better-off inhabitants. The latter were therefore disenfranchised people even though many of them did not belong to the subaltern classes. This was so because women could not vote,[35] and because males younger than 25 also could not vote in Berlin and in most provinces of Prussia (the Rhine Province being the exception). Clearly, we must subtract from the figure that gives us the number of enfranchised Berliners the figure that gives us the total number of female adult members of the big, middle and small bourgeoisie, as well as the total of the children of these combined class factions, if we want to get an idea of the numerical size of the subaltern classes. Shall we put, roughly, the total number of the human beings belonging to said class factions (women and minors) at 150,000, of which the biggest part belonged undoubtedly to the petty bourgeoisie? In view of a total population of more than 400,000, this lets us put the number of the more or less proletarian urban poor (often referred to summarily as the workers, of course by including their families) at roughly 250,000. But in view of the fact that the petty-bourgeoisie of Berlin included many factually pauperized, and thus "proletarianized," small shop owners and self-employed craftsmen, the size of the *subaltern classes*, as Gramsci would define them (as we know, he was using a term that became necessary when he had to use the "slave language" of a political prisoner who was allowed to write but saw his writings censored), would certainly be no less than 300,000, perhaps more. They formed in part the real and, at any rate, almost in their entirety, the potential base of any real and radical, rather than just tame "middle class"-defined revolution in Berlin.

We see the capital's well-to-do middle class and also of its petty-bourgeoisie very nicely revealed by perhaps typical figures in the book August Brass wrote. His book makes obvious that non-participants, in the armed struggle, like the judicial councilor Bergling or the banker Martin Heinrich Mendheim,[36] who lived in the posh Breite Strasse (Broadway),[37] or the middle class onlookers in Gustav Julius' reading room (among them officers), sympathized with victims of Prussia's army when it "enforced order" and "dissolved [so-called] tumults" during the days of March. When people who had attended a people's assembly at the Zelten were pursued by sabre-swinging soldiers on horseback one night during the days prior to March 18, quite a few people living in the expensive Linden Avenue (*Unter den Linden*, in German) opened the doors of their house and let them in. As long as absolutism, its bureaucracy, and the army were the common foe, many if not almost all members of the middle class in Berlin quite obviously sympathized to a greater or lesser extent with the petty-bourgeois, educated activists who organized open air meetings of the people and with the largely petty-bourgeois and working class listeners—and sometimes, speakers who attended this event. The "subaltern classes" were not alone in the days of the revolution and in its immediate aftermath, up to the burial of the dead fighters in Friedrichshain. Rüdiger Hachtmann attempts to deflate the number of participants in this revolution. Of course, when he refers to the armed fighters opposing the royal army, he is right. The guerilleros who landed in Cuba and the revolutionaries who defeated Batista's army and entered La Habana victoriously also did not comprise millions of Cubans. But the majority of the population sympathized with them and supported them, when there was a chance to do so. And able-bodied young men and women joined their ranks—at least the awake and courageous ones. It was much like this in Berlin: those who were against the revolutionary struggle clearly appeared to be a minority of conservatives and reactionaries, and even of those who stayed away and who formed delegations to the king, quite a few came across as at least neutral. So it does not make sense to deflate the numbers, in the name of an alleged realism, and to depict the armed revolution as the work of a minority.

Something that is also a questionable aspect of Hachtmann's otherwise "social" study of the Berlin March Revolution is the fact that it mirrors the fashionable ways of most 20th (and early 21st) century sociologists to "deconstruct" and dissolve the only existing potentially revolutionary subject in capitalism—the working class—usually by subscribing to the superb insight that there occurs what they call increasing internal differentiation (*Ausdifferenzierung*). In like manner, the professor of sociology I have studied with since 1966, before encountering Urs Jaeggi, tried to fantasize the "dominant class" away by pointing out the many divergent interests that often come into play. I embarrassed him, not by refuting what he maintained, for different class factions can indeed embrace, in specific contexts, particular interests; the pursuit of particular interests is in fact a characteristic feature of capitalism, in all classes. But I pointed out that at the very moment when their power as a dominant class is threatened, they "forget" about all of their particular interests, and embrace their overall interest as a class.[38] So let's say that Hachtmann is progressive and, like the professor I mentioned was in 1966–67, is in fact a bourgeois progressive like so many of them —Ulrich Beck, Luhmann, Lepenies, Berger, Luckmann, and all the rest. But the notion that the proto-industrial, and then the early industrial, and finally the modern industrial working class, when it formed in Germany in the mid-1820s or the early 1840s, were internally differentiated is such an old hat. And yet it offers such nice opportunities to many bourgeois scholars, to fantasize away *their general interest as exploited wage workers* that can—but must not come—into play again and again in capitalist societies, and *the awareness of which is decisive* for their—and our —potential human emancipation.

It is true that after the days of armed struggle in Berlin during the bloody days of March '48, divergent interests came into play. As far as many commoners mentioned by name in the book by Brass are concerned, quite a few of these bourgeois and petty-bourgeois people, who, largely, appear as supporters of the revolution (or who are mistaken for them), seem to have backtracked after initial flirtations with liberalism and a limited democracy. They did so due to a strange and—as it turned out—premature anticipation of their own defeat, not by the "old powers" in Prussia, for this they suffered and almost accepted, but at the hand of an unknown and yet demonized force: the awakening sectors of Germany's suppressed majority—the working class. For it was true that just as much as the *junkers*, Prussia's class of large, aristocratic landowners, had to fear the ire and revenge of the rural subaltern masses who still passively bore their yoke before 1848 and—despite moments of peasant insurgency in Silesia in the year of 1848—to a considerable extent even at the time of the March Revolution, quite in contrast to their brethren in France during that other major revolution that had occurred nearly 60 years before the German attempt,[39] the bourgeoisie and parts of the petty-bourgeoisie began to fear the "red peril" in the 1830s and 1840s. It could only increase their anticipation of unknown dangers that the mid-19th century saw the March Revolution erupt in Berlin and that they witnessed more revolts and insurgencies in other German locations.[40] As Marx had pointed out so clearly in the Communist Manifesto, a phantom was haunting the propertied classes in these very years, regardless of how weak and unorganized the urban proletariat obviously was, and this not only in German lands.[41] Fear of demands uttered by the "mob"—in other words, by the workers, the subaltern classes, in all their different ways and forms—was the main reason why the "citizen guard" turned so conservative in early April 1948.

* * *

There existed objective reasons for such fearful anticipation with regard to the pauperized and proletarianized subaltern classes. The example of revolutionary action by this "mob" (as historians—even British ones—called it and still call it today, at least in some cases) that made the news when it occurred in nearby France in 1789 and 1830, and then also that other fact of a successful uprising in Brussels (albeit by an alliance of the French-speaking bourgeoisie and the city's subaltern classes against a Dutch-speaking bureaucracy and king) had filled not only kings and aristocrats but even large parts of the bourgeoisie in Europe with anxious anticipation of the "worst" that might happen. Such sentiments braked liberal pressure for change not only among "capitalists," thus among those Marx referred to, at the time, as the "haute bourgeoisie" (the upper stratum of the bourgeoisie or '*hohe Bourgeoisie*'), but among all segments of the "propertied classes."[42]

In Prussia, during and after the March Revolution, briefly, at least, decidedly liberal and certainly prosperous "burghers" frequently changed their course. Many of the Rhinelanders among them had been socialized in a context that was quite different from Prussia's East Elbian heartland. The Rhineland had welcomed the *Code civil* when it was introduced in that region during the years of French rule. But now many "liberal" Rhenish entrepreneurs sought a *rapprochement* with the King and his bureaucrats—though not with his generals and *junkers*. This tendency rubbed off on other parts of the bourgeoisie, even in Berlin. With increasing political working-class activity in cities like Cologne and Berlin, and signs of unrest of the subaltern classes in rural areas and small towns like Calbe,[43] a new fear of the "mob," in the wake of March 18 and 19, gripped the well-off burghers and even many petty-bourgeois "souls" if they thought they had something to lose and little to gain. Rumors, spread by the conservative press, informed by government sources in possession of communist pamphlets, added to fear.

It is true—proletarian agitation existed; but at least initially, it affected mainly *the large number of journeymen* and thus that part of the working class which was the least modern, the most threatened by ongoing industrialization, but at the same, quite often, the best-informed and most clearly "self-educated" segment of a rapidly pauperized yet numerically growing, and at the same time geographically "mobilized" and thus undoubtedly modern, proletariat. The journeymen formed a stratum that included many autodidacts and many rebellious souls. If the working class as a whole was growing in numbers, it was in part due to the fact that "modern industry" had expanded, that the traditional mining sector had undergone modernization in Prussia, and that miles and more miles of railroads were built. Nevertheless, the "modern industrial proletariat"—the most recent segment of the working class in Berlin and the segment that gained so obviously in strength, at least numerically—still constituted a minority within the broadly defined class of working people, and this class as a whole existed only as a "class in itself" (*classe en soi*; Klasse an sich) and not as a "class for itself" (*classe pour soi*; Klasse für sich). Thus it was only beginning to become conscious of itself, its needs, and its rational route to emancipation.

Though the workers of the Borsig iron works would participate actively in the armed struggle during the days of March 1848, it has been maintained that, in the course of events during the spring, summer and fall of 1848, the skilled "machine makers" (*Maschinenbauer*, mechanics) employed by Borsig and a number of other factories in the mechanical engineering sector were playing an intermediate role by placing themselves between the angry, rebellious "crowd" of Berlin's subaltern population and the "Citizen Guard" (or "Civil Guard" or Burgher Guard) that functioned now as the Hansemann government's instrument of maintaining "law and order."[44] Some working class activists were actively joining the "Civil Guard," as did Stefan Born, the book printer and communist, in order to strengthen a small and therefore insignificant working class element in this troop.[45] By doing so, Born shouldered expenses for the uniform and probably also for the gun that few people could afford. And a militant "machine maker," Siegerist, played a notable role as a radical agitator edging the "people" on to storm the arsenal and avail themselves of weapons,[46] when almost three months after the promise of "arming the people" had been made, this had still not occurred, for the "Civil Guard" was no more than the armed instrument of the liberal bourgeois government and, as events prove, a repressive instrument to boot that would be used repeatedly by the Camphausen government against the "people" later when tensions in Berlin increased during the spring and summer of 1848.

But many mechanics seem to have identified with the moderate "liberal" stance of August Borsig and similar entrepreneurs. Thus it is impossible to assert that the workers of the mechanical engineering sector were clearly more progressive, on the whole, than their "moderately" liberal bosses. And these bosses wanted above all to enjoy the political influence and the rights they thought they had attained for good in the wake of the March Revolution. Like the government, they, too, aimed to exclude the vast majority of the population—the workers of Berlin and the common people in Prussia's cities, and as a matter of fact, also the peasants, the suffering class in the countryside—from genuine political power.

There exists a consensus among social historians that, by and large, it was the pre-modern "proletariat" of journeymen and other poor craftsmen, and not the growing mass of modern factory workers, who were "radicalized" by their unbearable situation and by the pamphlets and books to which their clubs, associations, and "reading rooms" gave them access. They are often politically awake, even in the 1830s and early 1840s, thereby surpassing the factory workers and miners in terms of political consciousness and readiness to take action. Whether this is still true or not in 1848 is hard to tell. The proletariat of the spinning mills in Gent and quite a few miners in the Borinage revealed in 1848 that, at least in Belgium, things were changing, and that these segments of the working class were ready now to take action.

For the "propertied classes," fear of revolt by the poor and exploited was nothing new. They had experienced it in early modern times already. The urban revolts of a by now already distant past had been the work of employed artisans, craftsmen, and, quite generally, the urban poor. But there were more recent examples that the affluent could keep in mind, even though these mostly concerned events that occurred abroad. After all, several revolutions had been unleashed in Paris since 1789 and they were carried to victory, not just by speeches and pamphlets of liberal clerics, liberal parts of the nobility, and radical burghers, but by the anger, effort and dedication of the subaltern classes: by those who had strong arms and were ready to fight. This was what modern history had shown since 1789. And since the very moment of the July Revolution in France in 1830, the insurrection of the Lyon silk workers in 1831, and the February Revolution of 1848 in Paris, the informed elements of the bourgeoisie were at least faintly conscious of the—perhaps very near, perhaps distant—possibility of a class-based revolt, a workers' uprising, a proletarian revolution, that could erupt also in German cities, and against which they and the state might be powerless. To avert this possibility, the most obviously financially saturated, most commercially successful bourgeois people who had been true advocates of so many patently lacking *bourgeois political rights* began to close ranks with the late absolutist state and royal governments even before March 1848. And thus, they drew nearer to those "powers" they had denounced silently and privately as "feudalist" only yesterday.

* * *

As it turned out, the March Revolution of 1848 in Berlin ended a period of armistice, of uneasy "peace" between subjects and an absolutist government or monarchical ruler that was maintained by psychological and physical force.

Death penalties against democratic university students (the *Burschenschaftler* condemned in 1836),[47] incarceration of troublemakers in military prisons, relegation of students, the firing of dissident professors, and last but not least the silent work of censors and police informers were all contributing in Prussia to a climate *typical of a period of restauration that prevailed in all of Europe*. Clearly those years bore the mark of a time when fear of death braked revolutionary longings that had once filled the hearts and minds of a Georg Forster (1754-1794) or Friedrich Hölderlin (1770-1843)—people whose thoughts were still faintly alive in the hearts and minds of progressives.

At first, the local insurgency in the Prussian capital, a major city by European standards, that became famous immediately as the *March Revolution,* was undoubtedly an unintended act of passive resistance of Berliners exposed to brutal acts of an army that had harassed those assembling in the streets, thus in the Opera Square, or who were returning from "unlawful" meetings. The army had finally been ordered repeatedly to disperse assemblies in the Palace Square. Such meetings and convocations were unusual because the law of the land banned and criminalized all such public get-togethers. The meetings occurred in response to the calls of reformist burghers—middle class "citizens" with demands that were political rather than social in character. But soon the newly popular meetings at the Zelten grew larger and the working-class component of those forming the public grew and became the majority. However, with the exception of a few people like Siegerist and Stephan Born, the speakers continued to come from the so-called "middle class." They comprised people of different persuasions, among them also people who would be referred to as so-called "moderates" today. But there were probably far more outspoken democrats, although republican ideas were hardly voiced publicly before March 18–19, in view of the danger of arrest that even less "radical" speakers were theoretically facing. A supposedly liberal chief-of-police tolerated these meetings, happy to keep track of what was said and how it was received, and seeing in it perhaps a way that allowed disgruntled Berliners to let off steam. Minutoli was reporting carefully what he had seen to the minister of the interior (since 1845), Ernst von Bodelschwingh, who shared his views. Clearly, the "liberal" aristocrat Minutoli was a defender of law and order and of the monarchy, but he was not stupid. Reactionaries in the officer corps of the Prussian Army later blamed him for having, by negligence, let the revolutionary situation unfold, as if it could have been stopped after word of the French revolution and of occurrences in Vienna and Munich reached the Berliners. Army officers, on the others hand, lacked the foresight of the president of the police and stoked the flames of angry resentment and revolutionary readiness that had been triggered by news from abroad. In charge of small troops of dragoons, they even carried out attacks on people who returned in droves from large mass meetings at the Zelten. And this practice got even more bloody when large crowds assembled unlawfully in the Palace Square, usually because they accompanied men selected to present petitions to the king.

Brass reports all of this in great detail, thus documenting a prerevolutionary phase which saw people who were harboring democratic, and, in some cases, social as well as democratic ideas, engage in the organization of what soon became real popular assemblies, the aim always being to articulate demands that were to be presented to the king in the form of petitions. The entire process of drafting petitions, and especially the way they addressed the king, seems tame and harmless by today's standards. But at the time it was new and daring to discuss such matters in public, and even by today's standards, the way the populace was participating, the way they debated and voted on popular demands, was truly democratic and participatory. It was an activity that would have been *well-nigh impossible* during the period of stern reactionary rule that persisted between 1815 and 1830. And because of the successful liberal July revolution of 1830 in France—or in spite of it?—it would also have been persecuted severely in the 1830s, until finally a certain relaxation set in under Frederick William IV who ascended to the throne in 1840. The new king had appeared almost ready to accept liberalization, but he soon backtracked, as the stymied attempts of the First United Diet (in 1847) to push for a constitution showed. It was clear that the February revolution in France gave German democrats a boost; the public was "electrified" by this unexpected and unexpectedly successful event, and the authorities began to comprehend the necessity of piecemeal compromises that even the stubborn Prussian king felt compelled to offer, in need as he was of newly consented money, thus a new convocation of the United Prussian Diet that had to vote on new taxes. It is true that the adamant refusal of the United Diet to accord consent to higher taxes in exchange for only insignificant concessions offered by the king had hardened the positions of both sides in 1847. But then, the anxiety of a King facing clamoring crowds in the palace square had made him ready to give in, and the news that Louis Philippe had been toppled and was forced to leave France had let him move forward more than an inch. So he offered concessions—perhaps too little for the masses, but enough for many among the bourgeoisie—on the morning of March 18. And it was only the brutal overreaction of troops that had been ordered to dissolve the crowd on March 18 that set in motion a chain of events that turned into armed resistance of the majority of Berlin's population in the face of an army that overstepped all limits of "normal restoration of order." The confrontation turned into a real revolution, a bloody fight nourished in the last analysis above all by implicit, though unvoiced grievances of the capital's urban masses.

All of this comes to light in August Brass' fresh, well-written eyewitness account. It is an account that reveals many aspects of this revolution and of the social forces engaged in it. And it also throws light on the bystanders, thus people like Pastor Sydow, a conservative figure, and on such "liberal" and at first sight morally decent and—seemingly—even in their fulfillment of duty, "neutral" persons like von Minutoli, a man who is portrayed by Brass as someone who tolerated, as chief of police, illicit meetings of democrats and who kept the city's police away from any participation in the armed struggle. There are others, not mentioned by Brass, who remained mere witnesses and bystanders in this struggle and who might also be named here—among them certainly Bettina von Arnim, an old aristocratic lady well-known for her correspondence with Goethe in earlier years, who was in contact with many key persons of the dominant "elite" in the government, the army, and the palace, and who nonetheless developed a certain sympathy for the revolution. The same can be said of Fanny Lewald, a middle-aged woman, in contact with almost the same circles (including Camphausen and Hansemann, in June 1848), who also shows sympathies for certain demands of the people in her diary.

The honest descriptions of the persons Brass singles out as important in the context of the March events is a strength of his book. These are subjective descriptions, no doubt. And sometimes—for instance with regard to Mr. Urban—we may wonder whether they are fair. Brass strived to be objective, and at the same time he was empathetic, revealing a remarkable understanding of the code of honor of those who fought for the king and thus for conservative interests, on the other side of the barricades. Perhaps their code of honor was *not that distinct* from his own. If it was not so, it reveals at least his attempt to be fair. With regard to bloody actions of the popular masses, when they led to the death of soldiers whose rifles were coveted, while they were standing guard in a hopelessly isolated and for them hopeless location, he sought reasons to justify acts and prove that the masses were "decent." He would not have liked the curses hurled by proletarian women, kids, and nearby fighters, when these "underdogs" threatened two officers on horseback—trapped, almost, while on a reconnaissance mission. Shouts like those then uttered—"Kill those dogs! Let's slay these bastards!"—were truly not his style. He did not feel the rage, it seems, that had formed for good reason in the hearts of that part of the population which lived "elsewhere," in parts of town he may have hardly known, in derelict houses at the edge of the center, in the part of a tenement building that was accessible only through a dark and narrow courtyard, of which there were many in the petty-bourgeois Königsstadt quarter (the "King's town," to the North and North East of Alexander Square, both to the left and right of New King's Road: *Neue Königsstrasse*) or in the old and new proletarian suburbs outside the capital's excise wall.

Brass was honest, as a writer, as a man participating in the armed struggle, informed by the classical ethos of ancient Greek historians that he had come to know in high school (the old-fashioned German *Gymnasium* where they taught kids Latin and Greek) and which he undoubtedly remained attached to as a student at the university of Berlin where he studied history and philosophy, graduating with a Ph.D. degree. Yes, the immediacy, the freshness of his observations, coupled with an attempt to be fair, honest and objective, makes his subjective descriptions that attempt to be factual and observing, yet also aware of "psychological meanings," exceedingly valuable. And this even more so, due to the fact that Brass, in more than one way, quite often did not understand the significance of what he saw and described. His good insights are as important as his illusions, and his capacity to misjudge situations and perhaps, at times, also major "players" in these events and developments, is telling us much about him, but even more about his class, his peers and his time. And this is good, indeed. It is easier for us, it seems, to come to other judgements than those he arrived at, for we are later ones and judge with the knowledge of those who evaluate the occurrences of these days, their immediate and long-range significance, based on additional sources, endowed with different perspectives, and also clearly in hindsight.

The people who remain in the shadow of his descriptive account are those Gramsci referred to as the *subaltern classes*, in the language adopted of necessity in his prison writings.[48] It is they who participate most actively in the insurrection, it is they who form the bulk of the fighters on the barricades, and it is they who all too often sacrifice their lives.[49] They are largely commanded by men belonging to a different class, people like Brass, people who "quite naturally" arrogate the position of officers of the people, of leaders on and behind the barricades. It was Marx who saw, as early as the 1840s, that "the teachers must be educated"—that a dialectic should exist between spokespersons or "leaders" and the masses (this is also what Jean-Paul Sartre demanded), and that we have to learn a lot, as petty-bourgeois educated people, from conscious and awake working people, those who comprehend that it matters "to rise with the ranks," that is to say, the rank and file, "and not from them," as Edward Dahlberg put it.

Many, if not most of the "officers" on the barricades, these "leading figures of the revolution," are "moderates"—befitting the general tendency prevalent among those of their stratum or class: they are educated men, by and large, and many are cunctatory men, full of illusions. They loved to address, and to speak of "das Volk" (*the people*) when they talked of the whole bunch of non-aristocratic Berliners (the "commoners," thus also the bourgeoisie); and sometimes, using the term "people" that was so dear to them, they were referring specifically to the "masses," the "crowd"—that vast mass of wage-employed and at times, also jobless people, in whom they saw the destitute folks of the capital. Undoubtedly, "das Volk" (in the latter sense of the word) carried the biggest burden during the fighting—they paid the highest price, because most of those killed during the struggle on the barricades belonged to the subaltern classes. One cannot repeat this often enough, because they were also the ones who were denied the fruits of their victory that they had hoped for: goals that they began to decipher and to express. For it is true that they were "revolutionized" by the revolution; the experience of resisting the army—and this victoriously—made them shed off their old "subservience," that hideous *cloak of seeming submission* to masters who employed them, to house owners, cops, and the government, beneath which they had been hiding their rage, their apparent weakness, their helplessness that could verge on apathy. But the petty-bourgeois speakers addressing mass meetings and those who fought on the barricades and remained politically active in the subsequent months, also paid a high price in several ways in the course of the revolutionary events of 1848–49.

It is true that an unknown number of these more or less liberal, sometimes radical or even republican and socialist democrats—who talked to and spoke of and attempted to lead "the *people*"—also paid a high price in several ways in the course of the revolutionary events of 1848–49. They had been ready to pay with their lives, if necessary, during the fight. But, strange as it is, they did not show this same courage when they appeared to have won. What kind of assessment of the situation, which reasons, and also which fears hindered them when they might have acted in a more determined manner, with clearer goals in mind? Why did only unnamed people—working people, it seems—shout out loud what they wanted: a republic. Why was there not an attempt at least to immediately form a provisional government on March 19, with the King as a mere figurehead who could have been sent into exile later?

After the revolution was finally vanquished, many known democrats were jailed, and others saw themselves compelled to emigrate in 1849. Some were sentenced to death. Not all of them were pardoned, in the context of a more general amnesty, years after the revolution had been defeated.

We know too little of the punishment that ordinary fighters on the barricades received after the victory of the counterrevolution in November if they had been identified as participants in the struggle. But let us remember forever that they—despite the readiness of democrats like Brass to give "all" that they were capable of—had borne the real burden of the armed struggle; it had rested on the shoulders of the insurgent majority of the city's population, the subaltern classes. It was *to this largely faceless and seemingly voiceless "people"* whose curses Brass preferred not to hear—or not to report—that the Woenigers,[50] Brasses, Mendheims,[51] Berends, Nauwerks[52] and Jungs owed their brief sense of victory in the glorious days of March 1848 that gave way so soon to a period of defensive street protests and similarly defensive people's assemblies that tried, during the spring, summer and autumn, to safeguard the little that had been attained for the masses, and to expand their rights peacefully, if possible. The masses saw that the revolution did not bring them what they desired: bread, work, existential security—this was never on the agenda of most of those educated men who deliberated in the name of the "people!" As for voting rights, they were granted, but in a distorted way, and this was clearly intended to cheat them, too: it was to muzzle their voice and limit the presence of their delegates in the new National Assembly that met in Berlin. So all there was for them was a semblance of democratic progress, with strings attached. As we know, even this would not last.[53]

* * *

If any serious analytical discussion of the immediate events in Berlin in March 1848 cannot but note the decisive role that was played by that part of the population which Brass refers to not only by using a vague expression—"the people"—but just as often by the term "protected clients," then the question arises of course: are these terms synonymous? No, we learn—they are not. But if they are not synonymous, who were they, these "protected clients?" As pointed out further above, they are the real majority of the Berliners—as August Brass also did not fail to point out. What do we know about them, about their social status, immediate goals during the revolution, ideals, thoughts, hopes and further intentions and expectations? In a way, very little, one must admit. This part of the Berlin population was the majority, that much is clarified. And, according to Brass, this group is *defined by its legal status as disenfranchised inhabitants* of Berlin, consisting of roughly 400,000 men, women, and children—whereas the so-called "citizens" numbered about 40,000 people, he said. Whether or not his figures are slightly exaggerated does not matter here so much. For it is apparent that these figures may actually camouflage the correct "real proportions" of *two groups objectively opposed in politico-economic, social, and soon also immediately political terms:* the bourgeoisie, with its ally, the complacent and relatively well-off part of the capital's petty-bourgeoisie and, on the other hand, the subaltern classes that comprised the wage workers and the large proletarianized and semi-proletarianized part of the petty-bourgeoisie. All of the latter were by and large disenfranchised Berliners. But as pointed out already, wives and dependent children below age 25 of Group One (the "die besitzenden Klassen," i.e. "propertied classes," in the language of the time) were also disenfranchised,[54] and the poor members of the petty-bourgeoisie who are counted as a part of Group Two may actually have been largely enfranchised, as they usually owned a house. If they were not exempted from paying the land tax (i.e., house tax), they enjoyed in fact the right to vote in municipal elections, and might even be elected city councilor. So all of our attempts to assess the objective, politico-economically defined proportions, and thus the relative strength of each group in purely quantitative, numerical terms, must of necessity remain vague. And this is even more true if we try to estimate the extension or "numerical strength" of each group in subjective, that is to say, ideological respect.

We simply can only guess that the overwhelming majority of Berlin's enfranchised members of the bourgeoisie consisted of men who embraced "moderately liberal" political positions and held socially conservative views with regard to workers and their political and socio-economic rights. We have the evidence that many joined the civil guard (a real "burgher" guard, and not at all the working-class militia that petty-bourgeois radicals and many workers desired), and that this "burgher guard" that initially protected the king against "mob pressure," until he departed for a long time to his Sanssouci palace in Potsdam, was a force of law and order in spring, and shot and killed protesting workers in the summer of 1848. This armed "guard" turned out to become very big as a force of order of "liberal" governments like the Camphausen-Hansemann government and the subsequent Auerswald-Hansemann government. Camphausen noted that 25,000 rifles were distributed—of course in the main to law and order loving burghers, even though divergent political opinions existed within the guard.[55] But the main tendency becomes visible in their actions. That they took part in the second, again symbolic, march to the grave of the killed revolutionaries in the Frederick's Grove (Friedrichshain) shows, of course, that the moderate liberals recognized to what extent the Camphausen government owed its existence to such fighters and to the days of struggle, even though this government denied the very fact of a revolution and preferred to speak of the "occurrences in March" as if these had been simply a tumult that got out of hand. When the threat of a reactionary backlash became more apparent and even the "good burghers" in their moderate complacency recognized it, the new provisional commander of the civil guard, Major Rimpler, recommended that workers should be recruited by the guard, too—and this in large numbers. He suggested that they should be armed with pikes, instead of rifles! This modest proposal was rejected by the bourgeois majority: by the "Magistrat" (i.e., the elected city government), by the majority of the city councilors, by the government, and in all likelihood also by the majority of delegates in the Prussian National Assembly, if the proposal was discussed in this assembly. They began to fear the reaction, as the workers and their democratic petty-bourgeois allies had done all along—but as true bourgeois Berlin liberals proud of their "moderate" stance they feared the workers, the majority of Berlin's population, even more. Only in the fall of 1848, when everything was already too late to turn, did the Civil Guard become somehow more democratic in orientation.

As far as the subaltern classes were concerned, the extent of their political awareness—the very result of being revolutionized in March—becomes apparent when we hear a conservative observer express, in a way that reveals surprise, anger, consternation, and bewilderment—his amazement that, in the weeks after the fighting, he saw Berlin's "women politicizing at every street corner." Their minds were focused on the situation—the political situation. They were standing at street corners, reading political posters, and discussed them with other women while their husbands, normally, were off to work. Who? What sort of women? Clearly working-class women and perhaps also some women of the petty-bourgeoisie. Working class women knew what drove their men to take part in political actions. They shared concerns, shared many goals, even though they must have resented the fact that none of those who spoke in favor workers' rights put the issue of female suffrage squarely on the table. As far as bourgeois women are concerned, they would hardly debate political matters in the street. The ladies of the bourgeoisie always would discuss things at home, in their so-called *"salon"*:[56] culture, fashion, the situation that existed with regard to business generally, and thus the regrettable fact of a recession, and that the revolution made everything worse. Certainly working-class "disturbances" were not seen as helpful by them. And thus, perhaps, they also "talked politics" at times—who knows.

The difficulties of determining the exact size of the combined numerical strength of Berlin's working class and other disenfranchised subaltern class factions notwithstanding, it is clear that the subaltern classes (with the working class as the core) must have formed the overwhelming part of the Prussian capital's "protected clients." This portion of Berlin's population, bigger by far than the other two groups—the well-off "citizens" and their protected family members—is the one that we should focus on now more closely. Were they actually a homogenous group, as members of Berlin's working class? This is not only doubtful: it is in fact not the case. There exist, basically, two ways of differentiating them, two ways that we can attempt to rely on, when trying to understand their basic composition. These analytical approaches are not related only to their function and position in the process of production: they also include socio-cultural factors.

If we focus on their geographical background, we can differentiate between those who are newcomers or at least fairly recent arrivals (respectively offspring of inhabitants who settled down in this city fairly recently), and on the other hand "old Berliners," entrenched in the city for quite some time already, yet due to their intergenerational poverty still without the rights of a "citizen." Newly arrived inhabitants might also be without voting rights if they chose not to buy this right; thus they would not necessarily belong to the subaltern classes—but in fact, most of those who did not pay the sum needed to buy the status of an "enfranchised" Berliner did probably belonged to the subaltern classes if they weren't briefly staying business people or students from other parts of Prussia and Germany. Therefore, we can safely assume with regard to the majority of "recent" (newly arrived) Berliners that they belonged to the subaltern classes. The geographically focused look at "protected clients" helps us to obtain a first differentiation: we get (1) poor "old Berliners" rooted for long in the town; (2) poor, proletarian "new arrivals" (the group that contributed most decisively to *urban population growth*,[57] apart from the high birth rate that must be noted generally, but especially with regard to the subaltern classes); (3) a small number of university students who arrived from other parts of Prussia or areas beyond Prussia; (4) travelers; and (5) merchants visiting the city because they had business to do within its walls.

Population growth in Berlin

Year	Number of inhabitants	Annual growth rate (%)	Year	Number of inhabitants	Annual growth rate (%)
1835	272,005	2.8	1842	339,153	2.0
1836	278,585	2.4	1843	349,110	2.9
1837	283,140	1.6	1844	363,424	4.1
1838	294,716	4.1	1845	380,040	4.6
1839	307,940	4.5	1846	396,535	4.3
1840	322,626	4.8	1847	410,116	3.4
1841	332,602	3.1	1848	411,509	0.3

Source: Statistisches Jahrbuch [Statistical Yearbook], edited the Amt für Statistik (Office for Statistics) of Berlin, Berlin: Berliner Wissenschafts-Verlag, 1998, p.26 f.

A group we are not likely to find present (though they would be present nowadays, among the urban poor) are the beggars. "Vagrants" would typically be confined to the Berlin "workhouse" (*Arbeitshaus*) and there were probably very few of them who would dare at all to enter the city voluntarily. It was the police that picked them up outside the city and transported them to Berlin. Thus, there existed in fact, among the huge subaltern part of the disenfranchised population of Berlin (6) the involuntary inhabitants of the workhouse and (7) the prison inmates as further groups denied citizen status—but are they "protected?"

If we focus, now, on *the role* of Berlin's non-citizens, its so-called "protected clients," *in the process of production*, we must say that most of them belonged to the sector of production that we can term *small-scale, pre-industrial production*: this sector entailed production in workshops—production, the methods of which may have improved, and they certainly did, due to science and technical progress, since the middle ages and early modern times, but whose dimensions were still more or less the same, and with them, the closeness of social "rapports" (thus, social relations between master and craftsman, master and apprentice or between craftsmen and apprentices). Patriarchic social relations were close in the pre-industrial sector; they were more "familiar," and thus different from those in *the second, no longer small-scale and already proto-industrial sector* that was formed during the second half of the 18th century when the silk processing industry boomed.[58] At the end of the century cotton spinning mills were added (they are found by the River Spree, in the Southeasterly suburbs), and with them came the calico printers, manufactories that applied fashionable designs to the cotton cloth. It was a cotton mill, that of Johann Georg Sieburg, that was the first enterprise in Berlin that used a steam engine (for its jennies), and this already in 1795. The steam engine had been imported from Britain. There were also other "manufactories" such as the "porcelain" [china ware] manufactory that was located in Fredericktown (Friedrichstadt), a spacious, socially bourgeois town expansion to the west of that old urban core which comprised the small historical center of Berlin, thus Old Berlin, Cölln, and New Cölln, as well as the royal palace. The emphasis of this proto-industrial manufacturing sector was placed on the production of luxury goods, and these entrepreneurs aimed at the aristocracy in Berlin, the court, and the city's bourgeoisie.

If the first sector dated back to the middle ages, the second had come into existence during the second half of the 18th century. Both sectors thus were not new facets of Berlin's "trades and industry" in the 1840s. They had been the material precondition of *early forms of a "proletariat"* that found paid work in Berlin in the sphere of production, rather than only as servants or maids of the king and aristocrats, and also of the bourgeoisie.

The third sector of material production was the most modern in the late 1840s. It was *the factory sector*. It was in part state-owned, thus a "Royal" industry that included above all the mint and the Royal iron foundry that produced cannons and other weapons as well as cannon balls. This *state-owned sector* had a long history, but it had expanded and had also been modernized. But more important was now *the private sector* with its factories. It surpassed *the older state-run sector* both in terms of the quantity of workers employed and in terms of its growth dynamics and technological advances. This latter sector was brand-new; it had come into being mainly since the early 1830s, it had quickly attracted new workers to Berlin, and it was located mainly outside the excise walls.

As noted already, the *state sector* was old; it had premodern origins, but it had expanded in size and had evolved technologically and in terms of its forms of organization, from the small to the large workshop to combined workshops—thus, it implied the existence of technologically related workshops under one roof or in adjacent buildings. And then, this constellation developed in ways that let it form the modern factory.

In said state-run sector, just as in *the two parts of the private industrial sectors* (comprising both the older, proto-industrial *Manufaktur* or "manufactory" sector, and the recently formed modern industrial sector, typically represented by the Borsig iron, steel, and "locomotive engines" producing complex), the *social differentiation* was clear: under the command of a director, there existed employed "master craftsmen" overseeing an elite of skilled workers and a certain number of helpers, thus unskilled or semiskilled workers and apprentices. Ranks and status mattered in these sectors, though in different ways. Skilled workers of "porcelain" manufactories enjoyed the reputation of "artists," for instance.

If we would have to quantify sections of the Berlin proletariat that existed during the 1840s, we can certainly say that those working in small and medium sized workshops still constituted a clear majority. Among them, those working in the textile sector as tailors formed a large group; a similar estimate is possible with regard to those working in the furniture-producing and carriage-producing sector (both part of the woodworking industry).

The construction industry, still pre-industrial, was another sector that featured an important number of workers. A large number of them were paid by the state when needed, and were thus subject to a changing pattern of alternation between employment and unemployment.[59] They formed a true "mass" of unskilled proletarians, as the more solidly skilled among them—master builders, and architects—were most likely kept on the payroll and respected as well, due to their expertise. These latter segments (Baumeister and Architekten), though state employees, were not—in any real social sense—proletarians. In view of their position as salaried personnel they were, strictly speaking, wage-laborers, but they still were seen as a part of the petty-bourgeoisie due to their reputation and the size of their paid compensation. The most renowned, with perhaps university or building academy degrees and with high salaries, formed a part of the upper petty-bourgeoisie that was "bourgeois" in status, though *not with reference to their role in the process of production*: they weren't owners of big industry or financial capitalists. And they were not even owners of small, pre-modern units of production, like those thousands if not—more likely—tens of thousands of independent, self-employed petty-bourgeois craftsmen and "artisans" who operated small workshops, many of them without employing anyone or, at most, one or two journeymen and apprentices.[60]

If the highly educated segment of *employees* could gravitate, in terms of status, and probably also ideology, to the bourgeoisie (with its reactionary, conservative, and "liberal conservative," or "moderately" liberal currents), the *self-employed* artisans and craftsmen found themselves more and more exposed, in certain branches of production such as the textile sector, to *pauperization* and *proletarianization*—something that could radicalize many and made them prone to accept and embrace democratic, sometimes radically democratic, "liberal" and, in quite a few cases, even socialist ideas and ideals. Poor "masters" of a trade were not much better off than badly paid, employed artisans, at least in terms of income, especially during a sharp downturn of the economy, like that of the crisis experienced in the late 1840s.[61] What kept both strata apart was property, for the master craftsmen usually owned an old house, owned by the family for generations, that also provided space for their workshop.[62]

If we can speak of the frequently painful poverty of many independent artisans during the 1840s, this can be noted with even more justification with respect to wage laborers in certain sectors of urban small-scale production, sectors that were increasingly exposed to the competition of a clearly expanding "big industry" that was only semi-modern at the time in some cases, yet nonetheless advanced when compared with cottage industry. The competitiveness of "industry" exerted pressure on prices, something that presented a danger for individual spinners and weavers who saw their livelihood and very existence threatened. But we should also note the situation of tailors. In the Prussian capital, Berlin, they had to cope with foreign competition. In Paris, for instance, an important center of fashionable textile production, tailors already worked in large "ateliers" that introduced an internal division of labor while employing large numbers of otherwise pre-industrially working journeymen "under one roof."

Journeymen, rather than manufactory workers and modern factory workers, were *the first to embrace republican and quite often, even socialist ideas in Germany in the 1830s and 1840s*.[63] The effects of the revolutions of 1830 in France and Belgium were felt in this social group. Pre-modern guild rules demanded, for instance, that carpenters should learn the trade by walking from town to town in search of employment, and this in order to expand their expertise by working under different master craftsmen. The practice of tailors was similar in that they sought work in flourishing foreign centers of textile production, thus Paris and London, but also Brussels and a number of towns in Switzerland. And in fact, in the 1830s and 1840s, there existed large communities of expatriate German journeymen (mainly, tailors?) in Paris and London. All of these European centers with major expatriate communities of German artisan, journeymen, or, generally, workers became also places of refuge and exile of persecuted German democrats in those years, and thus places of political debate, agitation, and recruitment.[64] As journeying was prescribed by respected traditional rules of the trade and also necessary, due to rising unemployment or bad wages and starvation at home, the fluctuation in the expatriate German journeymen communities abroad was considerable, and large numbers of journeymen returned home, "infected" (as the authorities feared) with radical republican, as well as "communist" or Chartist ideas.

If we talk, however, of the well-paid artisans in Berlin's manufactory sector that produced luxury goods—thus, for instance, by focusing on those who applied paintings to "porcelain"—we can hardly expect many among them who would easily show an interest in socialist publications like the writings of Wilhelm Weitling,[65] let alone the Communist Manifesto, published in 1848, and spread immediately by the small but active fold of workers and intellectuals who were members of the clandestine Federation of Communists.[66]

Still, one must say that the inroads made by "socialist" ideas among the subaltern classes—consisting to a large extent of such wage workers as the pre-industrial journeymen, craftsmen, artisans, apprentices, but also of some proletarianized, still self-employed master craftsmen—remained probably moderate prior to the revolution of 1848. Even republicanism seems to have remained "*minoritaire*": like the quest for equality and social justice, it was only a vague sentiment among the "masses," not an ideology, not a program, although there was a lot of dissatisfaction. There were real grievances, it is true; there were social demands like bread and jobs in the face of periodically increasing unemployment (a capitalist crisis made itself felt at the time!). Among the better informed, there was also a thirst, a desire vaguely crystalizing in such concepts as socialism. But if there was a general quest for more justice and an improvement of the situation, it was expected—if expected at all—faintly from "those above," kings and their government, in Germany's patriarchic, paternalistically structured society.

But still things were fleeting and changing, and not just in the form of an acerbation of poverty during the crisis. Those tens of thousands of German journeymen who had been in western European capitals like Brussels, Paris, and London or in big cities like Zurich and Lyon returned very often with hot republican ideals and a desire to spread them: Switzerland was a republic, after all, even though a strange, patriarchic one with many medieval traits. In France, republicanism had been strong since the 1790s. In a certain number of cases, especially among those returning from France, an impact of socialist ideas was noted by the watchful eyes and ears of the German authorities who relied on censors reading all the imported books and brochures and tracts they could get hold of, and on the police with its large network of secret informers at its disposal.

Workers' associations were formed. They provided a politically relevant infrastructure for those who desired change. In Paris, there existed a club of

German workers; in Brussels, expatriate Germans formed the *Association Democratique*. And everywhere, secret societies began to form: the Italian Carbonari, the German Federation of the Just, that later became the Federation of Communists. It included men like Moll, Schapper, Marx and Engels.

In the Prussian capital, in clear contrast to Paris, London, Brussels, but also in contrast to Genève and other urban centers in Switzerland, and to Cologne in the Rhineland, no substantial segment of the Federation of Communists had formed in the 1840s, although Stefan Born, an active and intelligent member of this clandestine group, was clearly seeking to win support in Berlin and perhaps was relatively successful among the book printers. Later, in the spring of 1848, the young radical democrat Schlöffel organized hungry, job-seeking or underemployed construction workers.

This much is clear, the tide—among the journeymen, at least—went in the direction of republicanism. By 1848, socialist ideas became attractive and affected more and more of the journeymen, though certainly not yet a majority among them. Journeymen were the "typical" workers of the time —there can be no doubt about this: they and not the workers in modern factories were forming an "avantgarde." They were the group with the most progressives; they were the "educated ones" among the proletariat. A large part of them sought to further themselves, to educate themselves. They formed "Workers' Educational Associations" (Arbeiter-Bildungs-Vereine), and these associations, financed by the small fees that members paid, subscribed to progressive journals and bought books that were available to members.

This should remind us of the Newspaper Hall in Berlin, established by Gustav Julius. True enough, as far as the paying customers are concerned, it obviously was a rather petty-bourgeois establishment: it found its readers among liberal intellectuals and a few liberal army officers—all of whom were seemingly too poor to subscribe to one or more newspapers, yet able financially to join the Hall and pay the fee it demanded.[67] The social composition of its subscribing members set Mr. Julius' Reading Hall apart from the typical Workers' Educational Association that featured a different "class character" and was offering less than his reading room. Contributions that workers were expected to make to their association were surely more modest than the considerable fee demanded from subscribers of the Newspaper Hall, which explains why the latter could offer readers a large number of newspapers and books, certainly more than an association of and for workers might afford without problem. But the pattern or model was the same: the progressive parts of the petty-bourgeoisie and of the working class met in their interest to absorb news from abroad. And obviously, such news came "from the West," as Brass does not fail to point out.

France, in the 1830s and 1840s was, politically speaking, causing attention: it caused the admiration of some and grave fears of others. It was here where— in the wake of the revolution of 1789, and of its abortion by Napoléon (who represented the interest of the *grande bourgeoisie*)—a reactionary monarchy had been installed by returning aristocrats, aided by foreign powers. But discredited in many ways, this monarchy had been toppled in 1830, and then insurgencies and revolutions kept occurring in a row: in 1831 (above all in Lyon), in February 1848 (above all, in Paris), and finally, in July 1848 (again, in Paris). In Germany, republicanism had led to no revolution in this same period: in the form of Jacobinism (Jakobinertum), it had only gained roots and become a strong factor in Western parts of Germany, such as Mainz (Mayence), and this when the French Republic had already annexed much of the West (the Rhineland, with Aachen and Cologne).

But then—also due to the draft imposed by Napoleonic occupation authorities in German states—an anti-revolutionary, nationalistic backlash had occurred that was exploited by the reactionary late absolutist German rulers. The King of Prussia, recovering from political paralysis caused by defeat in 1806 and advised by reformist administrators, resorted finally to a version of the French revolutionary strategy of a *levée en masse, a military mobilization of the masses,* something that *seemed* to transform the army (that old, yet defeated "standing army") into a *people's army* (ein Heer des "Volkes"—a thought and sentiment that would be echoed later, in 1848).

The reforms carried out under Stein and Hardenberg could have modernized at least Prussia, had they not been braked by the King. And if stepped up, they could have brought the transition from absolutist to constitutional monarchy in that state. But the aristocracy persevered and the Prussian kings regretted their reformism, forced upon Frederick William III by political necessity and armed defeat in the battles of Jena and Auerstedt in 1806. The petty-bourgeoisie, and also a large part of the bourgeoisie, remembered the promises of reform, however.[68] Between 1815 and 1830 there was much dissatisfaction felt in these circles. The students—kids of well-off families, mostly—agitated frequently for unity of all German lands and their populations. Liberalism was *en vogue* among wealthy commoners. Bankers and big commercial capitalists—especially in a city like Hamburg that was dominated by the commercial bourgeoisie, but also in Frankfurt, and even to some extent in Cologne—had international contacts and experience; their political vision and dreams were not imprisoned in the confines of a backward Germany whose rulers embraced reactionary views and resorted to repressive methods. Following suit in the tracks of big merchants and bankers, a new stratum of industrialist upstarts, especially in Prussia, had contacts abroad, as well. Technical innovation was coming from England, and many industrial entrepreneurs went to England in order to have a look and learn from British industry. Among the bankers, Jewish banking houses were especially networked internationally and bankers, merchants, and factory owners with Jewish roots were clearly the most liberal segment of the German bourgeoisie. With large families and offspring in other professions (education, science, law), the progressive ideas often adopted in families of certain financial capitalists with foreign business partners and their own experience abroad spread among the educated petty-bourgeoisie and—as it were—even among members of the aristocracy with jobs in the state administration, law, and education. As already noted, the liberal "democratic" impulse was also exceedingly present among university students, thus existing among young people from wealthy, usually bourgeois or petty-bourgeois and, in some cases, even aristocratic, families.

All of this explains in part the sentiments we discover during the March Revolution among many propertied commoners. Liberal tendencies were unmistakably present. They owed their existence to a large extent to resentment that these people felt because the King and the government had failed to carry out political reforms. And this because of a will, on the part of Frederick William IV, to defend absolutist prerogatives, and also because the reactionary majority of the aristocracy did not want to give up the outdated system of unequal "parliamentary representation" enshrined in the United Diet (Vereinigte Landtag).

But to this consciousness of broken Royal promises of reform was added the involuntarily suffered nuisance of having to accept censorship that made the publication of a free bourgeois press and the publication of critical books well-nigh impossible. Both slights merged with memories of the anti-Napoleonic "wars of liberation" (*Befreiungskriege*), with dreams of national unity, and with the myth that the "wars of liberation" had supposedly brought about an "armed people" for a short time. It was especially among young and middle-aged educated petty-bourgeois liberals that demands of constitutional reform coincided with criticism of the standing army (commanded overwhelmingly by members of the reactionary, "class-conscious" aristocracy) and with a quest to establish an "army of the people"—that is to say, a more bourgeois and petty-bourgeois, and in this regard very different, command structure. For it was clear to them that when they would have to serve in the military, or had served already, their chances of promotion were rather limited, and that meant that they faced aristocrats in the higher and highest ranks and the particular, sometimes ugly and condescending, treatment they received from them.

Among the workers (both journeymen and factory workers), the demand to form a people's army, if and when it was uttered at all, had another meaning: it implied posing the question of power. The demands of conscious segments—and also of less conscious segments—of this class always gave priority to the so-called "social question," however. And this regardless of whether the solutions offered were *reformist* (and even entailed perhaps illusions of paternalistic reform, carried out by the monarchy or the bourgeoisie) or assumed a *revolutionary* (democratic) character—in some cases even a socialist character. The main concerns among the working class were joblessness, or outrageously long working hours with insufficient pay, and hunger.[69]

The housing question assumed increasing importance only slowly, when certain cities, like Berlin, started to grow more rapidly. This does not mean that one can deny that the housing situation was miserable in many cases.[70]

In 1824, the first modern tenement buildings were constructed on the Garden Street (Gartenstrasse) at the Northern periphery, just outside the Hamburg Gate.[71] They were meant to accommodate workers streaming into the city. Although the way such workers were put up was not good, in view of the large number of people densely packed in such buildings, the situation would still deteriorate, as the century progressed and densification in big and medium-sized cities with growing industries and their expanding workforce increased side by side with "*slum lordism.*"

If the housing question, in all of its different forms, characterized the social reality of the subaltern classes—or, in other words, the working people, working class folks and also quite a few of the proletarianized self-employed (thus formally "petty-bourgeois) artisans—so did poverty. The failure of harvests and suspected or real ways of speculatively driving up prices of staple foods like potatoes were at the root of the food question and a main cause of the food riots in 1847, and also helped motivate angry action by Berlin's poor women and the street kids who joined them. Hunger could drive the poorest of the poor—especially those concentrated in the most proletarian suburbs of Berlin, just North of the city wall—to desperate deeds. This is what a monthly published in the capital, the *Bericht aus Berlins gesellschaftlichem Leben* [Report of Berlin's Social Life], told its readers in November, 1846:

> The gutters in Berlin are the gold mines of the poor, as we have occasion to notice day by day. Every thorough cleaning of the same would deprive many of our poor of their gain. Let's narrate this here, in order to shame our intelligentsia. While the day hardly dawns, these stagnant waters are being ransacked by hundreds of hoes, to get bones, leftovers of meals, and other things still of value for *poor people* out of their muddy depth. And so we saw recently a women performing this Herculean work; the bag she carried on her shoulder was still light; the evening already squinted down on all Berlin gutters and their ransackers [*scavengers?*], and with a sad face, the poor woman thought of her children in the Voigtland. But suddenly her eyes shone more brightly, she seemed to have found something good. And indeed, we saw how she brought to light from out of the gutter what was probably a few pounds of fish spawn, with which she hurried happily to the next street well where she cleaned it from its disgusting hangings. We could not refrain from asking her what she intended to do with her find, for a revolting suspicion arose in us. "This spawn I will cook tonight for my family—and, gentleman, *such* a supper we haven't had for a long time. My children have picked up left-over potatoes in the fields, and my husband has stolen wood in the Jungfernhaide (the Virginsheath)." "And what else do you have for supper, except the potatoes?" "The brine of herrings, sir, or scraped off left-overs of cheese, if we have any. Nothing else." Those surrounding her gave her a few dimes, but they were not able to convince the poor bony woman to throw the spawn back into the waters of the gutter.[72]

> № 7.   **Bericht**   1846.
>
> aus
>
> **Berlins gesellschaftlichem Leben.**
>
> Im Verein mit Mehreren herausgegeben
> von
> **Adolph Wolff.**
>
> Von diesem Bericht erscheint monatlich eine Nummer.   Preis für den Jahrgang 12 Sgr.
>
> ### Monat November.
>
> — Zum Vergnügen der Einwohner hiesiger Residenz ist gewiß von den Allerhöchsten Herrschaften wie von den Vätern dieser Stadt viel gethan, und es sind zu diesem Behufe zu allen Zeiten wohl große Opfer gebracht worden. Wir haben zur Erholung und Kräftigung der Gesundheit schöne Anlagen vor den Thoren, namentlich den weltberühmten Thiergarten, jetzt besonders so außerordentlich verschönerten Thiergarten. Es entsteht zu gleichem Behufe auf Fürsorge des hochedlen Magistrats und der Stadtverordneten der neue Friedrichshain vor dem Landsberger Thore, dessen weit ausgedehnte und mit Umsicht geleitete Anlagen große Summen kosten werden; aber dennoch bleibt den Einwohnern dieser sich immer mehr vergrößernden Hauptstadt noch viel zu wünschen übrig. Vieles fehlt uns noch, was andere ähnliche große Städte schon haben, und woran deren Einwohner besonders zur Frühlings- und Sommerszeit sich auch recht erfreuen, ich meine große, vor den Thoren sich befindende und von jedem Bewohner zu benutzende, gleichsam öffentliche Obstbaum-Pflanzungen, in denen sich die Bewohner der Stadt nach Willkür durch Lustwandeln oder auch an dem Genuß der für Geld zu erkaufenden Früchte ergötzen können. — Wollen wir uns aber eine Idee machen, welchen Reiz solche Obstbaum-Pflanzungen unserer sonst ja so lobenswerthen Hauptstadt gewähren würden, so brauchen wir uns nur im Geiste vor das Prenzlauer Thor zu versetzen, und uns zu vergegenwärtigen, welche Freude uns der Blüthenschmuck dieser an der Chaussee angepflanzten Obstbäume im Frühlinge und deren Früchte im Spätsommer verursachten. Wie öde war diese Gegend früher, vor dieser ihrer jetzigen Ausschmückung, und wie besucht ist dieselbe jetzt! Solcher Anlagen ließen sich vor Berlins Thoren gewiß auf gleiche Weise noch viele schaffen, und überall würden sie gewiß auch mit gleicher Freude benutzt werden. Hätte nicht in dieser Beziehung auch der neu angelegte Friedrichshain mitbenutzt werden können? Würden wir nicht alsdann, eben so wie z. B. die Bewohner Potsdams uns zur Blüthezeit und Fruchtzeit ihrer Kirschbäume u. s. w. einladen, auch diese und Andere zum Anblick der Blüthenpracht unserer Obstbaum-Pflanzungen im neuen Friedrichshaine einladen können? Die Waldbäume, so angenehm wir uns auch sonst, und zumal bei großer Sommerhitze, unter ihrem Schatten belustigen mögen, gewähren doch die Genüsse nicht, welche uns die Obstbäume besonders in fruchtbaren Jahren gewähren. Man könnte mit hier zwar einwenden: Obstbäume passen für eine große Stadt mit ihrer großen Einwohnerzahl nicht, denn wer sollte zur Erntezeit die Früchte solcher gleichsam öffentlichen Anlagen schützen? Pächter, erwiedere ich darauf ganz einfach, werden in Verbindung mit der Obrigkeit diese Anlagen mit ihren Früchten eben so schützen, wie die Anlagen ähnlicher Art jetzt vor dem Prenzlauer Thore von Franz Buchholz bin geschützt werden. Aber woher mag es kommen, daß Berlin gerade an solchen das Leben erheiternden Anpflanzungen immer noch großen Mangel leidet? Ich will es sagen und zu behaupten wagen, daß daran nur die begüterten Einwohner dieser Stadt selbst Schuld sind, indem diese in Berlin und seinen Umgebungen nicht solche Vergnügungen benutzen wollen, und lieber auf Reisen und in die Bäder ziehen, um sich solche Vergnügungen mit weit größeren Kosten außerhalb zu verschaffen. Dort ziehen diese mit ihren Familien erst zur innigen Freude ihrer Kinder nach den Obstgärten und vergnügen sich, meinend, so etwas Schönes sei doch in Berlins Umgebungen nicht zu finden. — Würden wir aber die Kosten zu solchen Anlagen hier nicht scheuen, sie würden in wenigen Jahren vollständig ins Leben treten, und wir würden die doppelte Freude hier genießen, erstens zu sehen, wie glücklich Familien aus den Thoren hinausziehen, um sich an den Blüthen und Früchten der Obstpflanzungen zu ergötzen, und zweitens werden wir selbst mit gleicher Lust Antheil an diesen Freuden nehmen können. Darum, Ihr Reichen und Ihr Väter dieser sonst so herrlichen Stadt, laßt Euch erbitten, und legt vor allen Thoren, auch auf Aktien, wenn Ihr wollt, große und schöne Obstbaum-Pflanzungen an, und seid versichert, Eure Kinder schon werden Eure guten Werke preisen und Euch noch in der Ewigkeit dafür segnen.   a.
>
> — Viele werden sich mit Vergnügen des großen Rosen-, Obst- und Weingartens in der Schillingsgasse Nr. 12. 13. 14. erinnern, zu dessen Besuch anständige Leute bisher stets ohne Weiteres zugelassen, ja in der Blüthezeit selbst durch die öffentlichen Blätter aufgefordert wurden. Das herrliche Grundstück soll, dem Vernehmen nach, nun verkäuflich sein, weshalb leider die Besorgnis nur zu nahe liegt, es möchte in die Hände von Spekulanten gerathen, da von solchen die Durchlegung einer Straße schon längst projektirt sein soll. Möglich aber doch, daß irgend ein wohlhabender Bewohner Berlins, dem es um

We have reflected on the "propertied classes" and we had a glimpse of the "subaltern classes." Perhaps we can even say with regard to Berlin in 1848 that the two main pillars of the revolution are clearly visible. And so is their ideological complexity, if not—in large part—their undecidedness. There is the petty-bourgeoisie (to the extent that it is intellectually awake) side by side with the liberal, progressive part of the bourgeoisie and certain liberal aristocrats, who are all—in their majority—envisioning reforms of one form or other that would *expand their political rights*, usually thought of as possible in the form of a constitutional monarchy, though there are some radicals who embrace republican or even socialist ideals. Among the politically active ones—those who do not simply remain spectators— quite a few are journalists, writers of pamphlets and of petitions that people's assemblies voted on and adopted or rejected. They were speakers in the weeks immediately before the fighting erupted in Berlin. Many will continue in that way. Some were able to cause enthusiasm, Friedrich Wilhelm Held, for, instance. Or Schlöffel, the radical student. The term used for them was "demagogues." They and those close to them saw it as a positive term—taking it to mean educators and motivators of the people, persons who could edge the people on, in a good, rational, morally justified way. This reflected very much the original Greek sense of the word. For those state bureaucrats, censors, cops, aristocratic landowners and army officers, and the conservative ones among the bourgeoisie who used the term in a derogatory way in the 1830s and 40s, they were bad guys, seducers, who tempted the people to revolt. Perhaps, finally, in 1848, many of these speakers and writers supported revolt, or joined it simply, like August Brass, when the fighting broke out. But by and large these men were not men of action; frequently, they were the ones who, during the spring and summer of 1848, warned the masses against rash and thoughtless action that might provoke the reactionary forces to step in and make an end to what had been attained. This is how many of them saw it. They warned, they were cunctatory; they were men of the word, not the deed.

But then there is, in 1848, also the suddenly truly revolutionary bloc formed by a part of the working class (and they are many, in Berlin, it seems, who belong to it), who feel and sense and know that thanks to the revolution, the subaltern classes have attained nothing. Nothing that counts. Nothing that improves their situation. Not even a voice in the Prussian (or the German) National Assembly that reflects in the slightest way their numerical strength and their basic concerns. Perhaps many of these men have only vague political ideals; but they have a clear consciousness of their misery, the permanent threats and sporadic experiences of unemployment, or of hunger, of accidents on the job, of dependence on poor offspring when they are sick or old and unable to work.

Many among them eagerly received the watchwords of the other (petty-bourgeois and bourgeois) liberal bloc: "a constitution"; "freedom"; "the arming of the people" in the days preceding the revolutionary eruption. But these words have a different material significance for them: not that of formal equality under a constitutional monarchy (or even in the way of a bourgeois republic that only very few petty-bourgeois intellectuals dared to dream of)— but *work*, an *end to hunger*, an *end of chicanery and suppression by masters* in their workplace, and *by the authorities*, the police. Equality was a dream and a wish, deep down in them. Material equality, not just equality before the law and equal political rights. Many did not know how it could be achieved, but briefly they were full of hope: they manned the barricades, a majority, side by side with the liberal petty-bourgeois intellectuals, the petty-bourgeois master craftsmen and shopkeepers. Many of the latter two were also members of the Rifleman association (the *Schützengilde*) at the time, if they were wealthy enough to buy the uniform and an expensive rifle: these men were truly modestly well-off "citizens" of Berlin, though not very rich and not important members of the citizenry. The workers stormed gun shops and snatched rifles from soldiers who stood guard in isolated locations of the city.

In contrast to quite a few young and middle-aged educated members of the petty-bourgeoisie, Berlin's bourgeoisie ("the very rich," the "owners" of banks or industrial firms)—a class still liberal in the early 1830s, perhaps even throughout that decade—had already been gripped by fear of change, feeling, sensing the ascent of unruly masses and radical thinkers. Intuitively, this class, in its majority, sided with the King, the reaction. And as the events in Berlin in the course of the year 1848 would show, a large part (and mostly, it appears, the *relatively* wealthy part) of the petty-bourgeoisie followed suit: for it was during the revolution that the masses revealed a new power, and began to voice new threats and new demands, and those who thought that they had to lose something (even if it was only a little) were shocked, and joined the Camphausens and other representatives of the big bourgeoisie, since early April 1848. Clearly such people, such class factions, such a petty-bourgeoisie and bourgeois "middle class" were on their path of surrender to royal authority and the Prussian "Obrigkeitsstaat" (authoritarian state) that was to survive till 1918.

Speculation with regard to a so-called national character is always problematic. Collective socio-cultural traits are never more than the abstraction of what appears to be *the average*. As we know, there exists a huge discrepancy between such *statistical abstractions* as average national income (a concept that prompts politicians in Germany to say nowadays that "Germans have never been that well-off before") and an *empirical reality* that comprises such contradiction as the huge income of the heiress of the Quandt dynastical fortune that amounts to several millions of Euros per day, and the money allotted by "welfare" for the food and drink of millions of children in Germany that is considered to be necessary for their healthy survival by our parliamentary majority in the 21st century: slightly above 2 Euros per day, less than the price of a cup of coffee in many restaurants. A statistical average includes and often hides the reality of the extremes, and of course there are all the intermediate values, as well: in this example, the intermediate "income groups." Statements about an average "national character" can hide a huge diversity of *individual* and of *group specific* traits, too. We may also ask whether *two cultures* still exist and, thus, if there are not divergent if not opposed "national character traits" of, on the one hand, the dominant social class, and on the other, the subaltern social classes.

Probably they do, at least *to the extent that nationalist discourses and the collective inanity of those who sought to be part of a "Volkgemeinschaft"* (the ethnically defined 'people,' as a supposedly homogenous mass) under the Emperor, then in the Weimar Republic, and in the most terrible way under Fascist Nazi rule, *did not succeed to level,* if not blot out (on the surface) *the differences between these two cultures*—in other words, between all of that which, on the one hand, constitutes the "cultural capital" of the bourgeoisie (that largely adopted the tastes and manners of the aristocracy over the last 150 or 200 years while compelling the latter to become more and more "bourgeoisified") and all of that which, on the other, constituted the spontaneous solidarity of workers and the traditional mentality—quite often, of mutual help—alive in village communities and in proletarian neighborhoods of the cities.

Today, we must admit, the village does hardly exist anymore; most often it has become a location of urban people who commute to the city where they work. And the trivialization of "high culture" by the media, after World War II, as well as the fact that the bourgeoisie wholeheartedly embraced Nazism in the not very distant past, must be considered indeed as important factors that broke down apparent class barriers on the surface, in the ideological sphere, in Germany, quite in contrast to what we see in Britain. Germany was "Americanized" in this way: the illusion of equality was reinforced while this society grew more unequal. And yet, whether the classes became more similar in attitude or not—is it acceptable to say that "national" or rather "collective" character traits exist in Germany, at least tendentially? I think that an answer to this question is also relevant with regard to 1848. Why did French revolutions succeed? Why were French petty-bourgeois revolutionaries more daring? Why did the French subaltern classes, especially the urban subaltern classes (the workers, the working women, the "mob," as historians called them) in Paris, Lyon and other cities rise up again and again? Why in 1789, and in those moments when they supported the *levée en masse* against the armies of the reactionary European big powers (Britain, Austria, Prussia, and Czarist Russia) in 1792? Why, during the French revolution of 1830, during the uprising in 1831, and then, during the revolution in February 1848 and the renewed and more radical revolutionary attempt by the French workers, in July 1848? Why nothing of the sort in Germany? Why did Holland achieve a conservative republic in 1588 that survived till 1795? Why did the Swiss manage to establish such a limited, conservative form of republicanism in about 1300 that endured till 1798 when the more modern Napoleonic political state supplanted it briefly?

The truth is probably that early modern times had seen decisive revolutionary attempts and bloody struggles, both in the countryside and in the cities of the "German empire" (a fairly lose construct that had increasingly allowed the development of large, factually autonomous, territorial states: Bavaria, Brandenburg, Wurttemberg, Saxony, and numerous, autonomous, yet smaller, states and "free cities"). The *Fettmilch insurrection* in Frankfurt in 1614 is but one example of the many urban revolts by dissatisfied independent, self-employed artisans, employed journeymen, apprentices, and small shopkeepers against the notables, the patricians—the alliance of urban-based aristocratic families and very rich "merchant houses" (a proto-capitalist mercantile class) that ruled the more important cities. These urban revolts were bloodily suppressed, if need be, by troops dispatched by the emperor. In the countryside, initially quite successful and widespread revolts of the peasantry occurred: these were the most widespread, most clearly mass-supported insurrections of peasants that occurred in all of Europe before the French peasants began to set the chateaus aflame in 1789. The uprising of the peasantry that led to a full-fledged "peasant war" against the aristocratic due-collecting and service-enforcing landowners as well as the tax collectors broke out in 1524 and mobilized several hundred thousand *armed peasants* and their families, in some cases supported by the burghers of smaller cities (at least, by their "small people"). More than 100,000 peasants perished in this war. The revenge taken by the victors was terrible. The memories of this defeat inscribed themselves in the collective memory of the population.

Less than 100 years later, war between the emperor and Catholic territorial princes coming to his aid, and—on the other side—protestant territorial princes and protestant towns, exerted another, even heavier death toll on the German population. Foreign powers (above all France and Sweden) intervened in this Thirty Years War (1618-1648) on the side of protestant governments that fought central authority, pretending to fight mainly for religious self-determination, while seeking, above all, de facto independence. According to some sources, 40 to 50 percent of the German population died. In the Duchy of Wurttemberg, about three fourth of its population perished. The most bloody conflict in European history, it saw acts of barbarism only surpassed by Nazi barbarism in conquered Russian territories and in Nazi death camps. This historical experience—just as the earlier one of the *peasant war*—inscribed itself in the German collective memory for a long time. It contributed to a spirit of arrogance among the victors, the German aristocracy, and to submissiveness among the German subaltern classes[73] that only gave way slowly in the late 18th and first half of the 19th century, when some people—and finally more and more people (but perhaps not enough) were encouraged by the success of the American and French revolutions and began to voice usually carefully phrased expectations and wishes. The requests submitted to the King in Berlin in 1848 and their very language attest to this.

It is in this context of German mentalities of aristocratic arrogance and submissiveness of the people—mentalities that were still alive in the 1830s and 1840s and that apparently affected the petty-bourgeoisie more than the "restless" and often angry proletarian *class base* of the revolution in Berlin in March 1848—that we must put the individual protagonists of the revolution singled out by August Brass[74] in his book and also by other writers describing the revolution: all those men who like Nauwerck (also spelled Nauwerk), Julius Berends, Oppenheim,[75] Jacoby, Jung,[76] Rudolf Löwenstein,[77] August Woeniger,

Löwenberg,[78] Dr. Löwinson[79] etc., appear as leading figures, important voices, democrats, perhaps in some cases even radicals. All of them are more or less well-educated members of the petty-bourgeoisie, like August Brass.[80]

Berlin Democrats, from top left, Löwenberg (a friend of Alexander von Humboldt), Oppenheim, Löwenstein, Brass, Berends, Nauwerck, the socialist Weitling, and Jung.

III.

The days between the King's ride through Berlin on March 21 and March 27, 1848 appear largely like days of indecision. Who was going to act, which side would assert itself and take the next step: the "crowd," in other words, the revolutionaries in Berlin—or the King and those figures and institutions that usually backed him? Was the ministry that had been hastily imposed by the King on March 19 to be taken seriously? Did it take any further steps apart from having asked certain people to organize a citizens' guard as the supposed initiation of something bigger that had been accepted by the king when he ceded, under great pressure, to the popular demand that the people must be armed? Nothing of note became known to the "crowd." If the ministry of Count Arnim was active, it was so in a silent, invisible way. It is not even clear that advisers like Count Arnim or Count Schwerin, the leading ministers of the new cabinet since March 19, had influenced and decisively contributed to the decision of the King when he was wearing the black, red and golden colors of the liberal movement for national unity on March 21 that were also the colors of the March Revolution, of both constitutional monarchists and left-leaning liberal democrats as well as all (socialist and non-socialist) republicans. On the contrary, it is likely that this was Frederick William's impulsive choice, and his distancing from this choice, revealed to Prince William, was also of his own making, unknown to Arnim and Schwerin, in all likelihood.

But still there remains the fact that silently, and perhaps even in uncoordinated fashion, as far as the institutions of Berlin's bourgeois "burghers" were concerned, an "anti-people camp" was forming in these days, between the purportedly "liberal" aristocratic advisers of the king, the new government formed on March 29, the executive body of "burgher self-rule" in Berlin—the "Magistrat"—and Berlin's assembly of city councillors.

A decisive element of the strategy of this "anti-people camp" consisted in the clear determination to deny, as much as possible, any kind of real democratic political representation to the majority of the people although everyone knew that this was what the people expected. The determination underlying this strategy was perhaps hardly clear to "the many" in March, though it had moved a liberal delegation from Breslau on March 21 to intervene in person, warning the king against relying on the United Diet. But when the strategy became more obvious it moved large parts of the crowd to action, and thus widespread voting rights agitation would take place in the months of April and May, including petitions and the attempt to stage a massive demonstration to the palace. This voting rights campaign would of course focus centrally on the overall issue of democratic national elections. The argument was that all people should participate freely and fairly in the election of a Prussian Constituent Assembly (the so-called Prussian National Assembly) that would be focused on the creation of a constitution valid in Prussia, and also in the election of the German Frankfurt-based "parliament."

If the national assemblies were important, the local elections in Berlin also required attention. As we know, the old Prussian "Städteordnung" (Municipal Ordinance) of 1808[81] that was still valid when the revolution broke out denied voting rights to the vast majority of Berlin's inhabitants. Very clearly, house owners were overrepresented in the capital's municipal representative body, the "Stadtverordneten-Versammlung" (Assembly of City Councilors). And as a consequence, the Magistrat, the executive organ that was the decisive authority representing municipal self-government (despite the presence of a royally appointed Governor of Berlin and a chief of police appointed by the Ministry of the Interior), reflected the composition of the assembly of councilmen: only the no. 1 of the Magistrat, the Lord Mayor of Berlin, required confirmation by the King. Of course, it was not insignificant who could elect councilmen: clearly no women, and no minors. But the vast majority of Berlin's inhabitants was also excluded, and so the conservative composition of the assembly of councilors, with its strong presence of representatives of the bloc of house owners, had always been a foregone conclusion. It had caused decreased interest in the municipal election in the past and explained the comparatively low turn-out in previous elections. This disinterest waned and gave way to a keen interest in voting rights after the days of March 18–19.

In these days, immediately after the revolutionary victory of March 19, the extremely conservative Lord Mayor, Krausnick, had been forced to resign after clear expressions of popular anger that took the form of "cat music" (that is to say, unwelcome noise) in front of his home at night, and protesting crowds surrounding his home during the day. He had to go into hiding and other members of the Magistrat as well as city councilors, among them probably his best allies, pressed him to resign.

It remains a rather amazing fact that similar pressure to resign was not exerted by "the street" with regard to the entire Magistrat and the undemocratically elected assembly of city councilors. But perhaps there was such pressure, or at least it was anticipated by members of these undemocratically elected bodies. Adolph Wolff mentions the "step of a general renunciation of their political mandate that had been taken by city councilors in their first zeal"[82] immediately after the days of fighting, but notes that it apparently was not meant to be taken as a serious intention; it had no other significance, he writes, than simply this: that they were ready to stand for election again, but according to the same rules and regulations foreseen by the Staedteordnung, which would mean that nothing would change. In other words, "the present assembly of councilmen was to be replaced by a very similar one, elected according to the old ... electoral law" that excluded so many.[83] This had already been envisioned before the days of fighting, and thus it is clear that in this respect nothing was to be changed if the majority of the city councilors—the overwhelming majority, in fact—could have their way. It had already been on March 15, 1848, that the Kgl. Privilegierte Berlinische Zeitung (i.e., the Vossische Zeitung) had published the following announcement:

Public Announcement

> Towards the end of March of this year, after three years have passed, printed forms destined to prove possession of municipal burgher rights (Bürgerrecht) are to be distributed in order to be filled in, in the houses of that third of the city, whose inhabitants, insofar as they possess local burgher rights and the right to take part in the election of the assembly

of city councilors in 1848, remain invited to take part. Since a precise filling in of the rubrics of these forms, the contents of which are later to be printed and distributed, avoids manifold complications and inquiries, we expect from the common sense of the homeowners concerned or their deputies that they are careful and accurate when filling in the rubrics according to the literal content of the "Bürgerbriefe" ("civil letters": i.e., documents confirming possession of municipal burgher rights), and that they will thereby allow such an acceleration to occur, as is necessary to make the district chiefs' job not unnecessarily arduous.

Berlin, March 1, 1848.
Lord Mayor, Mayor, and Magistrat of the Royal Residence[84]

Krausnick had stepped down. The members of the Magistrat knew that their continuation in office was imperiled, too. And thus, on March 23, these men who, not long ago, had so determinedly opposed all the petitions voted on and adopted by large crowds at the Zelten, had issued a "proclamation of the Magistrat" concerning the burial of the revolutionaries killed on March 18–19.[85] In this way, the executive body of the city of Berlin paid what may have been, at least to some extent, merely "lip service" to the revolutionary fighters, even though it is not possible to exclude a very moderate, yet nonetheless "liberal" satisfaction with the promises of a constitution obtained from the King.

The proclamation described the burial of the dead fighters as a "homage that our entire population paid to those fallen in the glorious battle" and at the same time as a homage to "all heroes who fought for the grand cause of political and social freedom and who have attained it for us by their fearless dedication that did not shun the danger of death."[86] The Magistrat's proclamation that was thus honoring the revolutionaries and acknowledging the revolution on March 23 had added these significant words, however: "To work for this, that, springing from liberty, the greatness, fortune, and welfare of our people may be constructed in the framework of the strictest order, this is and will be the task of all of us."[87] There could be no clearer way by which the main orientation of the Magistrat could have been expressed. A return to "normalcy," and thus law, order and stability, mattered most to these men. Basically, the orientation of the members of the Magistrat coincided with that of the City Councilors' Assembly: things in the city, things in Prussian society, should stay as they had been. To the bourgeois his bourgeois class interests mattered most; he had taken care of them before the revolution: now he saw his—but only his—political participatory rights expanded already by the Constitution that was still to be written. This was good; but otherwise most things should stay as they had been.

But verbally, at least on March 23, the "Magistrat" had not distanced itself from the revolutionaries and the revolution, even though this was what its members had by and large done at the moment of revolutionary struggle and in the days that preceded it. The wind changed in April when the government—

and then, the majority of delegates that would be elected in May to the Prussian National Assembly, but also a good deal of the bourgeois press and quite a few, not necessarily "moderate", burghers of Berlin—came out more openly in favor of a negative appraisal of the revolutionaries. They would distance themselves at least. For them, the struggle of March 18–19 would not be the March Revolution; they would rather refer to it as "that occurrence."

When law and order, thus bourgeois stability, was emphasized so much, the determination of the elected bodies of the Prussian capital—those two institutions that historically represented the so-called municipal autonomy or "self-rule" of Berlin's enfranchised burghers—to resist any further acts that could bring change, cannot surprise. And thus, the undemocratic municipal regulation concerning the election of the assembly of city councillors and the selection of members of the Magistrat (the aldermen and the mayor) is not scrapped in the course of the year 1848 but remains in force. Some 375,000 male and female Berliners (adults and minors, the latter defined as people younger than 25) out of a total of roughly 415,000—remain disenfranchised when the new municipal elections occur in the city in the May, 1848.

Already in March 21 or 22, an aristocrat, the bourgeoisified liberal platoon leader of the civil guard, Baron von Reden, a self-employed statistician by profession, had suggested a change with regard to the city councillors' assembly, as the *Kgl. Privilegirte Berlinische Zeitung* reported on March 23, 1848. His proposal was this: the civil guard should be the sole "law-making organ [or instrument] of the desires of the inhabitants."[88] If the civil guard had indeed been factually open to all Berliners, regardless of their class background, this would have indeed been a radical proposal, even if it was dangerous to endow a militia, a people's army, with legislative functions. As it turned out, the civil guard became the armed instrument of Berlin's bourgeoisie very quickly—that of the Magistrat and also, unnoticeably, that of Count Arnim's cabinet. Later, in April, and during the rest of the year, it would faithfully serve the bourgeois Camphausen government and other cabinets that succeeded it. By and large, at least—for even in this "Burgher Guard," there was a unit that would refuse to be used against the people, as Blesson, its commanding officer at the time, would notice on June 14. (The same thing had happened in the Prussian army in March.) But generally speaking, the Civil Guard was, above all, an armed tool of those now at the helm of the ship of state. And that was, as such, a good reason for regarding the proposal made by the platoon leader von Reden as dangerous. The justification of the proposal that Mr. von Reden offered, is interesting, however. Adolph Wolff paraphrases von Reden's argument in this way:

> After a political revolution, a different yardstick should be set for all things than before. If, in the past, the assembly of city councilors, alone or with the Magistrat, was the legal organ of the wishes of the citizens, and probably also of the inhabitants, they can no longer be regarded as such, "because obviously a part of their members is in contradiction with public

opinion. If the new advisers of the king want to get to know the wishes of the population of Berlin, Mr. von Reden concludes his speech, they should therefore explore these wishes only by relying on the civil guard and their brave allies, the students and the associations of craftsmen.[89]

As Wolff notes, this proposal was not backed by a majority in the very bourgeois civil guard itself, and it was not accepted by the assembly of councilors, the dissolution of which von Reden had practically demanded. This is not surprising. What is more interesting is that the subaltern classes did not press for a dissolution of said assembly and that there wasn't a greater effort to open the civil guard for everyone. With regard to the latter quest, a quest connected with the idea that the people as a whole should be armed against tyranny, the objective impediments, apart from a screening process, were clear; members of the civil guard, though supplied now with rifles by the government, still had to buy their uniform—and more importantly, those who were on duty during a given time, were on duty during their office or business hours. This was a big sacrifice for small shopkeepers and for self-employed craftsmen, whereas state officials joining the civil guard were simply allowed to stay away from work by their bureaucratic superiors. They were even encouraged by the authorities to join the civil guard and to contribute to its dependability. As to workers, they worked 12, 14, some even 16 hours per day, and no employer would give them time off in order to serve in the guard. None of them, or very few, managed to join the Civil Guard. Later—in July 1848 or, if not, at the latest, in August—Gus Hesse found a way to join the constables when this troop was created by the government as another "force of order" and soon reached a strength of 2,000 men. Hesse was criticized on account of the fact that he joined, by the Democratic "Berliner Krakehler,"[90] a satirical journal not unlike today's Parisian left-wing paper, *Le Canard enchaîné*. Did Hesse serve in the constable force merely on Sundays, in view of a likely working-class job?

When the assembly of city councilors had declared its dissolution soon after Krausnick resigned, a step that was immediately regretted, and then regarded as not having occurred at all—but what a wonderful chance it had offered to the masses, to insist that it had, and to elect their own assembly!—a judicial commissarius, Mr. Lewald, immediately critiqued this step as an act characterized by cowardice. According to him, it was essential to stay on and act according to the "new spirit of the time," a spirit expressed by the notion: "We are satisfied with what has been achieved, that is to say, with constitutional monarchy, and so on."[91] Lewald then went on to say:

> The opposing party wants new elections of the deputies [of the United Diet] before the United Diet is convened, and they want an election of the city councilors, but only if prior to this all the *protective clients* [die *Schutzverwandten*; i.e., the disenfranchised inhabitants of Berlin] have been declared [enfranchised] citizens.[92]

This summed up the position of the democrats very nicely, and it shows that they had tried to make themselves heard in March. But the meetings and debates in the assembly of city councilors were at the center of attention of the bourgeois press, and so were statements by the government. Circulation of daily papers like the *Spenersche Zeitung* and the *Kgl. Privilegirte Berliner Zeitung* (aka Voss'sche Zeitung) outstripped the combined number of sold and freely distributed copies of the progressive press by far. It is clear that workers could not afford a subscription; they relied on what they heard during mass meetings, what they read on wall posters, what they talked about among themselves, and what they "politicized" about in the streets. The writers and publishers producing the progressive newspapers and journals addressed progressive members of the petty-bourgeoisie, above all: it was a smaller fold than the camp of Berlin's "moderately liberal" bourgeoisie that was so determined to stall the emancipation of the hard-working, hungry and dissatisfied "mob" that clamored for fair, equal, and factually—not just seemingly—democratic elections.

To a person tied to law books like Lewald, who shared in this respect the opinion of the Camphausen government that would soon be appointed, continuity mattered. As he saw it, the new electoral law could only be changed by the existing powers. But what he concluded nonetheless, is interesting:

> The task of the representatives of the state [the Camphausen government] and the city, therefore, can only be to change the old rotten electoral law in accordance with the needs of constitutional freedom, and this is what we expect and demand from all who have participated in the struggle on the barricades, our representatives.[93]

But let us now return to the course of events, by looking more closely at "national" developments—those that concerned the entire Prussian monarchy as well as the German Confederation—in the wake of the proclamations of the King on March 19 and after his famous "ride on horseback" through the streets of Berlin on March 21, when Frederick William IV was wearing the black, red, and golden colors of the revolution.

In the morning of March 20, the King had granted not only an amnesty for "political crimes" and "crimes" that were known as press offenses ("Pressvergehen")—that is to say, the publication of criminalized content in the press. On March 20, a royal proclamation had also informed the public of what would be read as liberal intentions of the king. It is not clear whether Frederick William acted here on his own accord or was following the advice of men like Count Arnim. His proclamation said,

> [...] I have named the Dr. of Law Bornemann Minister of Justice and called upon the President of the Chamber of Commerce, Camphausen, to aid me as well from now on as a minister.[94]

If Count Arnim had advised the king to ask the well-known Rhenish "moderate liberal" Ludolf Camphausen, a leading Cologne banker and entrepreneur (thus, like Hansemann, a major investor in new railroad lines), *to join the cabinet* headed by him, Nitschke may be correct when he thinks that the Count who had been named prime minister before—and who had been dismissed not very gracefully by the king because of divergent opinions regarding "a constitution"[95]—was in a difficult position politically when Camphausen declined.[96]

Camphausen wrote Count Arnim, on March 25, 1848, that he would not join his government.[97] When the attempt to woe Camphausen failed, Count Arnim attempted to convince David Hansemann, the banker, railway investor and property speculator,[98] who had been a leading conservative-liberal voice in the Provincial Diet of the Rhineland since 1845, to join the cabinet. This attempt failed, too.[99] But Hansemann was interested in being named minister, even though he rejected the proposal of Count Arnim. He arrived in Berlin on March 26.[100]

That Count Arnim had turned to Hansemann was of course due to the fact that the latter was not only a merchant, banker, and investor in railway company stocks—in other words, up to a point a "trustworthy" member of the propertied classes, and as such quite "naturally" a conservative liberal (or as most historians say today, euphemistically, a "moderate" liberal), who had written and in part, published, memoranda directed to the king and government that outlined fairly clearly his views on pressing issues that his class was aware of. Another reason why the Count turned to Hansemann in March 1848 may be connected to the likely fact that the two men got to know each other in person during the 1830s. Hansemann, no native of the Rhineland, had been based in Aachen before opting for a bigger and more important commercial center, Cologne, and it may have been on Hansemann's own turf that the two met during the period of Count Arnim's erstwhile service as a Prussian bureaucrat in the Rhineland; to be exact, in Aachen. The *Deutsche Zeitung* notes, in fact, that Arnim was "well-liked" (beliebt) in Aachen.[101] Actually, Arnim had been in charge of the Aachen administrative district (Regierungsbezirk Aachen) as *Regierungs-Präsident* since March 4, 1834, under von Bodelschwingh as the *Ober-Präsident* [governor] of the Rhine Province.[102] Did Arnim support Hansemann's railroad company in 1836 and his subsequent railway connected property speculation—or did he stay aloof, or even oppose it? This is a touchy question. As Hoffmann notes, Hansemann—just like Camphausen—had a stake at the time in the project of a railway line that would connect Cologne and Antwerp. Hoffmann sees both as vehemently opposed to each other in the late 1830s because the projected route favored by Camphausen would have bypassed Aachen. Challenging Camphausen and his *Rhenish Railroad Co.* (Rheinische Eisenbahn-Gesellschaft), Hansemann founded an Aachen-based railroad company, the *Prussian-Rhenish Railroad Co.*, on March 31, 1836. Both companies merged in May 1837.[103] Of course, with regard to the quarrel about the route of the Cologne-Aachen railway line, it wasn't the Regierungs-Präsident at the time, who could settle the question; this was a matter to be dealt with by von Bodelschwingh and by the government in Berlin. But Arnim could give advice in this regard, and he could have intervened or adopted a laissez-faire attitude with regard to the brash large-scale property speculation that Hansemann was engaged in, as was, in all likelihood, Aachen's mayor and a few others. Did the Count's involvement or non-involvement in the late 1830s help foster a relationship and did it even improve relations; or was the opposite true? Hard to say, but anyway it remains significant that David Hansemann, just like Camphausen, gave Count Arnim the cold shoulder in late March, 1848. Nitschke explains it by writing that the leading business circles of the Rhineland obviously hoped to get rid of the "reactionary" Count Arnim.[104] But why? Because they did not want to be tainted by the bad reputation Count Arnim enjoyed in more democratic liberal circles?

On March 21, a proclamation by Frederick William revealed that the King had come to think of a reshuffled cabinet or at least a redistribution of the "responsibilities" of his ministers quite soon after he named new ministers on March 19. Now he decided that Baron von Arnim would join the cabinet. Nonetheless, Count Arnim was still needed—at least till early April, and thereafter, in other ways—as Prussia's envoy to Vienna, another hotspot at the time: a real hotbed of revolt. Clearly, the King and Count Arnim were focused in these days of March on the question of how to handle the problem of the constitution that Frederick William had been forced to give his "consent" to. Now, Baron von Arnim was to be the new man who would take charge of constitutional matters. And it was obvious to all of these men that the writing of the constitution was not a matter to be truly decided by the "people." The "powers that be" were ready to pull the strings and everything they did already, and were still going to do, was meant to largely determine the outcome of the entire process. And this despite the fact that a Constituent Assembly was to deliberate on Prussia's future constitution. As we will see, the people advising the king came up in this respect with a new "theory," their "theory of agreement." The constitution was to be agreed upon between the Assembly and the king. The idea of a sovereign revolutionary people that would determine a constitution of its own accord was anathema. And the election laws had to be framed in a way that would forestall a majority of delegates who advocated people's power. The proclamation said,

> Today I have appointed the previous envoy *[Baron Heinrich Alexander] v. Arnim*[105] Minister of Foreign Affairs, thus replacing *Count [Adolf Heinrich von] Arnim* who has up to now directed this department provisionally. Due to the necessary connection between general German and Prussian constitutional affairs, the [newly appointed] Minister will also be responsible for overseeing these matters. The Minister Count v. Arnim remains president of the State Ministry [i.e., the cabinet, thus Prussian prime minister] for the time being, without the administration of a special portfolio.[106]

The "previous envoy," Baron Heinrich (i.e. Henry) Alexander von Arnim, had held no insignificant position since 1845, for he had been stationed in Paris as the Prussian ambassador. As Gollwitzer writes, H.A. von Arnim was a "keen observer of conditions that became more and more ripe for revolution ("scharfer Beobachter der einer Revolution zureifenden Verhältnisse"),[107] and thus not blind but at the same time certainly no friend of the revolution. He was an adviser close to the king soon after the ripples caused in Germany by the revolutionary events in Paris prompted him to return to Berlin. Aware of the necessity of preventive steps, and driven by the impulse to make the monarch aware of the necessity to take appropriate preventive steps in order to avoid what for him and his ilk was "the worst," he had recommended certain concessions to the liberal bourgeoisie and the discontent liberals among the landed aristocracy as well as the higher (thus, normally aristocratic) echelons of the state bureaucracy. These suggestions had been outlined in his *memorandum* ("Denkschrift") presented to the king on the day before the outbreak of the revolutionary fighting in Berlin.[108] Here, he had urgently recommended that the king should give in to the repeatedly uttered *liberal request* that the United Diet should be convened.[109] The king followed this advice on March 18, when it was much too late and could no longer produce the desired effect of staving off the revolution. Gollwitzer maintains that Heinrich Alexander von Arnim had also recommended to the king that he should ride through Berlin and embrace the cause of German unity,[110] though it is not clear whether this advice, if it was really uttered, was decisive. The king may have had this in mind, too, or perhaps others also gave such advice. But its propagandistic ideological implications are apparent in so far as it bolstered the reputation of the King immensely that he was not so bad, but mainly ill-advised and misled by the "camarilla." It is remarkable that the former envoy to France, Baron von Arnim, had simultaneously advocated beefing up the military, perhaps also against "revolutionary" France (there were those, like Hansemann, who warned against a repeat of the war waged by the Holy Alliance against the revolutionary France of 1789) but more likely with home affairs in mind.[111] Thus, the former envoy's—and actually also Count H. von Arnim's and the king's—priority was the implementation of a *dual strategy, that of* (1) "*concessions*" and, thus, of a coalition with the "big bourgeoisie" (which, as we will see, entailed the promulgation of a flawed electoral law that would check the political influence of "the people," i.e. the subaltern classes or masses), and that of (2) a very specific way of keeping *the promise to arm the people*: the security situation, in the face of further "mob action" or, in other words, possible democratic and republican attempts to assert people's rights, had to be improved; the creation of the "*Bürgerwehr*" (the civil guard, or armed force of the enfranchised *burghers*) was the first step in this direction, but core attention had to be paid to the royal army; meanwhile the immediate disarming of the revolutionaries was another step that Count Arnim and von Minutoli immediately recognized as necessary, and initiated since March 19–20, 1848. But this, although entailing the decisive *practical* course of action that would be pursued, was not all that mattered, for the strategy pursued had an *ideological* component as well. It was a threefold strategy: the creation—or reinforcement of an existent—image of the "good king" mattered, as Rüdiger Hachtmann also points out. It was a conservative image transported in this way, for it entailed such concepts as *god* (a king by God's grace, endowed with his "divine right"), *fatherland* (i.e., Prussia, not Germany), and *fidelity* (Treue) of subjects, not citizens, to a king installed by God's "providence." It was a policy that would appear as compromising (which it was, up to a point, for the time being), mild, reconciliatory, and, at least tendentially, also surprisingly close to certain bourgeois "liberal" positions, whereas—in reality—the strategy was clearly counter-revolutionary in its basic medium-range and long-range orientation.[112]

This course was sketchily prefigured in the advice given by the former envoy, Baron v. Arnim, and it also underpinned the actions of Count Arnim since March 19. We will see this strategy *as basic*, in the months ahead, as it was actually pursued by the king and those close to him—most obviously throughout the spring and summer of 1848. On the other hand, the previous envoy's advice was springing from a position that *quite a few enlightened aristocrats* embraced.[113] As such it was not identical with the romantically reactionary views harbored deep inside by Frederick William IV, who loathed liberalism and who had always rejected every proposal that Prussia should have a constitution. After Frederick William had named Camphausen prime minister and wrote rather respectful, but often urgently demanding and insisting letters to him, he wrote not much later—in a letter to the envoy to Britain, Josias von Bunsen—these emotional words that reveal how he really thought about his new liberal political partners:

> Liberalism is a disease, just like an inflammation of the spinal cord.[114]

In other words, as he saw it, liberals had no guts, and were perhaps also mentally impaired—but the accent was clearly on guts, in view of the connotation of the German word *Rückgrat*, i.e., backbone. To say, in German, that someone *has no backbone*, implies that this person is someone who will easily cave in, who is not dependable, who does not have guts, and whose character is simply not "manly." All of this was present in Frederick William's utterance about liberalism, and by implication, about liberals. The king's words to Bunsen reveal the entire perspective, or rather, the "lack of a future," that could be ascribed to the king's "emergency alliance" with the Prussian liberal (big) bourgeoisie.

Quite obviously, the advice given by Baron Heinrich von Arnim that recommended, amongst other things, "concessions" throws more light on the liberalism of the "liberal faction of the aristocracy" than on the political preferences of the king who just accepted such advice in these days because they were "all lying on their belly": the king, the queen, and even the "Prince Case Shot," the *Kartätschenprinz*,[115] as he was known among the common people in Berlin, for the news had spread that he had been ready, like general von Prittwitz, to withdraw the troops but expose the capital of Prussia to a terrific artillery bombardment by units outside Berlin.

The position of Baron von Arnim, Count Schwerin, Count Arnim and other such advisers close to the king in the decisive days of March and early April, who all aimed at a flawed electoral law and sufficient presence of forces of law and order in the capital, was often very similar to that of the noted "moderate liberal," Camphausen, this member of Germany's *grande bourgeoisie*, who had played a role in the politics of the Rhine Province, in addition to being a banker and railway investor. Undoubtedly, when Camphausen came to Berlin to accept a political role in the capital, he enjoyed the respect—and in fact, could also be fairly sure of the sympathies—of a good portion, if not the overwhelming majority, of Berlin's well-off "burghers."

Both strata (or class segments) —the "moderately liberal" upper class and upper middle class (if I may use these more conventional terms for the "big" bourgeoisie and those who backed them to a certain extent at the time: the affluent "burghers") and, on the other hand, the progressive part of the old "elite," the "liberal" faction of the aristocracy—opted for political but, by and large, not social reforms. And this because it was a rational *preventive measure* for them to ward off "the worst;" that is to say, real steps leading potentially to an emancipation of the masses. Simultaneously, their alliance in the spring of 1848 reflected the desire of the aristocracy and bourgeoisie to achieve influence denied to them by absolutist power.

There are good reasons to assume that with respect to the future political development of the Prussian state and also with respect to Germany as a whole, the question of elections—and thus also of an electoral law—was squarely on the table several days before the government of Count Arnim—this purportedly "liberal" man with the added reputation of being, deep down, a reactionary—was forced to step down, after only ten days in office.[116]

Perhaps news leaked somehow that the "universal suffrage" demanded by the revolutionary people on March 19 and "consented" to by the king on that day might not mean what it seemed to promise. At any rate, as early as March 21, a group of progressives—a delegation dispatched by the citizens of Breslau—came to Berlin and was received by the king.[117] Breslau,[118] one of the larger cities of the Kingdom of Prussia,[119] was a center of liberal activism, and even a hotbed of democratic ideas. It was also a city where nuclei of organized working-class activity were forming. Breslau was in this respect comparable to other large Prussian cities like Königsberg (today Kaliningrad) and Cologne. On March 23, a document written by them was made known to the public that documented their demand made known to the king and the king's elusive and seemingly positive but, with regard to the key aspect of their demand, firmly negative reply. Apparently the Breslau democrats feared that the king would ask the United Diet to decide the electoral law that would determine the concrete way in which the delegates of the Prussian Constituent Assembly would be elected. Thus they asked him to decide the electoral law by himself, and in a way that would reflect his earlier (yet vague) promise of a genuinely popular constitution and genuine elections. It was quite clear to the delegates from Breslau and to those who had asked them to go to Berlin and make the wishes of the citizens of Breslau known to the king that a *ständisch*, estate-based parliament like the United Diet could not be expected to agree on an election law that would reflect their democratic desires. The fact that the king declined, taking recourse to the subterfuge that he had been asked by so many—but *before* the revolution! and as we know, in vain—to convene the United Diet reveals not only the fact that a seemingly far-reaching promise had been given in bad faith and purposefully in vague form; it also reveals quite clearly that a strategy to impose *indirect* elections had already been decided on by March 21. On March 22, the king made known the same reply that the Breslau delegates would publish, too.[120] It was a reply that culminated in the assertion that he would promulgate "a popular election law" (ein volksthümliches Wahlgesetz), which could mean everything or nothing, and in the explanation that it was necessary to respect of the will of the people, in so far as he had been asked so often to convene the United Diet before the revolution—thus a body that was hardly representative of Prussia's population in all its rank-based way of giving a voice to the country's aristocracy in the upper chamber and to certain commoners, with as many votes for the aristocracy as for the lower chamber. But before the revolution this assembly that could vote on taxes when convened, and that attempted in 1847 to push for some kind of constitution, had been the only institution of the monarchy that could challenge late absolutism, apart from exemplary, courageous liberal judges. In so far, the United Diet had been the straw that democrats—people like the brilliant Johann Jacoby in Königsberg—would cling to before the revolution, when they demanded an end to absolutism and wrote that the diet should be convened. By March 19, this "straw" had become obsolete, and not only obsolete, but something that could not be trusted, in their eyes. It smacked too clearly of class privilege and unequal representation. It represented the past.

The question of how to handle the electoral process was a pressing issue not only for the king. It was an essential issue for the aristocracy and the commercial bourgeoisie of the big cities, too. They all feared "instability" and social change that could negatively affect their privileged position in society. Of course, it would also become an important question for the subaltern classes, in another sense. For the masses, it would decide whether they would remain submissive *subjects* or become *citoyens*. As far as the urban commercial bourgeoisie was concerned, it had waxed rich due to international trading connections and branched out into banking. As we see in the case of Hansemann and Camphausen, it had discovered the profitable possibilities of investment in railways as well—thus in a new traffic infrastructure that was clearly of importance to the state and its economic prosperity, but also to its army. It was a sector that benefitted from carefully and selectively provided state subsidies but that people like the two just mentioned also saw as unduly regulated and thus hemmed in by the Prussian bureaucracy, an administrative apparatus run by members of the aristocracy. Bureaucratic neutrality sometimes had protected private landowners against expropriation of needed terrains by railway companies. At any rate, both camps, the wealthy commercial and banking bourgeoisie (an incipient "grande bourgeoisie" in Germany but too provincial and still too "poor" to compare with that of Paris or even London and New York) and the aristocracy, had a stake in the maintenance and, if possible, improvement of their situation, in a say in public affairs, and in control of the subaltern classes which they feared were becoming too vocal and infected by democratic sentiment. The aristocracy in Prussia is often referred to as the *Junkers* and depicted in some studies as a reactionary feudal class, but even though it played an overwhelmingly reactionary role after the March Revolution, and this throughout the period from 1848 to 1918, and again in the Weimar Republic where it, just like the bourgeoisie, represented the extreme right, aided right-wing and Fascist coup d'état attempts and finally helped to engineer the rise of Hitler to power, it had included carefully "progressive" and "liberal" elements among its ranks, from Stein and Hardenberg, to Count Arnim, the envoy Arnim, Auerswald etc. to Pfuel and Minutoli. All of these "liberals" pursued one main purpose, however: to safeguard the continued existence of the Prussian monarchy and, at the same time, to modernize it. They were intelligent enough to see that certain reforms were necessary, *that something had to change in order to make sure that nothing would change*, and that the basic structure of Prussian society and the Prussian state would be preserved. Of course, they saw *that the balance of power between an old dominant class*, disempowered to a large extent by absolutist kings, but economically important and socially influential in many areas of society (the countryside, the army, the bureaucracy, the court where its men were advisers), *and a newly evolving bourgeoisie was shifting*. But the aristocracy itself had changed, too, and was continuing to change. It was a once feudal "estate" (*Stand*, or rank) that had not shed all vestiges of its feudal past (certainly not, certain rights derived from it) but that had otherwise metamorphosed into a politically partly reactionary, partly "liberal" agrarian capitalist stratum of big, but often cash-squeezed, landowners, with sons and relatives in top and intermediate positions in the army and the administrative state apparatus. Gramsci's analysis of *immobile social strata that cling to the defense of the patrimony, of inherited privileges, and that venerate the purity of their blood-line linking them back to famous and important, in any case, noble ancestors* is not wrong if applied to the bulk of this *Junker* stratum.[121] But if Gramsci's analysis is applied here to the Prussian context of the 1840s (which he hadn't had in mind), it is clear that this does not take account of the *economic dynamics of the times* that unfolded even in the Prussian countryside, where lords of the manor sold wheat on the world market, where former serfs became small rent-paying tenants, small farmers, or mobilized farm workers, often seeking work, even abroad, as in the case of many *Heuerlinge*[122] from Prussia's province of Westphalia who would typically find work during the harvest season in Holland. Proletarization was a fact not only in the cities where more and more independent craftsmen lived in wretched poverty, but also in the countryside. It was the basis of much revolutionary ferment that both the aristocracy and the bourgeoisie were aware of. From the minute of revolutionary triumph of insurgent Berliners in the Prussian capital, and since they had heard Frederick William's promise of "popular election" that he made on March 19, though only coerced and fearing death, both major "classes" in Prussia—the old dominant stratum or "class" of the *Junker* aristocracy and the *grande bourgeoisie* as the most important class faction of a bourgeoisie that is often called a rising class (whereas its "middle class" section appears as stagnant and under great economic pressure, and its poor section, the *Kleinbürgertum* of independent craftsmen [with just one or no employee] and of small shopkeepers, as often threatened by decline)—knew they had something to lose.[123] Popular elections could become a way of redistributing the cards of the game. If they did not fear it, they at least saw the risk.[124] They—like the king, as it turned out—wanted to determine *how the cards were dealt*, and they wanted to reign in and control the measure of change permitted, and the way things would change if change was to occur.

On March 21, the delegation of concerned democrats from Breslau had seen the king in Berlin and demanded that he should not convene the United Diet for the purpose of debating and expressing its opinion, or actually passing, the anticipated electoral law, but should decide it himself, according to the spirit of democratic change that he had seemed to embody, all of a sudden, on March 19. But as we know, the king had decided during the night of March 17–18 that that United Diet should be convened on April 2, 1848. Despite the complete change of the situation brought about by the armed revolution and the defeat of the army, the king stuck to this and warded off all requests to change his agenda and course of action. Was it because the prime minister in office since March 19, Count Arnim, advised him to do so? At any rate, this much is clear: the king would convene the United Diet on April 2.[125] And, indeed, the United Diet would deliberate on two laws that were drafted covertly in the meantime by the Arnim government. They would deal with the foreseen elections. This upset the people of Berlin and many others in Prussia. Bergengrün comments that although the request of the population had previously been directed towards the "early convening of the United Diet, this request was now overtaken by events. Almost the entirety of the press that was now free of its shackles suddenly declared the United Diet antiquated on account of its outmoded rank-based (*ständisch*) foundations."[126]

In the meantime, attention had to be paid to the other pillar of the new strategy: the question of the promised arming of the people. We saw that Berlin's "civil guard" had been formed quickly on March 19–20 by Count Arnim with the help of Nobiling and others, relying mainly on the thoroughly bourgeois Rifleman Association as the core of this force. On March 25, Minutoli's "Provisional Rules" (or "Provisional Orders") concerning the selection of leaders of the "civil guard" were published. Hachtmann notes that the majority of the captains were "Fabrikanten," that is to say, employers, bosses in charge of small or larger Berlin-based manufacturing firms. The strategy of creating this bourgeois force as a force of law and order but also—for the bourgeoisie—as an embodiment of its political aspirations was flanked by a straightforward measure: orders were issued immediately after the revolutionary struggle in Berlin that all armed fighters had to hand in their weapons. To comply with this, in view of punishments threatened in case of contravention, was one of the big mistakes that many revolutionaries committed. Too many trusted promises that a new democratic beginning would occur.

Were the "people" active in this period? Yes, political clubs were founded: democratic ones, by progressives from the petty-bourgeoisie, speaking above all to workers; by "moderates," who were mainly bourgeois and petty-bourgeois constitutional monarchists; and by determined conservatives who admired the ancient regime that had just suffered such a heavy blow on March 18–19.

Among those educated democratic radicals mentioned in the book written by August Brass, an interesting person has already been mentioned further above. This was Gustav Julius, the publisher of Berlin's democratic journal Berliner Zeitungs-Halle (BZH) who was also the owner of the reading cabinet of the same name, the Berlin Newspaper Hall. Julius, and two other democrats who had been speakers at the Zelten during popular mass meetings —Carl Nauwerk and Julius Berends—were portrayed not only by August Brass but also by Adolph Wolff and others as courageous, outstanding progressives. It seems that Nauwerk and Berends were the only truly progressive councilmen elected to Berlin's assembly of city councilors. Gustav Julius comes across as a reformist much of the time, even though he embraced socialist ideals, obviously without revealing them clearly. His thinking was close to that of Karl Grün, initially, who had published, in 1845, the book *Die soziale Bewegung in Frankreich und Belgien. Briefe und Studien* [The Social Movement in France and Belgium. Letters and Studies].

In these decisive days when the course was set that would determine the fate of the revolution (to be precise, on March 27, 1848), the king named Ludolf Camphausen Prime Minister without asking the revolutionary people for permission, thus forming a calculated pact with the *grande bourgeoisie* of Prussia.[127] On the same day, March 27, an undated poster appeared in the streets of Berlin. The poster asked for a return of the military to Berlin![128] Three days later, on March 30, the *Voss'sche Zeitung* (Voss' Daily),[129] officially known as the *Kgl. Privilegirte Berlinische Zeitung* (the main paper of Berlin's more and more conservative "moderately liberal" bourgeoisie that was supporting constitutional monarchy and soon also indirect elections so wholeheartedly), reported that a Mr. Berends was among the undersigned, next to Mr. Urban and Mr. Eckert, who were also named on the poster. It is not unlikely that the Arnim government that was still in office until March 29, although Camphausen had already been picked as successor, had a hand in this. At any rate, the poster was put up by the authorities, or with their aid. The carefully calculated posting of this "citizens request" calling back army troops to Berlin is significant. In view of the fact that the next government in Berlin would not be headed by an aristocrat, but by a bourgeois prime minister, it may have seemed important to the King and his present advisers that a counterweight to the "bourgeois force of order"—the obvious instrument of the newly appointed Camphausen government, for the time being—would exist in Berlin. The impending change of cabinet clearly established an awkward alliance.[130] It was *reflecting a class compromise* that was *not based on trust*, as far as the king and people like Count Arnim, Baron Arnim, Count Schwerin and others are concerned. We do not have to speak here of people like Gerlach[131] and Radowitz[132] who did not even trust a supposedly liberal minister like Count Arnim.

It is not clear whether the person named on the poster calling for the return of the army, Mr. Berends, "cotton printer and cigar maker" by profession, was the progressive city councilor. In all likelihood it was a namesake, and it may be that this coincidence was used by the Voss'sche Zeitung in order to cause confusion and discredit the progressive councilman in the eyes of his partisans. This is even very likely. But it is also possible that Julius Berends was by profession a cotton printer and also a cigar maker, and that he signed the request for the return of the army. It is also possible that his name was added without his permission.

The book that republished this poster was published in 1849. Entitled "Persons and Conditions in Berlin since March 18, 1848: A Contribution to the Future History of Prussia" and published anonymously by Keil Publishers in Leipzig, the anonymous author (possibly a Mr. Petersen) squarely denounced "Urban and his buddies" (Urban und Consorten), and this above all in view of their naïve but dangerous proposal to call back the military that had just been forced by the revolutionaries to leave Berlin. Mr. Urban and his supporters apparently believed that their proposal would help to achieve a *rapprochement* between the revolutionaries or, in another sense, "the people," and a king whom they saw as well-meaning but misguided.

On April 1st, 1848, a statement by Dr. Woeniger, a liberal activist cherished by Brass, appeared in *Voss' Daily* [Vossische Zeitung] that it was he who was the actual author of the text; he phrased it after a conversation with Urban.

Whether Julius Berends was involved at all in the call to the authorities that the army should return is not clear, for he was a sober, clear-minded democratic. He is among those who had just signed a public statement that contained progressive demands. The petition, co-signed by Bisky,[133] Reuchardt, Meyer, Ries and Brill, appeared on posters making the demands known to the inhabitants of the capital on March 27th.[134]

This petition of March 27, directed by Bisky et al. to the King but in fact also to the government and to the people of Berlin, was still formally phrased in nauseatingly devote fashion, just like all the other petitions adopted in the context of (mainly open-air) *people's assemblies* in March (as if no armed, victorious revolution had occurred!). But it embraced a progressive, typically democratic agenda. It asked for (1) a Dept. of Labor. Other documents show that this demand entailed a department comprising, in a balanced way, both workers and employers, and elected by both; it was to be an organ that could mediate in labor conflicts, draft bills concerning labor relations that would curtail the power of employers and that could abolish repressive, clearly outdated decrees and regulations like the prohibition of so-called "coalitions" of workers (i.e., of trade unions), the prohibition of individual forms of "work refusal," and of all forms of collective action, thus strikes; and of course it was to abolish or rewrite the ominous "Gesindeordnung" ("Regulation of underlings," concerning the duties of servants and of journeymen and apprentices receiving accommodation in the house of their master, stipulating also the penalties, including prison terms, for being late, for talking back, for shoddy work, etc.).[135] Then it continued by focusing on the very important issue of the promised arming of the people by demanding (2) the reduction of the armed forces which should give way to a *Volksheer* (people's army). It then added the demand of (3) general, cost-free education of the people; of (4) a pension system for workers permanently injured by work accidents; and of (5) a fair government that avoids extravagant cost. It finally expressed the clear necessity of (6) an election law that grants the right to vote and the right to be elected to all male adults; and—most importantly—requested (7) the annulment of the decree that foresaw the convocation of the United Provincial Diet and simultaneously the immediate convocation of an assembly that would be freely elected by all.[136] Clearly the last two points, (6) and (7), reflected concerns that the elections might not be as democratic as expected, and they also revealed the fact that the democrats did not trust the undemocratically composed United Diet.

March 27, 1848 was thus a day when the cards of the political poker game were decisively remixed. The camp that was concerned about the survival of the dynasty, the further existence of the monarchy, so-called "law and order," and the stability of a social order, had been slyly on the offensive, taking steps that prefigured much of the future institutionalized political process. They had prepared drafts for elections that would not be as democratic as promised, and they had also taken steps to further a formal process that was meant to lead to a constitution which was anti-people and thus a "factor of stability." As people would see very soon, the principles that the king wanted to be enshrined in the constitution were sketched in his "Proposition Edict" that was made known to the United Diet on April 2, thus on the same day when the bills concerning the electoral law governing the elections of the Berlin-based Constituent Assembly (also known as the Prussian National Assembly) and the Frankfurt-based German Assembly were also introduced. The final coup had been the step that lead to the return of army units and the naming of Camphausen on March 27. By comparison, the democratic demands adopted during an open-air people's assembly and published by Berends, Bisky and others on March 27 were relatively tame and the tone was much too submissive. The democratic camp's voice wasn't more courageous and certainly not more determined than in the days immediately before the revolution although the "requests" were now more far-reaching. They were attacking, by forming demands, but the attack was weak and its mobilizing effect unclear. With bloody days behind them, and new forces of order in the city (the Civil Guard, and now also army units), the subaltern classes clearly shrank back from anything that could entail the risk of another bloody battle and accepted instead the things that occurred, especially insofar as they were told that they had nothing to fear from these troops: it was the same regiment that had refused to fire on the insurgent people in Magdeburg when commanded to do so, about a week earlier. In so far, the democrats and, with them, the people, the subaltern classes, the vast majority in Berlin, were on the defensive: an incomplete revolution was left to speakers, and the masses became listeners. Symbolic acts soon replaced real action. The democrats were, more and more, on the defensive—despite a few sudden outbreaks, short upturns, signs of returning energy and determination. One thing should have been clear to them, however: an *unfinished revolution* remains imperiled. A period of dual power or of other forms that reveal the undecidedness of the relation of forces must give way, sooner or later, to a different situation where it becomes clear who is in charge: the new social forces or the old "powers that be." This should also have been reflected on: those who fight—in whatever peaceful, or if necessary, armed way—can lose. But those who don't fight against the "powers that be" have already lost.

At any rate, it would become apparent during the next few month that with a few determined steps, which among those already mentioned included the very significant royal decision to name Camphausen prime minister on March 27, the decision to impose indirect elections (which had effects on the composition of the National Assembly), and the creation of a significant "force of order" based in Prussia's recently insurgent capital, the course of events—and perhaps the *rapport des forces*—in Berlin and therefore, indirectly, in Prussia was greatly changed for the moment.

On March 29 the "liberal" Rhinelander Camphausen[137] took office. He was the first bourgeois Prime Minister or head of government ever appointed in Prussia. When the king had decided, on March 27, officially, and unofficially perhaps much earlier, to replace Count Arnim, the fact that he sought an alliance with the big bourgeoisie, a clear proponent of "law," "order," and political exclusion of the masses, was undeniably established. Arnim, we must remember, had been hastily picked by the king as chief minister on March 19, and this mainly because Frederick William was so anxious to get rid of the government headed by Ludwig Gustav von Thile[138] that had been in charge during the days of armed attacks on the people. Now, Count Arnim was no longer needed. By dropping this "liberal-conservative," who was, in the eyes of many, a *reactionary* aristocrat with whom he had already had disagreed in 1845, and by choosing a well-known leader of the pre-revolutionary "liberal" Rhenish big bourgeoisie, Ludolf Camphausen, Frederick William IV opted for a strategy that could realistically underpin the hope of his own survival as monarch. The sacked chief minister, Count Arnim, saw that, too. And he probably worked in the same direction as Frederick William in those days, which would mean that both were recognizing the alliance with the *grande bourgeoisie* of the Rhineland as a necessity at this moment. These people knew that the so-called Liberal leaders in the Rhineland and in the first United Diet of 1847 had opposed the king's absolutism in the past; but they were also aware of *the class interest* that let men like Camphausen, Hansemann, Benecke, Mevissen etc. favor *a strong state*, a strong government, law and order, and *exclusion of the subaltern classes* from political power. It was very clear that such "moderate Liberals" preferred a monarchy (albeit a constitutional one) to a republic, a dream of some among the proletarian masses. In other words, it is possible and even necessary to say that the king, who was obviously aware of radical democratic tendencies in Berlin, acted very consciously in the interest of the preservation of his power, and this by building a new alliance that entailed a compromise that he had to accept for the time being. The conservative political "battalions" of the "old powers" in Prussia were too weak at that moment. The monarchy needed the support of the bourgeoisie, and if possible, of the more conservative elements among a wavering petty bourgeoisie (or "middle class"). In terms of Realpolitik, this was indeed a determined and clever move with immediate implications.

Quite soon after the change of government that made the bourgeois "liberal" Rhenish banker Ludolf Camphausen prime minister something else that was of significance occurred: the king left Berlin and went to his palace in Potsdam with his wife. As Frederick William's brother, William, the Prince of Prussia, had already fled to England immediately after the armed struggle in Berlin, because he was well aware of the negative feelings that most Berliners had towards him due to his openly reactionary stance, there was now no one of the royal family in the capital who might be exposed to forceful pressure by the masses knocking on the palace doors. The liberal *Unsere Zeit* (Our Time), supportive of Camphausen and Hansemann, commented on Frederick William's departure:

> Although in the stormy days of March he had continually expressed his satisfaction with what had happened and with the noble attitude of the metropolitan population, he breathed more freely when he had escaped happily from the intrusiveness and the onslaught of the parties without arousing suspicion.[139]

As far as the bloc of revolutionaries in Berlin is concerned, it was divided in terms of material interests and political goals. Its leaders went on drawing up petitions in ways not really different from what they had done before the bloody urban fighting in March. It did not help that the petty-bourgeois democrats lacked unity of vision. It did not help that some petty-bourgeois "leaders" or "spokesmen of the people" disregarded the working class while signing petitions or putting up posters of—all too often—irritating content. And it did not help that the enfranchised, mostly well-off (and in part, also not so well-off) "citizens" or "burghers" of Berlin—people who had also welcomed the promises made on March 19 and thus, gains that not all of them had actually fought for during the time of bloody fighting—expressed support for Camphausen, Hansemann, and indirect elections, desirous as they were of a constitution and enlarged political rights for their own good. But when it would have been necessary to support democratic calls to broaden democratic rights, they often stayed aloof or they actually opposed such attempts. As it turned out later, when the counterrevolution had waxed strong, they did not even dare to factually preserve at least all those gains and so-called "concessions" that had been made under pressure on March 19 by the king and that many thought of, at the time, as something they had already securely obtained. It was obvious that many if not most "middle class" citizens in Berlin (described as "moderates" nowadays) opposed all further action, seeking reconciliation with the king, not unlike the Rhenish commercial and financial "big bourgeoisie" and their textile industrial cousins.[140]

The fact that Camphausen had been chosen by the king gave a lot of apparent influence to their class, one might think. Frederic Engels even wrote in July 1848 that the bourgeoisie was in power in Prussia.[141] It may be necessary to contest that assumption. Camphausen and his ministers hadn't been installed by the people, of its own accord: they had been appointed by the king and received orders from him. He could sack them at any moment, in theory, even though this was not opportune at the moment. Later, the king would do it. For the moment, the king placed hopes in this Rhenish banker and entrepreneur. Entrusting them with building a new and hopefully stable institutional framework for the Prussian monarchy and "ship of state" was indeed a clever decision. Camphausen saw to it that David Hansemann,[142] another member of the Rhenanian financial bourgeoisie and on top of that a man with an industrial *portefeuille (d'actions)* and speculative interests in the quickly expanding railroad sector and in new, railway connected town expansions,[143] was named Minister of Finance by the king. The liberalism of both men was a very limited one; it was purely concerned with furthering their own economic interests and the interests of their class, the *bourgeoisie*. If we want to understand their "liberalism," we may compare them with Jacques Lafitte,[144] the banker, property speculator, and minister who served the French bourgeoisie and his own interests so well in the 1830s. Or we may be reminded—in an American context—of someone like Alexander Hamilton, an upstart who founded a bank in New York City in 1784 and who played a conservative role in the context of the so-called Compromise of 1790 (reached with Jefferson).[145] It is clear that members of Prussia's high aristocracy regarded Camphausen and Hansemann less positively than the king who needed them at that moment; they were commoners, but worse yet, they coveted—and obtained briefly—political influence at their expense.

We have seen that since March 29, not only Camphausen but also another "Rhinelander," Hansemann, was effectively at the helm of the royally appointed Prussian government. And thus, two wealthy members of the Rhenish grande bourgeoisie faced the responsibility to steer the ship of state on a course that would not break their alliance with the king. From the point of view of the revolutionaries, this amounted to treason, a betrayal of the subaltern classes—the real force behind the revolution of March 18–19. But Camphausen, like his political friend, an old business adversary in bygone days, and occasional partner, the newly appointed Minister of Finance and de facto No. 2 in the new government, David Hansemann, had never cared for the subaltern classes. Hansemann had been shocked by the Aachen "bread revolt" of August 30, 1830, and both must have been terrified by the revolt of the workers of the decentralized van der Leyen silk manufactory[146] in Krefeld on November 4, 1828 that was suppressed by a regiment of the Prussian army and that Marx referred to as "the first workers' insurrection in German history." Awareness of these events determined the political horizon of many leading figures among the Rhenish "moderately liberal" bourgeoisie.[147] It is necessary to savor and digest the epithet, "moderate," that was and still is customarily applied to both Hansemann and Camphausen, because they were advocates of enhanced bourgeois political rights, and thus the rights of their class that has always been a minority in every society throughout modern history; that is to say, under the dominant conditions of very real capitalism. These men were not only contemptuous but also fearful of the "lower classes," and this for quite some time, perhaps since 1826 and 1830 when workers revolted in the Rhineland, or since 1831 when news arrived of the insurrection in Lyon. In his Memorandum of 1830 that he sent to the king and that was printed and published in 1845, Hansemann had already been quite outspoken in this respect: "To believe that the transformation of the political conditions of Europe is without influence on Prussia's power, as conditioned by internal relations and relations with other countries, could be a dangerous way of indulging in illusions," he maintained at the time. He added ominously, "The first and foremost danger is an uprising of the lower classes. Unmistakably, these are now often seized by a spirit of excitement against legal order [...]."[148] The February revolution acerbated such feelings—for it had been the "rabble" or "mob" despised by them, the working class of Paris, that had proved to be at the forefront of republican revolution and that was thus visible as the main pillar of all those democratic political and social forces which overthrew the "moderately liberal" constitutional regime of King Louis Philippe in France. Like Camphausen, David Hansemann was shocked by the French February Revolution.[149] In hindsight, Hansemann wrote two years later: "The poet Lamartine, the naturalist Arago, the socialist Louis Blanc, along with several other dreamers [Schwärmer] and fantasists, seized the reins of a great state in which freedom, order and prosperity had developed in the last 18 years as never before."[150] It was an expression of his awareness of the business opportunities that the July Monarchy in France had offered to the

French bourgeoisie, thus an expression of his bourgeois sense of "realism," and likewise, the most blatant condemnation he could think of. On February 27, 1848, faced with the sudden overthrow of a political system he admired and would have loved to see established in Germany, he commented "that a large part of the propertied classes will not draw the conclusion from the events in Paris that one must give in [*sc.* to popular demands for democratic and socio-economic rights, to pressure from below], and this in time. But they will rather deliver themselves to Absolutism."[151] He was not quite ready to do so, as he clearly desired co-participation of his class, the "big bourgeoisie"; he wanted it to have a voice and real influence in politico-economic matters. But he thought that the subaltern classes—the masses, or as they said in France, *la peuple*, the people (*das Volk*, or *das einfache Volk*)—were not ready to have a voice in the "chamber," "assembly," or parliament he desired: "[...] Aristocracy taken in this sense, that the wealthier and more privileged of the state should have the most influence, is quite my system," Hansemann stated [in 1848], thus rejecting the "exaggerated democratic ideas" which he saw expressed especially by the [petty-bourgeois] representatives of liberalism in the smaller German states, as Boch notes correctly.[152] Clearly, people like Hansemann loathed the power of the Prussian bureaucracy;[153] it was the core element of his dissatisfaction with absolutist rule and his view that it had become untenable; it had already been a hindrance at times when he had pursued his railway projects. When he argued in his *Memorandum*, however, that "Prussia's genuine interest" required not only "the implementation of the ideas of constitutional freedom" but also "the unity of the Germans,"[154] this was hardly pure and simple nationalism. In fact, what he desired was one national market without internal customs barriers.

Count A.H. Arnim von Boitzenburg

G. L. Camphausen, banquier—Chief minister, March 19-29, 1848, in office 3/29 - 6/20, 1848; and David Hansemann.

The second important occurrence that graced this 29th of March appears to be indicative of something ostentatiously even more ominous, for the new governor of Berlin, the "liberal" General von Ditfurth and the "liberal" chief of police, von Minutoli, announced the actual return of Prussian troops to the capital. Their poster that made this fact public was formulated in a conciliatory tone and it downplayed the significance of this event by referring to it as *the impending act of a minor military redeployment*. But who can ignore that this "act of a minor redeployment" would be merely the first of various minor "redeployments" that increased the presence of troops in Berlin, no doubt as factors of order that governments like the Camphausen government could rely on, in addition to the civil guard, and that these occurrences would in turn—as would become clear in the winter of 1848—serve to prepare, if not even to *legitimize* to some extent, the return of a very *large* military force later on? That is to say that, objectively, this casually announced act of a "minor redeployment" was not only going to change the real situation in Berlin immediately, in so far as these troops buttressed the role of the "citizen guard" or "civil guard" as a "factor of order"; it can—and must—also be seen as a prelude to the reactionary military *Realpolitik* synonymous with the counter-revolutionary *putsch* of the king in November 1848, a coup d'état that entailed the dissolution of the elected Prussian National Assembly.[155] The announcement published on March 29 *referred explicitly* to the "wish" uttered on March 27 that the troops should return, thus pretending to be undertaken in conformity with the desire of the people to see troops as a factor of order in the capital that would relieve volunteers especially from the duty to guard the palace, the armories, and other public buildings. The poster displayed in Berlin's streets said,

> After the wish that troops should again be deployed in Berlin has been uttered from many sides, the King has permitted that the 4th Line Infantry Regiment, 2 batallions of the 9th infantry (sc. regiment), the 3rd

ulan regiment and the training squadron shall enter here on the 30th of this month and in the following days, in order to patrol the city together with the citizen guard (Buergerwehr) and to thus alleviate the burden of the duties fulfilled by the citizens with the most glorious dedication. It is self-evident that the preservation of public order is left exclusively to the citizen guard and that possible aid will be given by the military only in an extreme emergency and this only after having been asked to do so by the urban and civil authorities.

Berlin, March 29th, 1848.
Dittfurth. Minutoli.[156]

Thus the troops, though only a small avantgarde, had returned. The promise that the "arming of the people"—demanded by the revolutionaries—would put "the guns" into the hands of the people, was already worthless by now.[157] But it was the "liberal" government, the "cabinet" led by Camphausen, that now perverted, with grave and very negative consequences, the other Royal concession forced upon the king by the revolution: the promise of "general suffrage." And this certainly out of fear that democracy and thus increased political influence of the "mob" (for this was their term for the radical parts of the petty-bourgeoisie and for the suddenly awakening working class that had been encouraged by news from Paris and Vienna and "revolutionized," to use a word chosen by Engels, during the days of conflict with the army, thus on March 16–19) could harm the very interests of their class—Camphausen's class, the bourgeoisie!—but also because people like Camphausen probably sensed that this abortion of democracy reflected the wishes of a King who had merely felt *coerced* to grant that much; in this, the desires of the bourgeoisie, the King, and the "old powers" of Prussia coincided.[158]

On April 2, 1848, the monarchy's United Diet was convened by Camphausen. The date had been decided during the night of March 17–18 and made public the next morning, immediately before the outbreak of the revolution. That it should indeed meet in session, and that the date, April 2, should stand, was reaffirmed by the king on March 21 and this reflected also Count Arnim's position. That the decision—taken in the early hours of March 18—had become as obsolete, with the revolution, as the United Diet itself, which was to dissolve itself forever on April 10, was as purposefully ignored by Camphausen as it had already been ignored by the government headed by Count Arnim that was in office only for ten days. Decisive days, one must say.

The delegates met in the White Hall, the Salle blanche or *Weißer Saal* of the king's Berlin palace. This in itself was a scandal, for the palace had not been appropriated by a provisional government or the revolutionary people. It was the king's symbolic terrain. Later, when the National Assembly would meet in session for the first time, its newly elected members would also meet in the White Hall and only a few delegates, thus Julius Berends, would protest and stay away, well aware of the significance that must be attributed to the decision of the majority. It amounted to an act of surrendering the people's sovereignty that had been asserted in the revolution, as it is, on principle, asserted in every popular revolution that sets the people squarely against the powers that be. But if Berends understood this, did Camphausen, too? Obviously, yes, for he negated this sovereignty on April 2, addressing the United Diet with the words, "Esteemed Assembly! The King has commanded me to preside over the State Opening of the Second United Diet in His most highly esteemed name."[159] There was no better way than this to confirm royal sovereignty than by accepting in this way the *role of the subject* that obeys a *command*. Camphausen in this way accepted the role of a junior partner, of an accomplice. He had opted for an alliance, and it was an alliance against the sovereignty of the people. His opening speech is reproduced in full by Streckfuß in his book on the revolution.[160] Here Camphausen outlined the main tasks of his government. It was to (1) "newly strengthen the power of the State" (die Staatsgewalt neu zu kräftigen), to (2) "reinforce legal order," thus the old, prerevolutionary legal frame of reference (die Bande der gesetzlichen Ordnung zu festigen), to (3) "rekindle confidence" of business in the crisis-shaken economy (das Vertrauen zu beleben), to (4) "alleviate the credit crunch" (den geschwächten Kredit zu heben), and to work in the direction of (5) "economic recovery and rewarding [i.e. gainful] employment" (auf den Wiederaufschwung der Gewerbe und lohnende Arbeit [sic] hinzuwirken).[161] This was at once a *law and order program* and *an economic program* that reflected, above all, the concerns of the bourgeoisie even though it revealed an awareness of the scourge of fairly widespread unemployment and underemployment. There followed, in his address, a few general words regarding external peace (Frieden nach Außen) and internal peace (Frieden nach Innen), the latter an antirevolutionary program that would be put in action already in the second half of April when Prussian troops, formally under the command of the Camphausen government and beefed up by the 15 million Prussian dollars that Camphausen had asked the United Diet to allocate to the army, bloodily quelled the republican insurgency in the Southwest German grand-duchy of Baden, far away from Prussian soil. The Grand Duke of Baden, faced with a wave of three such armed uprisings in 1848–49, fled on one occasion to the Prussian Rhineland, but already by mid and late April 1848, Prussia, and with it the Camphausen government, was the mainstay of the reaction in Germany, as the intervention in Baden unmistakably revealed. That this government was nonetheless regarded by a "liberal" bourgeoisie in Berlin and Prussia as liberal says a lot about the liberalism of this law-and-order oriented class, whose main concern was the protection of property and the *hoped for* economic recovery.

The important bills that were submitted by the new Camphausen government and voted on by the undemocratic and prerevolutionary United Diet between April 2 and April 10 were these: first, the draft of the "Prussian election law" (*Preussisches Wahlgesetz*)[162] that would spell out the method and rules concerning the election of the future "Prussian National Assembly"—a constituent assembly that was to be formed in order to produce, after thorough debates, a draft of the Prussian constitution. This bill was changed in one important respect by the United Diet. The law, as passed by the Diet (and then promulgated by the king on April 8), no longer included an important section of § 1 of the government's draft that denied the right to vote to a considerable portion of Prussia's working people, in fact to all so-called "dependents"—that is to say, to all servants, apprentices, and journeymen who received accommodation "under the roof" of the same house where the master and his family dwelt. Living in the house of the master had been standard practice for a long time.[163] It entailed paternalistic social relations that could be very repressive and demeaning but that could also provide a certain measure of economic protection.[164] That this provision was voided was a measure that certainly reduced the likelihood of strong popular protests against the new law. The law as passed kept, however, two other restrictive sections of § 1. It confirmed the provision included in the Camphausen government's bill that denied the right to vote to those below age 24 in all of Prussia except in the Rhine Province, where the legal age for all vital matters was 21.[165] This amounted to unequal treatment of Prussia's male adults—women were anyway excluded—because the Rhineland received better representation. By excluding young adults age 21–23 in most areas of Prussia, the provision also revealed a class bias, in so far as many of those barred from voting were probably heads of young working-class households and had a lot of experience in life, especially when they had been working already as children below the age of 10. And in view of the larger number of children of proletarian families, thus a greater proportional share in the 21–23 bracket, and also the shorter life expectancy of the poor, the subaltern classes were proportionally losing a greater number of potential voters than other classes. The law finally confirmed another restrictive provision contained in § 1 of the Camphausen government's bill that also revealed a class bias, for it denied the right to vote to all those on public assistance due to extreme poverty (which Prussia's urban poor might receive when it was caused either by involuntary unemployment or by incapacitating illness). The United Diet also kept the important, very questionable clause favored by Count Arnim and by Camphausen as well as Hansemann that foresaw indirect elections, and this clearly with a purpose in mind. As Schilfert notes, the government's draft, and then also the law as actually passed, both aimed "to prevent the preponderance of the 'laboring classes' in the future 'Prussian assembly about to be established for the purpose of an agreement on the constitution' [...]."[166] The "agreement" referred to by Camphausen, Count Arnim, and others again and again when the future Constituent Assembly (the National Assembly in Berlin that voters were to elect) was mentioned was to be an agreement that the assembly was bound to reach with the king when a majority of the delegates in the assembly would have come up with a draft of Prussia's supposedly democratic constitution—a constitution "on the broadest base" (auf breitester Grundlage), as the king had said and as others were not ceasing to repeat. The term sounded harmless—it smacked of cooperation, not confrontation—but the provision limited the powers that the Constituent Assembly had when devising a constitution. Whatever they came up with had to be acceptable to the king in order to enter the final text of the constitution; if this final draft was not accepted by the king, a new draft was required. And in order to limit the presence of radical democratic representatives of the subaltern classes who might tend to write "unacceptable" provisions into the constitution (or press for laws repugnant to the king or the Camphausen government), the election law had its own limitations, quite in line with what was in all likelihood Count Arnim's royalist "theory of agreement." The government was probably surprised that the *ständisch* (rank-based) and therefore undemocratically formed United Diet mellowed the government draft of the Prussian election law, rather than passing it unchanged. But whether the draft was amended or not, the delegates of the Diet had at any rate been ready to provide a questionable seal of "democratic approval" which no such staged presentation of a fake democratic process could produce in the eyes of Berlin's and Prussia's progressives.

Hachtmann mentions the fact that the prime minister, Camphausen, who swallowed the changes regarding § 1 of the election bill, was not ready to accept any further revisions, particularly with regard to the question whether there should be direct or indirect elections. His words in this respect were clear, revealing the basic concerns of this bourgeois "liberal": he said that he was compelled to point out that "an assembly originating thanks to direct elections would lead to a republic, and that the survival of the present Government is intimately bound up with the [form of] suffrage enacted."[167]

Apart from the Prussian election law that regulated the way the delegates to the Constituent Assembly in Berlin were to be elected, the draft of an election law pertaining to the election of the future German National Assembly had to be debated and passed by the United Diet. The so-called "Vorparlament" (or proto-parliament—the preparatory committee of this National Assembly) was already meeting in the St. Paul's Cathedral (Paulskirche) in Frankfurt on Main. It turned out that objections of the "Vorparlament" finally forced Prussia to annul the election law pertaining to the election of the delegates that Prussians would send to Frankfurt. The crux of the matter—something that was apparently feared all along by such men as the free-thinking delegates from Breslau who had seen the King in this regard on March 21—was that the government was determined to stifle direct popular representation. It was not only a scandal that the draft that the Arnim government had worked on foresaw no direct elections with regard to the Prussian Constituent Assembly. This was already very clearly impairing the whole democratization process that many were hoping for in Prussia. Worse yet, the drafters of the second election law pertaining to the Frankfurt assembly, that had to be finally voided due to outside pressure, proposed quite shamelessly that Prussia's delegates to the future Frankfurt-based German parliament should not be elected by general suffrage at all (regardless of whether it would have been direct or indirect).

Instead, the delegates to Frankfurt should be named by the members of the undemocratic, prerevolutionary United Diet. If the German constitution would foresee an Upper Chamber (sort of a Senate) and a Lower Chamber, the Prussian delegates to the Upper Chamber were to be named by the United Diet's "Herrenhaus" (House of Lords, the chamber representing Prussia's high aristocracy and common gentry). This contradicted the very promise of democratic elections that the revolutionaries thought they had obtained on March 19 in the form of Royal consent to their unequivocal demands. And these anti-people drafts were covertly produced in the very same month of March by a seemingly silent, apparently do-nothing government headed by a prime minister some had always seen as a reactionary, but whom others mistook for a liberal. Count Arnim was indeed a "conservative-liberal"—not completely unlike Camphausen and Hansemann, von Minutoli, Auerswald, or von Pfuel; he was undoubtedly in favor of stability, law and order, defense of the monarchy and of the Hohenzollern dynasty, and a lot indicates that he had already been convinced in 1847 that a constitution was necessary, in order to stabilize the regime. As it turned out, too many suspected him to be a reactionary, and so he had to step down as prime minister to make way for a conservative-liberal representative of the *haute bourgeoisie*. When he made his final appearances, as ex-prime minister, in the United Diet, on April 2 and also during its second session on April 4, he said words that characterized, like nothing else, his way of thinking. Addressing the delegates, Count Arnim noted on April 2,

> how he, in taking charge of the government, had posed himself, above all, the task to stay at the helm until the convening of the United Diet is assured" and "that this was the reason why his government [not the King, who signed the document] had informed the delegates of the City of Breslau [who had demanded, in the name of Breslau's inhabitants, the immediate promulgation by the King of a truly democratic electoral law, without participation of the United Diet in this entire affair] that things would stand or fall with the principle that first of all the United Diet had to be convened, and that it was necessary to proceed in a legal way…[168]

thus acting within the frame of reference provided by prerevolutionary legality. As it were, Rönne quotes Count Arnim verbatim, fully aware of the legalism inscribed in the prime minister's approach.[169] On April 4, in a long speech, the Count said the following when addressing the members of the United Diet: "*It is better to make a step ahead, rather than to be washed away by the flood.*" (In other words: Give the "people" a little, if necessary, to avoid the worst.) He also said, again, during the second meeting of the United Diet, on April 4, that this was his principle, during the time of his administration: "Under the circumstances in which I led the ministry, it was advisable for us to stay one step ahead of the events rather than to be pushed by them […] As far as the principle itself is concerned, I think it is a quite right, *if* the time [i.e., the situation] demands it."[170] Von Arnim undoubtedly saw that flexibility was required in order to achieve long-term goals, most of all continuity, stability, the preservation of the monarchy, and control of the *"classes dangereuses"* that had furnished the bulk of the revolutionary fighters on March 18–19 and who had been themselves "revolutionized" to a considerable extent during the immediately prerevolutionary days marked by people's assemblies and during the actual days of revolutionary combat against the king's government and his army.[171]

Together with the draft of the electoral law that the United Diet received on April 2 for approval, or rather in order to endow the whole constitutional process with a semblance of participation by an (unequally) elected body, this pseudo-parliament received also the Royal "Proposition Decree,"[172] that is to say, the *Draft of an Ordinance on Some Foundations of the Future Prussian Constitution*. It was to debate this Ordinance, too, and it was obviously expected to approve it practically unchanged, which it did. This Ordinance laid down basic principles that had to be incorporated in, and/or respected by, the future constitution. The Ordinance stipulated that the draft of the future Prussian constitution that the government would submit later on to the *not-yet-elected* Constituent Assembly (i.e. the Prussian National Assembly) was not merely to be debated and agreed upon by at least a majority of the members of that assembly: the text of the constitution that would issue from these parliamentary debates would then have to be submitted to the king for approval. In order to reach an agreement with the king, it would in all likelihood become necessary to incorporate changes demanded by the monarch. Then, after changes demanded by the king had been incorporated, the constitution might be promulgated. Mutual agreement on the final draft thus was the underlying premise, and what the constituent assembly could write into the draft was restricted by the "principles" insisted on in the first place in the Proposition Decree. In that sense, too, strings were attached to the entire process of deliberating and of writing a document that was supposed to express the "will of the people."

The fact that the United Diet was asked at all to approve the electoral law and the Ordinance just mentioned was interpreted later on in public by David Hansemann and others as the decisive link that established a continuity between the period (and the governments in place) before the revolution and the period (as well as the governments in place) subsequent to March 18–19, i.e. the days when the people established its power and forced the king to agree to its demands. The assertion of such a continuity was mocked by Marx in the *New Rhenanian Gazette*, and in fact it is clear that without the revolutionary events of March 18–19, the governments that now followed, headed by bourgeois prime ministers, would not have come into existence.

Apparently, the "Royal" side (Count Arnim, Count Schwerin, Baron Arnim, von Minutoli, etc., with the king as "figurehead" or as symbolical "center") had been slyly, largely inconspicuously, yet quite effectively active between March 19 and April 2, even though it is not clear whether it is justified to say that they were already on the offensive, no matter how tamely and embellished with liberal words of pardons and amnesties granted, of misunderstandings that had to be clarified, of reconciliation, support for German efforts to realize national unity, and royal consent to the "arming of the people," and of a "constitution on the broadest base." It is clear that Frederick William IV and the queen had thought of themselves as humiliated and exposed to mortal danger on March 19 and that they also felt that the army has left them behind unprotected and exposed to the whims and will of an insurgent population. The immediate acts of the king, and much of the advice given on March 19–21, can be explained by this. But the thoughtful, or rather well calculated, steps taken by the group of leading figures, who were either members of the newly appointed government or otherwise close to the king (Minutoli, for instance) beg the question whether a defensive strategy became a low-profile, very carefully orchestrated strategy to undermine the opposite "camp" and shift the balance of power thereby in a direction that was favorable to the monarch and the monarchy. Did they know, in fact, that a defensive strategy, due the important, potentially decisive steps being taken, had mutated into a silent offensive strategy? Did they want to be on the offensive? How genuine were their promises of a constitution that might do justice to popular aspirations by being genuinely conceived "on the broadest possible base?" Did they really want that—and did Camphausen want it, did Berlin's municipal executive, the "Magistrat'" want it, did the majority of those sitting in Berlin's Assembly of City Councilors want it? We have already seen how Count Arnim, Camphausen and Hansemann—three early advocates of a constitution that gave no voting rights to the "subaltern classes," that is to say, to the vast majority of the population or Berlin and of Prussia—thought about constitutionally guaranteed freedoms. If they could have their way, the masses would be excluded from the sphere of politics. That the revolution forced the king to make concessions was regrettable; what mattered now was to interpret vague concessions that meant a lot to the common people, in the most restrictive way that was feasible, in view of the actual situation and the potential significance of revolutionary "people's power." This is what they did. It guided, one may almost say, their every step.

* * *

As far as the masses—Berlin's insurgent population: the revolutionary fighters, their helpers, sympathizers, and relatives—were concerned, they, too, and not only the soldiers of the army, were glad that peace was achieved. Many fighters and helpers were probably exhausted on March 19, but the mood they were in was not impregnated by exhaustion. There were those who greeted concessions by the king joyously, almost trustingly, when he spoke to them from the balcony of his palace on that day. There were those who were grieving. And there were those who were angry, who continued to see the king and his ministers with distrust, and many among them felt what some of them shouted: They wanted a republic. The king had to go; monarchy was no solution—not even a constitutional monarchy like the July Monarchy in France that Hansemann admired, because it was a bourgeois monarchy, a monarchy that was good for bankers, large merchant houses, and for property speculation, while showing the workers, the "classes dangereuses," "their proper place" thanks to a reactionary prime minister (Guizot[173]), a number of harsh ministers of the interior,[174] and an even more unscrupulous chief of police in the capital, Paris.

But by and large even these republicans were astonishingly passive right after the days of fighting. Symbolic acts, like the ones staged by the king—when he rode through downtown Berlin and even seemed to embrace the goal of German unity—caught much attention. And so did another act with great symbolic significance: the procession of tens of thousands of Berliners that accompanied the coffins of all the revolutionaries who had died in action, or who had been taken prisoner and were subsequently killed by the army. It was in fact a mass demonstration, from the church (Brass's church) where their coffins had been placed to Friedrichshain (Frederick's Grove)—a grove at the periphery of the capital, "outside the city walls."[175] On March 22, Berlin's notables—the members of the Magistrat (the city's executive body, consisting of aldermen and the mayor), the members of the city council, the professors of the university, and perhaps also some liberal state officials had joined the funeral procession, even though most of them had stayed away from the struggle of the people in the days past. They had ducked and sought cover. Now they joined, because that was the popular mood and, for them, the necessity of the day. The democratic agitator Georg Jung had been one of those who spoke to the crowd. He was an "assessor," a young law official, still quite young, just 34, but had been an outstanding orator in the days of March, shortly before the outbreak of the revolution, when he talked to the people who flocked to the large popular meetings at the Zelten in order to listen to democratic speakers, also some who were expressing sympathies for the cause of the workers, and who had made their very needs and worries their own. What Jung had said as he stood by the graveside, on March 22, in the Friedrichshain, was similar to the words of the worker Gus Hesse: it was ominous, or at least a thoughtful warning. Folks should be ready to safeguard "the testament of the dead fighters" that bequeathed to the entire people freedom and equal rights.[176] These were his words that he would remind his listeners of, only three months later, on June 4, again at the graveside, obviously taking stock.

Such symbolic acts as the mass demonstration on March 22 and the talks that were given on this occasion did very little, however, to further change the balance of forces in favor of Berlin's majority; republican and democratic intellectuals and workers did not dare to use this demonstration for the purpose of political agitation and for further mobilization of the masses. But neither did they achieve a seriously intended "broad united front" with the "middle classes," the burghers, against a lurking reactionary camp that was taking cover only for the time being. It was only superficially and for a brief moment that the funeral procession strengthened, in ideological respect, the tendency to value reconciliation, class cooperation, and peace between the king, the burghers, and the subaltern classes. But the self-organization of the workers also remained rudimentary. True enough, political clubs were founded: thus, on March 23, the "Politischer Club der Demokraten" (Political Club of the Democrats, for short: Political Club), an association that mainly counted "journeymen and intellectuals" among its members, and that was known as the "Demokratischer Club" (Democratic Club) since May 21, elected Jung president of the club. Another important member was Dr. Heinrich Bernard Oppenheim who hailed from a family of bankers in Frankfurt. Dr. Gustav Julius, mentioned above already as editor and publisher of the newspaper and reading room known as Berliner Zeitungshalle (Berlin Newspaper-Hall, BZH), and Dr. Arnold Ruge, who edited the "Reform" jointly with Oppenheim, were at least close to this club.[177] Other clubs and associations (Vereine) focused on politics in Berlin were the "Constitutionelle Club" (Constitutional or Constitutionalist Club); the left-wing "Volks-Verein" (People's Association, founded on March 30 during a people's assembly at the Zelten) that counted, above all, workers among its 3,000 members but also quite a few left-wing democratic intellectuals (Louis Levissohn or Loewinson and the philosopher Dr. Max Schasler were in charge; apart from having discussions, drawing up petitions, and organizing people's assemblies, the association published the journal "Volksstimme," i.e. Voice of the People);[178] the radically democratic "Volksklub" (People's Club);[179] the "Verein für Volksrechte" (Association for People's Rights);[180] the left-wing "Central-Arbeiter-Club" (the Central Workers Club, founded on March 29);[181] the red "Central-Komité für Arbeiter" (Central Committee for Workers) or, for short, "Arbeiter-Komité" (Workers Committee) founded by the book printer Stefan Born, a member of the League of Communists, on April 11)[182]; the leftwing democratic "Volkswahlkomité" (People's Election Committee, with 10,000 members, formed on April 19 during a people's assembly at the Zelten);[183] the "Bürgerwehr-Club" (Club of the Civil Guard or Burgher Guard, with M. Simion and J. Springer as leading figures);[184] and the "Bezirks-Central-Verein" (District Central Association) that counted A. Löwenstein, R. Löwenstein, L.K. Weyl, S. Stern, L. Zunz, and R. Remak among its key members.[185]

The program of the *Volksverein* stated that this association should be "a People's Association within which all classes are represented, but especially those who form the pithy core of the people, *the propertyless workers*."[186] Blos quotes the key points of the program adopted by the association that demanded, in this order, "genuine arming of the people, representation of the people, and education of the people" (wahrhafte Volksbewaffnung, Volksvertretung und Volksbildung), but also notes that the program contained no specifically "social" demands.[187]

In early April, a nationalist "moderately" liberal club was founded by the industrialist Werner Siemens, the publisher Franz Duncker, the pedagogue Adolph Diesterweg and the journalist Adolf Rutenberg.[188]

The Conservatives founded the "Patriotischer Verein"; it represented a tendency that was superficially for constitutional monarchy and thus a reform of Prussia's political frame of reference and state of affairs; but deep down, many probably were monarchist enough to desire no—or almost no—change of the pre-revolutionary situation. Despite the large number of clubs focused on politics that sprang up in quick succession, and the considerable membership that some of them could point to, it is obvious that the people organized in these clubs were clearly a minority of Berlin's population of more than 400,000 people, as even the larger organizations that formed—like the local chapter of the Buchdrucker-Verein (book printers' association), a nationwide "union" founded in June 1848 in Mainz, or the Berlin-based "Handwerkerverein" (a "trade-specific" association of employed artisans, thus journeymen, that existed already before the revolution) —had at best a few thousand members.

The lack of self-organization of the "masses" was certainly appreciated by all the royalists based in the palace, and, quite obviously, it was also in the interest of the saturated, well-to-do constitutional monarchists among Berlin's commoners who had joyously welcomed the promise of increased political rights, freedom of the press, juries, and the right to meet in public and to freely associate in clubs that the Berliners received on March 19. But they begrudged the workers these rights; that much is very clear. On March 27 or 28, thus immediately before Count Arnim stepped down as prime minister and Camphausen took over, several members of this rather class-conscious, in many respects truly conservative, but otherwise—in view of the prevalent anti-absolutist standpoint—"moderately liberal" stratum of well-off Berlin "burghers" founded the "Constitutional Club of Berlin"[189] that linked up quite soon with other Constitutional Clubs in Prussia and Germany. A law official at the Berlin supreme court[190], Mr. Ludwig Crelinger, and a journalist were elected key officials; but Dr. Prutz was perhaps its most influential and thus noteworthy member. Those belonging to Berlin's well-off "middle class" had always provided quite a few members of the city councilors' assembly and the Magistrat even though people from the poorer, but still tax-paying, and clearly petty-bourgeois stratum of shop-owning or workshop-operating houseowners also got elected; it was after all a stratum whose members knew that they were a lot better off than the hawkers and the proletarianized part of the small self-employed master craftsmen who could not even afford to employ more than one person (an apprentice, usually; more rarely, a journeyman), and who leaned to either more democratic or more reactionary positions than this saturated bourgeoisie. But they also felt the sting of being looked down on by the "big bourgeoisie" and the aristocracy, and they loathed the fact that they had to serve in the army but rarely under anything other than aristocratic officers.

What is painstakingly clear, however, is this: that despite well-attended popular meetings at the Zelten, despite the creation of a considerable number of politically active clubs, the subaltern classes did not really organize when the combat ended, even though a certain number of politically conscious working-class activists and petty-bourgeois intellectuals tried to work in that direction, and not without some success. Instead, most revolutionaries who had fought the Prussian army turned in their arms when the authorities asked them to do so in the afternoon of March 19 and during the next few days. This failure to achieve working class self-organization and the disarming of the revolutionary fighters were perhaps the most negative effects of the illusion of reconciliation among objective adversaries that existed in many minds in the final days of March 1848. It is in this sense that we must interpret the moments of merely symbolic "post-revolutionary unity" that appeared to be accomplished when Berlin's aldermen and the city councilors joined the mass demonstration on March 22 that headed to Friedrichshain. It was an empty and—in the case of many who had previously denounced the "mob"—dishonest gesture, and we must remember that the new election of members of the two traditional representative bodies of the city that would take place in the middle of May changed very little, as the regulations pertaining to the election of aldermen (Ratsherren) and city councilors (Stadtverordnete) were not changed. Just as in 1815 or in 1840, when Frederick William IV ascended to the throne, they were elected only by *the small minority of Berliners who were affluent enough to materially fulfill the conditions defined the Prussian "Law Concerning the Towns"* (Preußische Städteordnung) and in greater detail by Berlin's local regulations concerning the implementation of this law. Only some 25,000 out of more than 400,000 inhabitants of the city would be allowed to vote![191] And thus, despite their revolutionary victory on March 19, *the overwhelming majority of Berliners remained excluded from political participation in Berlin's municipal self-government;* their voice was hardly heard, for they were not represented. Few city councilors, mainly Nauwerk and Berends, made the cause of the excluded majority also their cause in the assembly of councilmen.

Still there existed a considerable number of those who remained active. And so it is not quite to the point that somebody would claim that the monarchists were slowly but surely, and in a quiet, unobtrusive, formally almost impeccable way, on the offensive, while the revolutionaries seemed to be on the defensive and the revolution was either stagnant or withering away. *The activists on the Republican side tried to turn the trend around—that at least cannot be denied.* And they had a certain *mass base* mainly among the subaltern classes, for the number of politically interested, curious, and awake working people who flocked to mass meetings, principally at the Zelten, was not small. The leading speakers addressing working people are undoubtedly Louis Levissohn (or Loewinson) and Friedrich Wilhelm Held; but also Georg Jung, Stefan Born, Gustav Julius and Julius Berends. All of them had been activists and speakers at the Zelten already before the days of revolutionary struggle on March 18–19. Gustav Julius, owner, as we know, of the democratic daily "Berliner Zeitungshalle" (BZH), is not only mentioned by Brass and others in their accounts of the March Revolution. Karl Marx referred to him, as he referred to Brass with whom he would meet (again?) during his brief stay in September 1848, after having met with revolutionaries in

Vienna and Dresden. Karl Marx was initially critical of Mr. Julius; he described him as an adherent of a naively German "socialist" current, the "True Socialists" (Wahre Sozialisten).[192] But he attended Mr. Julius' funeral in London in 1851, saying that Gustav Julius had later become remarkably conscious, developing in a more left-wing direction. Nonetheless, we know that Marx was generally skeptical with regard to Berlin's petty-bourgeois writers, regardless of whether they considered themselves democrats, republicans, or even socialists. In the book *Die deutsche Ideologie*, written during the spring of 1846, by Marx, jointly with Engels, we find a sarcastic characterization of their limitations that are very much owed to the relative backwardness of Germany's politico-economic and also socio-cultural condition that were at the root of Berlin's provinciality, if one was to compare it with London, Paris, or even New York. The passage *The German Ideology* here referred to is also quoted by Jacques Rancière, in the book *The Philosopher and His Poor*. It says that

> [i]n the case of a parochial Berlin schoolmaster or author […], whose activity is restricted to arduous work on the one hand and the pleasure of thought on the other, whose world extends between [the Berlin suburb] of Moabit and [nearby] Köpenich and ends, as if stopped by a crude wooden barrier, behind the Hamburg Gate,[193]

we should not expect too much. The conditions condition him. He is likely to have a limited horizon.

Mr. Julius had raised the question of the situation of Berlin's subaltern classes already in his BZH of March 23, 1848, pointing out that they—the main force of the revolution in the days of street combat and fighting on the barricades—were ignored and left in the lurch by the propertied classes. If this continued, he admonished, the two currents representing the anti-absolutist united front of March 18–19 might split. The result of his article was an uproar. Gustav Julius commented on it in a special issue of the BZH on March 24. It is worthwhile to quote from his article extensively, as it reveals the readiness of a notable part of the better-off "middle class"—and perhaps also of certain poor, yet nonetheless resolutely monarchist, petty-bourgeois shopkeepers and self-employed master craftsmen—to resort to bad threats and, if necessary, violent means in order to silence their critics. The two anti-absolutist currents had in fact split already. The words M. Julius used to defend his earlier article were these:

> When I wrote this essay, my intention was none other than to take such steps as seem suitable to open the way to a *lasting peace*, and to lay a *secure ground* for the welfare of all classes of the people.
>
> For I believe that a *momentary* calming, which is achieved by way of words, of encouragement, of *reassuring talk*, does not produce the result of *genuine* calming [—in other words, Mr. Julius was aware of the fact

that the workers were agitated and that words of the Magistrat, the city councilors, and ministers of the government tried to calm them down while the bourgeoisie was nervous and fearful; *the editor*], and that only *actions* can achieve the aim of an *improvement of the situation*.

Mr. Julius obviously saw that there existed a potential for revolt, because the situation of the subaltern classes was not improved by the revolutionary struggle and its results which consisted in the "concessions" or "promises" of March 19 that the bourgeoisie were also interested in, without wanting to extend political rights or grant socio-economic rights to the subaltern classes. Defending himself against the charge that he was offering an apologetic excuse for working-class "unrest" (Unruhe) or even inciting workers to be "restless" and engage in what the bourgeoisie, but also the court, may have regarded as something bordering on "tumult," Gustav Julius continued by writing, in the article here quoted,

> [...] I did not ask to prolong this [existing] provisional condition, this condition of absent rules, this unrest [almost a phase of dual power, a transitional phase where things were still undecided, where either side could win or lose?; *the ed.*]; on the contrary, I have given advice, to the best of my knowledge, as to what should be done in order to *get out of this*, to *emerge* from it unscathed [was this because he feared that otherwise things might get very painful?; *the ed.*]. I want the unrest to *end* [does he refer to the *open-air* workers' assemblies, to agitated debates, to general impatience of many members of the subaltern classes with *things as they are*?; or to fisticuffs, "cat music" etc.?; *the ed.*], and that's why I am pushing for *institutions* that can put an end to it [he may be thinking of a Dept. of labor that some workers demanded, or of new, Paris-style *ateliers nationaux* (national workshops) as a way to combat unemployment, etc.; *the ed.*], that's why I say: let's not rest until we have brought such [reformist] institutions to fruition.

Mr. Julius then went on to say:

> I have recommended two things to this end, both in such a manner that it proceeds from the king [sic]—one concerning the construction of our new constitution, the other concerning the establishment of a firm peace [which does not exist today; *the ed.*] and of a deep trust between the acquiring and the unemployed parts of the population. [...] [H]ow you can find it upsetting when somebody makes *constitutive* proposals for the *most rapid* accomplishment of a definite [Democratic?] *order* and for a *caring* authority [bent on welfare for the poor; the ed.], this, my fellow citizens, I do not understand.

> Some have taken offense already *with respect to this*, that I used the word "anarchic." But, gentlemen, do you think it is good that we conceal the true nature of the existing condition? Or is it not an anarchic state when

a friend of truth, a man who made use of the barely won rights of the free press to the best of his conscience [namely the publisher of the 'Berlin Newspaper Hall'; *the ed.*], is loudly threatened by his fellow citizens in the street that they will smash his windows, smash his printing presses, practice "popular justice" on him, "exterminate" him, "neutralize him?" So I ask, is this not an anarchic state? Gentlemen, these outbursts of anger, the threats, the storming of my house, the attempts to discredit my paper, my institute, all of this – what is it but proof that the condition is anarchic [...]? But - gentlemen, who extends the anarchic state? Someone who, in his own way and after his insight, makes proposals to establish an orderly state of affairs fairly quickly, or rather he who [...] threatens the writer? Who, I ask, gentlemen, promotes anarchy? Does that writer do it? or does this citizen do it? I am sure that those who uttered such threats yesterday [...] are ashamed of their proceedings today. You have proved yourself to be too brave, my fellow citizens, in the hour of struggle and danger, to cherish now a mean attitude in your hearts; you have shed too much of your noble blood, fighting for the goods of freedom of speech, freedom of the press, freedom of assembly, to be able to demean the same goods you have just won, the very next day; you have not relinquished the pressure of tyranny on your shoulders in order to practice repression and tyranny yourself; [...] you will not want to practice terrorism for the suppression of the free expression of opinion, you will always convince yourself more vividly that only from clear knowledge of the existing conditions an improvement of the same can take place [...]

I have expressed the opinion that the new *constitution* which we require must not be deliberated by the old diet, and that not even the new electoral law may emanate from it. I wanted to say that [...] the United Diet in its constitution and composition, the Diet as an *institution*, as this *corporative* body that it is, is utterly unfit to establish the new constitution. [...] I know that many of my fellow citizens are of the opposite opinion [...][194]

The article clearly reveals this much: If workers were agitated and resorted to nightly noise, so-called "cat music" in front of the house of ministers, officials, politicians they regarded as reactionary, and even targeted certain notably conservative burghers, some people among Berlin's relatively well-off so-called "middle class"—that consisted largely of constitutionally-monarchist, "law and order loving" yet anti-absolutist and in so far "liberal" burghers—were obviously getting militant, too. It also reveals Mr. Julius' awareness of existing social tensions and colliding political views that separated "burghers" and "workers," and he was arguing in favor of reforms, of considering the plight of the subaltern classes, in order to head off an outbreak of more militant working-class protests. He favored reconciliation—a continuation of an alliance that had existed between a part of the burghers and the working class during the moment of armed struggle.

His concluding words raise the issue how the constitution will be written and by whom. And the eminently related question of the suffrage law: Will there be direct or indirect elections?

Clearly, the article of Gustav Julius in the BZH helps us to understand the mood in Berlin that prevailed as the last days of March approached; it gives us a good idea of the tensions between, on the one hand, the "propertied classes" of Berlin—the "liberal bourgeoisie" with its auxiliary troops, the conservative and "moderately liberal" ones among the petty-bourgeoisie—and, on the other hand, the progressive camp of the workers, radical democratic writers, republicans, and socialists.

But Mr. Julius' article did not only reveal that this tension existed; it also revealed a desire that was still alive in him and in many that belonged to his "camp": the desire to preserve the "united front" between the "liberal bourgeoisie" and the progressives that had existed in the 1830s and perhaps even in much of the 1840s but that was already impaired in the days before and during the outbreak of the March Revolution.

There were others who had their own views of the situation that existed in late March, but also in April and May when a voting rights movement unfolded and tension between the camps increased. One of those who had a definite view was the king. In late May he wrote to his brother, William, the Prince of Prussia and heir apparent to the throne, who was still in exile in England, that it might become necessary "to take up the sword" (zum Schwert zu greifen) and to carry out a decisive blow, with the aid of his army and the supposedly conservative rural population, against the "disorderliness and the anarchy in Berlin" (Berliner Ordnungs und Zuchtlosigkeit).[195] As Rüdiger Hachtmann writes, the letter to William, from which these words are quoted, no longer gave a single thought to all the king had promised and said in public when he talked of reconciliation, and that he would swear to defend the constitution, and trusted the Civil Guard. Abandoning his mask, Frederick William used plain talk, as he did again later, in this year of deceptions and illusions, when he wrote that the only thinkable solution would be "victory over the revolution" (Sieg über die bewaffnete Revolution); "this," he said, as if foreseeing the moment of counter-revolution, "is my definite conviction" (meine entschiedene Überzeugung). The revolution had to be crushed; what little advance had been made had to be annulled. And only "my army crowned victoriously" (nur allein mein sieggekröntes Heer) can achieve it, he added.[196]

Mr. Julius' view of the situation in late March is certainly interesting, but it lacked the determination that the king's words that have just been quoted revealed in late May. We have, however, another, later, fairly realistic appraisal of the situation that existed in Berlin in late March, April, and early May when concern about the way the constitution—that was still to be written—might be intended by the government (and by the king, some may have thought), and with regard to the election law, moved many, especially among those parts of the population who feared that considerable segments of the subaltern classes would be excluded, something that was one of the factors at the root of working-class "unrest." This appraisal was written in hindsight in the course of the year 1848 by the republican university student Gus Schlöffel, who had already been very active politically in Southwestern Germany during the vibrant days of February and March 1848, but who immediately came to Berlin when he heard the news of the struggle on March 18 and 19. During a people's assembly convened by the *Volksverein* (People's Association) at the Zelten outside Berlin on April 2, Schlöffel had made some good and perhaps passionate speeches that seem to have left a deep impression on many of the workers that were present. Due to this verbal intervention, he was elected as a "speaker" of the "Arbeiter vom Tagelohn" (day laborers) on that occasion.[197]

In his appraisal, written after he had already been condemned to six month of imprisonment in a fortress of the Prussian army, the young Republican agitator painted a rather disillusioned picture of the situation in the Prussian capital. He clearly focused mainly on the despicable state of the liberals and the petty-bourgeois democratic radicals, on their lack of determination (as he saw it; in fact, very much like Marx) that he had tried to challenge and that nonetheless persisted in the weeks subsequent to the erstwhile victory of March 18–19, and that would determine the kind of action that was taken during the period of protests against the undemocratic electoral law that foresaw indirect elections. Thus he wrote that what had so far been achieved in Berlin and Prussia "goes no further than the content of the most derisive liberalism; [...] no further than the fulfilment of the promises of 1815." The liberals, he said, "restored the hobby horse that the German princes used to ride in their embarrassment: nationality"—an idea that was turned into a fetish.

> Wouldn't the princes have been fools, if they [...] had shunned the small version of the National Cockade and if they had not embraced the slogans [of backward-looking, nationalist professors] that were directed against France, Denmark, and the Polish [insurgents in Posen],

Schlöffel asked, mockingly, adding,

> The German people should have had the courage and the conscience to bring about the political execution [i.e. the demise of the absolutist regimes] as fast and as determinedly as possible. [...] But that was beyond the horizon of German erudition [...]. [It was] terra incognita for the childish aspirations of an affectionate middle class,[198] it was connected with sacrifices too big for the German radical party and it put their perseverance and decisiveness too much to the test. [...] – And so it happened that the middle class regarded every attempt with indignation that could diminish the gratitude that the "princely concessions were owed," by expressing a "further request"; [so it happened] that the bourgeoisie is flocking almost more readily around the thrones than the French one after the July Revolution [of 1830], and that they are—as

a black-red-golden Federal Diet, strengthened by some renegades of [democratic or republican] radicalism devoid of courage, in Frankfurt—playing the same color [nationalistically] against [...] the determined part of the people, as once the princes and noblemen did during diplomatic congresses after the liberation wars [when they used anti-Napoleonic, anti-French, and thus nationalist rhetoric] against the liberalism of the student movement.[199] And thus it happened [...] that the resolute ones, apart from a few of them, turned despondent at the first failure of a republican onslaught [...] In short, the so-called intelligentsia of the German nation did not comprehend its task [...], they did not see the crisis apparent in its hardly overlookable symptoms; they were blind and dejected; and, shying away from the work that was right before them, which was, to recruit the unhistorical nation from among the lowest of the masses, they abandon it to anarchy. The [liberal proponents of compromise and reconciliation,] men of peace, of order, are the true anarchists, and will soon find out how painfully they will inflict their own punishment, how little power is available to them [...]. You will see that the social turmoil, the social misery that we endure, must produce far more dangerous collision clamps than the war-struggles of a national struggle at the beginning of our century.[200]

Just three days after Gus Schlöffel first talked to the crowd assembled at the Zelten, on April 5, 1848, the first issue of a new bi-weekly journal (or should we call it a newspaper?) appeared. It was called *Der Volksfreund* (*The Friend of the People*). It was obviously a Republican publication; after all, it alluded to the paper *L'ami du peuple* that was published by Marat during the heydays of the French Revolution. Like Marat's paper, it sided with the wretched of the earth, the salt of the earth. Marat had been their spokesperson and he had advocated a radically democratic republic that would empower the poor masses and contribute to their well-being and social as well as political, and thus human, emancipation. Marat had produced a vigilant journal, determined to ward off every counterrevolutionary attempt. This is what Schlöffel had in mind, as well, when he published *Der Volksfreund*.

Wernicke notes that

Schlöffel's "Volksfreund" was published twice a week, its 2,000 copies apparently being paid for by the publisher, editor-in-chief and editorialist, out of his own pocket. Part of the circulation was distributed by him free of charge to the [so-called] earth workers, men who were employed in the context of public work projects[201] and who were widely known as "Rehbergers"[202] whereas their saucy appearance seemed to frighten both conservatives and middle-class liberals desirous of peace and calmness. In the "Volksfreund," Schlöffel proclaimed his program for the continuation of the revolution in two main directions:

the abolition of the old apparatus of power and the abolition of the exploitation of labor by capital. This radical position immediately made him enemies *en masse*, even among left-wing liberals [...][203]

A page of the Ami du Peuple

The opening words of the Berlin-based *Volksfreund*, edited by Gustav Adolph Schlöffel, were clear indeed:

> During the glorious days of the first French revolution,[204] the insurgent people [in the sense of "populace" or "poor people"] escaped those countless slings of its countless traitors only for this reason: that it had men who made it their holy task, even though persecuted and outlawed,[205] to have only its [the people's] well-being in mind with every step they were taking, [and] to be the intellectual guards[206] of the great cause of the people [cause du people; Volkssache]. The "Volksfreund" daily is renouncing each and every consideration of particular interests; it wants to pursue—unrestricted and without restraint in its discussions—only *one* goal, *one* decidedly embraced purpose, viz., the change of existing conditions by and for the people, that has been made confused by useless knowledge, and that still has a heart capable of comprehending freedom. And that has an arm to fight for it—through and for the working, suppressed and subjugated classes. They are the only ones who, in this rotten state of today, motivate us to fight, and whose cause one can love, the ones one can sacrifice one's life for. Yes, we believe in the *impending* rebirth of our society, but only when its rotten elements that swim on its upper surface, have been destroyed and dissolved, when the masses have been set in motion, when they cease to be masses and to be seen as such, when they form the foundation[207] on which, after the removal of all impediments, the State of the *Free* shall be built. Adopt our way of thinking,[208] [all of] you workers, you proletarians, you poor folks, you subjugated ones, with that trust which you are compelled to feel if you consider that it is youthful men who intend to serve you in this newspaper, young ones, without any particular interests of their own, regardless of other things, who dedicate their intellectual capacity and their carefully, though only briefly gathered experience, to your liberation, your cause. [...]

Another text that could be of interest to Berlin's workers also appeared in print on April 5. It was entitled "Demands of the Communist Party in Germany" and it was published by the *Berliner Zeitungshalle* (BZH), No. 82, the paper founded and edited by Gustav Julius:

DEMANDS OF THE COMMUNIST PARTY IN GERMANY

"Workers of all countries, unite!"

1. The whole of Germany shall be declared a single and indivisible republic.

2. Every German, having reached the age of 21, shall have the right to vote and to be elected, provided he has not been convicted of a criminal offence.

3. Representatives of the people shall receive payment so that workers, too, shall be able to become members of the German parliament.

4. Universal arming of the people. In future the armies shall be simultaneously labor armies, so that the troops shall not, as formerly, merely consume, but shall produce more than is necessary for their upkeep.

This will moreover be conducive to the organization of labor.

5. Legal services shall be free of charge.

6. All feudal obligations, dues, corvées, tithes etc., which have hitherto weighed upon the rural population, shall be abolished without compensation.

7. Princely and other feudal estates, together with mines, pits, and so forth, shall become the property of the state. The estates shall be cultivated on a large scale and with the most up-to-date scientific devices in the interests of the whole of society.

8. Mortgages on peasant lands shall be declared the property of the state. Interest on such mortgages shall be paid by the peasants to the state.

9. In localities where the tenant system is developed, the land rent or the quit-rent shall be paid to the state as a tax.

The measures specified in Nos. 6, 7, 8 and 9 are to be adopted in order to reduce the communal and other burdens hitherto imposed upon the peasants and small tenant farmers without curtailing the means available for defraying state expenses and without imperiling production.

The landowner in the strict sense, who is neither a peasant nor a tenant farmer, has no share in production. Consumption on his part is, therefore, nothing but abuse.

10. A state bank, whose paper issues are legal tender, shall replace all private banks.

This measure will make it possible to regulate the credit system in the interest of the people as a whole, and will thus undermine the dominion of the big financial magnates. Further, by gradually substituting paper money for gold and silver coin, the universal means of exchange (that indispensable prerequisite of bourgeois trade and commerce) will be cheapened, and gold and silver will be set free for use in foreign trade.

Finally, this measure is necessary in order to bind the interests of the conservative bourgeoisie to the Government.

11. All the means of transport, railways, canals, steamships, roads, the posts etc. shall be taken over by the state. They shall become the property of the state and shall be placed free at the disposal of the impecunious classes.

12. All civil servants shall receive the same salary, the only exception being that civil servants who have a family to support and who therefore have greater requirements, shall receive a higher salary.

13. Complete separation of Church and State. The clergy of every denomination shall be paid only by the voluntary contributions of their congregations.

14. The right of inheritance to be curtailed.

15. The introduction of steeply graduated taxes, and the abolition of taxes on articles of consumption.

16. Inauguration of national workshops. The state guarantees a livelihood to all workers and provides for those who are incapacitated for work.

17. Universal and free education of the people.

It is to the interest of the German proletariat, the petty bourgeoisie and the small peasants to support these demands with all possible energy. Only by the realization of these demands will the millions in Germany, who have hitherto been exploited by a handful of persons and whom the exploiters would like to keep in further subjection, win the rights and attain to that power to which they are entitled as the producers of all wealth.

The Committee:

Karl Marx, Karl Schapper, H. Bauer, F. Engels,
J. Moll, W. Wolff

On April 5—the day when the first issue of the "Volksfreund," the *Friend of the People*, appeared in print—the "Volksverein unter den Zelten" [Popular Association "Under the Marquees"], known as a democratic association with many proletarian adherents and sympathizers that organized people's assemblies at the "Zelten" location, protested against ongoing slandering of the working class.

The March Revolution: A Botched Revolution?

Poster put up by the "Volks-Verein."[209]
The first word—"Arbeiter!"—means "Workers!"

By way of a poster that the *Volksverein* published, distributed, and affixed to the walls of houses at street corners, the association noted that malicious rumors had been spread in the capital which insinuated that the purpose of meetings of this association was to deliberate on such things as the pillage of shops, and other, very similar matters. Such was the climate in Berlin, in the period when the elections of delegates to the Prussian National Assembly and to the German parliament in Frankfurt were prepared.

People like Schlöffel—the editor of the Volksfreund—and the democratic intellectuals who were active in the *Volksverein*, were in all likelihood a minority among the democratic petty-bourgeois intelligentsia of Berlin. If republican liberals constituted the leftwing of the liberal tendency in Berlin, "red republicans" like Schlöffel were positioned even farther to the left. The same was true of Stefan Born, an active organizer among the working class, especially among previously unemployed workers who had obtained jobs in a public works program, the construction of the Spandau barge canal. Most of these workers lived in a northern suburb of Berlin, the area of the so-called Deer Mountains (Rehberge), in fact not an area of mountains but of low hills, for there are no genuine mountains worth that name in or near Berlin.

In addition to the voting rights issue that dominated liberal and democratic discourse in late March and in April, 1848, other pressing issues like unemployment, low wages and high food prices, overly long working hours, domineering, paternalistic attitudes of employers, and the prohibition to form "coalitions of workers" in the context of disputes with employers undoubtedly existed. But the key issue in early April was the undemocratic election law that the Camphausen government wanted.

On April 8 and April 10,[210] respectively, the new, flawed election laws had been passed. Soon, the government announced that on May 1, the first round of the election (the "Urwahlen") should take place:[211] this meant that Berlin voters could determine the "electors" (Wahlmänner) by choosing them from among the number of citizens previously approved as candidates by the Magistrat. Some 60,000 Berliners, out of the city's population of over 400,000, would be permitted to vote in this first round. Those among the officially screened candidates that Berliners voters were allowed to vote for, who would run successfully in the first round of elections, would then form the electoral college that could select 10 delegates representing Berlin in the Prussian National Assembly and 6 delegates representing the Prussian capital in the Frankfurt-based German National Assembly.[212]

Protest against the two election laws immediately erupted. An active "Wahlrechtsbewegung" or voting rights movement formed "immediately after the new election law[s] were adopted."[213] Blos notes that the Democrats were not only protesting against the intention of the United Diet to name the delegates to the Frankfurt assembly (a decision the Diet was soon forced to annul due to the intervention of the Frankfurt proto- or pre-parliament), but just as much against the fact that the delegates to the Berlin-based Prussian Constituent Assembly should be determined by way of indirect elections.[214]

A petition (or rather, an "Adresse," i.e., list of demands "addressed" to the King) that was passed in a popular meeting convened by the Volksverein and then sent to the prime minister, Ludolf Camphausen, asked determinedly for direct elections, age 21 as the legal voting age (rather than 24), and the right to stand for election ("passive suffrage") for those 24 and older.[215] Camphausen merely promised that the ministers would deliberate. They would discuss the matter, but it is clear that neither he nor Hansemann were inclined to give in and abandon their intention to conduct indirect elections. Just like the "Volksverein" (People's Association), the democratic "Political Club" also opposed indirect elections; and they were the ones who also protested against the provision of the Prussian election law that barred dependent employees (Gesinde; Dienstboten etc.) and those who received alms, from voting.²¹⁶ But the "Constitutional Club," as the main voice of Berlin's *constitutional monarchist* bourgeoisie, was clearly in favor of the Prussian election law.²¹⁷

Poster addressing the voters in Berlin, signed by Georg Jung

"After a number of people's assemblies had decided in favor of direct elections, a large people's assembly at the Zelten decided on April 10 to form an election committee that was to work for direct elections."²¹⁸ Among the speakers who argued in an especially effective way in favor of direct elections, the writer Dr. Eichler is mentioned by Blos. The committee that was formed comprised the following members: the writer Baader; the city councilor Julius Berends; the law official (Assessor) Bergenroth; the gold worker Bisky; the printer Stefan Born; the merchant Constant; the writer Dr. Eichler; Prof. Dr. Erman; the wine merchant Fähndich; the writer von Förster; the law official (Assessor) Hammerfeld; the journalist and retired lieutenant Friedrich Wilhelm Held; the physician Dr. Hexamer; the writer Hoppe; the law official (Assessor) Georg Jung; Dr. phil. Köppe; the plumber Krause; the naturalist Kümmelau; the student Lange; the physician Lessing; the economist Count zur Lippe; the city councilor Mertens; the student Monecke; the plumber Fritz Müller; the city councilor Nauwerk; the writer Dr. Prutz; the Chairperson of the Handwerkerverein, Dr. Ries; the student Salis; the journalist Dr. Schasler; the student Gustav Adolf Schlöffel; the highly qualified mechanic Siegerist; the highly skilled turner Steffens; the physician Dr. Thümmel; Dr. jur. Türke; and the writer and physician Dr. Wiß. [Blos, ibid, pp.227f.] Clearly the workers were in the minority. It was this committee that came up with the idea of a large civil rights demonstration that would demand voting rights for those excluded, and above all, direct elections. The fact that the "Arbeiter-Komité" (Workers Committee) was formed on the next day by Stefan Born and other workers highlights the importance that the voting rights campaign had for awake and perhaps also concerned and angry workers in the capital. Still a day later, on April 12, Schlöffel published, in the third issue of his *Volksfreund*, the call for a massive demonstration to the palace that he said should crucify Camphausen, that is to say, topple his government.

* * *

The authorities reacted in a repressive manner when they got wind of the planned demonstration. The time of free, unannounced, unpermitted demonstrations was over. The right that the "people," the "common" people, had seized—the right to take to the streets and reclaim the streets—was suddenly scrapped and such acts were defined as a crime. The old Tumult Law of 1835 was applied again and a new Tumult Law, updated by the Camphausen government, was envisioned.

The government sent a formal reply to the chief of police, Mr. von Minutoli (the "spymaster") after it received notice of the planned demonstration. This is what it said:

> Your Excellency indicated to us, that it is intended by a local [i.e., Berlinian] people's assembly to bring a petition asking for a change of the existing electoral law to the palace by way of a massively attended demonstration and to hand it to the Prime Minister on the next Thursday, the 20th of this month. We cannot accept such a demonstration, that suggests the intention to intimidate the authorities and that is likely to

disrupt public peace and order, as legally permissible, and we therefore request Your Excellency to oppose its realization, if the same, despite your warnings, should be attempted, by confronting it with the means at Your disposal, with the help of the Civil Guard, whose commander[219] has received from us a copy of this. We do not doubt that the local citizenry [Bürgerschaft; this excludes, legally, inhabitants without a "citizen letter" of "Bürgerbrief"] will willingly respect the orders given in the interest of the defence of the laws and of public peace and that they will support them.

Berlin, April 18, 1848.
The Government.
Camphausen. Count Schwerin. Von Auerswald.
Bornemann, [Baron von] Arnim. Hansemann. Von Reyer.[220]

The natural right of the people was thus disregarded, and this by taking refuge to antiquated "laws" passed by the dominant so-called "elites" in their own interest. If the Camphausen government was prepared to outlaw the demonstration, it had the full support not only of Minutoli (who notified the government of the planned demonstration) but also of Berlin's anti-democratic, though formally correctly-elected Magistrat.

A public announcement (Bekanntmachung) was published in the press that said,

Bekanntmachung

We have been officially informed that, based on a decision taken by a people's assembly that took place at the Zelten, a massively attended demonstration shall hand the government tomorrow, [on] the 20th of this month, a petition that seeks to attain a change of the constitutionally[221] adopted electoral law. [...] The government has declared that it is ready at any time [...] to accept petitions. [...] It does not consider it legitimate, however, to exercise the right to petition in a way that can lead to a disturbance of public order and peace in the city. Called upon to protect these first requirements of civil liberty and welfare, we turn first with complete confidence to the presidents of corporative associations [Vorstände, *sc.* der Korporationen], master craftsmen [Meister], and journeyman associations [Gesellenschaften] of all local trades with the urgent request not to join this unlawful project. The intended petition cannot succeed, whatever one's views with regard to the underlying idea of a direct electoral system may be, because the ministry cannot arbitrarily modify the constitutional electoral law; because, if it could make such a change, the interests of Prussia and Germany would be most painfully violated by the impossibility of timely representation of the Prussian people at the German Ntl. Diet; and because at last such a measure could only be taken if the voice of the whole country had been heard about it, and would have opted for it. We therefore expect that all our fellow citizens, including those who, due to their political conviction, consider direct elections to be the more correct way, will refrain from demonstrations which, in so far as they express a party view, could not find the approval of the [supporters of the] contrary opinion held by a large part of the country that would see in it a presumptuous act directed against it.

Berlin, April 19, 1848. The Magistrat.[222]

Minutoli was precise: the key message that his urgent address (Dringende Ansprache) to the Berliners got across, was this:

The Royal State Ministry [i.e., the government] has prohibited the popular demonstration scheduled for today that aims to change the electoral law.[223]

By publishing these, and other, similar statements in Berlin, during these days of April, the *Kgl. Privilegirte Berlinische Zeitung*—the main voice of the "moderate," and thus fairly conservative, anti-absolutist, but nonetheless monarchist bourgeoisie of the capital (the "middle class," as they preferred to be called)—revealed the anxieties of the government, the Magistrat, the overwhelming majority of the city councilors, and of the "propertied classes," not to speak of the king and his advisers.

Clearly, mass demonstrations make the authorities nervous. They fear that they can get out of hand, that the masses are angry and will storm not only the Winter Palace, but the Elysée, the White House, and Congress. In Berlin, the majority of the delegates that had been elected, by way of a flawed electoral law, to the Prussian Assembly were nervous. Some would be harassed soon, in the street, when they left the Sing Academy, where they met in session. The government was the most fearful of them all; the king had preferred to stay in Sanssouci, his summer palace near Potsdam, and the Camphausen cabinet had slipped into his shoes—its cabinet meetings took place in the palace of the king in downtown Berlin, the most hateful place of the entire monarchy. In fact, they represented him; they defended the continuity that otherwise he would not have been able to cling to, in the fatal, decisive days of March. If they could maintain His law and order, He would be saved—even if they should fall.

But did the organizers know—and did the people know—what a determined march meant? The events of March 18 should have told them. On March 18, the crowd was confronted with bullets, the firing of guns, the blows of sabres, and they had answered in like measure. All else would only be a symbolic act. And the "powers that be" can swallow and digest a lot of such "symbolism"—at least up to a point.[224]

Something else came to mind to some of the organizers, however. On March 19, the army was weakened decisively in bloody street fighting, and the king—who was completely at a loss, "*lying on his belly,*" as he told Ranke—was practically their hostage. Now Frederick William was absent, the army replenished and outside the city, able to bombard it from afar. Could the relations of forces be properly accessed? What were the risks? How responsible was it to insist on the mass demonstration when the Camphausen government revealed not only its concerns and fears, but also a determination to let the civil guard shoot, if need be, on the demonstrators?

It was clear to quite a few that the Camphausen government was aborting the democratic process, that something had to be done. Perhaps the opportunity had been missed for good in the days of March, perhaps there existed a second chance. It was hard to tell, but a second revolution was an option—it was "silently longed for" in April, May, and also in June, and sometimes, speakers during mass meetings at the Zelten, would call for a republic, and some would appear with red flags.

Every revolutionary attempt is as if people are playing dice. They can win or lose.

* * *

In hindsight, in the context of his book on the German Revolution of 1848–49,[225] Wilhelm Blos comments sarcastically on democrats like Berends and Nauwerk.[226] The people's assembly, massively attended by workers, had opted for a mass demonstration in order to exert pressure. The common people knew that the bourgeoisie can be polite: sometimes they pretend to listen to all and sometimes they accept all petitions. But while they dine at night with their ilk, and meet with them in back-rooms in order to talk "business," they don't waste much time with the petitions of ordinary folks At most, they give a brief, formalistic reply that explains why, unfortunately, they have to say no. More often the petition is thrown into the wastepaper basket with a contemptuous gesture. The answer the petitioner gets is silence. This is business as usual in all bourgeois democracies. The common people knew it in the past. They were more immune to the fantasy that there exist no classes and that all are equal. Their very situation told them that it was not so. That is why they were ready to fight and to take risks. Still, they had not learned yet to speak in public, even though they "politicized"—that is to say, they *talked politics*—in the street and in the work place. They were impressed by the "educated way" the educated talked. They thought that they needed leaders, petty-bourgeois educated men, not spokespersons elected among their own midst. The leaders—most of those who had at first talked enthusiastically to them about the big demonstration when they met at the Zelten—deserted them. When counter-pressure was brought to bear on the bloc of discontent workers and democratic petty-intellectuals, all the "sober" men among the democrats called it off. All of them, Held, even Jung, opted out and left the organizing committee. And discouraged and disappointed, most of the working people stayed away from the demonstration on the 20th of April—only 2,000, instead of the envisioned 50,000, marched as far as Alexander Square. Some carried red flags, reports say.

And thus Blos is compelled to note how little resistance was put up against a law that said that, now and in future, delegates to the National Assembly would have to be elected *indirectly*.[227] Yes, the workers protested by resorting to "cat music," even to fisticuffs when they encountered a reactionary delegate in front of the National Assembly; they tried to make life in the street uncomfortable for ministers walking home (they had no Cadillacs, in those days, and—yes—they walked quite often, shunning the carriage). But the petty-bourgeois democrats who offered resistance were few. One of those who did—a man who grew famous because he was immediately targeted by the authorities—was Schlöffel. It was he who wrote that pressure of the masses should be organized, that tens of thousands knocking on the door of the palace would make the King wake up. Schlöffel was put on trial and thrown into a dungeon. The demonstration of workers who demanded direct elections revealed the reactionary role of the Civil Guard: the workers had not got very far on their march to the Palace when they were stopped by the Guard; their march was impeded; this "Citizen Guard" (Bürgerwehr) put together in March under the supervision of Nobiling and Minutoli (two guardians of law and order, who were in close contact with the King and his ministers) had confronted the peaceful workers with their raised bayonets on Easter Thursday.[228]

Focusing not only on Schlöffel and the obstructed march, but also on the election campaign as such, and its speeches, Wilhelm Blos writes,

> During the election campaign, the most confused views were brought to light, as it was the first time that one could vote. The Berliners had no right to mock the "blind Hessians" because they were said to have demanded "the republic with the Grand Duke" [at the top]. Mr. Julius Berends said in his printed articles of faith: "We want a republican government and at its head a king, who outwardly gives up—as a representative of the people—all other powers, in order not to limit the liberty of the people." The programs of Held, Jung, Oppenheim (who was then already beginning to accept defeat—which he later continued to do, so persistently), Ruge, and Nauwerk were not much better. [All of them were known as Democrats. (*My addition; AW*)] The Constitutional Monarchists managed, of course, to produce far more confusion and phrase-mongering than the Democrats. But the retention of indirect suffrage had the desired effect: the Democrats remained in the minority and the representatives of the center parties as well as the covert reactionaries triumphed. The following [persons] were elected as members of the *Constituante* [i.e. the assembly that was to agree on a constitution; the German term used here—Vereinbarungs-Versammlung—is very antiquated]: the Prosecuting Attorney [Staatsanwalt] v. Kirchmann, the Secret Councilor [Geheimrath] Waldeck, Lord Mayor [Oberbürgermeister] Grabow, the Secret

Councilor [Geheimrath] Bauer, Alderman [Stadtrath] Duncker, Pastor [Prediger] Sydow, Dr. Johann Jacoby, City councilor [Stadtverordneter] Berends and Graduate Civil Servant [Assessor] Jung. As delegates to the Frankfurt parliament, Berlin elected only one Democrat, Dr. Nauwerk, and otherwise [the Prussian Prime] Minister, Mr. Camphausen, Major Teichert, Colonel Stavenhagen, Professor Raumer, Dr. Veit. It proved fatal that so many Democrats, among them Nauwerk, had accepted an indirect election [...]

As Wilhelm Blos notes, and as I repeat here, the delegates elected to the *Constituante* (i.e. the Prussian National Assembly) that would meet in session between May 22 and December 5, 1848,[229] had to be elected indirectly, because this was the method that the government led by the so-called "liberal" Prime Minister, Mr. Camphausen, had prescribed, meeting with little or no resistance from the petty-bourgeoisie of Berlin and even less from its bourgeoisie. The capital's delegates to the assembly were thus not elected by all male voters of Berlin directly, as desired, but by a small electoral college that had been formed in every precinct of the city (and likewise, in other cities of Prussia). And this on the basis of the number of votes each elector obtained in a process that has been described as complicated and bureaucratically controlled, via a screening process that let the county president determine whether potential electors where acceptable. This method, decided on with cleverness by the government, had the effect of attaining the intended goal; it effectively limited the influence of the subaltern classes and thus, in effect, that of "left-wing" democrats in the assembly.

In one of the first sessions of the Prussian National Assembly, Camphausen justified the way the broad masses were conned, by saying the following about his, Hansemann's, and Count Arnim's strategy of getting the electoral law that they wanted, and the kind of composition of the National Assembly, once it had been elected, that they could live with or at least tolerate:

> [...] By no means have we judged the situation to be such, that a complete upheaval has resulted from this occurrence [the March Revolution], that the entire structure of our state has been overthrown, that everything that exists has ceased to be legal and that all conditions must be placed on a new legal basis. On the contrary. The Government agreed from the moment of its initial meeting to regard it as essential for its own future that the then convoked United Diet meet in reality, regardless of the petitions received opposing such a course, and that the new constitution evolve from the existing structure with the legal machinery offered by it without the bond which ties the old to the new being severed. This incontestably correct policy has been maintained. The electoral law has been submitted to the United Diet and passed with its advice. Later on, the attempt was made to induce the Government to alter this law on its own authority, in particular to change the indirect electoral system into a direct one. The Government

did not yield. The Government did not act in a dictatorial way; it could not and would not act in such a way. The electoral law has in fact been implemented strictly according to the letter. It was on the basis of this electoral law that the electors and deputies were chosen. [...][230]

Marx commented,

> The doctrinal trick by which Herr Camphausen has evolved the new constitution from the existing structure with the legal machinery offered by it develops as follows: An illegal occurrence turns Herr Camphausen into an illegal person within the meaning of the "existing structure" and of the "old state of affairs": that is into a responsible Prime Minister, a constitutional Minister. The constitutional Minister illegally transforms the anti-constitutional, dear faithful "United Diet," based on the estates, into a constituent assembly. The dear faithful "United Diet" creates unlawfully the law of indirect elections. The law of indirect elections creates the Berlin Chamber, the Berlin Chamber draws up the Constitution and the Constitution produces all successive chambers from here to eternity.

Thus, a goose is transformed into an egg and an egg into a goose. Thanks to the Capitol-saving cackling the nation soon realises, however, that the golden eggs of Leda, which it laid in the revolution, have been stolen.[231]

* * *

Basically, only workers—in view of the fact that the protest march had been forbidden, a surprisingly large number of them—had dared to demonstrate against the Camphausen government's decision to outlaw the big voting rights demonstration that had been planned. There were about 2,000 of them, in Alexander Square, on April 20, and with them a tiny number of petty-bourgeois radicals, most notably, that courageous young man, Mr. Schlöffel, editor of the *Volksfreund* and still a student at the university of Berlin. He had sided with them.[232] It is true that he had published an article calling for mass protests, a text interpreted as seditious in content. Schlöffel had written:

> On Easter Thursday [April 20, 1848], we want to celebrate the Lord's Supper with the Camphausen government, so that it may be crucified. Once upon a time, the Jews released Barnabas in order to hang a great "Volksaufwiegeler" (i.e., a man who stirs up the people) and a revolutionary who was revered as a "god" for millennia. Tomorrow we do not want to release the Barnabas Camphausen, and we want to forever save our freedom, which we see in the popular elections at the moment. Therefore, do not trust those scribes and Pharisees in the Constitutional Club and those royal soldiers in the guard houses of the Burgher Guard, and that Pontius Pilate, Minutoli, who all tell you how good and excellent

Barnabas is, and how dangerous that political "Christ," the Democratic Electoral Law is (for it leads to the Republic), and don't be talked out of going in big numbers with us to Golgotha right in front of the royal palace, where that barbaric Friedrich Wilhelm Titus let them shoot on you 4 weeks ago [...]. We do not want to [...] become tacit murderers of our own freedom and admit that [...], thanks to the bad election law, the rich and order loving camels go through the bottleneck of the county president's election control."[233]

But it appeared only in print, belatedly, after the demonstration of Berlin's more conscious or desperate proletarian workers was already under way and had already been stopped by armed might. The printer was slow, or others had caused a delay. As I pointed out already further above, Schlöffel was to pay dearly for his courage.[234]

It was the first political trial in Berlin, since the March Revolution, and neither the prosecutor, Dr. Kirchmann, nor the judge, gave a damn for the law that guaranteed freedom of the press.

Dr. Kirchmann (a "moderate liberal!") would soon be elected as a delegate to the National Assembly whereas Mr. Schlöffel would suffer in prison.

But Schlöffel was no dreamer; he saw facts—social facts, sociologically obvious conditions. When Schlöffel had addressed the workers of Berlin during the election campaign in this month of April, 1848, the large number of unemployed and underemployed construction workers constituted the greatest potential for renewed acts of effective protest—and, if the situation would become extreme, perhaps even of real resistance.

Among all sections of the working class, the construction workers employed in public works projects were perhaps the most distressed. They needed written endorsements by the city government (the "Magistrate") to get a job in the first place. Public construction projects like the canal construction project did not have jobs for everyone; other public and private construction had been slowed down or put on hold, due to financing difficulties during the protracted economic crisis of 1847–48. Furthermore, wages were insufficient, as public work projects were considered just another way of charitably providing minimal subsistence to jobless and starving Berliners. It must also be remembered that it was not only the situation in the job market that was bad, putting pressure on wages. In this period, 1847–1848, crop failures and food shortages drove up prices in Berlin and in Prussia, just as in other regions of Europe. All of this had added to hopelessness and despair, then to voiced grievances, to recurrent meetings and assemblies, and surely—in March—to an increasing readiness to act. Was it like this again now? Could it still drive people to action? Schlöffel had seen this possibility and had thought it would do so. Objective preconditions existed. In addition, the bulk of Berlin's construction workers—above all the unskilled and semi-skilled men, employed in the context of the large public works projects—constituted a fairly homogeneous mass, a relatively large "army" of workers with few if any internal divisions due to differences in terms of skill and pay. At the same time, many shared the same social space, working in the same construction site, which made self-organization a lot easier. What could they not have achieved if armed properly, and if other segments of their class had joined their effort! But as it were, save for their picks and shovels, they were unarmed when the Civil Guard, the "Bürgerwehr" or defensive arm of the bourgeoisie—the "citizens"! —stopped the march of this large crowd that sought to reach the Royal Palace.

Schlöffel was arrested on April 23. The young revolutionary commented sharply:

> In the midst of this situation, [just] 6 weeks after the attainment of freedom of the press, the anxious hopelessness [of the government, and thus also of the reaction it wittingly or unwittingly serves] avails itself of the instrument of a press trial [a trial against the press] and believes itself to be saved if it imprisons some literary figures. The constitutional bourgeoisie begs the absolute *Landrecht*[235] to protect it against the people. [...] It does not know what to do with the friend of the people, who, despite the general depression, does not lose courage."[236]

His trial took place on May 11 before the Supreme Court in Berlin. Wernicke writes,

> Though its significance was recognized by few contemporaries at the time, the trial was a milestone with regard to the efforts of blocking the process towards a democratic Prussian state that had been initiated with the fight on the barricades of March 18-19. For the first time [since March 19] it was demonstrated by a supporting pillar of the state [the judiciary] that the revolutionary events which had taken place had by no means created revolutionary legality; instead, the law which had been in force since 1794 continued to be applied as if nothing had happened. If the provisions [of the Tumultgesetz (Tumult Law) of 1835[237]] had not been applied *post festum* against the barricade fighters, this was only due to the royal pardon! The accusation of prosecutor Julius von Kirchmann (1802-1884) accused Schlöffel of "incitement to commit acts of physical ill-treatment against the Prime Minister, Camphausen" as well as "attempted incitement to revolt."[238]

Schlöffel had been active in the voting rights campaign that demanded direct elections, not indirect ones—the latter the brainchild of Rhenish "liberals," Ministers with dual loyalties to their class, the "big bourgeoisie," and to the king, but not to the people. Now, in late May, he was already incarcerated in a fortress prison of the king's army.

When on May 25 the fact that the Camphausen government was submitting its draft of a constitution to the Prussian National Assembly became known thanks to newspapers like the *Kgl. Priviligirte Berlinische Zeitung*,[239] the concerns about a likely abortion of everything that was democratic were fanned again. The draft of the constitution foresaw two Chambers, and the census suffrage foreseen with respect to the First Chamber or Upper House foresaw such outrageous barriers that only the richest of the rich could vote for its delegates or be elected to it. Even Berlin's merely moderately wealthy "burghers" were enraged.

* * *

EARLY JUNE FOUND BERLIN'S SUBALTERN CLASSES RESTLESSS. Perhaps more restless than usual. Rumors circulated in the city that the Prince of Prussia was coming back.

After a difficult flight via Hamburg, the heir-apparent to the Prussian throne, William, Prince of Prussia, had stayed in England where he had arrived in March 27, 1848. But the correspondence between him and his brother Frederick William, the king, and also Frederick William's correspondence with the Prussian prime minister, Mr. Camphausen, reveals that both Hohenzollerns were thinking often enough about a way to secure William's return. The king asked Camphausen to lobby in favor of William, who was hated by many among the subaltern classes, probably the majority. They had declared his palace in Berlin "national property"—something that angered and hurt William, and he said that he could not return honorably unless he got his property back. Camphausen knew that the Prince of Prussia was loathed by the masses, that he had the reputation of a really dangerous reactionary, and that people were aware that it was he who had recommended the bombardment of Berlin by Prussian artillery from safe positions outside the city. Camphausen knew that having William back too early might make the explosive situation, that existed due to the voting rights protests, turn even more explosive, as he would come back, undoubtedly, as an unwelcome guest. So he told the king, *Let's do it slowly*. But he cooperated, and it is even possible that Camphausen drafted William's declaration of allegiance to the "new constitutional order of things" that William then sent from Brussels to the king and had simultaneously published in the press.

No matter how much Camphausen was coaxed, it is apparent that, formally, it was the government, *and thus he*, who "called back the prince-regent from exile in England in May 1848"[240]—thus at a time when the king already dreamt of using his "sword," the army, against the revolution (or rather, wrote about it, in an angry letter, speaking contemptuously of Berlin's "anarchy").[241]

Steinmetz thinks that at a time when William's return was planned and finally achieved,

> Friedrich Wilhelm and his informal advisers consciously calculated (indeed, they outright yearned for it) that the so-called "agitators" and the "riffraff"

from elsewhere, a large number of whom had allegedly gathered in Berlin, would use the return of the prince of Prussia or other acts of the government as a reason for violent action. In his private correspondence with friends and family members—which included the Tsar of Russia and the Kings of Hanover and Saxony—Friedrich Wilhelm IV repeatedly indulged in civil war scenarios and made it obvious that he wished for a fight. Leopold von Gerlach prayed for a war against republican France, and, as he could not have it, he hoped at least for a proclamation of a republic in Berlin. "If it comes to a conflict with ministries, rabble, constituent assembly, all the better." [...]"[242]

That Camphausen really thought that it was not good to hasten the return of the Prince is not only expressed in one of his letters to the king; he confirmed it on June 6 during the 11th session of the Prussian National Assembly when he said,

> that we did not have any reason that might reflect the interest of the country, to apply earlier for the recall. I do not hesitate, however, to add that we do not believe we have to recommend a step that would have produced a worrying excitement at an inappropriate time. If we are reproached on account of it, we must submit to it. But as the date of the convening of the assembly that is to lay the foundation of the future constitution of the country drew nearer, we considered it indispensable that the heir to the throne be present in the country; we considered it our duty to apply for the return.[243]

Leaving Brussels on May 30, Prince William arrived on May 31 in The Hague, on June 4 in Arnheim, then in Wesel. Going first to Mecklenburg now, he was in Charlottenburg on June 7 and arrived in Berlin on June 8.[244] The conservatives welcomed him, the "moderately liberal" bourgeoisie may have taken it more nonchalantly, and the democrats and republicans did not fail to protest. Of course, his presence in Berlin caused great commotion among those who remained faithful to the revolution.

The first official news of the return of the prince was contained in a report published by the prime minister in the State Gazette (Staatsanzeiger) that appeared on June 4. This report was accompanied by a letter which the prince had purportedly addressed to the king from Brussels on May 30. The publication of the letter was a real propaganda coup.

Prince William's letter, possibly based on an earlier draft by Camphausen, said in the tamest of voices:

> (...) I think that this is the most appropriate time to reiterate openly my opinions that are already known to your Majesty. I am filled by the hope that the free institutions, for the more solid foundation of which Your Majesty now convened the representatives of the people (...), will develop

more and more for the good of Prussia. I will devote all my strength to this development with confidence and faithfulness, and I am looking forward to the moment when I will express my recognition of the Constitution, which Your Majesty, after conscientious consultation with your people, is about to agree on, and which will present the definitive constitutional document for the heir to the throne.[245]

It tallied strangely with the uncensored expression of the king's real sentiments in late May, when he said he was thinking of using the sword, das Schwert, or rather the army against the hated situation in restless Berlin.

* * *

Perhaps the uneasy feeling caused by William's return, coupled with Camphausen's renewed refusal, on April 18–20 and on May 30, to change the law that required indirect elections, contributed to the desire to hear the National Assembly confirm, very explicitly, that they did not disown the March Revolution, without which this assembly would not have come into existence.

So it does not surprise that a flyer, produced by Berlin workers and journeymen at the beginning of the month, sounded a wake-up call in view of the attitudes of the majority of delegates deliberating in the Prussian national assembly and of a bourgeois government—institutions that both seemed to heap insults on the revolution and its heroes, rather than showing in the slightest manner that they still honored the barricade fighters of March 18–22. Something that worried them especially is that they—the workers and craftsmen who had borne the brunt of the struggle on the barricades—were largely excluded from a Civil Guard that they had thought would be an army of the people.

"Citoyens, be vigilant!" the flyer said. "Just look, what sort of difficulties they are having, to place the sole, and full guarantee in your hands, that secures the unalienable rights of the people! How stubbornly they are trying to impede this, that the arming of the people becomes a true fact."[246]

As we know, it was Julius Berends, the well-known democratic delegate elected to the National Assembly by an election district in Berlin, who submitted the motion that the Assembly should "recognize" the March Revolution. How weak must a revolution be if it needs to be "recognized!" And this not by the true sovereign, the people, but by the authorities and a questionable institution whose members were elected on the basis of an undemocratic electoral law!

Marx, for one, ridiculed the relevant motion submitted in the National Assembly on June 8. The very fact that they asked a legislative body created by the powers that be—and not by them—showed the absurdity of the quest put forward by "revolutionaries." They should have dictated the terms; instead, they asked to be recognized. By this, they themselves annihilated revolutionary sovereignty, and sought refuge under the cloak of pre-revolutionary legality.

Perhaps this is what these Democrats had done since the moment the call, Peace! Peace! resounded in Berlin on March 19. They had been in charge of the capital; the king *could not* but cave in, and instead of dictating the terms, they had thankfully listened to promises. They gave a piece of sovereignty back to a king "lying on his belly," and he saw the chance. It was the old subservience. Only those seemingly faceless masses whose beautiful faces we see so rarely, and whom we hear so seldom speak on public occasions, on grandstands, in television, on the radio, and who do not speak to us ever (or almost never, except quoted at will by "Lohnschreiber") in the press—only these people, moving into the palace yard as a big, black, dark-faced cortège, a massive demonstration of ire and grief, had guts, as they shouted, angrily and disrespectfully, "Hat off!" to the king, and as the tabooed word resounded: "A republic!"

But anyway, as a certain Mr. Benda told readers in the press, the idea of asking the National Assembly to "recognize the revolution" had already been floated as early as May 31, when the steward of the Association of the Fifth Electoral District had requested,

> that an application should be addressed to the National Assembly in the same form that was later chosen by Mr. Berends for his motion (submitted to the Assembly), [noting] that the proposal had been voted on by the members of the Association who had unanimously adopted the motion, which was then handed over on June 4 to the delegate Mr. Jung who had been elected in said Electoral District, in order to let him submit it to the National Assembly, while several hundred copies of it were also printed. Why the motion was submitted by Mr. Berends and not by Mr. Jung, about this, said Mr. Benda, "these gentlemen may have a conversation.[247]

Adolph Wolff notes that the fifth district council, comprising 28 electoral districts, stated that the Assembly should declare on record "that those who fought for liberty in Berlin on March 18 and 19 have truly served their homeland." He adds that the address glorifies the March fighters, after having mentioned the reactionaries. It is worthwhile to look closely at a part of the text he quotes from the motion, because it reveals a thirst for peace, fear of civil war, a grave concern both with regard to a government that cannot be trusted and the darker spectre of the "reaction" that is becoming more and more vocal:

> [...] Some reactionaries try to turn the provinces against Berlin. They are threatening the fatherland with civil war and destruction, they call the glorious revolution of March a "crime," and the immortal heroes of those days "criminals." That happens only two months after freedom was won with the noblest blood. But these reactionaries are encouraged in their actions, because the government that emerged immediately out of the March Revolution fearfully avoids recognizing this revolution and the merit of those who fought for it, whereby it fills the hearts and minds of

all true friends of the fatherland with restlessness, distrust, and concern regarding the unclear intentions of the government and prevents a return to peace and order. It is only the more that painfully the reactionary incitements are felt [on account of this], especially in so far as they appear to be caused mainly by intrigues and machinations of government officials who do not only question the achievements of the revolution but even the security and continued existence of the fatherland. [...]²⁴⁸

Adolph Wolff adds: More comprehensive wishes are expressed by the *Friedrichs-Wilhelmstädtische Bezirks-Verein* in an address of June 5. Like the previous one, this address also mentions that the government actually recognized the revolution on March 22. It is now the duty of the Assembly to acknowledge before the whole Prussian people that only these struggles have achieved the concession of true and full freedom. He then quotes the following verbatim from the motion of the *Frederick-Williamtown Election District Association*:

> The people's representatives cannot deny this, because it is unadulterated in the annals of history. [...] The foundation of the revolution is by no means synonymous with anarchy. On the contrary, wanting to deny the revolution means to evoke anarchy, which makes revolution necessary again. To restore order and calm after the revolution, a vigorous government must handle the principles of law that have become valid in the revolution, it must fully recognize the right of the revolution without reserve, and break with a past that was alienated from the aspirations of the people long ago. The Assembly of Representatives in its current [no longer rank-based] composition is a child of the revolution and it would be bad for the Assembly if it did not honor its generosity.²⁴⁹

Obviously, it was the concern felt by many about demeaning commentaries on the revolution that occasioned the demands that the "revolution" be "recognized." The wish was variously expressed in Election District Associations and it was the subject matter of the motion submitted on June 8 in the National Assembly by Julius Berends. But already four days earlier, on June 4, a big demonstration had taken place to the Frederick's Grove (Friedrichshain), the burial ground of the fighters of March 18–19 who had paid with their lives. The figures given with regard to the number of participants vary. As we know, the police and hostile observers always diminish the number of protesting participants in a demonstration, if they are unsympathetic to their cause. Bourgeois historians, in the name objectivity, follow suit. Yes, to see things factually—as objectively as possible—matters. But who can say that the democrats whose guess puts the number of demonstrators at 100,000²⁵⁰ were blind and that such estimates are completely mistaken?

The Camphausen government that had prohibited a mass demonstration to the seat of the government in the palace on April 20 couldn't care less. Even the numbers hardly mattered. The demonstrators would walk to the outskirts of Berlin and listen to talks at the graveside of the killed revolutionaries. Even though it mobilized many—even quite a few burghers—it was merely symbolic. It was just—talks.[251] A straw fire for the moment, without consequences. The government could almost ignore it. The Camphausens had nothing to fear from it, if that was all.

The debate about the questioned recognition of the March Revolution was commented on by Frederick Engels in the New Rhenanian Gazette on June 14 as follows:

Fred. Engels, "*The Berlin Debate on the Revolution*"

Cologne, June 13. At last the Agreement Assembly has made its position clear. It has rejected the idea of revolution and accepted the theory of agreement.

The matter the Assembly had to decide was this.

On March 18 the King promised a Constitution, introduced freedom of the press together with caution money, and made a series of proposals in which he declared that Germany's unity must be achieved by the merging of Germany in Prussia.

These sum up the real content of the concessions made on March 18. The fact that the people of Berlin were satisfied with this and that they marched to the palace to thank the King is the clearest proof of the necessity of the March 18 revolution. [What about the angry ones who brought the coffins, who shouted *Mütze runter—Cap off?!* And what about the ones who shouted A Republic?! What about the many republican tricolored flags and the red flags during the fighting of March 18-19?—(AW)] Not only the state, [many of Berlin's burghers and even of the workers still had to be revolutionized—but how many among the subaltern classes, how many workers, how many impoverished youngsters, were revolutionary, yet much too mute, too dependent on the organizers of people's assemblies, on the speakers who had talked to them during these mass meetings—who finally failed them, in the decisive moment on March 19 and in subsequent days—and later also as delegates in the Prussian National Assembly..? (AW)] its citizens too had to be revolutionised. Their submissiveness could only be shed [and was to a large degree shed in those days of March, March 16–19 when they were taking to the street, and finally] in a sanguinary liberation struggle.

A well-known "misunderstanding" led to the revolution. There was indeed a misunderstanding. The attack by the soldiers, the fight which continued for 16 hours and the fact that the people had to force the troops to withdraw are sufficient proof that the people completely misunderstood the concessions of March 18.

The results of the revolution were, on the one hand, the arming of the people, the right of association and the sovereignty of the people, won de facto; on the other hand, the retention of the monarchy and the Camphausen-Hansemann Ministry, that is a Government representing the big bourgeoisie.

Thus the revolution produced two sets of results, which were bound to diverge. The people were victorious; it had won liberties of a pronounced democratic nature, but direct control passed into the hands of the big bourgeoisie and not into those of the people.

In short, the revolution was not carried through to the end. The people let the big bourgeoisie form a Government and the big bourgeoisie promptly revealed its intentions by inviting the old Prussian nobility and the bureaucracy to enter into an alliance with it. Arnim, Kanitz and Schwerin became members of the Government.

The big bourgeoisie, which was all along anti-revolutionary, concluded a defensive and offensive alliance with the reactionary forces, because it was afraid of the people, i.e. of the workers and the democratic bourgeoisie.

The united reactionary parties began their fight against democracy by calling the revolution in question. The victory of the people was denied, the famous list of the "seventeen dead soldiers" was fabricated, and those who had fought on the barricades were slandered in every possible way. But this was not all. The United Diet convoked before the revolution was now actually convened by the Government, in order post festum to fabricate a legal transition from absolutism to the Constitution. Thus the Government openly repudiated the revolution. It moreover invented the theory of agreement, once more repudiating the revolution and with it the sovereignty of the people.

The revolution was accordingly really called in question, and this could be done because it was only a partial revolution, only the beginning of a long revolutionary movement.

We cannot here go into the question as to why and to what extent the present rule of the big bourgeoisie in Prussia is a necessary transitional stage towards democracy, and why, directly after its ascent to power, the big bourgeoisie joined the reactionary camp. For the present we merely report the fact.

The Agreement Assembly had now to declare whether it recognised the revolution or not.

But to recognise the revolution under these circumstances meant recognising the democratic aspects of the revolution, which the big bourgeoisie wanted to appropriate to itself.

Recognising the revolution at this moment meant recognising the incompleteness of the revolution, and consequently recognising the democratic movement, which was directed against some of the results of the revolution. It meant recognising that Germany was in the grip of a revolutionary movement, and that the Camphausen Ministry, the theory of agreement, indirect elections, the rule of the big capitalists and the decisions of the Assembly itself could indeed be regarded as unavoidable transitional steps, but by no means as final results.

The debate on the recognition of the revolution was carried on by both sides with great prolixity and great interest, but with remarkably little intelligence. One seldom reads anything so unedifying as these long-winded deliberations, constantly interrupted by noisy scenes or fine-spun arguments about standing orders. Instead of the great passion of party strife, we have a cool, placid temper which threatens at any moment to sink to the level of amiable colloquy; instead of the biting edge of argument we have interminable and confused talk rambling from one subject to another; instead of trenchant retorts we have tedious sermons on the essence and nature of morality.

Nor has the Left particularly distinguished itself in these debates. Most of its speakers repeat one another; none of them dare tackle the question resolutely and speak their mind in frank revolutionary terms. They are always afraid to give offence, to hurt or to frighten people away. Germany would have been in a sorry plight if the people who fought on March 18 had not shown more energy and passion in battle than the gentlemen of the Left have shown in the debate.

* * *

During the night of June 13–14, people noticed that the army that had routinely stationed some soldiers at the Berlin central armory, the Zeughaus, was carting off weapons from the Zeughaus, loading them on river barges, either because authorities feared that the restless subaltern classes clamoring for the arming of the people would avail themselves of these weapons, or because the army needed them, or for both reasons. The news caused great commotion, and in the course of developments of this day, a confrontation of the crowd with the civil guard and the army occurred. The civil guard shot, and people died. In the end, after fairly short negotiation, the commanding officer of the army unit withdrew—something that even prompted even the creation of a song that got fairly popular at the time and that praised him, whereas, on the other hand, the man was heavily criticized by the authorities. That he withdrew at all can remind us of course of the regiment in Magdeburg that had disobeyed commands to shoot at the people in March 1848 and of the incipient revolt of soldiers in Potsdam in 1848. We have seen in more recent years how nervous the reaction got in Chile when parts of the army, including officers, switched their loyalty and became allies of the young Allende government, and the same is true with regard to Portugal during the mid-1970s. NATO generals and politicians were very aware of it and very concerned. In 1848, the more conscious activists of the democratic movement clearly attempted to reach those the king referred to as "my soldiers"—but liberals and most democrats warned against it, fearing it would rock the boat.

The civil guard was also withdrawn on June 14, and the crowd, entering the Zeughaus, made off with weapons in a haphazard, chaotic and entirely unorganized way. No units of the armed people were formed on the spot, no officers were quickly and provisionally elected. Obviously, the storming of the Zeughaus had not been planned; it was a spontaneous—defensive rather than offensive—act of a nervous crowd fearful of a scheming reaction.[252]

It is likely that memories of the planned mass demonstration in April, that had been forbidden by the authorities and stopped by the civil guard, had contributed to a desire of the people to get into possession of arms. Clearly, the fact that the workers had been unarmed had meant helplessness and momentary defeat of their project to enforce direct elections by exerting pressure "from below" on April 20. It may have provided a lesson for the more determined among the subaltern classes. Many were angry that they could not join the Civil Guard in order to transform its social character. They knew that their working hours coincided with the hours they would have to be on duty in the guard. They also could not afford to buy the uniform of a member of this guard. And they were aware of the formal process of applying and being accepted: they knew that they were at any rate not welcome. Perhaps this sentiment and the memory of occurrences like the defeat of the people's march on April 20, on top of the things that had happened in the preceding night and during the day, contributed to working class action in the evening of June 14, 1848 that became known as the Berlin "Zeughaussturm": the Storming of the Arsenal.

The Storming of the Arsenal has often been denounced by bourgeois historians as a provocative and unnecessary action of the crowd or the mob that precipitated the fall of the "liberal" Camphausen government. But it was the courageous attempt of radical parts of the populace, on this evening of June 14, 1848, to arm independently. Frederick Engels saw in it the preannouncement of a "Second Revolution." He used the metaphoric expression "Wetterleuchten" (sheet lightning) in his article that was printed in the Rhenanian Gazette.

Interestingly, Stefan Born, a good man and courageous socialist activist present in Berlin, and someone who was actively engaged in working towards the formation of an organized workers' movement, was not enthusiastic about the spontaneous attempt of the crowd to avail itself of weapons. In this respect,

Born, like other cunctatory democrats in Berlin, disagreed with Engels. Born, who had been close to Frederick Engels and Karl Marx when they all were members of the *Association Démocratique* in Brussels (and also of the *League of Communists*), had been among those workers who had succeeded to join the Civil Guard. A leftist under the command of a Civil Guard officer who was determined to establish law and order, Born had participated in disarming men who had taken part in the "pillage" (as it was called) of the Arsenal. Later, he uttered the suspicion that the attack on the Arsenal had been consciously provoked by Prussian reactionaries in order to brake political developments and reverse even the modest gains made under the Camphausen government. This suspicion is not entirely unfounded. In fact, an act that provoked the people who had taken to the street to voice their protest had occurred on June 14, *preceding* the storming of the "Zeughaus": a crowd had assembled in protest in front of the Sing Academy, the site where the Prussian national assembly was meeting in session, and also in front of the Ministry of War, where they were apparently demanding the "promised" arming of people. They had been quickly dispersed by units of the Civil Guard that determinedly resorted to the use of armed force against unarmed demonstrators. In front of the Ministry of War, an unknown number of demonstrators had been wounded by gunshots and two persons had died.

The apparent failure—from the point of view of the authorities—of both the commander of the civil guard, Blesson, and the commanding officer of the army unit at the Zeughaus, Natzmer, to act ruthlessly, that is to say, "in determined manner" when it was "necessary to deal with the crowd," caused an investigating committee to look into the matter. The commission report presented in hindsight the following assessment:

> Before reports are [were] received [by the Central Office of the Civil Guard with respect to what was happening in front of the Zeughaus], at the request of the mixed commission, the Central Bureau [was] relocated from Wallstrasse to the palace. No sooner than Mr. Blesson [had] arrived here, he sees a man wounded by gunshots carried across the Palace Square [= Schlossplatz]. A crowd of people follows with a red flag, and exclaims, "Long live the republic." Mr. Blesson now suspects that a republican movement has broken out and is worried that he will no longer be able to count on the battalions 20, 21, 22, and 23, which have not yet been used. This view is particularly confirmed by the fact that when he soon afterwards moves the Central Office back to Wallstrasse, reports are received that barricades with red flags were being erected in Landsberger Strasse, at the Frankfurter Tor, and elsewhere. After all, especially among the men of the 22nd Battalion (Sametzky), there was a great deal of excitement [thus, in several units of this civil guard battalion] later on, and a company almost refused service when it was commanded at night to proceed to the armory. [...]

Blesson thought it necessary at this moment to reach a decision whether the military should be asked to step in. The chairman of the assembly of city councilors was of the opinion, however, that—in view of the change in the assembly of city councillors [the election of new councilors]—he lacked the authority to give his consent; a view shared by mayor Naunyn. City Councilor Scheffer thought that their consent was not necessary. The three gentlemen departed, leaving it up to Mr. Blesson to take the responsibility for asking the military to step him, which he did not dare to do." With regard to the members of his staff it is noted that Mr. Glaue fulfilled his duties from the very beginning personally and facing danger. Dr. Woeniger was ill, but nevertheless he appeared immediately in the central office [of the civil guard] when the alarm [the Generalmarsch, "general march"] was sounded. [...][...] Soon after shots had been fired at the armory [Zeughaus], several deputations of the people, of the civil guard, of the students, of the Handwerker-Verein [craftsman or artisan association] appeared in the central office. They demanded more or less vehemently [stürmisch] that the battallions [Natzmer's] that had fired should be withdrawn from the armory, and also the withdrawal of the military from inside it. A deputation of the *Handwerker-Verein* was especially vehement, depicting the ire of the people [Wut des Volkes] as terrible [entsetzlich] and begging imploringly to withdraw the battalions, in so far as the student association [Studenten-Verein] and the *Handwerker-Verein* were ready and strong enough to protect the armory; they only needed permission to enter the building. The demand that the military should be withdrawn could not be consented by him, Mr. Blesson said, pointing out that a deputation regarding this matter should see the Minister of War. And he ordered Dr. Woeniger to accompany them to this location with a written statement that he, Blesson, had no objections if the military was withdrawn. During this time, the ministry refused this request. Mr. Blesson gave in to the request of the *Handwerker-Verein* in the following way. As he had only 12 to 16 men of the civil guard at his disposal which he could position inside the armory, he ordered Dr. Grosse [Große] to negotiate with the troops in the armory regarding the concern of the *Handwerker-Verein*, and at the same time he gave orders that all of the civil guard [at the armory] should withdraw. This order was given in writing. The report of the commission criticized Mr. Blesson in the sharpest possible way.[253]

The juridical aspect of the storming of the arsenal was taken care of by the State Prosecutor, Mr. Temme, in this way:

Notice

It has become known to the public prosecution today that during the attack on the local arsenal last night, a considerable number of rifles, several valuable weapons, and other items belonging to the equipment of the army were forcibly removed from it. I ask everybody who is able to aid the investigation by giving definite information about any individuals to inform me about such facts. [...]

The Prosecutor at the Royal Criminal Court, Temme[254]

* * *

While the Civil Guard had been shooting at the people in front of the Ministry of War (and dispersing those in front of the Sing Academy?) on June 14, the bickering between conservative constitutional monarchists, liberal moderates, and openly reactionary, anti-democratic factions, all of whom supported the monarchy, continued, and the petty-bourgeois Left in the National Assembly remained an isolated minority. All the while, the reactionary press continued to bedevil republicans and radical democrats as enemies of the old Prussian monarchy, something that was undoubtedly expected by the king who had already exhorted Camphausen in the past to get things published in the media that would denounce anarchy and the republican peril. In this context, all attempts by the more progressive members of the Prussian National Assembly to *bourgeoisify* the command structure of the armed forces were bound to fail.

* * *

As we know, a "ministerial" or government crisis ensued in the wake of the storming of the arsenal. The minister of war, General August von Kanitz, who had been appointed on May 1, when the voting rights campaign was in full swing, stepped back on June 16, two days after the Zeughaus had been occupied by the angrily protesting crowd that had feared machinations of the authorities when they heard about the clandestinely attempted—or already ongoing—transport of weapons from the Zeughaus to an unknown destination outside the city.

Mr. von Kanitz was not the only one who expressed his apparent lack of confidence in Camphausen. Count Schwerin—who had been part of all cabinets since March 19, also declared that he would resign, and so did Baron von Arnim. Camphausen made their resignation known to the Prussian National Assembly on March 17.[255] The press immediately reported it. Under the date of June 16, the *Kgl. Privilegirte Berlinische Zeitung* reported in the column "United Germany" regarding the events in Berlin: "According to reports, the ministers Arnim, Graf Schwerin and von Kanitz have asked for their dismissal."[256]

This short message was immediately followed by the following news:

Yesterday afternoon at 5 o'clock, Major Rimpler who is replacing Major Blesson after the latter suddenly resigned, was elected almost unanimously as interim commander of the civil guard by the captains and platoon leaders gathered in the Marstall. [257]

Obviously, the Storming of the Arsenal had repercussions not only on the immediate political level, but also with respect to the Civil Guard and, most likely, within the army as well. The Berlin chief of police, Julius von Minutoli, also felt compelled to step down. Like Blesson, he was in all likelihood under great pressure to do so.[258]

The fact that Count Schwerin—the minister who enjoyed perhaps the closest personal rapport with the king—formally ended his term of office on June 25 was the most problematic part of the government crisis that Camphausen briefly attempted to resolve but failed to cope with. Even though he tried hard, "Camphausen could not replace Schwerin."[259] And so the prime minister told the Prussian National Assembly on March 20, that he, too, would request his dismissal.[260]

As we know, a measure of continuity ensued when Camphausen offered his resignation, in so far as "Hansemann stayed on until September as finance minister in the [new] Auerswald Cabinet [...]"[261] that was to be formed. The decision to appoint Rudolf von Auerswald prime minister must have been taken between June 20 and June 25. As a replacement for the minister of war, von Kanitz, the king selected the lieutenant general von Ludwig Roth von Schreckenstein. Yes, really Schreckenstein; *nomen est omen*?[262]

The crisis and fall of the Camphausen cabinet and the appointment of Auerswald as prime minister on June 25 prompted the satirical Berliner Krakehler to comment,

> And there originated a government of the Right, as a likeness and image; as an image and likeness of the Right, it originated. And there originated a little man and a little woman, and they were called: Auerswald and Hansemann. And the Right blessed them [...][263]

They had no illusions about its orientation, regardless of the "liberal" reputation of both Auerswald and Hansemann. If it was a government of a politically "rightist" persuasion, it was not a secure government, however. It lasted only 75 days, even less than the short-lived Camphausen government.

Quite obviously, among those in power, security concerns continued to prevail after the storming of the arsenal and the creation of barricades by workers with red flags that had been seen in various parts of the city on June 14. But all of this had hardly been an organized way to start a second revolution—or was it? Fears had been largely at the root of the "people's" assault on the arsenal and this indicates that as far as many participants in the attack were concerned, it was largely prompted by the determination to stave off the removal of weapons that might be needed by the army for the feared reactionary attempt that would replace the conservative "liberal" Camphausen government by a state of siege and outright reactionary rule.

The creation of the constabulary by the Auerwald-Hansemann Cabinet was the direct result of the above-mentioned concern about the security of the government.

"On Saturday, the swearing-in of the constables took place all day long in the Exercierhaus in the Köpnicker Feld. They will be operational from Monday," the Kgl. Privilegierte Zeitung reported on Sunday, July 23.[264]

The fact that even the army was no secure foundation for the security of those in power may have been an added factor that contributed to the desire to be able to have several "pillars of support" at the disposal of the government:

- The Civil Guard with about 25,000 men armed with rifles distributed to them, who were obviously not well trained.
- The Constabulary, with 2,000 men—as a first intervention force stationed even in the unruly suburbs, that would be able to intervene more quickly and that was to quell "outbreaks" on the spot, and this immediately, in their incipient phase.
- And yes, in addition to the Civil Guard and the new Constabulary, there were—I think—two regiments of the army that were garrisoned in Berlin since the army had been "recalled" in late March.

In the already mentioned issue of the *Kgl. Privilegirte Berlinische Zeitung,* this bourgeois paper noticed what it described as "a nasty spirit" of insubordination in the 24th regiment stationed in Berlin. Apparently, the rebellious tendency, that was alive in many working-class people, had rubbed off on ordinary soldiers of the Prussian army, as it had on parts of the civil guard. It is remarkable that this happened despite the relatively successful efforts of the government to control disturbances and other "outbreaks" of anger that were driven by working-class dissatisfaction with the socio-economic and political situation. Of late, such "misdemeanors directed against subordination" as the paper mentioned, had occurred frequently ("mehrfach"), and it had required the "calm and determined intervention" by officers of the regiment to suppress them.[265] The fact that it was reported at all in the bourgeois press, rather than being passed over in silence, reveals clearly the importance attributed to it, and thus the worries about a breakdown of discipline in the army that had gripped not only the authorities, but the bourgeois press and its readers, as well.

Already in June, the fall of the Camphansen government and the appointment of the Auerswald-Hansemann cabinet had occasioned a number of articles in the *New Rhenanian Gazette* that was founded by Marx at the beginning of this month in Cologne, the "liberal" center of the Rhine Province. Let us briefly look at some excerpts from articles that were probably written by Marx himself, or jointly with Frederick Engels, in the days since June 20, and that are highly interesting.

In an article written on June 21 that was published on the following day in the *New Rhenanian Gazette*, either Marx or Engels wrote on the situation in Berlin:

> For days now we have been predicting the downfall of the Camphausen Government. And we added: Either a new revolution or a definitely reactionary Government.[266]

The conclusion, after the event of June 14, as expressed in the *New Rhenanian Gazette*, of June 22, clearly was ominous: "The attempt at a new revolution has failed." [267]

Bowing to pressure from the king to better guard against "disturbances" caused by the "mob" or, in fact, angry workers, the Camphausen government had introduced a measure intended to better secure "public order" in Berlin: the creation of the constabulary. Soon there were 2,000 constables, among them, as already mentioned, the heroic barricade fighter, Gus Hesse. On June 23, the government decided that this new force of order—a bit like the Magistrat's "force of protection" that had attempted to police downtown Berlin in the days before the outbreak of revolutionary fighting—should establish a dense network of police stations in the entire city, including the unruly proletarian suburbs outside the walls, in order to quell disturbances at the moment when they were forming, and in order to be able to notify the civil guard immediately.[268]

When it was already being predicted that the Camphausen government would be toppled—as it indeed was, two days later—the *New Rhenanian Gazette* wrote this obituary on the first "liberal" government in Prussia:

> The Camphausen Government has covered the counter-revolution with its liberal-bourgeois cloak. The counter-revolution now feels strong enough to shake off this irksome mask. It is possible that the Government of March 30 will be followed for a few days by some untenable Government of the Left Centre. Its real successor will be the Government of the Prince of Prussia.
>
> Camphausen has the honor of having given the absolutist feudal party its natural boss and himself a successor.
>
> Why pamper the bourgeois guardians any longer? [...] Is not the bourgeoisie tired of revolution? [...]
>
> The Camphausen Government seeks to snatch a pennyworth of popularity, to stir up public compassion by the assurance that it is making its exit from the stage of the state as a dupe. It certainly is a case of the deceived deceiver. Since it served the big bourgeoisie, it was compelled to try to cheat the revolution out of its democratic gains; in combating democracy it was forced to ally itself with the aristocratic party and become the tool

of its counter-revolutionary aims. The aristocratic party is now strong enough to throw its protector overboard. Herr Camphausen has sown reaction as envisaged by the big bourgeoisie and he has reaped reaction as envisaged by the feudal party. One was the well-meant intention of the man, the other his evil fate. A penny's worth of popularity for the disappointed man.[269]

When Rudold von Auerswald was made prime minister by the king, the *New Rhenanian Gazette* commented on the appointment of the new government headed by Auerswald but dominated by Hansemann as follows:

"The hangman stands at the door," a reaction and the Russians are knocking and before the cock will have crowed thrice, the Hansemann Government will have fallen despite Rodbertus and despite the Left Centre. Then good-bye to the Prime Minister's office, good-bye financial plans and gigantic projects for the elimination of want; the abyss will swallow them all and best wishes to Herr Hansemann when he quietly returns to his humble civil hearth and can contemplate the fact that life is but a dream.[270] ("The Hansemann Government," in: Neue Rheinische Zeitung, No. 24, June 24, 1848)

In an article published on June 25 that was entitled "Threat of the Gervinus Zeitung," the New Rhenanian Gazette commented sarcastically on the entire situation and mocked especially the "prestige" of Prussia coveted by the reactionary defenders of the Prussian dynasty and absolute monarchy. Obviously, Prussia's and Frederick William's "prestige" was lost on the day when absolutism was forced to push a "'written scrap of paper,' soiled by plebeian blood, between itself and its people, and when the Court was compelled to place itself under the protection and supervision of bourgeois grain and wool merchants," the author commented (Neue Rheinische Zeitung No. 25, June 25, 1848).[271] But in view of the fact that the New Rhenanian Gazette was anticipating a reactionary coup, one wonders whether this view, that was probably justified at the end of March and in early April, was still correct in June. Perhaps the "prestige" was really gone, and a true return to the *status quo ante* no longer possible after the Royal "consents" of March 19—in other words, after the visible way in which Frederick William had been forced to cave in, in an absolutely humiliating manner. But the question of not "prestige" but power had remained at the forefront—and undoubtedly the day drew nearer when the already accomplished hidden defeat of all liberal bourgeois dreams of political co-participation in power would turn into the spectre of the openly visible breakdown of all such illusions.

If it would not show tragic self-deception or lack of courage or, as others maintain, conscious treason of bourgeois delegates elected on a "moderate" democratic platform, all the ways in which illusions of a "democratic monarchy" in Prussia were expressed would only seem ridiculous to us. But they were a political reality. Thus we note that on July 1, 1848, the delegate C. G. D. Nees von Esenbeck introduced a bill to this effect.[272] Their dream of a "democratic monarchy" remained an empty and meaningless proposal. The more reactionary delegates elected to the assembly had anyway secured royal backing and they aimed at other things.[273]

How "democratic" the democratic monarchy could be when the Auerswald-Hansemann government was in charge was revealed by a progressive publication in Berlin, the satirical *Berliner Krakehler*, on July 22, 1848. It revealed that the political trial against Schlöffel was perhaps the first one after the days of barricade battle in March. But it had by no means remained the last one: "Schlöffel sitzt," it wrote, "Monecke sitzt, Siegrist, Lövinsohn, Korn und Urban sitzen." It commented ironically, "Das Sitzen der Volksmänner ist leider erfolgreicher als die Sitzungen der Volksvertreter."[274]

This small comment published by the Berliner Krakehler on the political persecution of democrats entailed a play with words. The verb *sitzen* means *to sit*, and a *Sitzung* (plural: Sitzungen) is a *session*. But a colloquial use of *sitzen* is made here; it now means "to 'sit' in jail," that is to say, "to be in jail." And so, let's now translate the whole thing into proper English, while of course quite regrettably the pun is lost: "Schlöffel is imprisoned, Monecke is imprisoned, Siegrist [aka Siegerist, the mechanic] is imprisoned. Lövinsohn [aka Loewinson] is imprisoned, Korn is imprisoned, and Urban is imprisoned." "Regrettably, the [practice of] imprisoning the [democratic] men of the people is more successful than the sessions of the delegates [are]" in the Prussian National Assembly and of course also in the Frankfurt-based Assembly.

Focusing on a German parliament meeting in Frankfurt, Frederick Engels demasked the prevalent phrases then current. He wrote,

> It certainly speaks in favor of the Left in Frankfurt that, apart from a few exceptions, the deputies of the Left were perfectly delighted with Citizen Ruge's speech on Poland, a speech which contained the following passage:
>
> *"Whether we have in mind democratic monarchy, democratized monarchy (!) or pure democracy, let us not quarrel about this; on the whole we want the same thing—freedom, national freedom, and rule of the people!"*
>
> Are we expected to be enthusiastic about a Left that allows itself to be carried away when someone says that it wants "on the whole the same thing" as the Right, as Herr Radowitz, Herr Lichnowski, Herr Vincke and all the other fat or lean knights? A Left whose head has been turned with rapture and which forgets everything as soon as it hears a few empty slogans, such as "national freedom" and "rule of the people?"

But let us leave the Left and return to Citizen Ruge.

> "So far, no revolution that swept the world was greater than the revolution of 1848."
>
> "As regards its principles, it is the most humane revolution" for these principles have arisen as a result of the glossing over of the most contradictory interests.
>
> "It is the most humane revolution as regards its decrees and proclamations," for they represent a compendium of philanthropical fantasies and sentimental phrases about fraternity produced by all the feather-heads of Europe,"[275]

Engels commented sarcastically, continuing by pointing out in sharp manner the realities of repression in Posen and counterrevolution in Paris, Kraków, and Prague:

> "It is the most humane revolution as regards its actuality," that is, the massacres and barbarities in Posen, the murderous incendiarism of Radetzky, the ferocious cruelties committed in Paris by the victors of June, the butcheries in Cracow and Prague, the rule of brutal soldiery everywhere—in short, all the outrages which constitute the "actuality" of this revolution today, September 1, 1848, and which have spilled more blood in four months than was spilled in 1793 and 1794 taken together.
>
> The "humane" Citizen Ruge![276]

The keen analysis of the treason of the *soi-disant* "liberal bourgeoisie" during the years of 1848 and 1849 that both Engels and Karl Marx offered already in 1848 has been confirmed by a number of progressive historians, among them Walter Schmidt. Public and private statements by Camphausen and Hansemann show how much they resented political participation of the masses and direct elections. They were not the only ones. People like Gustav Mevissen and Hermann von Beckerath[277]—both were bankers[278]—were afraid of the subaltern classes and though they loathed the bureaucratic "tyranny" of Berlin's often aristocratic administrative officials, fear of the proletarian masses draw them closer to the king. Another "Liberal" from the Rhine Province, Baron August von der Heydt—the banker and delegate elected to the Rhenish Provincial Diet for Elberfeld (who also represented Elberfeld's bourgeoisie in the first United Diet in 1847)—was more than ready to represent the Rhenish big bourgeoisie as Minister of Commerce, Trade, and Public Works in the reactionary Brandenburg-Manteuffel government. He assumed office on December 4, 1848. His reputation was impeccable; he could boast a brother, Carl von der Heydt, who already "[gave] a speech advocating absolute monarchy" as early as August 1848, thus before the actual reactionary coup d'état.[279]

As far as August Brass is concerned, so much is clear: he was an educated man—it is enough to remind the reader again of the fact that he had received a Ph.D. from the university in Berlin where Hegel had been teaching. The opening sentences of his book about the March Revolution in his native city reveal already the impact of Hegel's philosophy. What Brass gives the reader here is metaphorical language that equates "time" (history) with "god," thus making it the absolute and supremely reigning reality. This is basically a popularized version of Hegel's idealistic conception of the dialectical course of "History" as the movement of the absolute "Geist" (consciousness, "spirit") that, of necessity, becomes conscious of itself in the process. *Everything that is, is reasonable (vernünftig)*, Hegel maintained—in other words: it is hypostasized Reason (Vernunft) that manifests itself, *in an increasing way*, in the course of history. Every stage of history, for Hegel, thus represents the historical form (or stage) of Reason that has been attained. What becomes unreasonable, is bound to disappear; it will cease to exist. Obviously, *Formwandel*, change of (logical) forms, is a primary concept inscribed in Hegel's philosophic system. In a different sense, it became also a central category of Marx.

For people like August Brass, influenced by Hegel, the historical process, thought of as autonomous, self-propelled "movement" of the hypostasized, abstract [thus abstracted, and therefore implicitly: general(ized) human] "spirit" or "Geist" (i.e. dialectical evolution of consciousness, advances of Reason) meant *that the consciousness of concrete human beings had increased*, it had *matured*. And this demanded that they should no longer be treated like children, by an absolutist, even though supposedly (since the times of Frederick II) "enlightened" monarchical government. The time and conditions—above all, the *Geist*, spirit, consciousness of citizens, of the people, in his native city of Berlin, in all of Prussia, all of Germany, even in all of Europe—had *matured* (of necessity, in the course of what was "the historical process," as propelled by Reason itself). And thus, time had become ripe for change.

Marx was to put it differently—the other way, "vom Kopf auf die Füße" ("from the head on the feet"): he was thus rejecting a view that was privileging the ideas that develop in history, the evolving consciousness of people, etc., that Hegelian idealists regarded as the primary reality and true motive force. And he was turning it around, making it thus "stand on its feet," by asserting that it was above all politico-economic conditions that had matured.

And therefore, the "maturation" of the consciousness of most people reflected the material process.[280]

Marx, and also Frederick Engels, later on rephrased this basic insight by emphasizing that it is not only *the real, "material" social relations* (class relations and relations of production) that affect the forms and the development of consciousness, but that *prevailing forms of consciousness* (mental customs, everyday knowledge, ideologies, theories, etc.) *in turn* affect "material social reality."

The relationship between the "material" social forms and processes and the sphere of ideas and ideologies thus is regarded as *reciprocal*, or in other words, it is characterized by *interference* (a term borrowed from "wave mechanics," studied in the field of optics, of acoustics, etc.). But both Engels and Marx did not leave us in doubt that they considered the real social processes, especially the process of material production, and the real form(s) of class conflict, as primary.

If we compare this view—which, in its basic form (that was implying the accentuation of material developments), had already been embraced by Marx and his collaborator, Engels, at the time when they wrote and published the *Communist Manifesto* in 1848—with the respective views expressed by Brass in 1848, it becomes clear how much August Brass was, by all means, separated from the position of Marx. As most educated Germans at the time, he remained an idealist, and though somehow attached to Hegelianism, he did not proceed to a position that could be called, with good reason, "materialist."

Still, it is true that people like Brass, Oppenheim, Jung, Jacoby, Löwenstein and so on had clear demands when they chose political activism in 1848. Some of them, if not all, were radical democrats, and all of them had sympathies for the subaltern classes. What they wanted, was clear: as educated men, if not intellectuals—and as members of the more or less well-off part of the petty bourgeoisie—they wanted freedom of the press, a constitution, the right to vote (and this expanded—thus "generalized"—and in ways typically thought of at their time; thus they, too, were excluding women).

Yes, and, as a matter of fact, they wanted an end to discrimination based on religion.[281] This is understandable and was justified. People like Brass and Woeniger shunned prejudice and discrimination, and those with Jewish roots —democrats like Oppenheim, Jacoby, or Löwenstein—were sick of it. Despite so-called emancipation of Jews in Prussia, anti-Jewish prejudice remained widespread in everyday life, and the State violated its own decree and promises when, for instance, educated Jewish Prussians, despite their university degree, could not become officers in the army at the time. So all of these men of the petty-bourgeoisie had demands and voiced them; it amounted to a Democratic bourgeois [or petty-bourgeois] program.

Did Berlin's workers also have a program? We hear nothing about this—or do we?—that would appear as specifically proletarian, in the account of the revolution provided by Brass.

Marc Reynebeau says of the subaltern classes—the social forces that were so decisive everywhere when they fought on the barricades in 1848—that they had neither demands nor a program nor were they organized at all.[282] He refers to the Belgian proletariat in the factories of Gent, in the manufactories of Brussels, and in the Borinage mining region. But he refers also to France, and what he says, could be said with the same justification or lack of justification about the subaltern masses—the proletariat—of Berlin.

But then, what made them join the revolution and why did they bear the brunt of the sacrifice during the fighting?

A simple working-class woman put it across vis-à-vis Frederick Engels in a street of Paris in 1848 when he confronted her, wearing the uniform if the national guard, called upon to defend the Republic against the "emeute" of the workers. Le people souffre tellement!, that's what she said, more or less. That was the sentiment expressed. The people suffer so much. Or to quote Engels verbatim: *One doesn't have to shoot at the people. It is so unfortunate!*[283]

It expressed everything.

It expressed why these men clad in the blue blouses of workers were fighting on the barricades.[284] Yes, it is true, in Berlin, too; *the blouses bleues des travailleurs* could be seen, worn by men of all ages who manned the barricades. They were a frequent sight, far more than the feathered hats and green coats of the Rifleman's Association. The blue blouse was typical: in Paris, in Brussels, in Berlin, for it was cheap yet sturdy.

But is it true that these fighters, these men clad in blue, that this *unfortunate people*—conscious, as it was of its unhappy situation—had no demands?

It is true that they would only have adopted demands formulated by bourgeois and petty-bourgeois democrats if they had repeated their list. They did not have to; they had heard these words; these utterances were known to them, and whether they reverberated in their minds or not, they were not against them—and there must have been those among them (probably many, at that time) who recognized their importance and took them seriously. Freedom of the press. Juries that were elected. No discrimination due to religious beliefs. The vote, general suffrage. But were these demands "their demands," would they have been on the top of their list, had they drawn up a list *in the polished way and submissive tone* of the petitions submitted in Berlin in March, 1848? No—it was not how they spoke: they spoke more directly, with guns, with stones thrown from roofs, and curses hurled at Prussian officers. Their demand was clear to them: they wanted an end to their suffering.

Something else also becomes very clear—in the simple words directed at Engels by a "simple" woman of the people: To people like Brass—educated men, lawyers or writers or philosophers or even physicians, certainly brave men, democrats who manned the barricades when all their petitions remained without answer, or rather, were answered by soldiers using their sabres and guns—the concept that was so central to them in their discourse, the term "people," had either an ethnic significance, or a quite general political meaning, as an abstract concept referring to all inhabitants of a country, seen as possessors of natural, political, "civil" rights they should own.

To the working woman in Paris, quoted by Engels, and very likely to most fellow working people at that time, the meaning of the word people *was not that abstract at all*, and it also did not construct a unity defined by a shared language or a sense of belonging to a "nation" or "tribe."[285]

To her, it was clear, and intuitively so, that the unity the word "people" referred to excluded the rulers, the government.

Neither did it comprise the bourgeoisie.

"Moderate" (de facto, often rather conservative) Liberals representing the German bourgeoisie in 1848: David Hansemann is the 2nd, counting from the left margin, in the upper row; the 4th is von Auerswald, the 5th is Waldeck. The 2nd in the front row is Ludolf Camphausen.[286]

It excluded even *the petty-bourgeois citizen* who was well-off—in contrast to the master craftsman who toiled, hurt by the crisis, in his workshop, deserted by journeymen he could no longer pay. He might be an owner of a wretched abode, and yet he starved and was unable to save his wife and children from hunger.

The people, to her, were those who suffered.

The people were those who knew that it wasn't just.

If "Speak bitterness meetings" had taken place in the days of March, 1848, immediately after the bloody struggle, while men of the people presented the dead to the pale, defeated king, would they have spared his life and that of the Prince of Prussia, or that of his ministers, of the generals who served him, shooting at them, any more than France spared the life of Louis XVI?

Marx knew what the Jacobys, the Woenigers, and the Brasses didn't know: there is no unity possible between those who suffer and those who profit from it: from a world of inequality and separate classes, opposed in their interest.[287] The bourgeois spirit might be aware of such unequal existence, but they shrank back from the change required. They thought that charitable acts, paternalistic *bienfaisance*, Wohlthätigkeit, *a kind word* would suffice—if they cared at all.

For someone like Marx, the illusions did no longer exist that the class was harboring *into which fate had thrown him at birth*. In an essay published on June 29, 1848 he said it clearly, speaking of *the French nation*—but it could have been *any nation* by then, certainly the German nation, as well—and what he said should resound and should make us listen. What he saw in these days, and what he clearly expressed, was the deep gap that divided the nation "into two nations, the nation of the owners and the nation of the workers."[288] Two worlds, two nations within a society—two cultures. They even spoke different languages, for they gave the same words a different meaning.

It was this that let Marx, and that could let us today, recognize what the subaltern classes and, most of all, the workers are capable of. Ernest Mandel called it their "revolutionary potential."[289]

And nonetheless, these women and men—devasted by work, struck by strains of bad luck, insulted too often—still lack clarity. It was so in 1830. It was so again in 1848. People learn slowly, and yet they fought. Today, in numerous countries—also in the U.S., in this 21st century—it is true of many who suffer *that they have no program, no understanding of a theoretical sort* that would let them see clearly and make them aware in a practical sense of the route they must take to emancipation, self-emancipation as a class, human emancipation—let us put it like this.

Workers have grievances; even if speechless, they have demands. They feel them, they sense that so much is lacking, THAT THINGS ARE NOT GOOD. And so it is clear that they desire change. But not any change, and certainly not just the word and the slogan as an empty promise. Still, in how many hearts did that empty promise of Obama kindle hopes? And today? We know that millions who voted for Bernie Sanders and for Mr. Trump were workers: people with grievances, suffering people, in many ways. Don't kid yourself: America is a rich country—but the majority, the working class, is not well-off. They suffer: the insecurity of life when hiring and firing is so easy. Debt, private debt, not just because they were seduced; after all, everything is so expensive. There exist needs. You need a car to get to work. You lease it, and the payments hurt. But what hurts even more is the climate of rightlessness on the factory floor, the fact that you must swallow commands and insults, that you can never speak up and clarify your point-of-view, or draw on experience, better experience quite often, though only in minor matters like *how the job should be done*. You know it, but they don't listen. You ask for a pay hike, and they fire you. You want time off, because your kids are sick—and they say No.

Was it like that in France when the workers rebelled? Was it like that when they took to the barricades in Berlin?

Yes, these men and women were thirsting for an end to their suffering.

Their sisters and brethren today thirst for it now, but don't know it, as yet.

But the time will come when they will open their eyes and see things more clearly, and act.

The July insurgency was defeated, as we all know. The workers in Paris had risked all and lost. Repression and persecution were the reply. This is the possibility one has to reckon with. But the lesson of the March Revolution of 1848 is that the revolutionaries have to topple the *powers that be* when these seem to have reached the point of their greatest weakness—rather than agreeing to compromises, accepting "concessions granted," and seeking reconciliation. The right moment exists only once. It is synonymous with final defeat if they let it pass unused. It is always "them" or "us"—there are no "win-win" situations.

Other reports say that an old woman standing in the crowd cried out, Don't believe him. He is lying. He has always lied. She was silenced by plainclothesmen.

Endnotes

1. From a letter to the editor, *Süddeutsche Zeitung*, Dec. 13, 2018, p.22.
2. Marx variously dwelt on this topic. Among more recent contributions, it is worthwhile to notice Alexander Gerschenkron, *Economic Backwardness in Historical Perspective: A Book of Essays*, Cambridge, Mass.: Belknap Press, 1976. A 29-page essay by Gerschenkron on this subject was first published in 1952.
3. In March 1849, Marx wrote, "If [...], in the recent period a few branches of German industry have to some extent improved their position, they owe it solely to the English period of prosperity. From the whole of the history of commerce the Germans should know that they have no commercial history of their own, that they have to suffer for English crises, while in periods of over-production in England, a minute percentage is all that falls to their lot. But they have nothing to thank their Christian-Germanic governments for except accelerated bankruptcy." (Karl Marx, "The State of Trade", in: *Karl Marx and Frederick Engels, Collected Works* (MECW). Vol. 9: *Marx and Engels: 1849*. Moscow: Progress Publ., 1977; XXXIV, 661 S.; republished as: *Collected Works* (MECW), Vol. 9, transl. by Jack Cohen et al. London: Lawrence & Wishart, 1985, p. 3.) –It is clear that the relative belatedness of the development of a financial bourgeoisie, of agrarian capitalism in Germany, and then also of some notable early industrial progress since the 1830s, is related to the country's relatively peripheral geographic location with regard to the two countries that saw the fastest capitalist development, England and France. In both countries, buccaneers based in the Atlantic seaboard cities had co-profited from the Spanish colonialist exploitation of the New World that transferred enormous riches to Europe which never set off the kind of bourgeois proto-capitalist development on the Iberian Peninsula that it was to propel in cities like Liverpool, London, Bordeaux, Nantes or Rouen. In Spain, it was not necessary at the time to trade for the sake of profit; it was not necessary to develop proto-industries—the "enterprising" members of the lower classes found it easier to go West, to the colonies, in order to get rich, and the dominant strata that were directly profiting from colonial exploitation due to their positions of power could rely safely on imports of luxury goods from poorer neighboring countries. But the on-going plunder of the New World, piracy, and then the slave trade—the "triangular" Atlantic trade—had contributed enormously to original accumulation in the two countries named. In major seaboard cities of England, France, and then also Holland, the upper segments of the late medieval and, then, early modern commercial class of merchants became a fairly modern commercial and, at the same time, financial bourgeoisie—and a less affluent, middle segment branched out into production. Modern British textile industry in the Manchester regions largely relied on Liverpool-based capital; the proto-industrial 18th century textile manufacturers in Elbeuf and other locations near Rouen relied on investment of commercial capital accumulated in Rouen. In comparison with these regions of dynamic capitalist growth, Germany—ravaged also by the Third Year's war in 1618–1648—was a peripheral region in the 17th and 18th century.
4. The question whether the representative bodies of Berlin's enfranchised burghers (according to one source, there were 30,000 of these burghers out of a population,

in Berlin, of more than 400,000) should apply to the government for permission to form a "burgher guard," or civil guard, was discussed in the assembly of city councilors shortly before the outbreak of the revolution, on March 11, 1848.(See Adolf Wolff, *Berliner Revolutions-Chronik: Darstellung der Berliner Bewegungen im Jahre 1848 nach politischen, socialen und literarischen Beziehungen* [Chronicle of the Berlin revolution: An account of the Berlin movements in 1848 in political, social and literary respect], Vol. 1. Berlin: Gustav Hempel, 1851, pp. 37–41) Several city councilors advocated it; most of these, fearful of food riots like the one in April 1847 that may have caused damage to their business, because they wanted to employ it against the "mob" (they used the word a few times during the debate); a small minority of two, who sympathized with the demands of "Volksbewaffnung" (arming of the entire people) raised in people's assemblies, probably advocated it because they wanted to push in a direction that could be tantamount to giving democratic commoners the nucleus of a military force of their own. The question was shelved, as the majority was convinced that the government would not allow a "civil guard." The entire idea of a civil guard, the way it figured in the minds of many "conservative-liberal" burghers, had taken root more clearly since the French July Revolution of 1830 and the Belgian revolution of 1830 that produced "civil guards." If we keep this in mind, it becomes clear that to many if not most of Berlin's enfranchised burghers, the idea of a civil guard implied something totally different from a people's militia. At best, a burghers' guard would be a tool against those below them (the "subaltern classes," a term used by Gramsci in his prison cahiers as a synonym for the working class and related strata), and a weapon against those above, if their grievances were not addressed by the authorities. This view reflected the Belgian experience: When the revolution in Brussels erupted on Aug. 25, 1830, numerous groups of people, emerging from the theatre where they had seen a play that triggered their readiness to revolt, went to such sites in the city as the house of the chief of police, De Knyff, and the minister of justice. De Smet writes that soldiers were disarmed, furniture was taken away, and the houses of these officials that represented Dutch rule were set aflame. Troops arrived and engaged in skirmishes with the burghers but soon ceased to shoot and withdrew to their barracks and to the palace of the king. It was then that a "garde bourgeoisie" was formed, under the command of Baron Emmanuel d'Hooghvorst, and a bit later the tricolored flag of Brabant that was to become the Belgian flag fluttered above the town hall. (Joseph Jean de Smet, *Histoire de la Belgique*, 5th revised and augmented ed., Vol. 2, Ghent : Vanryckegem-Hovaere, 1840, p.317)

In the wake of the successful revolution in Brussels in the late summer of 1830 that echoed the July revolution in Paris, a proclamation was issued in the insurgent city on Sept. 3, according the which the King invited its inhabitants to present their demands to him in the Hague. The troops were withdrawn from Brussels. The final sentence of this proclamation says, "The Bourgeois Guard (or Burgher Guard) commits itself to accept no change of the dynasty and to protect the city and especially the palace." ("La Garde bourgeoise s'engage sur l'honneur à ne pas souffrir de changement de dynastie et à protéger la ville et spécialement les palais." – Quoted in : Auguste de Wargny, *Esquisses historiques de la révolution de Belgique en 1830.* Bruxelles : chez H. Talier, 1830, p.101) The House of Orange, as the ruling dynasty in both the Netherlands proper and that part which came to be known as Belgium, lost Belgium, of course. But the ambiguous nature of the guard as an organ of revolution and a coveted military guarantor of stability, continuity, and order became apparent. The *garde bourgeoise* in Belgium was soon referred to also as the *garde civile*. After Oct. 4, 1830, when a "declaration by the Provisional Government [...] marked the birth of the Belgian state" (Claude Roosens, "Première partie (1830-1914)," in: Rik Coolsaet; Vincent Dujardin; Claude Roosens [avec la collaboration de Vincent Delcorps et Anne-Sophie Gijs], *Les affaires étrangers au service de l'État belge : De 1830 à nos jours*. Bruxelles : Mardaga, 2014, pp.16ff., here: p.17), it continued to function as a factor of law and order. Since 1830, "burgher guards" (Bürgergarden) existed also in Hesse, Saxony, and Brunswick where sovereigns had also bowed to popular pressure and had swallowed the necessity of a constitution. (Ralf Pröve, *Stadtgemeindlicher Republikanismus*, ibid, p. 180) These burgher guards, *though demanded not only by outspoken petty-bourgeois and bourgeois liberals, but also by politically aware and frequently radical members of the subaltern classes*, remained "bourgeois" in orientation. The "conservative-liberal" Karl Schöchlin, based on his experience with civil or burgher guards in Central or Southwest Germany, clearly revealed the "Bürgerwehr" as what is was, or turned out to be: "due to the forceful and law-abiding sense of individual municipalities [in fact, this refers to the leading figures; the mayor, aldermen, those sitting in the city councilors' assembly, and at most, to the majority or a significant portion of the enfranchised citizens], [...] the civil guard [Bürgerwehr] became what it should be: a protection of bourgeois order, and at the same time the basis for the restoration of the undermined state of affairs." (nur durch den kräftigen und gesetzlichen Sinn einzelner Gemeinden wurde [...] die Bürgerwehr, was sie seyn sollte: ein Schutz der bürgerlichen Ordnung, und zugleich die Grundlage zur Wiederherstellung des erschütterten gesetzlichen Zustandes. - Karl Schöchlin, *Geschichte des Großherzogthums Baden unter der Regierung des Großherzogs Lepold von 1830–1852. Nebst einem Rückblick auf die frühere Geschichte des Landes*. Karlsruhe: A. Bielefeld, 1856, p.365.) The same assessment of civil guards in found in the Acta of the Saxonian Diet (Landtag). After having first of all discussed older forms of patriotic arming of the population (mainly against foreign adversaries), the Records of the Saxonian Diet for the year 1837 (*Landtags-Acten vom Jahre 1837: Beilagen zu den Protocollen der zweiten Kammer* [Acta (or: Records) of the "Landtag" for the Year 1837: Supplement regarding the minutes of the Second Chamber], Zweite Sammlung [2nd Collection]. Dresden: Kgl. Hofbuchdruckerei of Meinhold and Sons, n.d., p. 544) mention the decree of March 22, 1828, "Concerning the Creation of Burgher Guards" (die Errichtung von Bürgergarden betreffend) and continue by praising the *positive contribution* of these burgher guards that was owed to their "sense of faithfulness and their dedication to the duty of safeguarding the law and order of the fatherland, which inspired and united the well-thinking of every age and class during the ominous period of the year 1830" ("dem Sinne der Treue und dem Pflichtgefühle für Aufrechterhaltung des Rechts und der Ordnung im Vaterlande, welches die Gutgesinnten jedes Alters und Standes in der verhängnißvollen Periode des Jahres 1830. begeisterte und zu einem festen Bund vereinigte. – *Landtags-Acten*, Ibid, p.544.), thus at the time of revolution. This is a clear indication that (at least up to a point) the integration of the burgher guards had been achieved; or should we merely assume that this was only the perception of those close to the authorities? It is possible that this view may miss a fact—the ambiguity of the political position of burghers who desired law and order and the submissiveness of the subaltern classes, but who nonetheless wanted to attain and to expand political rights that the absolutist monarchy had always denied them and that constitutions like those accorded in Hesse, Saxony, etc. could only grant in an inadequate way.

At any rate we must not forget that it is for good reason that Jean-Pierre Vivet refers to the period of 1830–1914 as a period characterized by the dominance of the bourgeoisie in Europe. (See Jean-Pierre Vivet, *Les Mémories de l'Europe: L'Europe bourgeoise, 1830-1914*. Paris: R. Laffont, 1972.) Pröve points out, however, that the bourgeois character of the "burgher guards" formed in 1830 in some of the smaller German states featured a progressive aspect (or element) that reflected the political aspirations of the so-called "middle classes": "thus the burgher guards were meant not only to care for the maintenance of public security [above all, the security of private property, i.e. the economic interests of the propertied classes], but they were also expected to play a positive role with regard the 'preservation of the constitution' and the 'furthering of a community spirit' [...]" (... sollten die Bürgergarden ... nicht nur für die Erhaltung der öffentlichen Sicherheit sorgen, sondern auch bei der 'Aufrechterhaltiung der Verfassung' mitwirken und der 'Beförderung des Gemeinsinnes' dienen; Pröve, ibid, p.180; the words 'preservation of the constitution' and 'furthering of a community spirit' quoted by Pröve are from the entry "Volksbewaffnung," in: *Rheinisches Conversations-Lexicon* [Rhenish Encyclopedia], 3rd ed., Vol. XII, 1836, pp.18-23.)

With regard to Saxony in the 1830s, see also the article "Entstehung und Charakter der Kommunalgarden im Königreich Sachsen 1830/31" in: *Jahrbuch für Regionalgeschichte* [Yearbook for Regional HIstory], Vol. 14 (1987), pp.228ff. The author writes that it was significant that the *Kommunalgarden* [guards of the municipality (in German, Kommune), organized and overseen by the bourgeois *elected* authorities of the provincial towns and smaller capitals (that, as a rule, counted only a few enfranchised burghers among their inhabitants)] continued to exist after the end of the revolution of 1830–1831, and this in so far "as a well-organized armed institution of the citizenry [Bürgertum, this refers to the class character and to the institutional or 'political' form of its acknowledged mode of limited self-rule in German cities] was preserved *that could become the point of departure for a revolutionary arming of the people in the case of a new revolutionary upturn.*" (Emphasis by me [AW]; the passage, in German, is: "denn es wurde eine gut organisierte bewaffnete Institution des städtischen Bürgertums erhalten, die bei einem neuen revolutionären Aufschwung den Ausgangspunkt für eine revolutionäre Volksbewaffnung bilden konnte." - Yearbook, ibid, p.242) The radical democratic concept of such an "arming of the people" that transcended the limited concept of a "garde bourgeoise" or "garde civil" as an instrument of law and order, to be employed against the "mob" during periods of revolutionary unrest, was articulated quite openly already prior to the revolutionary outbreak of 1848. Ralf Pröve mentions that, as early as 1847, democrats voiced sharp criticism with respect to the "military constitution" of the German Confederation (the "Bundes-militärverfassung") because it did not permit a general arming of the people (allgemeine Volksbewaffnung). (Ralf Pröve, "Politische Partizipation und soziale Ordnung; Das Konzept der Volksbewaffnung und die Funktion der Bürgerwehren", in: Wolfgang Hardtwig, ed., *Revolution in Deutschland und Europa 1848/49*, Göttingen: Vandenhoeck & Ruprecht, 1998, pp.79ff., here: p. 114.)

As far as the radical democrats were concerned, it is obvious that their conservative adversaries could decipher their ultimate intentions when men belonging to the democratic current demanded again and again, even after the formation of a civil guard in 1848, the promised arming of the people. In 1848, the democrats sought safeguards against counter-revolutionary attempts by the social forces that had supported absolutism for so long; they desired to deepen the revolutionary process and attain further democratic rights, above all socio-economic rights of the subaltern classes, and perhaps some of them really thought of "Volksbewaffung" as a necessary condition of the formation of a republican army, as Schöchlin—referring to the situation in Southwestern Germany in 1849—writes in hindsight. Schöchlin says, "durch die Volksbewaffnung hoffte man ein republikanisches Heer zu bilden" (by way of the arming of the people, it was hoped to create a republican army)! (Karl Schöchlin, ibid, p.365.)

5   In early March 1848, both concepts had figured and both views, as well as the implicit interests connected with them, collided, though not openly, in the context of such debates as the one that took place between city councilors in the city councilors' assembly of Berlin on March 11. In this debate, and even more in the difference that stands out between the talks of "conservative-liberal" city councilors in the assembly and speeches given by democrats in *people's assemblies* ("Volksversammlungen") in Berlin since March 6, the class background (or even class antagonism?) underlying both positions became apparent. This should be kept in mind if we try to assess the decision of Count Arnim "and Co." on March 19 to proceed quickly with the formation of a citizen guard, thus exactly the "institution" that had seemed unacceptable to the Prussian government and the king just a few weeks, if not days, ago.

6   In 1848, at least according to Pröve, the arming of the people ("Volksbewaffnung") was "the first of the promises and demands, the fulfillment of which was attained" ("die erste der Verheißungen und Forderungen, deren Erfüllung bewerkstelligt wurde"), when the revolutionaries voiced their demands in 1848. (Ralf Pröve, *Stadtgemeindlicher Republikanismus und die 'Macht des Volkes': Civile Ordnungsformationen und kommunale Leitbilder politischer Partizipation in den deutschen Staaten vom Ende des 18. bis Mitte des 19. Jahrhunderts.* Göttingen: Vandenhoeck & Ruprecht, 2000, p.166)

As if to alert us to the ambiguity of both the demand and the promise, Pröve quotes Carl Schwebemeyer (Pröve, ibid, p.166), who stated in 1848, "The arming of the people, the creation of a civil guard, was—as it were—regarded as the palladium of all other freedoms, as the Minerva behind whose protective shield the rights of the people just attained in struggle" would be "secure and not endangered" (in German: "Volksbewaffnung, die Einrichtung eines Bürgerwehr, wurde gleichsam als das Palladium aller übrigen Freiheiten betrachtet, als die Minerva, hinter deren schützendem Schilde die soeben erkämpften Rechte des Volkes [...] sicher und ungefährdet" – Carl Schwebemeyer, *Die Volksbewaffnung, ihr Wesen und Wirken* [The Arming of the People: Its Character and Its Practice]. Wriezen: n.p., n.d. [1848], p.3).

The equation of both concepts, "arming of the people" and "creation of a civil guard," that we find in Schwebemeyer's book says everything about the naivety and the illusions that existed at the time in the minds of many contemporaries. Pröve is one of those who is aware of the wishy-washy way this concept "arming of the people" was employed, as he says poignantly (Pröve, ibid, p.166) that it is recommended—"[r]egarding the unclear idea of a concrete arming of the people" ["[z]ur unklaren Vorstellung einer konkreten Volksbewaffnung"]—to see: Friedrich Vischer, *Das Bürger-Institut oder: Ist der Jammer noch länger zum Ansehen? Eine bitterliche Klage und dringliche Bitte an das wirtembergische Ministerium.* [The Citizens Institution or: Can we bear any longer to see its woeful condition? A bitter complaint and urgent request to the government of Württemberg] Stuttgart 1849. He quotes the following (from Vischer, p. 14): "Thus the masses thought [...] that they were permitted to carry arms. On this basis [...], a part [of the population] thought: 'the government is armed, the people should also be armed.'" ("So dachte die Masse des Volks [...] Waffen tragen zu dürfen. Auf dieser Grundlage [...] dachte ein Theil so: die Regierung ist bewaffnet, das Volk soll auch bewaffnet sein.")

7   As Leopold von Ranke (1795-1886)—the noted Prussian historian who was in close contact with the king in all those years—wrote in his biographical entry on Frederick William IV, published in the *General German Biography* (ADB), the monarch later on said quite often to him that he, the royal family, and those in top positions in the military and the government were all "lying flat on their bellies" and taking cover in those days and weeks when they felt the effects of a sudden defeat suffered so unexpectedly on March 18–19, 1848 ("Damals lagen wir Alle auf dem Bauche." These were the king's words). See Leopold von Ranke, "Friedrich Wilhelm IV., König von Preußen", in: Allgemeine Deutsche Biographie [General German Biography (= ADB)], Vol. 7, Leipzig: Duncker & Humblot, 1877, pp. 729–776, here p. 770.

8   Ranke wrote, "This moment occurred [...], [when]—stepping on the balcony of the palace—he acknowledged the popular movement, as it were." ("Jener Moment trat ein [...], [als er] auf den Balkon des Schlosses tretend, die Volksbewegung gleichsam anerkannte." – Leopold von Ranke, ibidem, p.770.) Ranke's conclusion is plausible because Frederick William IV had so stubbornly resisted constitutionalism and because it was a moment that forced him to obey demands, rather than acting in accordance with his own will, as a monarch.

9   A.W. Ward describes Count Arnim, Count Schwerin, Alfred von Auerswald, and of course also Camphausen who became prime minister at the end of March, as "avowed Liberals, though of no extreme type." (A. W. Ward, "The Revolution and the Reaction in Germany and Austria. I. (1848–1849)," in: *The Cambridge Modern History*, ed. by A.W. Ward, G.W. Prothero and Stanley Leathes, Vol. XI: *The Growth of Nationalities*, Cambridge: Cambridge Univ. Press, 1909, p.159) This is, of course, the view of staunchly bourgeois 20th century British "Liberals"— but it misses the point in so far as loyalty to their aristocratic class background and to the monarchy made people like Arnim, Auerswald and Schwerin merely ready to concede just a minimum of *political rights* and *power sharing* to the bourgeoisie, and this only because "the time"—the historical moment of undeniable royal defeat—required it. What they shared with the Camphausens and Hansemanns was the fear of further revolutionary "unrest" attributable to an "unruly" mass of workers and pauperized members of the petty-bourgeoisie. It prompted all of these men, who had their own reasons to wish for a constitution, to desire a constitution that would increase the say of their class in political affairs while excluding the masses from all genuine participation.

10 As August Brass reports in his book, the "King, accompanied by his spouse and two of his ministers, Count Arnim and Count Schwerin, stepped onto the balcony." Both Count Adolf Heinrich von Arnim-Boitzenburg (1803–1868) and Count Maximilian von Schwerin (1804–1872) had just been appointed as ministers on March 19, 1848 and Arnim was charged with heading the new government on the very day of the occurrences here discussed. This may explain why they were present at this moment and may have been asked initially by the king to step on the balcony, in his stead.

11 When Frederick William IV stepped on the balcony to face the bodies of Berliners killed by his soldiers, the angry call that he should take off his helmet in a show

of respect had forced him to do it. The roles were reversed. Frederick William IV bowed his head in front of his subjects, and even in front of those insurgents who had died fighting him. The king always remembered this moment later on as extremely humiliating.

12 The words "Jetzt fehlt uns nur noch die Guillotine" (Now the only thing that is missing for us is the guillotine) were a significant indication of the ability of the king and queen to comprehend the dangers inscribed in the situation at a moment when the troops had left the capital and not even a small detachment had remained stationed in the palace to protect the king. He and the royal family were de facto hostages of the revolutionaries at this moment. The statement ascribed to the Queen is quoted by W. Blos in his review of a publication by major O. who heard and who reported it. – See: W. B. = Wilhelm Blos, "Die Flucht des Prinzen von Preußen, nachmaligen Kaisers Wilhelm I. Nach den Aufzeichnungen des Majors O. im Stabe des Prinzen von Preußen. Stuttgart, Greiner & Pfeiffer" [book review], in: *Die Neue Zeit: Wochenschrift der deutschen Sozialdemokratie*, 32.Jg.(1913–1914), 1. Bd.(1914), Heft 24, pp. 916-918. The exclamation was reported (in his published "Notes") by major O., an officer in the staff of William, Prince of Prussia. The major was present on the occasion, and then accompanied the prince on his flight to Hamburg. The quotation was later confirmed by a document found in official archives.

13 After the developments Brass witnessed during the spring and summer of 1848 in Berlin and in Germany, his assessment seems to have changed. At least, this is indicated by the fact that Brass founded a newspaper in October, 1848 that he called "The Republic." The "National Gazette" in Vienna, a self-described "political people's newspaper advocating democratic aspirations," quotes the following from a statement of purpose (or political platform) of *The Republic*—thus quite obviously sentences from an editorial written by Brass: "The Republic will strive with all its might to convince people of the correctness of this principle—that a Republican can only be a good fellow, and that we must all become good fellows if we want to become Republicans." [Die Republik wird aus allen Kräften dahin streben, die Leute von der Richtigkeit jenes Grundsatzes zu überzeugen, daß der Republikaner nur ein braver Kerl sein kann, und daß wir alle brave Kerle werden müssen, wenn wir Republikaner werden wollen.] See *Nazional-Zeitung, Politisches Volksblatt für demokratische Interessen*, 17.Okt 1848, p. 288. The colloquial term "brave Kerls" that Brass used cannot be rendered easily in English. "Brave" in German is not the equivalent of "brave" in English; brave kids are kids that behave well. But "Kerls" (guys) has a macho connotation and soldiers in Prussia were often referred to as "Kerls." Brave, when used in combination with "Kerls" connotes "honest, straightforward" etc., but there is also an undertone that implies courage, though this is not the primary semantic component. As a political statement, this introductory comment, directed to the prospective reader, is remarkably naive, at or at least non-theoretical, It is in line with the political poetry of this "red poet": it is above all addressing *the emotional side* of readers, not so much his *intellectual* capacities. Perhaps Brass saw that as the way that was necessary to win people to "the cause" and perhaps he did not regard the sharp and clear language of Marx that appealed to reason as a successful strategy. It is a well-known fact that Marx respected the poetry of Heine, because it was clear and to the point. He scoffed at and satirized the writings of overly emotional authors like Wilhelm Weitling who were propagating their ideas about socialism and communism before Marx turned socialist.

14 Pröve has variously discussed the semantic history of the concept "Volksbewaffnung" ("arming of the people") in the context of German debates. Thus he writes that "the semantics varied considerably" ("variierte die Semantik ganz erheblich" – See Ralf Pröve, *Lebenswelten: militärische Milieus in der Neuzeit : gesammelte Abhandlungen*. Berlin: LIT-Verlag Dr. W. Hopf. 2010, p.125) He thinks that there is a clear evolution of the concept—from an earlier, "patriotic" (one might say, authoritarian, i.e. "obrigkeitsstaatliche") toward a more democratic, but still limited content, reflected by the way the term was interpreted as coinciding with the material significance of the "burgher guards" established 1830–1831 and in 1848 and with the class interests that this form of realizing the "arming of the people" represented. Thus he writes that the "debates on 'Volksbewaffnung' set in during the 2nd half of the 18th century in the context of *Spätaufklärung* [so-called 'Late Enlightenment' in German-speaking areas] and of debates on patriotism" and that there existed *three waves of practical application* of "Volksbewaffnung"— the anti-Napoleonic "arming of the people" in 1806–1815, and the revolutionary upturns in 1830–1831 and 1848–1849. (See Ralf Pröve, ibid., p.125) But he is missing the contradictions inscribed in the understanding of the concept and in its application from the very beginning, thus during the "Wars of Liberation" when a *revolutionary* concept of *levée en masse* was adapted, in the Prussian context, to *reactionary* purposes. The same or rather, a similar ambivalence or ambiguity, in other words, a Janus-headed quality was characteristic of the term and the way it was being interpreted by opposing social forces (or "political camps") in a different, "more advanced" historical situation in German states during the revolution of 1848–1849. Pröve is correct when he writes that as a consequence of the triumph of the reaction in Germany in 1849–1850, the conservative or reactionary social forces established their discursive hegemony for a few decades and that the term became unequivocally synonymous with its reactionary "patriotic" (or rather, nationalist, if not chauvinistic) interpretation. Its revolutionary interpretation surfaced again in 1918–1923 in a tentative way, but Pröve does not discuss this, as far as I know.

15 In German: "Bis zum 16. März [1848] standen [in Berlin] insgesamt zwanzig Tote und 150 Verwundete […] [im] Anklagebuche [der in den Tagen der vorrevolutionären Agitation, Volksversammlungen und Zusammenkünfte auf dem Schloßplatz vom Militär immer wieder malträtierten Bevölkerung dieser Stadt]. Bürgerversammlungen berieten, wie man sich bewaffnen könne […]" (Source: *Preußische Monatsbriefe*, No. 18/ March 2013, URL http://docplayer.org/65245851-Berichte-kommentare-glossen-und-despektierliches-fuer-aufgeklaerte-muendige-schichten.html – Accessed 5 June 2018, 7:15 AM) The figures given reveal the extent to which the army intervened in the weeks of March prior to the revolution, since about March 6, against anything that appeared to them like an incipient "tumult." These bloody interventions were legally possible due to Prussia's "Law Pertaining to Tumults" (Tumultgesetz) of 1835. There are those like Haenchen who think that dangerous subversives had been active in Berlin all along, even before March 6. (See also Karl Haenchen, "Zur revolutionären Unterwühlung Berlins vor den Märztagen 1848" [On Revolutionary Subversion in Berlin Prior to the Days of March 1848], in: *Forschungen zur Brandenburgischen und Preußischen Geschichte* [Research Contributions on the History of Brandenburg and Prussia] (FBPG), Vol. 55/1944, p.114.) But censorship and the presence of police spies that were part of Minutoli's network of surveillance had toned down all liberal debate, and leftist agitation was carried out by very

few persons, in more or less clandestine fashion, and thus unable to reach the masses. It was the news from France, Baden, and Vienna, in early March, that blew the lid off the pot. Berlin's petty-bourgeois radicals (mostly liberals, plus a few "utopian socialists") and workers (among them a few members of the League of Communists) saw the chain reaction that the French February revolution was causing in South West Germany and Austria—and so the dam broke. They knew that the time to courageously press for democratic change had come. Thus Engels was right when he wrote, "The February events in Paris precipitated the imminent German revolution [...]." (Frederick Engels, "Marx and the Neue Rheinische Zeitung (1848–49)" [Marx and The New Rhenanian Gazette (1848–49)], in: Der Sozialdemokrat [The Social Democrat], March 13, 1884; reprinted in: Karl Marx and Frederick Engels, *Collected Works* (MECW), Vol. 26: *Frederick Engels 1882-1889*, London: Lawrence & Wishart, 1990, p. 120.)

16   Thus, in Cologne. A list of demands that was drawn up there in March 1848 included as item 3 the "dissolution of the army and the realization of a general arming of the people (Volksbewaffnung, i.e. a people's militia) with leaders freely elected by the people" ("Aufhebung des stehenden Heeres und Einführung einer allgemeinen Volksbewaffnung mit vom Volk gewählten Führern." (Hans Stein, *Der Kölner Arbeiterverein (1848–1849): ein Beitrag zur Frühgeschichte der rheinischen Sozialismus* [The Cologne Workers' Association 1848–1849: A Contribution to the Research on the Early History of Rhenish Socialism]. Köln: Gilsbach, 1921, p.27) – In Cologne, as everywhere in similar German contexts, the impact of the French Revolution that erupted in February 1848 was decisive. This new revolutionary upturn surpassed that of 1830–1831 when "burgher guards" had been formed in France, Belgium, and in smaller German states. The social and political developments that culminated in 1848 brought forth more far-reaching concepts of "popular arming" under the influence of radical democrats and outspoken republicans. Their ideas found the widest echo among people with considerable social grievances, thus especially in diverse segments of the working class (defined in the widest possible sense). For Nauwerk in Berlin, a people's militia or army of the people would be completely different from the type of army that served other interests than those of the people under the command of existing governments: "An armed citizenry was not to be equated with 'brute force', it was a thoughtful force" [an intelligent force, a thinking force; eine denkende Macht]; "for brute force exists only where everyone blindly obeys, and not when every could act himself [wo Jeder selbst handeln könne]." This is what he said according to the minutes of the meeting of the Berlin assembly of city councilors that took place on March 11, 1848. (Adolf Wolff, *Berliner Revolutions-Chronik*, ibid, p.40).

17   Actually, a "Burgher Guard" (Bürgergarde) had been demanded already previously in Berlin, usually in popular assemblies like those taking place at the "Zelten." But the petition adopted by the popular assembly at the "Zelten" on March 9, 1848 (the text of which is included in full in the book by August Brass) was unequivocal in demanding, as item 7, the "diminution of the army and the arming of the people with free choice of leaders." This petition was subject to a brief debate in the assembly of city councilors on March 11, 1848. The vast majority of the assembly—in fact all except Mr. Nauwerk and Mr. Berends (who had introduced it here)—refused to deal with it or to "forward" it to the king. The concept—burgher guard—was a muddled one, and some democrats, like Berends and Nauwerk in the debate on May 11, seem to have used it in certain contexts in order to camouflage the more far-reaching demand to "arm the people." The city

councilors had their own debate on the question whether they should apply to the government for permission to form a burgher guard (or civil guard) on March 11. Most of them were motivated by fear of the "mob" and concerns regarding the "security of (private) property." (See Adolf Wolff, *Berliner Revolutions-Chronik*, ibid., pp. 37-41. The book is also available as a reprint.)

Ralf Pröve refers to a petition by the "committees of protection" *in favor of a "burgher guard"* that was adopted in Berlin on March 17, 1848. He mentions these four key demands:
1. Zurückziehung der militärischen Macht [Withdrawal of the troops]
2. Organisation einer bewaffneten Bürgergarde [Organization of an armed Burgher Guard]
3. Pressefreiheit [Freedom of the press]
4. Einberufung des Vereinigten Landtags [Convocation of the United Diet]

(See Ralf Pröve, *Politische Partizipation und soziale Ordnung: Revolution in Deutschland und Europa 1848/49* [Political participation and social order: revolution in Germany and Europe 1848-49], Göttingen: Vandenhoeck & Ruprecht, 1998). The same demands that were articulated on March 17 are also mentioned by Franz Mehring, who writes that all the burghers who were members of the "commission of protection" had decided and proclaimed that a "peaceful demonstrations of the masses" should take place "in front of the Palace" (thus in the Palace Square) on March 18 at noon, and that the following demands should be made known to the king on this occasion: "Withdrawal of the troops, organization of an armed burgher guard, the granting of unconditional freedom of the press, and fast convocation of the United Diet." (Franz Mehring, *Geschichte der Deutschen Sozialdemokratie* [History of German Social Democracy], Vol.2. Paderborn, Europäischer Geschichtsverlag, 2015, p.8. Reprint of the 1909 edition.) Prittwitz, the commanding general in Berlin during the fighting on March 18 and 19, refers to the same petition mentioned by Mehring and Pröve that was adopted on March 17th. He writes that the gathering that adopted it came to pass because of encouraging "suggestions from several sides" (Anregungen von verschiedenen Seiten), that it consisted of "burghers and inhabitants" (Bürger und Einwohner) who all served as members of the "committees of protection" in thirteen different boroughs of Berlin, and the demands that were strongly supported included not only the demand no. 4, "the arming of the burghers" (Bürgerbewaffnung) that is mentioned by the other two authors when they refer to a "burgher guard," but also no. 5, "resignation of the cabinet" (Rücktritt der Minister), and no. 6, "Consideration of the working classes." But because items 5 and 6 met also with considerable opposition, they were dropped. Prittwitz mentions in passing that the final text of the petition was phrased by the writer Dr. Woeniger. The petition was presented to the king in the Palace Square on March 18. (See Prittwitz' account, edited by Gerd Heinrich: Karl Ludwig Prittwitz, *Berlin 1848: das Erinnerungswerk des Generalleutnants Karl Ludwig von Prittwitz und andere Quellen zur Berliner Märzrevolution und zur Geschichte Preußens um die Mitte des 19. Jahrhunderts*. Bearbeitet und eingeleitet von Gerd Heinrich. Berlin; New York: de Gruyter, 1985, p. 102) – Clearly, these demands mentioned by the three authors were political demands and it is apparent that items 1 to 4 could find broad support (although item 4 could be interpreted in different ways, depending on one's political convictions); items 1 to 4 expressed *a desire of political emancipation shared by most members of the bourgeoisie, the "awake" parts of the petty-bourgeoisie and practically all politically conscious members of the working class*. But it is notable that not a single social demand of the journeymen, factory workers, and other members of the subaltern classes was included in this petition, even though social demands must have certainly been voiced in popular assemblies taking place at the "Zelten" and in other locations of Berlin during the pre-revolutionary period, and they surfaced vaguely on March 17 in the meeting mentioned, as item 6 (that was dropped) clearly shows. The fact that it was dropped reveals a decisive rift between the conservative respectively "conservative-liberal" parts of the petty-bourgeoisie (and bourgeoisie) on the one hand and progressive "middle class" and working-class democrats. The fact that "social questions" belonged to the key questions that had to be solved is fairly obvious, not only in view of the general conditions of the working class, wage conflicts, inadequate housing conditions, etc. but most obviously because of the food question that became very acute in the late 1840s and that triggered Berlin's so-called "potato revolution" (disturbances or "food riots" that occurred due to the high price of food, thus even potatoes) in April 1847.

18 This becomes especially obvious in the account provided by the commanding general in Berlin, von Prittwitz, who was present in the Royal Palace at the time and who is thus a key witness. Von Prittwitz was barred from publishing his account by the authorities during his lifetime and it was thus unknown to Brass. It was edited by the historian Gerd Heinrich and published posthumously, jointly with other source material on the March Revolution, as *Berlin 1848: das Erinnerungswerk des Generalleutnants Karl Ludwig von Prittwitz und andere Quellen zur Berliner Märzrevolution und zur Geschichte Preußens um die Mitte des 19. Jahrhunderts* [Berlin 1848: the Account of Lieutenant-General Karl Ludwig von Prittwitz and other sources on the Berlin March Revolution and the history of Prussia during the mid-19th century]. Edited and with an introduction by Gerd Heinrich. Berlin; New York: de Gruyter, 1985.

19 Liberalism undoubtedly had very progressive effects in Germany during the "Vormärz" (Pre-March) period of the 1830s and much of the 1840s. The bourgeoisie and even part of the aristocracy, including bureaucratic state officials and army officers, started to have doubts about the late absolutist "old regimes" in Germany. Many, especially among the *petty-bourgeoisie* and the big bourgeoisie in the larger cities, started to become oppositional. The centers of progressive liberal opposition to absolutism could be found in the German regions West of the River Rhine (thus, Cologne and Mayence [Mainz], but even Trier, Aachen [Aix-la-Chapelle], and smaller towns) and in South West Germany (mainly in the Grand Duchy of Baden), but also increasingly in the large Prussian centers East of the River Elbe, in Berlin, Breslau [Wrocław], and Königsberg [Kaliningrad]. The working-class riots in the Rhine Province made many members of the liberal Rhenish *haute bourgeoisie* turn to more "moderate" (that is to say, conservative) political views, however, whereas quite a few petty-bourgeois liberal writers and a small number of intellectuals in Baden, in Berlin, Breslau, and Königsberg drifted to radical democratic and in some cases even left-wing positions. Bergengrün speaks of the "split of the liberal party" ("Spaltung der liberalen Partei"; see Alexander Bergengrün, *David Hansemann*. Berlin: J. Guttentag, 1901, p. 401)—a "dissensus," disagreement or split that is also noted by Rudolf Boch (see: Rudolf Boch, *Grenzenloses Wachstum?: Das rheinische Wirtschaftsbürgertum und seine Industrialisierungsdebatte 1814 - 1857* [Limitless Growth?: Rhenish Businessmen and Their Industrialization Debate 1814-1857]. Göttingen, Vandenhoeck + Ruprecht, 1991, passim). Of course, the term "party" at the time—used also by

Marx in the Communist Manifesto and elsewhere—does not refer to a political party in the modern sense. Here, "party" refers to an ideological tendency, to political beliefs that are shared more or less by an indefinite number of people who may or may not be loosely connected. – For Marx, the terms "bourgeois party" and "proletarian party" implied the two vast social camps that are opposed objectively to each other in modern bourgeois, capitalist society: on the one side of the "barricade," the bourgeoisie (all of its strata or class factions, with their diverse *particular* and their basically shared *general* interests; all of its particular ideological currents) and on the other, the working class, in view of its objective need of self-emancipation (of which not all of its "elements," its subdivisions, and individual members were subjectively conscious during his lifetime, as they are not today). In German states, during the 1840s, capitalism was clearly emerging, feudalism was a dead dog with antiquated rights still surviving that were "inherited" by the aristocratic landowners, but in a context of agrarian capitalism that was becoming dominant since 1820 at the latest. Liberalism was the ideological expression of the objectively developing modern capitalist economy, and it needed a bourgeois political form; bourgeois society (the social relations that came into existence since the days of French revolutionary republican, and then Napoleonic influence) made absolutism an anachronism. This was objectively true, and this was also how the bourgeoisie felt. But the threat of working-class revolts made many bourgeois German "liberals" increasingly seek protection by moving closer again to the princes whose absolutism they had questioned. This explains their penchant for "constitutional monarchist" views. For "liberal" army officers and bureaucrats critical of the old absolutist Prussian monarchy, it was clear that the continued existence of their status and relative "privilege" depended on the survival of the monarchy, regardless of its form.

[20] In German, it says: "Die Bürgerwehr zählte bis zu ihrer Auflösung Mitte November lediglich Berliner in ihren Reihen, die das Bürgerrecht besaßen, also ein Haus besaßen oder über ein bestimmtes Mindesteinkommen verfügten. Angehörige der Unterschichten waren aus dieser im Wortsinne bürgerlichen« Wehr ausgeschlossen. Anfang April war die Bürgermiliz im Unterschied zum Sommer und Herbst 1848 überdies noch stark konservativ getönt." (Rüdiger Hachtmann, "Die Macht des Gerüchts in der Revolution von 1848 – Das Berliner Beispiel" [The power of rumors in the revolution of 1848 – The case of Berlin], in: Michael Grüttner, Rüdiger Hachtmann and Heinz Gerhard Haupt (eds.), Geschichte und Emanzipation. Festschrift für Reinhard Rürup [History and emancipation, Festschrift for Reinhard Rürup], Frankfurt/Main: Campus Verlag, 1999, pp. 189-216; here: p. 212, Footnote 7)

[21] "Das Bezeichnende an der Persönlichkeit des Königs ist, daß er eine Hamletnatur war und sich ihrer auch bewußt war, daß er überquellend gemüthaft und träumerisch war, daß er aber diese Schwärmerei auch nur vorspielen konnte und sich dahinter durchaus auch Verstand und Berechnung verbargen. In dieser Hinsicht greift also die Charakteristik Rankes zu kurz, der einmal von der Politik des Königs gesagt hat, daß sie "aus keinerlei Art von Berechnung" entsprungen sei.(31) Eher ist dem österreichischen Diplomaten Georg Esterhazy zuzustimmen, der im Februar 1856 seinem Kollegen Rechberg schrieb:(32) "Merkwürdig ist, daß es Leute giebt, [...] die sich noch immer durch die sog. ‚P i e t ä t' des Königs Friedrich Wilhelm IV. dupiren lassen, des vollendetsten Komödianten der Gegenwart und e i g e n t l i c h unseres giftigsten Gegners." See Winfried Baumgart, "Zur Außenpolitik Friedrich Wilhelms IV. 1840-1858," in: Büsch, Otto (ed.), Friedrich Wilhelm IV.

in seiner Zeit. (= Einzelveröffentlichungen der historischen Kommission zu Berlin, Bd. 62 = Jahrbuch für die Geschichte Mittel- und Ostdeutschlands 36), Berlin 1987, pp. 132-156, here: pp. 146f. Also online:URL: https://publications.ub.uni-mainz.de/opus/volltexte/2011/2642/pdf/2642.pdf

22 "Insgeheim [...] schreibt er seinem Bruder, dem Prinzen Wilhelm: 'Die Reichsfarben musste ich gestern freiwillig aufstecken, um Alles zu retten. Ist der Wurf gelungen [...], so lege ich sie wieder ab!' [...]") The quotation is from an article by Volker Münchow entitled "Am 10. Juli 1868 gründeten 72 Bürger in Langenberg einen Ortsverein des ADAV: Gustav Adolf Köttgen arbeitete eng mit Friedrich Engels zusammen", in: Kerstin Griese and Peter Zwilling (eds.), *Lesebuch zur Geschichte der Sozialdemokratie im Kreis Mettmann*, Mettmann: rotation, n.d., pp. 161ff., here: p. 162 – ISBN 978-3-942972-09-3; this utterance made by Frederick William IV on the day after he rode through Berlin, wearing the black, red, and golden colors that had been flown on the barricades, is also reproduced online: URL http://hartbrunner.de/fakten/d_fakten.php?id=9578 – accessed June 3, 2018, 10:12 AM.

23 See Document No. 17. *Bekanntmachung vom 19. März 1848 betreffend die Neubildung des Ministeriums* [Proclamation of March 19, 1848 concerning the new cabinet]. Reprinted in: Wilhelm Angerstein, *Die Berliner März-Ereignisse im Jahre 1848. Nebst einem vollständigen Revolutions-Kalender. Mit und nach Actenstücken, sowie Berichten von Augenzeugen. Zur Feststellung der Wahrheit und als Entgegnung wider die Angriffe der reactionären Presse*; zusammengestellt von Otto Wigand. (=*Seit 1848. Beiträge zur preußischen Geschichte. Erster Theil: Die Berliner März-Ereignisse im Jahre 1848*) [The Berlin March Events in the Year of 1848. With a complete calendar of the revolution. With and based on official records, as well as eye witness reports. In order to determine the truth and as a response to attacks by the reactionary press; compiled by Otto Wigand. (= Since 1848. Contributions to Prussian History. Part One: The Berlin March Events in the Year 1848)] Leipzig: Verlag von Otto Wigand, 1864, p.99. – The proclamation informed the public that Count Arnim, who was regarded by the king as a liberal, would be prime minister and in charge of *matters concerning the promised constitution*. This was important and must be kept in mind! Count Schwerin, also perhaps seen by the king as a liberal and certainly mistaken for a fresh new face, was to be in charge of religious affairs; Count Stolberg would be the new minister of justice; and the conservative General von Rohr would stay on as Minister of War. It is interesting that Fanny Lewald, an intelligent woman whose political position as a liberal was certainly progressive, if compared with that of Hansemann and Camphausen (men she met and conversed with repeatedly in 1848), did not regard Schwerin as a liberal at all . As she saw it, quite the contrary was true. In her account of the days of revolution, Fanny Lewald writes: "Count Schwerin is certainly (...) no minister who makes concessions to get or keep his portfolio. He acts out of conviction. Unfortunately, this conviction is deeply rooted in the past (...) Being orthodox excludes tolerance; yet recognition of freedom of religion—making this principle a law—is the task of a Minister of Culture in present Prussia which cannot continue in the footsteps of [the reactionary] Eichhorn's ministry. Yet Count Schwerin seems determined to do so."

(Quoted from: Hanna Ballin Lewis (ed.), *A Year of Revolutions: Fanny Lewald's Recollections of 1848*. Translated, edited, and annotated by Hanna Ballin Lewis. New York and Oxford: Berghahn Books, 1997, p.96.) Hanna Ballin Lewis gives this sketchy assessment: "Count Schwerin although a moderate liberal, voted with the Right at the Frankfurt Parliament." She adds, "He was a Minister of

Culture during Camphausen's short-lived ministry." (Hanna Ballin Lewis, ibid, p. 95, footnote 9) Of course, the qualification "moderate" should be digested thoughtfully. It was hardly by chance that Count Schwerin voted with the Right.

24 This transformation that Frederick William IV underwent, as far as his image was concerned, was in part prefigured, however, in his self-image. It is a confirmed fact that even as an intransigent absolutist monarch who rejected most quests to introduce liberal reforms and to accord, most of all, a constitution, he saw himself as a good king. And when he addressed his "beloved Berliners" (thus on a poster) during the days of revolutionary fighting, he seems to have genuinely felt that only a "mob"—insurgent due to agitation of devilish foreign scoundrels—and some seduced and misinformed, but basically well-meaning subjects had taken up arms against him. All that was needed to win back their hearts was clarification of misunderstandings and the unmasking of evil elements and their lies.

25 The journal "Berliner Omnibus," edited by Adolph Wolff, notes in July 1848, that it was "necessity" that made Frederick William IV adopt a "liberal" (freisinnige) position: "The king is more liberal than the National Assembly. In the days of March—when, of course, virtue was taught him due to necessity—the king approved the general arming of the people with the free choice of leaders." ("Der König ist freisinniger als die National-Versammlung. In den Märztagen – die freilich die Tugend aus Noth lehrten – genehmigte der König die allgemeine Volksbewaffnung mit freier Wahl der Führer." – N.N., *Berliner Omnibus, Volks-Zeitschrift für Unterhaltung, Politik und gesellschaftliches Leben*, Vol. 2, No. 28, July 1848, p. 172.) The view expressed by the *Berliner Omnibus* indicates a relatively permanent change enforced by the conditions of March 18–19. Hachtmann seems to share my view that it was a temporary *change of course* when he writes that, in his address entitled "To My Beloved Berliners," Frederick William IV suggested that the people had misunderstood him, thus nourishing the image of "a good king" who had the genuine intention to pursue a liberal course: "The thesis of a 'misunderstanding'" —coupled with the image of a good king merely ill-advised by the so-called camarilla—"was [...] successfully used in the following months [...]. The image of the 'good king' radiated before this background [...]" and had a political effect among the "moderately" liberal burghers and even among some democrats. Hachtmann thinks that such a strategy was used "to ward off more far-reaching participatory demands of the Democrats and the people" (Rüdiger Hachtmann, *Berlin 1848: eine Politik- und Gesellschaftsgeschichte der Revolution*. [Berlin in 1848: A Political and Social History of the Revolution]. Berlin: Dietz Verlag, 1997, p. 170.)—which suggests that the author may assume that at least temporarily the king adopted a genuinely "moderate liberal position," whereas I hold that he never genuinely embraced it but feigned it, for a time, choosing a temporary tactical alliance with the Rhenish *grande bourgeoisie* and thus an extension of an already existing class compromise, and this out of necessity. A bourgeois class faction with considerable economic and social "weight" was allowed to have a limited say in government for some time, even though this was hard to swallow for the king, the aristocratic layers of the bureaucracy, aristocratic army brass heads, and the aristocracy in general. – The *change of course* set in prior to the days when it became apparent to most (March 19–21, 1848), however. It was perhaps anticipated by people like Count Arnim and the envoy Heinrich von Arnim, but also by General von Pfuel and the Berlin chief of police von Minutoli who all belonged to the "liberal" faction of the aristocracy and who saw in all likelihood the inescapable necessity of some "moderate" reforms and of a constitution for the

Prussian monarchy, based on "conservative-liberal" principles, and this as early as 1847, if not earlier. For such small steps it was already too late in March 1849. As far as the king is concerned, the *change of course* occurred between March 16, when the news of revolutionary victory arrived in Berlin (a triumph perceived not only by educated liberal and democratic readers of newspapers, who spread the news in the city, but also noticed by the court) and the night of March 17–18, 1848 when the text of a decree published the next morning in the *State-Gazette* (Staats-Anzeiger) was hastily written which proclaimed that the United Diet should not be convened on April 27 but already on April 2; simultaneously, a law concerning freedom of the press (Preßgesetz) was issued that was also published the next morning. The speed with which these steps were taken reveals a perceived urgency. (See N.N, "Friedrich Wilhelm IV., König von Preußen", in: *Unsere Zeit. Jahrbuch zum Conversations-Lexikon*; Vol. 6. Leipzig: F.A. Brockhaus, 1862, pp. 1-26, here: p.17 where we read "On the 16th of March the events of Vienna became known there [i.e., in Berlin], and the opinion began to prevail in the highest circles that now, for Prussia, too, a formal constitution had become necessary," in German: Am 16. März wurden daselbst die wiener Ereignisse bekannt, und es begann sich die Ansicht in den höchsten Kreisen Geltung zu verschaffen, daß nunmehr auch für Preußen eine förmliche Constitution zur Nothwendigkeit geworden sei." The author then continues by mentioning the steps taken until the early morning of March 18.) On March 14, the king had still announced the planned meeting of the German princes that was to take place in Dresden due to an agreement that the Prussian envoy von Radowitz (a reactionary general and close adviser to the king) had reached during his talks with the Austrian government in Vienna on March 10. (See N.N, "Friedrich Wilhelm IV., König von Preußen," in: *Unsere Zeit.* ibid, p.17.) The days of March 10–14 thus still reveal the intention of devising a coordinated counter-revolutionary strategy in response to the effects that the French February revolution had in Germany. Obviously, much more measured concessions to the liberal bourgeoisie were intended than those the monarch saw himself compelled to make on March 19. On March 14, the United Diet's convocation on April 27 had been made known. The intended way of handling things in this *ständisch* institution seemed to pose few risks that things would get out of hand.

26 The Constituent Assembly is also known as the Prussian National Assembly; it was created by way of indirect elections that would determine a number of "electors" (*Wahlmänner*) who in turn would usually favor the appointment of one of the local 'notables' as the delegate of their election district. The notables (in German, "Honoratioren") chosen guaranteed a large "moderate" bloc of delegates in the constituent assembly, as they tended to be propertied and/or educated commoners known for their ability to give talks, often also with political experience gained in the city council (Stadtverordneten-Versammlung) or as aldermen (members of the so-called "Magistrat": the municipal government). This "moderately liberal" bloc surpassed the number of those middle-class delegates who embraced more or less outspoken (in some cases, even radical) democratic positions. But it was at best slightly bigger than the conservative bloc of delegates, among them quite a few members of the state bureaucracy and many aristocratic landowners, the latter largely elected indirectly in small towns and rural parts of Prussia where they were influential. It was clear that the main task of this assembly, apart from controlling the appointed government, was to draw up the Prussian constitution that had been demanded for several decades already by many Prussians.

27 "[T]he [Prussian National] Assembly [...] had no eyes for the concentration and organization of Counter-Revolutionary forces, which that [...] ministry carried on pretty openly. At last, the signal being given by the fall of Vienna [Oct. 31, 1848], the King dismissed its ministers, and replaced them by "men of action," under the leadership of the present premier, [Otto Theodor von] Manteuffel. Then the dreaming Assembly at once awoke to the danger; it passed a vote of no confidence in the Cabinet, which was at once replied to by a decree removing the Assembly from Berlin, where it might, in case of a conflict, count upon the support of the masses, to Brandenburg, a petty provincial town dependent entirely upon the Government. The Assembly, however, declared that it could not be adjourned, removed or dissolved, except with its own consent. In the meantime, General Wrangel entered Berlin at the head of some forty thousand troops. In a meeting of the municipal magistrates and the officers of the National Guard, it was resolved not to offer any resistance." (Friedrich Engels, Revolutions und Konterrevolution in Deutschland. Berlin: Dietz, 1963; 4. verbesserte Auflage = 4th, corrected edition; English language edition: Revolution and Counter-revolution in Germany. Peking: Foreign Language Press, 1977; Frederick Engels, Germany: Revolution and counter-revolution. With the collaboration of Karl Marx. Ed. by Eleanor Marx. London: Lawrence & Wishart, 1969. Also online: https://www.marxists.org/archive/marx/works/1852/germany/ch13.htm – Accessed June 5, 2018, 8:15 PM) "On 14 November [1848], Karl [Marx] declared that it was 'the duty of the Rhine Province to hasten to the assistance of the Berlin National Assembly with men and weapons.'" (Gareth Stedman Jones, Karl Marx: Greatness and Illusion. Cambridge, MA: Belknap Press of Harvard University Press, 2016, p.283)

28 Walter Schmidt, in the interview by N.N. with Walter Schmidt, "Der einzige legitime Erbe," in: *Neues Deutschland*, March 17–18, 2018, p. 27. – Both Fredericks Engels and Karl Marx had already noticed this "treason of the bourgeoisie" in context of the French February Revolution of 1848, and they lambasted it in their articles published in the *New Rhenanian Gazette* (Neue Rheinische Zeitung) in 1848–1849. Werner Meyer also states very clearly that "the bourgeoisie abandoned its [policy of] opposition against the King and the old social forces" ("die alten Mächte") as soon as the first "revolutionary actions of the workers, peasants, and artisans occurred in the year of 1848." Apparently, fear of disorder, attributed to the "mob," and anticipation of "red" threats to bourgeois property were prompting them to engage in a "policy of cooperation [pact-making] with the Princes" ("eine Politik des Paktierens mit den Fürsten"). See: Werner Meyer, *Vormärz: Die Ära Metternich 1815 bis 1848*, Potsdam: Potsdamer Verlagsgesellschaft, 1948, p.123. – The term "die alten Mächte" (*the old powers* or *old social forces*) obviously refers above all to *the land-owning (high) aristocracy* and *lower (also land-owning) gentry* in Prussia (both jointly forming an originally feudal caste that was evolving into a class of very big and big land-owners interested in modernizing agricultural methods, while holding on—as far as possible—to anachronistic, originally feudal rights and privileges, like enforcement of unpaid labor from dependent peasants and due collection from this same group of peasants). But the term includes also the main allies of this land-owning class, viz. *the upper levels of the state bureaucracy* (positions that had been put almost completely into the hands of sons of the aristocratic land-owners), and *the upper and medium levels of the armed forces* (totally in the hands of the same social group).

29 Rudolf Boch, *Grenzenloses Wachstum?*, ibid, p.117.

30 Rudolf Boch, ibid, pp. 117f.
31 See Angerstein, Document "No. 28. Proklamation des Königs vom 22. März die Volksvertretung ec. Betreffend" – where item to pronounces the "right to freely associate and freely meet in public." (Angerstein, *Die Berliner März-Ereignisse im Jahre 1848*, ibid, p.105)
32 See the commentary that appears under the heading "Vereinigtes Deutschand" in the Kgl. Privilegierte Berlinische Zeitung of May 25, 1848, p.1.
33 In comparison with London and Paris or compared with Hamburg, Frankfurt, and even Cologne, Berlin was not an important financial center in the 1840s. But here, just as in Frankfurt, Jewish bankers played a leading role. Steven Lowenstein notes a "change in the economic activities of Berlin Jews in the second half of the eighteenth century [that] took place in the field of credit and moneylending. Credit operations became more complex and the larger money-changing operations (Wechselgeschäfte) took on more and more of the characteristics of private banks. Pawnbrokers became less important and bankers became more important as sources of credit. [...] Jews became important as brokers. In 1765 eight Jews were sworn in as legally recognized brokers (Mäkler). The financial importance of Jews at the turn of the nineteenth century can be seen by the fact that the committee creating the Berlin stock exchange in 1803 consisted of an equal number of Jewish and Christian representatives." (Steven M. Lowenstein, *The Berlin Jewish Community: Enlightenment, Family and Crisis, 1770–1830*. New York; Oxford : Oxford Univ. Press, 1994, p.29.) – Generally speaking, the Jewish community in Berlin was known for its progressive, liberal stance and included many educated men and women, including such noted philosophers as Moses Mendelssohn. In 1848, several young, well-educated Berlin Jews can be noted among the activists of the decidedly democratic political current. But as Lowenstein notes, "the Berlin Jewish intellectuals did not constitute a single social class; they were from many different places and many different backgrounds. Although some came from influential Berlin families, most did not. In fact, quite a few remained economically dependent on, and therefore socially far removed from, the Berlin [Jewish] elite that helped set a modernizing style in Berlin." (Lowenstein, ibid, p.36.)
34 The figures given here are those provided by August Brass in his account of the March revolution. They must have been estimates then current in Berlin. The approximate number of Berlin inhabitants must have been indeed somewhere between 400,000 and 440,000—considering the constant influx of paupers in search of work that took place during the economic crisis that seems to have peaked in 1847 but was far from over in 1848. Hans Herzfeld quotes official statistics that assert a total of 403,596 inhabitants in 1847. Sixteen years earlier, in 1831, the total had been 201,138 inhabitants; it had more than doubled in 16 years. The average population growth thus was ca. 12,650 persons per year—due to excess of the birth rate over the mortality rate and above all, due to new arrivals. The figure of ca. 40,000 enfranchised citizens provide by Brass seems doubtful; he most likely overstated the number of those permitted to vote in municipal elections. Based, it seems, on official records, Herzfeld provides the following data: 13,640 citizens in 1830; 18,700 citizens in 1840; 27,000 citizens in 1850. (Hans Herzfeld, "Erstes Kapitel: Allgemeine Entwicklung und politische Geschichte", in: Hans Herzfeld and Gerd Heinrich (eds.), *Berlin und die Provinz Brandenburg im 19. und 20. Jahrhundert* [Berlin and the Province of Brandenburg in the 19th and 20th Century]. Berlin: de Gruyter, 1968, p. 48) Thus the number of at least relatively well-off commoners in Berlin was significantly smaller than Brass

assumed when he assumed that 40,000 male bourgeois commoners and relatively well-off, male petty-bourgeois commoners formed the enfranchised citizenry of Berlin. – In addition, it must be pointed out that there is at least one group that remains unaccounted for in this calculation of Brass that divides Berlin's inhabitants into ca. 400,000 "protected clients" and ca. 40,000 enfranchised "citizens": the aristocracy—admittedly a very small minority (but including the king and the royal family). It is highly unlikely that they could take part in the election of city councilors. Had they been able to vote in this election or to run for office, there would have been aristocratic city councilors, in view of their prestige. Somebody like Alexander von Humboldt might have been elected. But this would not have reflected the "dignity" of aristocrats, and it would also have violated the bourgeois character of this representative body. In other words, the aristocrats were no "citizens" because they were no commoners; and they don't figure in the numerical list of inhabitants presented by Brass, which is a mistake—even though they were most likely relatively few in numbers. There is another group, as well, besides the aristocracy, that does not figure in the calculation of Brass— and this because they were not reflected by the total of Berlin's inhabitants established by the census. It is the army present in Berlin, both regular troops confined to the barracks, and the royal guard. The census disregarded army units because they could be redeployed, and actually were transferred now and then, and replaced by other units; but the size of the troops stationed in Berlin may also have been regarded as a military secret. The army officers who owned or rented a house or who rented an apartment in Berlin may have been registered by census officials, however.

35   It is really important to emphasize this fact that, if we merely deduct from the total number of Berlin's inhabitants, the figure of its "protected clients" (people without voting rights), we do not automatically get the figure that indicates the total numerical strength of the subaltern classes, that is to say, of the "lower classes," those tied in particular ways as economically and socially dependent people to a dependent role in the context of the relations of production existing in this city in the 1840s. It is true that we get the number of people who were not paying direct taxes and who did not own house in Berlin. Women and children of the bourgeoisie were also economically and socially dependent people— they did not pay direct taxes and did not own the house—and so they are legally speaking "protected clients" at the time. But they are dependent on their bourgeois husband or father, not on a capitalist employer as wage workers. They "own nothing" perhaps, but still they are not materially poor—they enjoy the wealth accumulated by the head of the household: they are part of the bourgeoisie. (The same can be said about those who belong to the well-off or economically at least modestly secure part of the petty-bourgeoisie.) Obviously, married women, unmarried adult women, young men under 25, and all other minors of the propertied classes were paternalistically suppressed at home (in objective, not necessarily subjective) respect, and they shared, with the subaltern classes, a situation of political disenfranchisement, i.e. the denial of the right to vote in municipal affairs.

But although it is true that this subgroup of bourgeois and petty-bourgeois wives and children (who are included in the huge figure of Berlin's disenfranchised) did have good objective reasons to complain that they did not enjoy political rights with regard to the affairs of the city, they were at least indirectly represented by an adult male member of the family who was a citizen. And they shared, probably, his social status, and more importantly, they belonged objectively to the same class.

36   More information on Mendheim can be found in Nadja Stulz-Herrstadt's book on Berlin's bourgeoisie of the 18th and 19th century. See Nadja Stulz-Herrnstadt, *Berliner Bürgertum im 18. und 19. Jahrhundert : Unternehmerkarrieren und Migration, Familien und Verkehrskreise in der Hauptstadt Brandenburg-Preußens, die Ältesten der Korporation der Kaufmannschaft zu Berlin.* Berlin; New York: de Gruyter 2002, pp. 105f, 114-116, and 119.

37   The Breite Strasse (Broadway) as well as the nearby Brüderstrassse (Brothers' Street) and the Schloßplatz (Palace Square) were respectable addresses, probably because they were so close to the Palace. Nadja Stulz-Herrnstadt mentions that the renowned firm of Jean Paul Humbert and Louis Gärtner was located in the Brothers' St., that François Rousset, a manufacturer of silk stockings, lived here, but also the banker Joachim Wagener, and Mr. Bronte, a manufacturer of textiles made of silk.(Nadja Stulz-Herrnstadt, *Berliner Bürgertum*, ibid, p. 134) When such streets became scenes of harassment and even of sabre attacks carried out by dragoons against innocent—in all likelihood bourgeois—pedestrians returning to their homes, this quite naturally incensed well-bred burghers like Mendheim, a senior member of Berlin's "corporation" of bankers (Korporationsältester). Such acts reinforced anti-absolutist sentiments of the bourgeoisie and caused bitter feelings with regard to the army.

38   In fact, when I first encountered this professor who taught at the Ruhr University in Bochum, he was relatively open-minded and friendlier than most German professors. I liked him, in a way, because he admired Schumpeter and Schumpeter, who like Max Weber combatted Marx, learned a lot from Marx; he was not dumb, and at the time I thought that, put into another theoretical context, some particular insights of Schumpeter and also of Max Weber might be useful. This professor, let's add this as an aside, was still very friendly to students in 1966 or 1967 when I attended his seminar. His name was Ioannis Papalekas. He was a nice guy at the time in a way, much preferable to conservatives like Roman Schnur or Koselleck, let alone Lübbe. But Papalekas changed in 1968, I heard from other students, when the criticism of students got harsher, and I have the impression that almost all of those named formed a *fronde* and made life as difficult as they could for Jaeggi, driving him practically away from Bochum, to New York and Berlin.

39   In *absolutist* and, during the first half of the 19th century, *late absolutist* Prussia, this class—the *junkers* (or land-owning aristocracy)—had ceased to be an all-powerful feudal "stratum": nevertheless, it was a powerful social force that the king—who represented absolute political power within the monarchic system—had to take into account when he needed their approval of new taxes and when the royal cabinet (of ministers appointed by him and, if he thought it necessary, dismissed by him at will) wanted to issue new government bonds, just as the king had to take the affluent commoners of the provinces into consideration for the same reason. Both social classes were sending delegates to the pre-modern parliament, the "provincial diet" or "Landtag" formed by two assemblies representing the provinces of the kingdom: an assembly of aristocrats or "junkers" and an assembly of enfranchised (urban) commoners. With piecemeal reforms by which the state sought to abolish feudal property relations and relations of dependency (so-called bondage), in order to mobilize property and increase its marketability, a dissolution of old feudal relations in the countryside was under way, though too slowly and clearly pursued by the government in a half-hearted manner because its slightly liberal ministers were themselves aristocrats, because almost all the

officers of the king's army (and all the high-ranking commanding officers) were aristocrats, and because the conservatism of kings braked everything that would severely alienate the aristocracy. Thus it can be said that this aristocracy, in the 1820s, 1830s, and 1840s, revealed vestiges of feudalism, but it was no longer a genuinely feudal "estate" (*Stand*) or "corporation" (*Korporation*) defined both by its rank and its unlimited feudal *property* of the acreage *owned* by feudally dependent peasants who had to respect their lord's overwhelming, all-encompassing *superior property rights* to the land they and their ancestors owned perhaps for many generations: the old dualism of different rights to the same plot or tract of land—enshrined as it was in the terms feudal (superior) *property* and subaltern, dependent, limited *ownership*— had become an obstacle to further development; it was rather obvious that the land had to be mobilized, its marketability was necessary because an agrarian financial market was developing, and lenders needed the possibility of foreclosure and sale of what had to be "modern agrarian property," in view of the fact that a borrowing *junker* might become bankrupt. The more progressive ones among the *junkers* had begun already in the 18th century to invest money in "amelioration" of their directly held land, and when—later on—in the course of the reforms, bonded peasants could obtain full property rights to the lands they owned, they had to give a big percentage of their land to the *junker*, the once feudal lord, in compensation for the full property rights they obtained. In addition, they had to indemnify the former overlord in cash for giving up his right to exert unpaid labor from them. This process of step-by-step abolition of legally defined economic and social *dependency of bonded peasants on the junker class* was still under way in 1848. Bad harvests, payments due to *junkers* in compensation, and loss of a considerable percentage of the arable land a peasant family had owned aggravated the poverty of the rural subaltern class, the peasantry, in the 1840s. There were also those still held in bondage because they could not pay. Nevertheless, the development of agrarian capitalism was underway, first tentatively in the late 18th century (affecting only the most progressive aristocrats and their holdings) and then quite fast and across the board, especially in the 19th century when grain exports picked up. Prussian grain was largely exported to Britain, but after the Corn Laws were passed and enforced since 1815, and with particularly painful effects for Prussian grain exporters during the years from 1842 to 1846, other markets—mainly in Germany —gained importance. It was this situation that made the *junker* class, with its large landholdings mainly East of the Elbe River, sharply aware of the necessity of Prussian railroad construction. According to Werner Meyer, such economic interests came into play when the *junker* class (referred to in his book as the "feudal" social forces) opted for a pact with the bourgeoisie in the wake of the March Revolution of 1848, signaling its willingness to vacate certain political positions in favor of these commoners. (See Werner Meyer, ibidem, p.124)

[40] Ernst Cassirer writes about the atmosphere prevalent among the (educated?) "middle classes" in Germany after the French revolutionary period had *ended*, step by step, with the establishment of the Napoleonic empire, with its wars and final demise, that "[t]he first enthusiasm [for this revolution] was followed by a deep disillusionment and mistrust. [...] [O]ptimistic hope [occasioned by it] seemed to be frustrated once for all. All the great promises of the French revolution remained unfulfilled"—or so, it seemed. (Ernst Cassirer, *The Myth of the State*, New Haven and London: Yale University Press, 1961, p.179) Doesn't this sound very much like a description of the atmosphere prevalent among some workers, a part of the petty-bourgeoisie and among "progressive" intellectuals in the wake

of the October Revolution, and then in the later period of disillusionment and distrust that affected the working class increasingly, in many countries? *Both revolutionary and post-revolutionary periods (1789–1814 and 1918–1989/90) were characterized by deformations and the final demise of a "system."* But of course, the petty-bourgeois and then bourgeois French republic of 1792 experienced several moments of "rebirth" and rejuvenated "returns" later on, and it is still around. As far as the impression is concerned that the "French events" left in the dominant social forces of the various states of Germany (all those kings, dukes, other princes, the aristocracy, and also the commercial and financial bourgeoisie), the revolution of 1789—and later also the revolutions of 1830 and February 1848—appeared to contain only one disquieting message: "The political and social order of Europe"—in other words, the late absolutist order that still featured the birthmarks of an older, feudal social structure, preserved in so many remnants— "seemed to be threatened with a complete breakdown." (Ernst Cassirer, ibidem, p.179) It was due to such fears that Frederick William IV, who had briefly appeared to be leaning towards liberal positions upon his ascension to the throne in 1840, was so decidedly determined to preserve old institutions and ward off anything that smacked of constitutionalism even if it assumed only the backward form of an equal voice of the aristocracy and "the rest" in the United Diet that had been requested by an enlightened, liberal faction of the Prussian aristocracy and by a more self-confident bourgeoisie ever since the anti-Napoleonic Wars of "liberation." Frederick William IV finally convoked the United Diet for the first time in 1847, compelled to do so because he needed approval of Prussia's Provincial Estates for new taxes. The United Diet was basically nothing but an assembly of the delegates of the eight Provincial Diets or "Provincial Estates" (Provinziallandtage) meeting in joint session; powerless as it was, but still certainly "feudal" in its unequal representation that privileged the not very numerous aristocracy, it nonetheless appeared to this Prussian king as almost "a Prussian parliament" which he did not want.

41 Though it reached few workers in Germany when it was published in February, 1848 in London, thus shortly before the March Revolution in Berlin, the "Communist Manifesto" did not go unnoticed; police informers, customs officials, the conservative press, and governments were aware of it. Fears, fanned by reports of "subversive activities" and rumors concerning "clandestine associations" that prepared an onslaught on the "old order" added to prevailing concerns and anxieties that haunted Royal and princely courts since 1789. In addition to red pamphlets found by the authorities when they controlled journeymen returning from Paris, Brussels, London, or Zurich, conservative and reactionary publications fanned fears of "social revolutions," thus, for instance a book by Adolphe Thiers edited by Sloman and translated to German: Adolphe Thiers/ Henry Brarens Sloman, *Kurzgefaßter Inhalt des in Frankreich erschienen Werkes von M. Thiers Eigenthum, Communismus u. Socialismus*. Hamburg: Hoffmann & Campe, 1848. ["Shortened Content of Monsieur Thiers' Work *Property, Communism and Socialism*, published in France"], an abridged version of *De la propriété - Du communisme, du socialisme et de l'impôt*. The policy of repression of freedom of association, of strikes, of free speech and debate, of freedom of the press, and so on, that resulted due to the prevailing anxieties caused by the revolutions of 1789 and 1830 in France, and more recently also by the "specter of communism," was characteristic of the entire late absolutist era. This repression that was intensified between 1815 and the mid-1840s was also a reflection of the rottenness of these absolutist regimes.

42   The term "Kapitalisten" (capitalists) was current at the time, popularized by many authors and many pamphlets in the early 19th century. It was a loosely used term, and by the 1830s and 1840s it referred above all to large financial and commercial capitalists, to bankers like Hansemann who invested in speculative projects, such as railway speculation. The term Marx used at the time when referring in the *Rhenanian Gazette* to this stratum or faction of the bourgeoisie, was "hohe Bourgeoisie"—*high bourgeoisie*, a translation of the term current in the French press, *haute bourgeoisie*. *Grande bourgeosie* was a synonymous term, but perhaps later, and then became current in Germany as *Großbourgeoisie*.

    Of course, these terms, *bourgeoisie, petty-bourgeoisie*, etc., were not really current in England or the United States; they became so only due to the reception of Marx's writings in these countries. But in France, they were the widely accepted (pre-Marxist) terms when discussing social reality, i.e. ranks, a stratified society, or a class society: *Aristocratie, bourgeoisie, paysannerie*—the nobility, the citizens, and the peasants (*paysans*); these were the three apparent classes even in the 18th century, and the first two, together with the "clerus," were represented in the pre-modern parliament, the "Estates." Then, in the revolutions, another "class" was noted: the workers (*ouvriers*). In Germany, the corresponding terms of *aristocratie* and *bourgeoisie* were *Adel* and *Bürgertum* and there existed derogatory terms for the poor segments of the *Bürgertum* when these appeared as obviously politically backward (for instance *Pfahlbürger, Spießbürger* [babbit]). As to the German equivalent of the French *paysannerie* (which revolted and emancipated itself in the French revolution of 1789, up to a point), it was still a diffuse mass in the 1830s and 1840s, consisting of non-aristocratic, yet free, peasants (*Bauern*), of bonded persons (*Hörige*), of peasant partially freed from feudal duties, and increasingly also of "free" agricultural workers (*Heuermänner*, etc.), workers, "mobilized" rather than "tied" to the land of a landlord (estate owner; Gutsbesitzer [i.e. the landed higher aristocracy and the still land-owning part of the gentry]), and free to sell their labor (Arbeitskraft), based on "free" contracts. But as far as I know, it was already unlikely to encounter real "Leibeigene" (*serfs*), as in previous times. The term *Arbeiterklasse* (classe ouvriere; working class) was a modern term, in the early and mid-19th century; utopian and later other, more advanced socialists became aware of the fact that workers formed a *class* due to their active and important role in the various French revolutions of that time and also to their increasing numbers and the visibility of the misery and poverty this class experienced. Here, too, modern terms that referred to this class originated in France; the expressions "classes dangereuses" and "classes laborieuses" were current in the French bourgeois press. At least the first one, of these two terms, was genuinely French and alluded to recent French historical experience. In England, the term "laboring classes" appeared perhaps at the same time as its French equivalent, and the Germans translated these terms, thus commonly using "die arbeitenden Klassen." This expression, by using the plural form, diluted the concept of class, but reflected its internal differentiation. It was probably Marx who coined the sober and precise term Arbeiterklasse, working class that stressed its unifying character constituted by "wage labor" (Lohnarbeit). The term working class is now current and accepted even in America but shunned in Germany. Marx endowed the terms *bourgeoisie* and *working class* with precise meanings by defining them (and thus class relations) with respect to their role and position as owners of the means of production respectively non-owners of the means of production and sellers of their "labor power" (Arbeitskraft), thus in terms of the existing *relations of production*. The term petty bourgeoisie (*Kleinbürgertum*) refers to an intermediate position between the bourgeoisie (owners of capital, of—directly or indirectly—the means of production) and the working class. The typical petty-bourgeois owned only his own immediate means of production: the *independent craftsman* his tools and workshop, the *intellectual* his pen, his books, his study. This intermediate class was subject to proletarianization and disappearance; and the absolutist state had already produced a new variety of an intermediate stratum: middle and lower-ranking public servants who, as such, were no independent "owners" of any means of production but state employees, and who—due to their income and status—were still considered by current opinion as a stratum forming a *new* segments of the well-off respectively (in case of the lower, badly paid public servants) the poor petty-bourgeoisie. This prefigured the rise of the stratum of *clerks*—objectively a segment of the working class, selling its labor, that is considered as "socially" an intermediate or middle class, due to its consciousness of relative "privilege" and due to the relative respect (or "prestige") it may or may not experience. Terms used by bourgeois sociologists who are tempted to negate the existence of a *class society* translate the precise terms that identify classes—and that have existed for long!—into a vulgar jargon; thus the terms "high bourgeoisie" and "bourgeoisie" become rendered as alternatively "upper class" (if this "segment" is acknowledged at all) and "upper middle class"; the better paid clerks and skilled workers are considered "middle class," the badly paid workers are lower middle class, and thus—by a magic linguistic trick—all classes have disappeared because there "exists" only a differentiated "middle class." But more recently, due to increasing tendencies of lengthy mass unemployment and increasing misery (*Verelendung*), the term "lower class" and the term "underclass" have become used, and of course, media still use the term "mob," as in 1848.

43   I single out only one out of many small-town examples. "In the villages of the district of Calbe there were protests and revolts in the spring of 1848 [...] The many dead and wounded on March 18 caused consternation and feelings of solidarity among the people in Calbe. They did not want to remain inactive and organized a memorial service on Sunday, March 26, in honor of "heroes fallen for freedom in Berlin." (Dieter Horst Steinmetz, "'Die teuer errungene Freiheit gilt es zu erhalten!' – Das Wirken des Demokraten Wilhelm Loewe von der März-revolution bis zur Septemberkrise" (Geburtswehen der deutschen Demokratie, Part 2), in: "Sachsen-Anhalt-Journal" (Journal of the Landesheimatbund Sachsen-Anhalt; LHBSA), No.3 (2016) |URL http://journal.lhbsa.de/cpt-articles/geburtswehen-der-deutschen-demokratie-teil-2/)

44   It has been asserted that a detachment of skilled "Maschinenbau" (i.e., mechanical engineering) workers joined the "Civil Guard" after its formation in March, 1848. They were highly skilled specialists with a certain prestige and above average pay and it seem that they formed an acknowledged detachment of armed workers, cooperating in certain cases with the Civil Guard and like this Guard dedicated to the preservation or law and order and the protection of the "liberal" Camphausen/Hansemann government, thus of a certain conquest of bourgeois political influence that had been attained, in comparison to the situation existing in Prussia before March 18–20. It is very likely that the armed unit(s) of "machine makers" came into existence under the supervision of their "moderately" liberal factory owners.

45   It is necessary to note here already that the Civil Guard was established by covert Monarchists in close contact with the Court who posed as "conservative Liberals" and that it was numerically dominated by relatively well-off "middle-of-the-road" liberals.

46   This was on June 14, 1848. See Wilhelm Blos, *Die Deutsche Revolution von 1848 und 1849*. Paderborn: Salzwasser Verlag, 2015, p.325. (Reprint of: W. Blos, *Die Deutsche Revolution: Geschichte der Deutschen Bewegung von 1848 und 1849*. Stuttgart: Dietz, 1891, reprint Stuttgart: Dietz, 1898, and Berlin: Dietz, 1878.) – The mechanic Siegerist had already played a noteworthy role as a speaker outlining key demands of the workers during a popular assembly on March 26. (W. Blos, *Die Deutsche Revolution*, ibid., p.220)

47   This refers to the year 1836 when the Berlin Kammergericht (Superior Court or "Chamber Court") tried a large number of students suspected of subversive activities and formation of a clandestine student association. About 1,800 students were arrested in Prussia. (See Werner Meyer, ibidem, p. 128) Among the 206 students sentenced on August 4 of that year, 39 young men were sentenced to death on account of their alleged membership in the secret nationalist and democratic student association, a so-called Burschenschaft. Others received long jail sentences. Contrary to their later reactionary role in German society, student associations known as a Burschenschaft advocated the achievement of German unity and democratic civil rights at the time. The death sentences were commuted subsequently by the Court of Appeals and the students were now sentenced to 25 years of imprisonment under severe conditions in military prisons (Festungshaft). (See: Walter Schmidt, "Die vom preußischen Kammergericht am 4. August 1836 zum Tode verurteilten Burschenschaftler. – Die Umwandlung der Todesurteile in Festungshaft, die Begnadigung vom März 1838 und die anläßlich des Thronwechsels erfolgte Amnestie vom 10. August 1840" in: *Für Burschenschaft und Vaterland: Festschrift für den Burschenschafter und Studentenhistoriker Prof. (FH) Dr. Peter Kaup*. Edited by Bernhard Schroeter. Jena : Burschenschadt Arminia auf dem Burgkeller, 2006, pp. 121-122)

The repressive steps taken against students considered "subversive" by the reactionary Prussian government in 1836 were not the first such steps, they were only only the most severe, and other German states persecuted students, too, if they were thought to be democratic and on top of that, advocates of German unification. An example is William Wesselhoeft, a young man sentenced to a prison term during the early years of the Metternich era, thus after 1814 and before 1824. "As a young man, William Wesselhoeft joined the German student protest movement, known as Burschenschaften, an activity that landed him in prison, from which he escaped after four months. He later moved to Switzerland, studied medicine at the University of Basel, and was appointed to the faculty as an anatomy demonstrator. When German authorities ordered the extradition of political refugees from Switzerland, he left Europe for the USA where, in 1824, he initially settled in a German-speaking Pennsylvania community." (Source: https://www.researchgate. net/figure/Robert-Ferdinand-Wesselhoeft-and-family-1843-With-permission-Special-Collections-of_fig1_286373274)

48   It is a good term, in a way: it helps to lump together the poor masses, the "multitude" that included (a) the city's impoverished "citizens" (i.e., the lowest spectrum of Berlin's petty-bourgeoisie - including poor self-employed "artisans" [thus "masters" or "master craftsmen"], many small shopkeepers, underpaid teachers, unsuccessful, therefore badly paid writers without other means or sources of income that could be deemed sufficient (a category that included the proverbial "starving" writers, unable to earn a living in that profession and totally without other sources of income, e.g. a steady job or "rents" derived from an inherited bourgeois or petty-bourgeois fortune); (b) employed artisans ("journeymen") working for the owners

of a small workshops (thus, for independent, self-employed artisans, referred to as a "Meister" ["master" or master craftsman]), (c) male and female "workers" in the diverse new and old branches of what was called "industry"; (d) male and female servants (except the better-paid *highest category of servants* employed by the Royal household); and (e) the "lumpenproletariat."

49 "The journeymen, together with the workers, formed the majority of those who fought on the barricades." (Werner Meyer, ibidem, p.122 – My translation, AW)

50 August Theodor Woeninger had studied law and philosophy and obtained a Ph.D. He founded, in 1843, the first liberal monthly journal in Berlin. It was named "Der Staat: Monatsschrift für öffentliches Leben" (The State: A Monthly Focused on Public Life). It seems that the issues of volume 2, 1844 were the last ones that appeared and that the monthly ceased to be published due to difficulties with the censors. (See the data base on censorship of the University of Vienna / Wiener Universität, Vienna, Austria: http://www.univie.ac.at/zensur/?dbv=6u5 f1pn&d=xwyk1V%252BNo1K%252BiwG5BxCbPA&q=rotteck%1Estaats& l=FFFFFFFFF&ol=FFFFFFFFF&c=77&mi=1500&ma=1848 .) In 1847, Woeninger published a book on the Prussian United Diet—in other words, on the assembly of the two Estates meeting jointly in session, its members, laws passed, deliberations, and history. The United Diet was a late absolutist, in a way still pre-modern parliament with limited competence that polemical voices could denounce as a heritage of "feudalism." (See: A. Th. Woeniger (ed.), *Preußens Erster Reichstag. Eine Zusammenstellung der ständischen Gesetze, der Mitglieder und der Verhandlungen des ersten vereinigten Landtags, neben einem geschichtlichen Umriß seiner Verhältnisse. Achter Theil.* Berlin: Stuhr'sche Buchhandlung, 1847.) The United Diet, not convened for long, was needed in 1847 by a government and king short of money and started to discuss the matter of new taxes that it was asked to approve, while connecting this with the demand for the constitution that had been promised in 1817. This demand annoyed Frederick William IV and he dismissed the United Diet, saying when pressed that he might convene it again in four years. In early 1848, thus in the year of the March Revolution, a committee of the United Diet, the "Vereinigte ständische Ausschuß" (United Committee of the Estates), met in session in Berlin repeatedly since January 17, 1848. (See Adolf Wolff, *Darstellung der Berliner Bewegung im Jahre 1848*, Paderborn: Salzwasser-Verlag, 2015, p. 7f. Reprint of: Adolf Wolff, *Berliner Revolutions-Chronik: Darstellung der Berliner Bewegungen im Jahre 1848 nach politischen, sozialen und literarischen Beziehungen.* Vol. 1, Vol. 2, and Vol. 3. Berlin 1851; 1852; 1854). The United Diet was convened again shortly after the revolution, on April 2, 1848, and met, it seems, for several days. It was needed by the government headed by Count Arnim in order to give a stamp of legality to a draft of the new electoral law that it had not written and that it was expected to approve basically unchanged. Upon completing this job, it was dissolved and met never again in its old form. – As far as Woeniger, author of the above-mentioned book on the United Diet, is concerned, he ran for office during the election of city councilors in 1848 as a candidate in the Brothers Street precinct, thus in Old Coelln. The merchant George Bröcker won with 74 Yeah Votes and 57 Nay votes. Woeniger and the incumbent, city councilor Johann Samuel Ludwig Becker, both received 73 Yeah votes and 58 Nay votes. Drawing lots, Woeniger was lucky and was named deputy city councilor (Stellvertreter). (Manfred A. Pahlmann, *Anfänge des städtischen Parlamentarismus in Deutschland: Die Wahlen zur Berliner Stadtverordnetenversammlung unter der Preußischen Städteordnung von 1808.* Berlin: Akademie-Verlag, 1997, p.115) Perhaps to single out Woeniger and the others I

name here as people representative of a stratum (the educated petty bourgeoisie) and as embodiments of a 'spirit' or attitude (that was liberal, petty-bourgeois, democratic, yet flawed by illusions and political misjudgments) is not fair, despite the fact that I name them in the plural (thus using their names as a 'pars pro toto'). There were far more of this caliber than those I name. But as Brass shows and other historical accounts show, Dr. Woeniger—a writer—was very active in the turbulent days of early March, 1848, when people were repeatedly meeting illegally at the *Zelten*, in the Newspaper Hall and in other "etablissements" in order to debate the "demands of the people" (initially referred to as 'The demands of the young people"—or of youth), and in order to draw up petitions and vote on them.

51 The banker Mendheim, located in Brothers Street, was in charge of the Bankhaus M. H. Mendheim. (See Prittwitz, ibid., p. 14; see also: Hugo Rachel and P. Wallich, Berliner Großkaufleute und Kapitalisten. Vol. 3. Berlin 1967, pp. 295 and p. 297. – 2nd edition). His role in the March Revolution is not only noted by Brass and by Prittwitz but also by Adolf Wolff. (See Adolf Wolff, *Darstellung der Berliner Bewegung im Jahre 1848*, Paderborn: Salzwasser-Verlag, 2015, p. 48.)

52 Carl Nauwerk, also Carl Nauwerck (b. 1810 in Salem (Duchy of Lauenburg) – d. 1891 in Riesbach nr. Zurich) was living in Berlin since 1835, the year he was "habilitated" (i.e. submitted successfully his post-doctoral thesis) at the university of Berlin. He was subsequently an (unpaid?) Associate Professor (Privatdozent) teaching at this university from 1836 until 1844. His strong advocacy of freedom of the press is revealed in his review of Nicolai's book *Die Preßfrage: die Preßfreiheit in England, mit besonderer Bezugnahme auf das Libell,* published in: Deutsche Jahrbücher für Wissenschaft und Kunst, No. 50, No. 51 and No. 52 (1842). The university dismissed him after he had been denounced by the King as "revolutionary." In 1845, he published a work that was documenting and discussing important decisions of the Prussian (United) Provincial Diets during the first half of the 1840s (C. Nauwerck, *Uebersicht der wichtigeren Abstimmungen der Preußischen Provinziallandtage 1841, 1843, und 1845*. Berlin: Veit, 1845). In 1847 and 1848, Nauwerk was a city councilor in Berlin, and according to August Brass, he and Julius Berends were the most progressive ones in this assembly. He was elected in 1848 as a delegate to the German Parliament in Frankfurt where he adhered to the faction of the so-called Left that also included such delegates as Jacoby and Wigand. This group met regularly in an *établissement* known as Der Deutsche Hof, which is why it was also known as the Deutsche Hof faction. Nauwerk then joined another faction, the *Association of March* (1848) or, in German, *Märzverein*, that included such democratic, left-leaning liberal progressives as Ludwig Bamberger, Ludwig Feuerbach, and also Andreas Gottschalk, the Cologne-based socialist critiqued by Marx. In 1849, Nauwerk fled to Switzerland, like many revolutionaries. He was sentenced to death in absentia in Prussia in 1851 (and amnestied ten years later). His book on the United States, *Statistisches Wörterbuch über die Vereinigten Staaten*, appeared in 1853, published by Wigand in Leipzig. He also worked briefly for the *Neue Zürcher Zeitung*, later on had a small shop, selling tobacco and cigars, and continued also to be active among expatriate Germans, thus as President of an association that aided extremely poor German refugees in Switzerland and as a member, since 1860, of a political association advocating German unity (most likely not under Prussian hegemony).

53 With the Prussian counterrevolutionary coup d'état of November 1848 and the constitution of 1850, the extent to which the political wishes of what was, above all, a cunctatory class, were met, was reduced even more than it had been in the preceding months of that year by compromising "liberal" governments, even though this harsh reactionary turn was coupled with further measures of economic "liberalization" that reflected bourgeois interests.

54 Wives and offspring still under age, and other possibly dependent family members still living in the same house as the head of a household who was a citizen, did not enjoy the political—participative—rights enjoyed by him, as far as the affairs of the city were concerned. But they partook, more or less, in his bourgeois or petty-bourgeois status. Objectively, they swelled the number of the class faction that the head of the household belonged to. Whether they shared his standpoint (his "class-based views") or not, is a different matter. Let us remember that Frederick Engels was the son of a wealthy manufacturer in Elberfeld. In 1848, he had many tough arguments with his—either moderately liberal, or perhaps conservative—father.

55 See Adolph Wolff, *Berliner Revolutions-Chronik*, Vol. 3, p.145. Wolff quotes prime minister Camphausen verbatim: "It is indeed certain that more than 25,000 rifles and between 5-6000 side rifles have been distributed to the civil guard and armed corps in Berlin. [And there were about 25,000-30,000 enfranchised (male) burghers in Berlin... (AW)] This is so great a quantity in relation to the needs of the whole country, that it cannot be continued without the danger of undermining the effectiveness of the army, if in other places the distribution is carried out in similar proportion, from the available supplies. The government therefore hesitates to proceed with the continued distribution of weapons in Berlin prior to the adoption of a law, which is to be presented to the Assembly, that will establish the manner, and the extent to which the State is to issue weapons to the civil guard." (In German: "Es steht thatsächlich fest, daß an die Bürgerwehr und bewaffneten Corps in Berlin über 25,000 Schießgewehre und zwischen 5-6000 Seitengewehre vertheilt worden sind. Es ist dies eine so bedeutende Quantität im Verhältnis zu dem Bedürfnisse des ganzen Landes, daß wenn in anderen Ortschaften die Vertheilung in ähnlichem Verhältniß aus den vorhandenen Vorräthen ausgeführt und damit fortgefahren werden sollte, dies nicht ohne Gefahr, die Wehrhaftigkeit der Armee auf's Aeußerste zu beeinträchtigen, geschehen könnte. Die Regierung trägt daher Bedenken, mit der ferneren Verausgabung von Waffen in Berlin vorzugehen, bevor nicht durch ein Gesetz, welches der Versammlung vorgelegt werden soll, die Art und Weise, sowie der Umfang festgestellt ist, welcher bei der Ausgabe von Waffen an die Bürgerwehr Seitens des Staates maßgebend sein soll.")

56 The "salons" of some erudite women became very famous, thus for instance those of Henriette Herz (1764–1847) and Rahel Levin, née Rahel Varnhagen von Ense (1771v1833) that were noted for offering public as well as private lectures of scholars which would addresses an invited bourgeois public. See: Jean-Édouard Spenlé, *Rahel Mme Varnhagen von Ense : histoire d'un salon romantique en Allemagne*. Paris: Hachette, 1910; Nikolaus Gatter, "'... die freundlichsten und zartesten Bezüge zugleich durch Bildung und Freiheit begünstigt ...': Henriette Herz und Karl August Varnhagen von Ense, " in: Studia niemcoznawcze, Vol. 59 (2017), pp.369-384, ISSN 0208-4597; Irina Hundt (ed.), *Vom Salon zur Barrikade : Frauen der Heinezeit* [From the salon to the barricade: women at the time of Heine]. Stuttgart: Metzler, 2002. See also: Handbuch der historischen

57   *Buchbestände in Deutschland* [Handbook of historic books preserved in Germany], Vol. 14. Berlin. Part 1. Edited by Friedhilde Krause in collaboration with Paul Rabe; adapted by Alwin Müller-Jerina and Friedhilde Krause. With a Preface by Bernhard Fabian. Hildesheim; Zurich; New York: Olms-Weidmann, 1995, p. 24.

The period between 1830 and the crisis of the late 1840s was characterized by "rapid growth of industrial production" (Werner Meyer, *Vormärz: Die Ära Metternich 1815 bis 1848*, Potsdam: Potsdamer Verlagsgesellschaft, 1948, p .120) and as a consequence, centers of modern industry like Berlin experienced a significant influx of job-seeking proletarians. At the same time, "the misery of the masses increased". (Werner Meyer, ibidem, p. 120. – My translation, AW)

58   "The heyday of the Jewish manufacturers of silk and other luxury goods was in the twenty-year period after the Seven Years War. Beginning in the 1780s a crisis hit many silk manufacturers, which resulted in the reduction or closing of many of the [protoindustrial] silk factories. Those Jews who went into the production of lighter [less luxurious, cheaper] cotton goods, however, were able to prosper even in the later years. Isaac Benjamin Wulff (a relative of the Itzigs) was the most important cotton manufacturer in Berlin in 1785 with 110 looms, 100 cloth-printing employees, and goods worth 100,000 Thaler produced annually." (Steven M. Lowenstein, *The Berlin Jewish Community: Enlightenment, Family and Crisis, 1770-1830*. New York; Oxford : Oxford Univ. Press, 1994, p.29)

59   Most workers in this "industry" are "employees whose employment is limited timewise, irregular, provisional and uncertain and who are thus underemployed or partially employed and who are nonetheless at the same time both overexploited and underpaid [...]." (Carlo Donolo, *Ungleichmäßige Entwicklung und Auflösung gesellschaftlicher Strukturen* [Unequal Development and Dissolution of Societal (or: Social) Structures], Berlin: Merve, 1974, pp.14f.)

60   Carlo Donolo speaks of a "sector of formally independent workers (poor peasants, artisans, small shopkeepers)" and describes it as a "sector" [of the population] characterized by "structural underemployment ('hidden unemployment')"; he also notes the "low productivity [of this sector], especially with regard to agriculture and petty commercial activities [...]." (Carlo Donolo, ibid. p.14f.)

61   "During the second half of the [eighteen-] forties, the German economy was affected by a severe overproduction crisis. [...] Companies that closed their doors and joblessness were its consequence. In Berlin, Leipzig, and Stuttgart, strikes as well as confrontations [of workers] with the army occurred. In addition to all of this, there was a food crisis due to the crop failures of the years 1847-1847 [My translation – AW]." (Werner Meyer, ibidem, p .120)

62   With regard to many if not most master craftsmen, Werner Meyer notes both their economic difficulties that increased during the 1830s and 1840s due to the growing competition of modern industry, and the fact that this stratum that found itself in an "intermediate position between the bourgeoisie and the proletariat," still remained *ideologically attached to the bourgeoisie*, and this obviously in contrast to the journeymen they employed. (See Werner Meyer, ibidem, p.122)

63   "Artisans suffered more and more [during the 1830s and 1840s] due to the competition of [modern] industry, [...] there existed great misery in these circles. [...] Tensions increased between masters and journeymen became more and more apparent; this became especially obvious in 1848."(Werner Meyer, ibidem, p .122)

64   In Paris, the Club of German Workers (Club der deutschen Arbeiter) was formed and in Brussels, the Association Démocratique (Demokratische Gesellschaft).

65 Sections of the secret Bund der Gerechten (Federation of the Just) and after its dissolution, of the Federation of Communists (Bund der Kommunisten) existed in Paris, Brussels, London and Switzerland. See Ernst Schraepler, *Handwerkerbünde und Arbeitervereine 1830-1853. Die politische Tätigkeit deutscher Sozialisten von Wilhelm Weitling bis Karl Marx*. Berlin; New York: de Gruyter, 1972. See Waltraud Seidel-Höppner, *Wilhelm Weitling. Leben und politisches Wirken*. Leipzig: Rosa-Luxemburg Verein, 1993; see also: Waltraud Seidel.Höppner, " Zu einigen theoretischen und methodischen Fragen der neueren Weitling-Forschung," included as the introduction in: Hans-Arthur Marsiske, *"Wider die Umsonstfresser": der Handwerkerkommunist Wilhelm Weitling* [Against Those Who Eat Free-of-Charge (Against the Free-of-Charge Guzzlers): the Artisan-Communist Wilhelm Weitling], Hamburg: Ergebnisse-Verlag, 1986.

66 Decisive documents of the Federation of Communists have been published in: *Der Bund der Kommunisten: Dokumente und Materialien. Band 1: 1836-1849*. Compiler or editor (Redakteur): Herwig Förder. Edited by the Institute for Marxismus-Leninism attached to the Central Committee of the SED and the Institute for Marxism-Leninism attached to the Central Committee of the Communist Party of the Soviet Union. Berlin: Dietz, 1970; *Der Bund der Kommunisten: Dokumente und Materialien. Band 1: 1836-1849*, ed. by Herwig Förder. Berlin: Dietz, 1983; and *Der Bund der Kommunisten: Dokumente und Materialien. Band 3: 1851-1852*, ed. by Herwig Förder. Berlin: Dietz, 1984.

67 This "reading room" ("Lesekabinett") was not the only one in Berlin, as Adolf Wolff notes (See Adolf Wolff, *Darstellung der Berliner Bewegung im Jahre 1848*, Paderborn: Salzwasser-Verlag, 2015, p. 5)—but it was the one that received the most attention, especially during the March Revolution. This may have been due to the liberal democratic position of its owner, Julius Berends, and due to the selection of newspapers, journals, and books that he offered.

68 This is discussed in a clear manner by Frederick Engels. He writes,

"[…] The treaties of Vienna are the epitome of the great victory of reactionary Europe over revolutionary France. They are the classic form in which European reaction ruled for fifteen years during the Restoration period. They restore legitimacy, monarchy by divine right, feudal aristocracy, clerical rule, and patriarchal jurisdiction and administration. But since victory was won with the help of the English, German, Italian, Spanish and especially the French bourgeoisie, concessions had also to be made to the bourgeoisie. While the sovereigns, aristocrats, priests and bureaucrats divided the rich spoils among themselves, the bourgeoisie was put off with promissory notes drawn on the future, which were not honoured and which nobody had any intention of honoring. Instead of examining the real practical content of the treaties of Vienna, Herr Ruge assumes that these empty promises are their true content, and that reactionary practice is merely an improper misinterpretation!

One must indeed be an astonishingly good-natured person to believe, after 33 years, after the revolutions of 1830 and 1848, that these promissory notes will still be paid and to imagine that the sentimental phrases in which the illusory promises of Vienna are wrapped up have still any meaning in the year 1848.

Citizen Ruge appears as the Don Quixote of the treaties of Vienna.

Finally, Citizen Ruge reveals a great secret to the Assembly—it is only the fact that the treaties of 1815 were broken in Cracow in 1846 which caused the revolutions of 1848. Let this be a warning to all despots!

To sum up, Citizen Ruge has not changed in any way since we last met him in the field of literature. He still uses the same phrases which he had learned by heart and repeated ever since he worked as the door-keeper of German philosophy at the *Hallischen* and *Deutschen Jahrbücher*; there is still the same confusion, the same jumble of views, the same lack of ideas, the same gift of presenting the most banal and nonsensical ideas in a pompous manner, the same lack of "knowledge," and, in particular, the same pretensions to the approbation of the German philistine, who has never heard the like in his life."

Source: Frederick Engels, "The Frankfurt Assembly Debates the Polish Question" (several articles without title in the *Neue Rheinische Zeitung* (New Rhenanian Gazette) since August 7, 1848.) The quoted passage is from *Neue Rheinische Zeitung*, No. 96, September 7, 1848. https://www.marxists.org/archive/marx/works/1848/08/09.htm.

69 See Erich Jordan, *Die Entstehung der Konservativen Partei und die preussischen Agrarverhältnisse von 1848* [The emergence of the Conservative Party and the Prussian agricultural relations of 1848]. Berlin: Duncker & Humblot, 1914, pp. 103-116, on the "Hungersnot of 1846-1848" (famine of 1846-1848) in Prussia. See also Manfred Gailus and Heinrich Volkmann (eds.), *Der Kampf um das tägliche Brot: Nahrungsmangel, Versorgungspolitik und Protest 1770-1990* [The Fight for the Daily Bread: Food Shortages, Policies of Provision, and Protest during the Years 1770-1990]. Opladen: Westdeutscher Verlag, 1994. – The famine of the 1840s was a European phenomenon. See: Eric Vanhaute, Richard Paping and Cormac Ó Gráda, "The European Subsistence Crisis of 1845–1850: A Comparative Perspective," in: Cormac Ó Gráda, Richard Paping and Eric Vanhoute (eds.), *When the Potato Failed: Causes and Effects of the Last European Subsistence Crisis.* Turnhout: Brepols, 2007.

70 By the mid-18th century, those renters of house and apartments who paid annual rents in excess of 20 Thaler were considered well-off and were compelled to pay a special tax in order to help the city repay a debt incurred when ransom money had to be paid to the General of the Austrian army so he would refrain from burning down Berlin in 1757. The poor, however, were exempt. The sum paid by renters gives us an idea of the value of the Thaler. (See Richard Borrmann (comp.), *Die Bau- und Kunstdenkmäler von Berlin*. [Berlin's Architectural Heritage and Monuments]. Compiled by Richard Borrmann, with a historical introduction by Paul Clauswitz. Berlin; Heidelberg: Springer, 1893, reprint: 2013, p.96) – In 1848 many Berliners were exempt from payment of this tax, due to their poverty.

71 See for instance Werner Hegemann, *Das steinerne Berlin. Geschichte der größten Mietskasernenstadt der Welt*. Berlin: Ullstein, 1963; Isabelle Weis, *L'urbanisme berlinois et les Mietskasernen (1840-1914) : réalités, discours et représentations*. Ph.d. thesis, Université de Reims Champagne-Ardenne, 2017.

72 The quoted text appeared in *Bericht aus Berlins gesellschaftlichem Leben*, issue No. 7, Nov. 1846, on p.27.

73 Of course, the successful commercial and financial bourgeoisie of the late 18th and of the early and mid-19th century never assimilated this submissive stance completely or made it truly part of its collective character, as this would have marred and contradicted its self-confidence as a decisive stratum of a socially "rising" class. The same is true of a number of brilliant individuals with a petty-bourgeois background like Schiller and Büchner, or of Goethe—a son of Frankfurt's bourgeoisie (whose father owned a large house in that city, which attests to parental wealth). Goethe, becoming a friend of Carl August, Duke of Saxe-Weimar, was

nobilitated and in that respect, symbolized the closeness of the upper layers of the bourgeoisie to existing late absolutist regimes (especially when a ruler appeared to them as "enlightened"). A number of economically important bourgeois financial capitalists (for instance Simon Oppenheim, ennobled in Austria in 1867) and important industrialists (like the Krupps) were also nobilitated sooner or later, at any rate, before 1918. Interestingly, the hypothesis of authoritarian character traits that may have been a frequent phenomenon among Germans in their country's old and recent history (and that may still be present today) is confirmed by Marianne Birthler, the woman who had been put in charge of the government office that focused on clarification of past activities by the East German internal secret service (the "Stasi")—but not on those of its West German equivalent that had its own networks of informers and repertoire of dirty tricks. Ms. Birthler refers to a long collective history of paternalistic traditions and authoritarian structures that characterize German history. (See: Marianne Birthler, "Vierzig Jahre Teilung brauchen vierzig Jahre Heilung: Die Deutschen haben eine lange gemeinsame Geschichte vormundschaftlicher Tradition und autoritärer Strukturen," in: Neue Zürcher Zeitung, International edition, April 28, 2018, p.28.) Perhaps it is also not by chance that the German social context gave rise to key publications focusing on authoritarian character structures, thus: Theodor W. Adorno, *The Authoritarian Personality*. New York: Norton, 1980 (1969); Erich Fromm, *The Super-ego: the reign of authority and the reign of conscience*. North Hollywood: Center for Cassette Studies, 1974 (audiobook); Erich Fromm, *Autorität und Familie : Geschichte und Methoden der Erhebungen*. München: Edition Erich Fromm, 2016. It must be noted that experiments conducted in the United States have also shown a strong prevalence of authoritarianism. Thus, many test persons were ready to carry out "orders" that would hypothetically harm others if the person ordering such actions was believed to be a man or woman in possession of scientifically underpinned "authority" (see the Milgram experiment, and subsequent research that confirmed its findings). We should keep in mind, however, that character traits are not natural facts and/or genetically transmitted. They are socially produced and should be explored—in social contexts, thus changing situations—as the processual rather than static psychic reality that they are. In other words, it matters to comprehend the dialectics between such traits and socio-economically as well as politically determined historical conditions.

74 August Brass (b. 1818, d. 1876) was also the author *of Chronik von Berlin, Potsdam und Charlottenburg, vom Entstehen dieser Städte bis auf die neuesten Zeiten,* published in Berlin in 1843, and of several prose works, thus *Die Mysterien von Berlin* (The Mysteries of Berlin; 5 Vols.), published in Berlin in 1844. He is also the author of a publication comprising only 8 pages that was published by him in 1848 and printed by Lohmann; it was entitled: *Drei schöne, neue, rothe Lieder, gemacht in diesem Jahr* (Three Beautiful, New, Red Songs, created this year), and of another publication, again comprising eight pages and printed by Lassar, that was entitled: *Das neue Lied vom blutigen Kaiser: nach einer wahren Begebenheit, so sich zugetragen hat in den Landen Oestreich im Jahre des Herrn eintausend achthundert und achtundvierzig, nebst einer Hinweisung auf die göttliche Gerechtigkeit / in schöne Reime gebracht von August Braß.* (The New Song of the Bloody Emperor: Based on a True Occurrence, As It Happened in the Lands of Austria in the Year of the Lord One Thousand Eight Hundred and Forty-Eight, Accompanied by A [Warning] Note on Divine Justice / Presented in Beautiful Rhymes by August Brass.)

75 Heinrich Bernhard Oppenheim (1819–1886) was jurist, writer and philosopher. Together with Arnold Ruge and Eduard Meyen, he was the editor of "Die Reform: Politische Zeitung" in 1848. Jointly with Arnold Ruge and Ludwig Schreckenstein, he was the author of "Aufruf an das Volk!" (Extrablatt der "Reform" ["Call to the People!", special edition of the "Reform"] in 1848).
    The letters exchanged between H.B. Oppenheim and Bettina von Arnim (1785–1859) between 1841 and 1849 have been published in 1990. See: Bettina von Arnim and Heinrich Bernhard Oppenheim: *".. und mehr als einmal nachts im Thiergarten." Briefe 1841–1849*. Herausgegeben, eingeleitet und kommentiert von Ursula Püschel. FSP Verlag, Berlin 1990. H. B. Oppenheim was the author of: *Das Bürgerthum der Juden* (The Citizenship [i.e., Civil Status, Civil Right and Civil Commitment] of Jews). Grünberg; Leipzig 1842; also of: *Der freie deutsche Rhein: Geschichtliche und staatsrechtliche Entwicklung der Gesetzgebung des Rheins*. Stuttgart; Tübingen: Cotta, 1842 [Reprint: Paderborn: Salzwasser Verlag 2016]; also of: *Ueber das Verbot ganzer Verlagsfirmen*, Karlsruhe: Groos, 1846 [a book that discussed censorship]; also of: *Philosophie des Rechts und der Gesellschaft* [Philosophy of Law and Society] (1847), edited and with an appendix by Hermann Klenner. Stuttgart: Frankh, 1850 [Reprint: Freiburg; Berlin; München; Würzburg; Zurich: Haufe Mediengruppe, 2007], also of: *Über Armenpflege und Heimatrecht*. Berlin: Heymann, 1870 [a book that advocated help that should be given to the poor and the homeless, vagrants, etc.]; also of: *Der Katheder-Sozialismus*, Berlin: Oppenheim, 1873 [republished, edited as a new edition with comments by Hansjörg Walther, Frankfurt am Main: Libera Media, 2016]; also of: *Die Judenverfolgung in Rumänien*, also of: *Gewerbegericht und Kontraktbruch: Zur Revision der deutschen Reichs-Gewerbeordnung*, Berlin: Oppenheim, 1874; and of *B. F. L. Waldeck, der Führer der Preussischen Demokratie* [Waldeck, the leader of the Prussian Democratic Movement (or Current)]. New edition, Berlin: Oppenheim, 1880.

76 Georg Jung (b.1815 [or 1814] in Potsdam, d. 1886 in Berlin) was a liberal, relatively progressive democrat in 1848. It was he who was the key orator speaking to those present during the burial of the slain revolutionary fighters in Friedrichshain, a talk featured *in extenso* in the book on the March Revolution written by August Brass and published separately as *Rede am Grabe der am 18. und 19. März gefallenen Kämpfer, gehalten am 22. März 1848*. Braunschweig: Götte, 1848. Jung was a member of the Prussian National Assembly in 1848. He was the author of *Der Magistrat von Berlin: Seine Begriffe von Ehre, sein Muth, sein Verstand*. Leipzig: Schulz, 1848 and of *Die Reactionäre: was sie wollen; was für Leute alles dazu gehören; an welchen Redensarten man sie besonders erkennt: ein Handbuch für das Volk* [The Reactionaries: What they want, what kind of people belong to them; which phrases make it especially possible to recognize them: A Handbook for the People], Berlin: Hofmann, 1849; and also of *Drei Ansprachen an meine Wähler und Abschied von denselben*. Berlin: Adolf, 1849. Merely a year after the revolution of 1848–1849, he published *Geschichte der Frauen. Teil 1 (i.e.Part 1) : Geschichte der Unterdrückung der Frauen und ihrer allmählichen Selbstbefreiung, bis zur Erscheinung des Christenthums*. Frankfurt am Main: Literarische Anstalt, 1850 [a book focusing on the suppression and emancipation of women]. Like Brass, Georg Jung adopted a "national liberal," thus fairly conservative position later on.

77 Rudolf Löwenstein (b. 1819 in Breslau, d.1891 in Berlin), was a liberal writer living in Berlin who was compelled by the authorities to leave Prussia due to his political activities in 1849 (the year of reactionary victory). Prittwitz refers to him in his account of the revolution as an intellectual suspected of democratic agitation.

Löwenstein was able to return to Berlin already in 1850 when he became editor again of the satirical journal Kladderadatsch, of which he had been a co-founder in 1848. He is the author of: *Aus bewegten Zeiten. Politische Gedichte von Rudolf Löwenstein* [Turbulent Times / Political poems by Rudolf Löwenstein]. With a preface by Albert Träger. Frankfurt: Lehmann, 1890.

78 Julius Löwenberg (1800–1893), who appears in accounts of the revolution as a democrat and thus one of the "intellectual troublemakers" during the days of March, 1848, belonged to the circle of Bruno Bauer, Max Stirner and "The Free Ones" ("Die Freien"). Adolf Wolff refers to him as a "young scholar" (junger Gelehrter) in the early 1850s. (See Adolf Wolff, *Berliner Revolutions-Chronik: Darstellung der Berliner Bewegungen im Jahre 1848 nach politischen, socialen und literarischen Beziehungen* [Chronicle of the Berlin revolution: An account of the Berlin movements in 1848 in political, social and literary respect], Vol. 3. Berlin: Gustav Hempel, 1854. Also *as a reprint:* Paderborn: Salzwasser-Verlag, 2015, p. 5). Prittwitz notes that Löwenberg presided during the debate that took place at the Zelten on March 9, 1848 ("Shrove Tuesday"), an assembly attended by about 600 persons. (Karl Ludwig von Prittwitz, *Berlin 1848: das Erinnerungswerk des Generalleutnants Karl Ludwig von Prittwitz*, ibid., p.19).) Löwenberg was a friend of Alexander von Humboldt, and published a bibliography of Alexander von Humboldt's writings, included in the three volumes of Karl Bruns, *Alexander von Humboldt – Eine wissenschaftliche Biographie*. Leipzig: Brockhaus, 1872. In the post-1849 period, Löwenberg became a journalist of the Voss'sche Zeitung. He also published scholarly works focused on geography in the 1860s, 1870s, and 1880s.

79 Dr. Löwinson (i.e. Louis Lewissohn) was Secretary of the "Volksverein unter den Zelten" (People's Association under the Marquees), and thus he held an elected position as the key leading figure of this association in the spring of 1848. According to Prittwitz, Dr. Löwinson was—like Löwenberg—a member of a deputation that had been elected during the session of a popular assembly taking place at the Zelten, to present a petition to the king in person, something that Minutoli (the chief of police), present during the meeting, vowed to impede—if necessary by force. They should rather send it by mail. According to Prittwitz, both Löwinson and Löwenberg (the two named by Prittwitz) declared that they had not been empowered by the assembly to do so. Thus, Löwinson was also a key figure and a widely respected man among those meeting at the Zelten in order to debate and vote on democratic petitions. As Prittwitz saw it, these meetings in early March must be seen as the "embryo of the revolution" ("Die Polizei war mit Embryo der Revolution in Unterhandlung getreten..." – Prittwitz, ibidem, p.21)

80 Both the necessity of active involvement of intellectuals in revolutionary situations and movements and their often rather questionable role must be reflected here. See also: Ernest Mandel, Die Rolle der Intelligenz im Klassenkampf (The Role of the Intelligentsia in Class Struggle; in French: Les étudiants, les intellectuels et la lutte des classes). Frankfurt/Main: ISP-Verlag, 1975.

81 See: *Die Preussische Städte-Ordnung vom 19. November 1808: mit deren durch die Kabinetsordre vom 4 Juli 1832 erfolgten ergänzenden und erläuternden Bestimmungen*. [The Prussian Town Ordinance of November 19, 1808: with the supplementary and explanatory provisions of the Government Decree ("Cabinet Order") of July 4, 1832]. Anclam : Druck und Verlag von W. Dietze, 1844, 48 pp.; see also: *Die preußische Städte-Ordnung vom 19. November 1808 nach Doctrin,*

Praxis und Gesetzgebung, ergänzt und erläutert von Ed. Zimmermann, Dr. der Rechte, Bürgermeister von Spandow, Obergerichtsassessor [The Prussian Town Ordinance of November 19, 1808 with respect to doctrin, practice and legislation, supplemented and explained by Ed. Zimmermann, dr. of Rights, Mayor of Spandow, High Court Attorney]. Dresden: Adler und Dietze, 1847, 96 pp.

82 In German: "der im ersten Eifer von den Stadtverordneten gethane Schritt einer allgemeinen Mandatsniederlegung" (Adolph Wolff, *Berliner Revolutions-Chronik: Darstellung der Berliner Bewegungen im Jahre 1848 nach politischen, sozialen und literarischen Beziehungen* [Chronicle of the Berlin revolution: An account of the Berlin movements in 1848 in political, social and literary respect], vol. 1. Berlin: Gustav Hempel, 1851, p. 432.)

83 In German: "hatte keine andere Bedeutung, als daß dieser Versammlung eine ganz ähnliche, nach dem alten exclusiven Wahlgesetze gewählte folgen sollte." (Wolff, *Berliner Revolutions-Chronik*, vol. 1, ibid., p. 432.)

84 In German:
Bekanntmachung. Gegen Ende des Monats März d.J. sollen wiederum, nachdem 3 Jahre abgelaufen, gedruckte Nachweisungen in den Häusern desjenigen Drittheils der Stadt zur Ausfüllung vertheilt werden, deren Bewohner, welche das hiesige Bürgerrecht besitzen, und zur Wahl der Stadtverordneten pro 1848 eine Berechtigung haben, dazu eingeladen bleiben. Da eine genaue Ausfüllung der Rubriken dieser Nachweisungen, deren Inhalt später zum Druck und zur Vertheilung gelangen soll, mannigfache Weiterungen vermeidet; so erwarten wir von dem Gemeinsinn der resp, Hausbesitzer oder Stellvertreter, daß Sie sich einer sorgfältigen und genauen Ausfüllung der Rubriken, nach dem wörtlichen Inhalt der Bürgerbriefe unterziehen und dabei eine solche Beschleunigung eintreten lassen werden, welche erforderlich ist, den Herren Bezirksvorstehern ihr mühevolles Amt nicht unnöthig zu erschweren.
Berlin, den 1. März 1848. Ober-Bürgermeister, Bürgermeister und Rath hiesiger K. Residenz
Berlin, den 1. März 1848.
Ober-Bürgermeister, Bürgermeister und Rath hiesiger K. Residenz." (*Kgl. Privilegirte Berlinische Zeitung*, No. 63, Wednesday, March 15, 1848, 1. Beilage = First Supplement, p.8.)

85 The document is reprinted by Angerstein. See "Bekanntmachung des Magistrats nach Bestattung der Gefallenen," in: Angerstein, ibid., p. 106.

86 In German: "Huldigung, welche unsere ganze Bevölkerung den in dem ruhmvollen Kampfe Gefallenen [...] [darbrachte]" and "Huldigung" to "allen Helden [...], die für die große Sache der politischen und sozialen Freiheit gestritten und [die] sie uns durch ihre todesmuthige Hingebung erkämpft haben." (Angerstein, ibid., p. 106.)

87 In German: "Dafür zu wirken, daß aus der Freiheit sich jetzt die Größe, das Glück und die Wohlfahrt unseres Volkes in festester Ordnung aufbaue, das ist und sei jetzt unser Aller Aufgabe." – Angerstein, ibid., p. 106.

88 Adolf Wolff quotes von Reden's words, "gesetzliche Organ der Wünsche der Einwohner" from the Kgl. Privilegierte Zeitung, also known as Voss Zeitung, Voss'sche Zeitung, and Vossische Zeitung. He writes, "Die Bürgerwehr, hatte ... v. Reden ... vorgeschlagen, solle fortan das alleinige 'gesetzliche Organ der Wünsche der Einwohner' sein." (Wolff, *Berliner Revolutions-Chronik*, vol. 1, ibidem, p. 432.)

89 In German: "Nach einer politischen Umwälzung sei an alle Dinge ein anderer Maßstab zu legen, als früher; sei früher die Stadtverordneten-Versammlung allein

oder mit dem Magistrat gesetzliches Organ der Wünsche der Bürgerschaft und wohl auch der Einwohnerschaft gewesen, so können sie als solches jetzt nicht mehr betrachtet werden, "weil offenkundig ein Theil ihrer Mitglieder sich im Widerspruch mit der öffentlichen Meinung befindet.""

"Möchten deshalb, so schließt Hr. v. Reden, die neuen Rathgeber des Königs, wenn sie die Wünsche der Einwohnerschaft Berlins genau kennen lernen wollen, diese Wünsche nur durch die Bürgerwehr und deren wackere Verbündeten, die Studirenden und Handwerker-Vereine zu erforschen suchen." (Adolf Wolff, *Berliner Revolutions-Chronik*, vol. 1, ibidem, p. 432. As noted already, Wolff relies here on, and quotes in part verbatim, from the Voss. Z. of March 23, 1848.)

90 See the brief newspaper commentary in *Berliner Krakehler*, No. 17, Wednesday, August 2, 1848, p.2. The jargon of the Berlin working class features the verb *herumkrakehlen* or simply *krakehlen* as a synomym for loud and perhaps even coarse shouting as a means to get attention.

91 In German: "Wir sind zufrieden mit dem, was erreicht ist, das ist das constitutionelle Königthum u.s.w." (Wolff, *Berliner Revolutions-Chronik*, vol. 1, ibidem, p. 432)

92 In German: "Die Gegenpartei wollen neue Wahlen der Abgeordneten vor dem Zusammentritte des Landtages und Wahl der Stadtverordneten, wenn zuvor alle Schutzverwandte zu Bürgern erklärt seien. Das neue Wahlgesetz könne aber nur durch die bestehenden Gewalten abgeändert werden." (Wolff, *Berliner Revolutions-Chronik*, vol. 1, ibidem, p. 432)

93 In German: "Aufgabe der Vertreter im Staate [the Camphausen government] und Stadt kann es daher nur sein, das alte verrottete Wahlgesetz nach den Bedürfnissen constitutioneller Freiheit abzuändern, und dies erwarten und fordern wir Alle, die am Barrikadenkampfe teilgenommen [haben], von unseren Vertretern." (Wolff, *Berliner Revolutions-Chronik*, vol. 1, ibidem, pp. 432f.)

94 The original German text says, "Zum Justiz-Minister habe Ich den Dr. der Rechte Bornemann ernannt, und den Präsidenten der Handels-Kammer Camphausen zu Mir berufen, um mir fortan gleichfalls als Minister [without portfolio?] zur Seite zu stehen." The entire proclamation is published by Angerstein. See Document No. 20: *Berufung der Minister Bornemann und Camphausen am 20. März 1848* ["Naming" (i.e. appointment) of the Ministers Bornemann and Camphausen on March 20, 1848], reprinted in: Wilhelm Angerstein, ibid., p. 101)

95 Count Arnim who was named interior minister by Frederick William IV in 1842 was compelled to resign in 1845 due to the fact that the King disagreed with his position regarding constitutional matters. Count Arnim seems to have been in favor of a constitution that would give some rights to some parts of population, which gave him the reputation of a "liberal" among Prussia's arch-conservative supporters of the late-absolutist status quo and which also accounts for the fact that the king, who profoundly rejected and loathed a constitution, saw him as a liberal, thus remembering him as a likely "liberal" choice for the post of prime minister when the *force des choses* left him with no alternative but that of bowing to popular pressure. More democratically inclined liberals and many among the subaltern classes in Prussia and Germany saw Count Arnim as another embodiment of the reactionary regime in Berlin. A major reason for this can be seen in the fact that his condemnation of Heinrich Heine's poem *The Silesian Weavers* became famous and made the poem even more famous, practically a treasure of the common people. As the editors of the "secular edition" of Heine's Collected Works (originally published by Akademie-Verlag in East Berlin) note, Heinrich Heine's poem *The Silesian*

Weavers was not only published by the Paris-based Socialist German-language newspaper *Vorwärts* [Forward!] that was edited by Karl Marx. Soon it was also distributed in its original and in often more militant abridged form in Germany in the form of pamphlets and one-page leaflets. (See: Heinrich Heine. *Heinrich Heine: Werke, Briefwechsel, Lebenszeugnisse. Bd.2: Gedichte 1827–1844 und Versepen.* Kommentar, Teilband 1 [Works, correspondence, life testimonies. Vol.2: Poems 1827–1844 and Verse epics. Commentary, sub-vol. 1] ("Säkularausgabe," compiled by Irmgard Möller in cooperation with Hans Böhm). Berlin: Akademie-Verlag, 1994.) Such clandestinely distributed material was of cause noted by the authorities. Aware of the poem, Count Arnim, as minister of interior, reacted sharply in 1844 by calling the poem "an address to the poor among the people that is seditious with respect to its tone and that abounds with criminal utterances." (See Dagmar Ernst, *Gedichtinterpretation: "Die schlesischen Weber" von Heinrich Heine* [Poetry Interpretation: Heinrich Heine's "The Silesian Weavers"]. Norderstedt: GRIN Verlag, 2008, p. 1, footnote 1 with the exact quotation in German: "eine in aufrührerischem Ton gehaltene und mit verbrecherischen Äußerungen angefüllte Ansprache an die Armen im Volke.").

96   Nitschke thinks that Arnim's "position as [the king's] civilian crisis manager" ("die Stellung seines zivilen Krisenmanagers" since March 19) "was damaged since March 20" and that his position as prime minister became "increasingly untenable." He bases this assumption on the fact that the king had hoped at the time to get Ludolf Camphausen—who was seen as a "moderate" liberal with some prestige, and a true representative of the Rhenish bourgeoisie—to join the new government as a minister under Count Arnim, but this attempt failed. Wolf Nitschke, *Adolf Heinrich Graf v. Arnim-Boitzenburg (1803-1868). Eine politische Biographie* [A.H. Count Arnim-Boitzenburg (1803–1868): A Political Biography]. Berlin: Duncker & Humblot, 2004, p.219.

97   The letter by Camphausen that Nitscke refers to here is reprinted in: Joseph Hansen (ed.), *Rheinische Briefe und Akten zur Geschichte der politischen Bewegung 1830–1850* [Rhenish Letters and Records on the History of the Political Movement 1830-1850], Vol. 2, Part 1 [Jan. 1846-April 1848]. Essen: Baedeker, 1942, pp.647-650.

98   Regarding Hansemann's leading role in the speculative development of a new town quarter in Aachen (in the context of the production of the new Cologne-Aachen railroad line and the construction of the Aachen railway station), see: Jürgen Wennemann, "Actenmäßige Untersuchung der Entwicklung des 'Eisenbahnviertels' zu Aachen um die Mitte des 19. Jahrhunderts. Ein Beitrag zum Terrainverwertung durch private Eisenbahngesellschaften" [An investigation, based on records, of the development of Aachen's 'Railroad Townquarter' (Eisenbahn-Viertel) during the mid-19th century. A research contribution on [speculative] valorization of terrains by private railway companies], in: Gerhard Fehl and Juan Rodriguez-Lores (eds.), *Stadterweiterungen 1800–1875: von den Anfängen des modernen Städtebaues in Deutschland* [Town Expansions 1800–1875: On the Beginnings of Modern Production of Towns in Germany]. Hamburg : Christians, 1983, pp. 205-233; see also: Everhard Kleinertz, "Die Bau und Bodenspekulanten in Köln 1837 bis 1847" [Speculating Builders and Property Speculators in Cologne 1837–1847], in: Friedrich-Wilhelm Henning (ed.), *Kölner Unternehmer und die Frühindustrialisierung im Rheinland und in Westfalen (1835–1871): Ausstellung des Rheinisch-Westfälisches Wirtschaftsarchivs zu Köln e.V., 17. Sept. 1984 bis 30. Nov. 1984* [Cologne Entrepreneurs and Early Industrialization in the Rhineland and Westphalia (1835–1871): Exhibition of the Rhenish-Westphalian Economic

Archives in Cologne, September 17 – November 30, 1984], Köln: Rheinisch-Westfälisches Wirtschafsarchiv 1984, pp. 147-170. In Aachen, the affluent among its burghers "fled" the densely built-up walled city since the 1830s and preferred the modern, spacious town quarter that was being created outside the Marschier-Thor (a large gate for marchers leaving the city, presumably marching units of the army) between the new railway station (which was certainly a positive attraction) and the town wall. The railway company, with the then Aachen-based Hansemann as a key shareholder (and vice president) proceeded like a typical "terrain company." It had anticipated a big increase of the level of the land rent and acquired the area foreseen for the entire development before its railroad construction plans and an associated town quarter became widely known. Under the July Monarchy that Hansemann admired so much, a banker turned politician, Jacques Lafitte (adviser and minister under Louis Philippe), had also been involved in property speculation. Somehow, Hansemann appears as Lafitte's provincial copy. It is interesting to see the U.S. railway companies building new lines in Ohio and in the Middle West also engaged in land speculation very early on. And that the Aachen example of the mid-19th century was copied very recently in Stuttgart (also in connection with a new railway station), a strategy that gave rise to massive, but unsuccessful, public protests, and that had the belated result of ending decades of conservative CDU rule in Baden-Wurttemberg and the state capital, Stuttgart. The new mayor is now a man of the Green Party, and the state government was formed by a coalition of the Green Party and, as minor partner, the CDU. The new prime minister is a conservative member of the Green Party, a devout Catholic and former Maoist.

[99] Nitscke, ibid, p.220.
[100] See Alexander Bergengrün, *David Hansemann*, Berlin: J. Guttentag, 1901, p.421.
[101] See *Deutsche Zeitung* [German Newspaper, this is the name of the paper], No. 95 of April 4, 1849, 2nd supplement. Nitschke refers to it; see Nitschke, ibid., p. 392, footnote 5.
[102] See: Nitschke, ibid, p. 75; see also the *Amtsblatt der Regierung zu Aachen* [Official Gazette of the (District) Administration in Aachen], Jg. 1835, for instance p. 143, p. 354, etc.; regarding von Bodelschwingh, see for instance p. 13.
[103] See Bernd Franco Hoffmann, Stillgelegte Bahnstrecken im Rheinland [Disused railway line in the Rhineland]. Erfurt: Sutton 2014, p.17.
[104] Nitscke, ibid, p.220.
[105] Heinrich Alexander von Arnim, b. 1798 in Berlin, d. 1861 in Düsseldorf.
[106] Document No. 26. *Ernennung des Gesandten v. Arnim zum Minister am 21. März 1848* [Appointment of the envoy v. Arnim to the post of minister (sc. in the cabinet of prime minister Count Arnim) on March 21, 1848], reprinted in: Angerstein, p.104.
[107] See the entry by Gollwitzer on von Heinrich Alexander [von] Arnim, known widely as Alexander Arnim, in the German-language biographical dictionary *New German Biography*: Heinz Gollwitzer, "Arnim-Suckow, Alexander Freiherr von" in: *Neue Deutsche Biographie*, Vol. 1 (1953), p. 368 f. [Also online:] URL: https://www.deutsche-biographie.de/pnd118810596.html#ndbcontent
[108] The memorandum entitled "Denkschrift über die französische Februar-Revolution und ihre Folgen für Deutschland" was presented to the king on March 17, 1848. See Wippermann's entry on Count Arnim in the biographic encyclopedia General German Biography: C. Wippermann, "Arnim-Suckow, Alexander Freiherr von," in: *Allgemeine Deutsche Biographie*, Vol. 1. Leipzig: Duncker & Humblot, 1875, pp. 571–574.

109 Wippermann, ibid.
110 Gollwitzer, ibid. – The assumption that baron Arnim was behind the king's idea to ride through Berlin is plausible in so far as Heinrich von Arnim seems to have thought of the possibility that "embracing the concept of German unity" might greatly enhance again the damaged popularity of the king. An unnamed "liberal" wrote in hindsight in *Unsere Zeit*: "The appointment of Heinrich von Arnim as minister of foreign affairs, dated March 21, proved to be of the gravest consequence, as it tore the king so rapidly in such a decisive way onto the path of a Teutonic nationalist policy." (Am folgenschwersten […] erwies sich die vom 21. März datirte Ernennung Heinrich von Arnim's für das Auswärtige, denn sie riß den König in kurzer Zeit so entschieden fort auf der Bahn einer deutschthümlichen Politik […]). See N.N., "Friedrich Wilhelm IV., König von Preußen," in: *Unsere Zeit. Jahrbuch zum Conversations-Lexikon.* Vol. 6. Leipzig: F.A. Brockhaus, 1862, pp. 1-26, here: p. 18. – The entry on Baron von Arnim confirms that the former envoy to France prodded the king to embrace (or to appear as if he embraced) the cause of Germany unity: "On his advice, therefore, the King promised a large delegation from Cologne on March 18 to assume a leading role during that Congress and to work for the appointment of delegates of the German people." In German: "Auf seinen Rath versprach daher der König am 18. März einer großen Deputation aus Köln, die Führung jenes Congresses übernehmen und eine Berufung von Abgeordneten des deutschen Volkes bewirken zu wollen." (C. Wippermann, "Arnim, Heinrich Alexander [Freiherr v.A.]," in: Allgemeine Deutsche Biographie, Erste Lieferung, Leipzig: Duncker & Humblot, 1875, pp.571-574, here: p.572)-
111 Gollwitzer, ibid.
112 Thus it becomes clear that the king did not act out of conviction but because he accepted a "rational" argument when he rode through Berlin on March 21 and when he pronounce himself in favor of German unity.
113 This relatively enlightened, somehow "liberal" anti-absolutist tendency among a part of the Prussian aristocracy that can be observed during the 1840s was not simply a matter of *being educated*, rather than remaining condemned to share "the idiocy of the village" (Marx) with other rural folks. It had a lot to do with the fact that agrarian capitalism was slowly becoming dominant in much of the Prussian countryside during the first half of the 19th century. Engels discovered its effects when he analyzed the politics of the first United Diet that met in session in 1847: "The sitting of the united Committees [of the United Diet] proved that the spirit of opposition was no longer confined to the bourgeoisie. A part of the peasantry had joined them, and many nobles, being themselves large farmers on their own properties, and dealers in corn, wool, spirits, and flax, requiring the same guarantees against absolutism, bureaucracy, and feudal restoration, had equally pronounced against the Government, and for a Representative Constitution." Frederick Engels, *Revolution and Counter-revolution in Germany*, ibid. (The book is made up of a series of articles written in 1851.) Also online: https://www.marxists.org/archive/marx/works/1852/germany/index.htm. Accessed: June 5, 2018, 8:15 PM.
114 In German, the king's revealing words were: "Der Liberalismus ist eine Krankheit, gerade wie die Rückenmarksdarre." See Wilhelm Blos, *Die Deutsche Revolution: Geschichte der Deutschen Bewegung von 1848 und 1849.* Stuttgart: Dietz, 1891, reprint Stuttgart: Dietz, 1898, and Berlin: Dietz, 1878, p. 304, footnote. The book by Blos was recently reprinted as *Die Deutsche Revolution von 1848 und 1849.* Paderborn: Salzwasser Verlag, 2015.

115 Literally, "case shot prince." Perhaps this can be rendered as "Shrapnel prince."
116 If it is necessary to speak here of the politically "mixed" character of Count Arnim's cabinet, this is because it included, side by side with the progressive liberal Bornemann, such arch-conservatives as the Minister of War, von Rohr. Friedrich von Rohr, one of the generals who had opposed the withdrawal of the troops from Berlin on March 19, 1848, had been Minister of War since October 7, 1847; he resigned from office on April 2, apparently unwilling to serve under Camphausen. Wilhelm Bornemann, a commoner, served as Minister of Justice under Count Arnim and Camphausen; he handed in his resignation in June 1848, when Camphausen stepped down.
117 See Angerstein, ibid., pp. 104-105.
118 For good reason, Breslau is known since 1945 as Wrocław. Poland, like the former Soviet Union, suffered badly due to Nazi Germany's aggression and the changes of borders and population exchanges after World War II, catastrophic as they were for many, were but the after-effects of the chaos created by the Fascist war. It was understandable that Poland claimed Silesia, not only because of areas they ceded in 1945 to the Ukrainian SSR and the Bielorussian SSR. Like all of Silesia, of which it is the capital, Breslau has been a part of Poland until 1335 when it became a part of the lands governed by the kings of Bohemia, residing in Prague. Since 1526, it was ruled by the Habsburg dynasty that was governing it from its Austrian capital, Vienna. Silesia, and with it, Breslau became part of Prussia after the First Silesian War in 1742 and more securely after the Seven Year's War (1756–1763). Like the Ruhr District, Upper Silesia (with the famous mines and iron works in new industrial centers like Königshütte) was a key area of Prussian early-industrial development in the 1830s and 1840s, with emphasis on heavy industry. Breslau was a commercial city like Königsberg and Cologne, but like Cologne with a growing sector of small industry.
119 Breslau's population was 62,504 according to the census of 1811 and 92,305 in 1840. By 1852, the total had reached 116, 235 inhabitants. (See *World History at KMLA*, URL: http://www.zum.de/whkmla/region/germany/sildemography.html. Accessed Nov 18,2018, 11:23 PM)
120 See the text of the King's proclamation of March 22, 1848 concerning the representation of the people, reprinted in: Angerstein, ibid, p. 105. The key passage that is repeating the king's reply to the Breslau delegation is: "After I have promised a 'constitutional' constitution [i.e., *no republican constitution*; the term *die Konstitutionellen* (pl.), current at the time in Germany, referred to 'constitutional monarchists,' in other words, those who wanted monarchy mellowed by 'constitutional rule,' checked by a parliament, often a parliament elected unequally, thus by a *Zensus-Wahlrecht* (census suffrage) for instance, an electoral law that tied the right to vote to a certain income, or property, or a certain sum of direct taxes paid! – (AW)] on the broadest foundations, it is My will to issue a popular electoral law, which is capable of producing a representative assembly based on original elections and representing all the interests of the people, without distinction of religious creeds, and to submit this law to the United Diet for review, whose speedy convocation I must take to be the general desire of the country, in view of all the petitions I have received. I would decisively violate the previously expressed wishes of the country if [...] I wished to issue the new electoral law without obtaining advice from the estates."
121 Maria-Antonietta Macciocchi alerts us to this. She quotes Gramsci as follows: "La tradition et la civilisation nées de la richesse [i.e. surplus production; AW] et de la

complexité de l'histoire [i.e. the evolution of classes and class societies; AW] ont déposé une multitude de couches sédimentaires résistantes, à travers une série de phénomènes de saturation et de fossilisation du personnel étatique [in Prussia, a bureaucracy that is "conservative" and even reactionary in certain respects; aw] et des intellectuels, du clergé [certainly true in Prussia in 1848–1849; AW] et des propriétaires fonciers [*Junkers*!], d'un commerce de rapine et de l'armée [the Prussian army, especially its commanding officers, as a bulwark of the reaction; AW]... On peut même dire que, plus l'histoire d'un pays est ancienne [e.g. Prussia, not the United States, in 1848; AW] , plus nombreuses et pesantes sont ces couches stratifiées de paresseux et de parasites qui vivent du « patrimoine » des « ancêtres » , de ces retraités de l'histoire économique" (Maria-Antonietta Macciocchi, *Pour Gramsci*, Paris: Éditions du Seuil 1974, p.182). The quoted text by Gramsci is from: Antonio Gramsci, *Note sul Macchiavelli*, Torino 1949, p.313. Gramsci may have been thinking of the landed aristocracy of the *Mezzogiorno* and of Southern Italy's respected conservative intellectuals, clergy, etc. His analysis could be applied to late Qing China as well, with its Mandarins, its gentry, its evolving comprador bourgeoisie; as we know, a lot of this persisted during the early decades of the Republic. The terminology is often largely due to the fact that Gramsci was writing while in custody of the Fascist Mussolini regime. It is a language that seeks to replace Marxist terminology by categories that sounded scholarly, yet not suspicious to those who allowed him to write what they must have regarded as "serious" historical and philosophical studies, due to a certain very Italian respect for erudition—something that German Nazis lacked completely, by and large.)

[122] The terms *Heuerlinge* (hirelings) and *Heuermänner* (hiremen, men for hire) began probably to be used since the 1820s or 1830s and they were prominent especially throughout the mid-19th century for those among the village poor who were forced to engage in paid agricultural work, often as seasonal migrant workers. Paid farm labor increased when obligations to do unpaid agricultural work for the lord of the manor (so-called *Hand- und Spanndienste*) were gradually abolished in Germany in the course of reforms that were indecisive and that were also factually implemented in imperfect ways, in order not to rock the boat, that is to say, in order to respect the economic interests and social as well as political position of the big aristocratic landlords in the countryside.

[123] Of course, the wealthy middle layers of the bourgeoisie (*das Bürgertum*) and even the stratum most threatened by proletarianization, the self-employed artisans, frequently thought so, too, fearing more from the "lower classes" than from those economically powerful capitalists whose competition threatened to ruin them—and often did. But these intermediate layers have often proved to be wavering, in modern history. In Germany, too. They did not only produce a particularly reactionary "phenotype" (remarkable because it formed the key mass base of German Nazism) but also remarkably progressive petty-bourgeois radicals that linked up with progressive, class-conscious workers.

[124] Hansemann, for instance, considered "[...] monarchy as a [...] conservative protection against the lower more dangerous democratic elements." Moved by apparently similarly considerations, the "liberal" banker and railroad entrepreneur Ludolf Camphausen, in his function as Prussian prime minister, thought it even fit or opportune to call "back the prince-regent," the widely loathed William, Prince of Prussia (a reactionary advocate of immediate and harsh repression of all democratic activities during the days of prerevolutionary agitation in Berlin, and

a proponent of such brutal military measures against the population of Berlin as shelling the capital "from outside the walls" when Prittwitz' strategy of engaging in street and house-to-house combat on March 18 and 19 failed), "from exile in England in May 1848 and never abandoned his hope of unifying Germany under the Prussian monarchy." (James M. Brophy, *Capitalism, Politics, and Railroads in Prussia, 1830–1870.* Ohio State University Press, 1998, p.12) Another Rhenish banker, Carl von der Heydt (brother of the "liberal" Elberfeld banker and railway investor August von der Heydt who accepted the job of minister of trade, industry, and public works in the reactionary Brandenburg-Manteuffel cabinet on December 4, 1848) had even declared publicly in August 1848 (!) without being asked that he was "advocating absolute monarchy." (James M. Brophy, ibidem, p. 203; Brophy refers to Jonathan Sperber, *Rhineland Radicals*, Princeton, NJ: Princeton Univ. Press 1991, p. 329.) Perhaps this sheds some light on a tendency not untypical of the Rhenish *grande bourgeoisie*.

125 It is good to remember here that the United Diet (known in April 1848 as the *second* one, for the *first* was convened, met in session for some time, and was dissolved in 1847) was still composed as usual of the delegates of Prussia's estates or *Stände* (=ranks); in other words, it was a *ständisch* parliament that consisted of an Upper House, i.e. the Herrenkurie (curia of "Lords," the high aristocracy) with its subsection, the Ritterschaft (the "knights," i.e. lower aristocracy; gentry) and a Lower House, the Drei-Stände-Kurie (curia of the three lower estates) that represented the three non-aristocratic estates (with delegates sent from *the towns* [thus, enfranchised "burghers"], from *the rural counties* [notables from the countryside, mainly wealthy landowners], and in some cases also from among *the clergy*). In the case of the Province of Prussia (i.e. East Prussia with Königberg [today Kaliningrad] and West Prussia with Gdansk or Danzig) the number of delegates in the Upper House was 50 (5 members of the Herrenkurie, 45 members of the Ritterschaft; their number in the Lower House (Drei-Stände-Kurie) was 51 (21 for towns that sent delegates, 22 for rural counties, none for the clergy; among the delegates of rural counties, there were quite a few big landowners, so-called *Gutbesitzer*). The 50:50 or rather 50:51 proportion was typical for the entire United Diet that consisted of the total of the Provincial Diets (provincial rank-based participatory bodies in each of the provinces of the kingdom) meeting in joined session. It was totally unrepresentative of the population of the kingdom, as it factually excluded the majority (the subaltern classes) and overrepresented a relatively tiny class: the aristocracy. It must be kept in mind, however, that the aristocracy as a decisive pillar of the Prussian absolutist monarchy, though economically not without weight and politically influential, had seen itself disempowered by Prussian absolutism, not completely unlike the French aristocracy before 1789 that had also lost its old relative territorial autonomy under absolutism since at least the mid-17th century. Consciousness of this loss had engendered a thirst for a relatively "mild," thus "conservative-liberal" form of constitutional monarchy among the more enlightened members of this class. Increasing business relations with the bourgeoisie and the growing importance of agrarian capitalism in the countryside bolstered this trend and turned the more "liberal" aristocrats into potential political allies of Prussia's *grande bourgeoisie* or *haute bourgeoisie* ("big bourgeoisie").

126 Alexander Bergengrün, *David Hansemann*. Berlin: J. Guttentag, 1901, p. 426.

127 The first, still unofficial session of the cabinet that was formed by Camphausen after he had been appointed by the king took place in the evening of March 28,

when the new government was not yet in office. (See Alexander Bergengrün, ibid. p.429) As Count Arnim still had his hand in the political undertakings of the government on April 2 and 4 when he appeared in the United Diet, the days from March 26 to April 4 can be regarded as days of a soft transition characterized by largely shared immediate political priorities of the outgoing and the new government. Count Arnim, dismissed officially on March 29, together with the ill-reputed Minister of War, Mr. von Rohr, who was replaced the next day by another man the king trusted, by Lieutenant General von Canitz (Ludwig von Rönne, *Das Staats-Recht der Preußischen Monarchie. Vol. 1: Das Verfassungs-Recht* [The National Law of the Prussian Monarchy. Vol. 1: Constitutional Law]. Leipzig: F. A. Brockhaus, 1856, p.31, footnote 3), simply had the wrong, "reactionary" reputation that made him unacceptable to many members of the liberal bourgeoisie in Prussia. He was sacrificed by the king for that reason. A bourgeois prime minister became necessary, in order to "calm things"—at least, as far as the bourgeoisie as well as the better-off and the backward, provincial, not yet radicalized parts of the petty-bourgeoisie were concerned.

[128] The text of the poster was:

Mitbürger Berlins!

Das Vertrauen, das uns ein Theil der Mitkämpfer für Recht und Wahrheit in den heißen Tagen geschenkt und die Liebe für das Gesammtwohl gaben uns Muth und Kraft, vor unseren König zu treten. Um den Thron mit dem Volke fest zu verbinden, stellten wir zur Begründung einer ruhigen Zukunft folgende Bitten:

1. daß Militair in unsere Stadt zurückkehre,

2. daß bei dem Militair eine Amnestie für alle Subordinations-Vergehen eintrete, wie beim Civil für alle politischen Vergehen.

Beide Punkte wurden uns sofort von Sr. Majestät gewährt und wir zur Ausführung des ersten Punktes durch eigenhändige Kabinets—Ordre ermächtigt.

Brüder! Wir haben unseren König gesprochen, wir haben uns überzeugt, wie herzlich und innig er uns liebt und wie mächtig sein Vertrauen in den Tagen der Gefahr gewachsen ist. Wir bitten Euch im Namen des Königs, im Namen des Vaterlandes, im Namen der ganzen deutschen Nation: lasset uns seine Freunde sein, lasset uns einig bleiben in dieser ernsten Zeit, wie wir einig waren in den Stunden des Kampfes. Ein jeder stehe an seiner Stelle unerschütterlich fest, jeder wirke nach Einscht und Kräften zur Vermittlung und Versöhnung zwischen Volk und Fürst, zwischen Bürger und Militair, zwischen Parthei und Parthei.

Dann erst ist unser König mit vollem Vertrauen umgeben, von Bürger und Soldat geliebt und wird als ein wahrhaft konstitutionelles Oberhaupt unsere Rechte vertreten, und sie für uns heilbringend bewahren können. || [p.17] Nur dann kann jede gerechte Bitte erfüllt, jeder Mißbrauch abgewendet, Haß und Feindschaft vernichtet und Liebe und Einigkeit in die Gemüther zurückgeführt werden; – Brüder! zum Siege der Freiheit sind traurige Tage nothwendig gewesen, viel liebe und theure Opfer sind gefallen, Gott wird solche Tage nicht wiederkehren lassen, wenn sie nicht durch Mangel an Liebe hervorgerufen werden. Gehen wir daher mit gutem Beispiel voran, reichen wir denen, die gegen uns gekämpft, die versöhnende Bruderhand und vergeben wir von ganzem Herzen das Geschehene. Es wäre eine Schmach für Berlin, für Preußen, ja für das ganze deutsche Vaterland, wenn wir wegen Ueberschreitung Einzelner das Ganze ausstoßen und die, welche ihre Pflicht gethan, als die Schuldigen ansehen wollten. Die gräuelvolle Ueberschreitung menschlicher Schranken wird in den Einzelnen ihren inneren Richter finden, sie werden die Stellung aufgeben, die sie so schrecklich missbrauchten.

Bedenken wir, daß viele von uns einst auch an ihrer Seite standen, bedenken wir hauptsächlich, daß für die militärische Erziehung eine neue Gestaltung, eine bürgerliche Grundlage errungen ist. Auch sie, die Soldaten einer verflossenen Zeit, sind durch unseren Kampf belehrt worden, daß mit starrer Gewalt—mit Kugeln und Schwertern—eine moralische Ueberzeugung nicht zu besiegen ist, und so wird mit Gottes Beistand kein deutscher Fürst ferner die ihm von Gott anvertraute Macht gegen sein Volk missbrauchen. Gleich wie nun die lieben Gefallenen in Eintracht und Frieden ruhen, so lasst uns, die Ueberlebenden, brüderlich ||
[p.18] und einig sein und das schwer Errungene bewahren. Friede und Einigkeit schützt, belebt und nährt; Brüder, lasset die, die unseren Muth und unsere Ausdauer kennen gelernt haben, auch unsere Liebe kennen lernen, sie werden, sie müssen uns wieder lieben. Versöhnung sei der Grundstein zu dem neuen Bau des Vaterlandes.
Also vorwärts Ihr Brüder,
Mit Gott für Vaterland und König!
Im Auftrage des Komitee der ersten Volks-Versammlung.
Urban praktischer Thier-Arzt
Eckert, Bürger u. Kleidermacher
Berends, Kattundrucker u. Cigarrenmacher
Source: Anonymous [i.e. Mr. Petersen?], Personen und Zustände Berlins seit dem 18. Maerz 1848: ein Beitrag zur kuenftigen Geschichte Preussens. Leipzig (Keil) 1849, pp.15-18.

129 Adolph Wolff's journal *Volks-Zeitschrift* provided this characterization of Berlin's papers: "The Prussian State Gazette, the *Vossische*, the *Spenersche* and the *Neue Berliner Zeitung* are the bearers of the outmoded absolutism; the *Reform* and the *National-Zeitung* are the organs of modern liberalism, the *Zeitungs-Halle* and the *Berliner Abendzeitung*, the two evening papers, announce the morning of a modernizing ultra-liberalism; the newspaper *Bürgerwehr-Zeitung*, a midday paper, is said to have started, as we hear, its eternal nap, i.e. it has blissfully given up its life." – In German: "Der Preußische Staats-Anzeiger, die Vossische, die Spenersche und die Neue Berliner Zeitung sind die Träger des unmodern gewordenen Absolutismus; die Reform und die National-Zeitung sind die Organe des modernen Liberalismus, die Zeitungs-Halle und die Berliner-Abendzeitung, die beiden Abendblätter, verkünden den Morgen eines modernisirenden Ultraliberalismus; die Bürgerwehr-Zeitung, ein Mittagsblatt, soll, wie wir hören, den ewigen Mittagsschlaf begonnen haben, d.h. sie ist selig entschlafen." (*Volks-Zeitschrift für Unterhaltung, Politik und gesellschaftliches Leben* [People's Magazine for Entertainment, Politics and Social Life], Vol. 2, No. 27, July 1848, p.1.

130 The view that an alliance was formed was first expressed by Frederick Engels. He writes that "the alliance between the bourgeoisie and the supporters of the overturned system was concluded upon the very barricades of Berlin. The necessary concessions, but no more than was unavoidable, were to be made, a ministry of the opposition leaders of the United Diet was to be formed, and in return for its services in saving the Crown, it was to have the support of all the props of the old Government, the feudal aristocracy, the bureaucracy, the army. These were the conditions upon which Messrs. Camphausen and Hansemann undertook the formation of a cabinet." (Frederick Engels, Revolution and Counter-revolution, ibid. Also online: https://www.marxists.org/archive/marx/works/1852/germany/index.htm. Accessed: June 5, 2018, 8:15 PM.

131 Leopold von Gerlach (1790-1861), a Catholic general and the king's adjutant, was for long the éminence grise among the reactionary advisers of Frederick William IV. He was a key figure of the so-called "camarilla." With respect to the "camarilla" at the Prussian court in 1848, see for instance: David E. Barclay, "The Court Camarilla and the Politics of Monarchical Restoration in Prussia, 1848–1858," in: *Between Reform, Reaction, and Resistance: Studies in the History of German Conservatism from 1789 to 1945*, ed. by Larry Eugene Jones and James Retallack, Oxford: Berg, 1993, pp. 123-156.

132 Joseph von Radowitz (1797–1853), a reactionary general and Prussian diplomat in 1848–1849, was a Conservative protestant whose ideology made him defend Prussian absolutism. He was another important figure among those who were considered as the "camarilla"—the group of informal, yet influential conservative advisers to the king who sought to embody "the old [anti-democratic and authoritarian] Prussian virtues"—values that were typical of the aristocratic officer corps.

133 Bisky was an active figure in Berlin as a member of the *Bund der Kommunisten* (Federation of Communists), the organization named previously *Bund der Gerechten* (Federation of the Just). Its members were by and large socialist and communist workers, intelligent people like the journeyman Wilhelm Weitling (1808–1871) whose pamphlets did much to popularize the ideas of Etienne Cabet (1788–1856) and others, but also his own brand of Christian communism, among working people in Germany during the late 1830s and the 1840s. The Federation of the Just was renamed shortly after Marx joined it.

134 The text of the petition was as follows:
Allerdurchlauchtigster, Allergroßmächtigster, Allergnädigster König und Herr!
Die am Sonntag den 26ten März stattgefundene Volks-Versammlung hat die unterzeichnete Deputation beauftragt, Ew. Majestät die von derselben ausgesprochenen Wünsche unterthänigst vorzutragen. Es bittet die Volksversammlung Ew. Majestät allergnädigst anzuordnen:
1. die Errichtung eines Arbeiter-Ministeriums, welches aus Arbeitern und Arbeitsgebern zusammengesetzt und von diesen selbst gewählt wird;
2. die Verminderung des stehenden Heeres, so dass dieses nur die Vorschule für die Volkswehr bleibt;
3. die allgemeine Erziehung des Volkes auf Kosten des Staates;
4. Versorgung der Invaliden der Arbeit;
5. Einführung einer wohlfeilen Regierung;
6. ein Wahlgesetz, nach welchem jeder großjährige Mann Wähler und wählbar ist;
7. Zurücknahme der Einberufung des vereinigten Landtags und sofortige Einberufung einer aus Urwahlen hervorgegangenen Versammlung.
Indem wir diese Wünsche des Volkes Ew. Majestät vorlegen, verharren wir Ew. Majestät allerunterthänigste
J. Berends. Bisky. Reuchardt. Meyer. Ries. Brill.
Berlin den 27ten März 1848

135 Among the things which the *Verfassung für die Stadtgemeinde* (municipal constitution) of 1747 regulated, we find among many other items (such as the control of farmers' markets, of inns, of "measurements and weight," or attention paid to pavement and bridges, to the safety, lighting, and cleanliness of streets, to precautions against fire, to wells), the "Gesindeordnung" or "Regulations concerning dependent employees," describing their duties and the rights

and obligations of employers. See Richard Borrmann (comp.), *Die Bau- und Kunstdenkmäler von Berlin*, ibid., p.82.
136 Anonymous [i.e. Mr. Petersen?], Personen und Zustände Berlins ..., ibidem, p.21.
137 Ludolf Camphausen (b. 1803 in Geilenkirchen near Aachen, d. 1890 in Cologne) was a member of the Rhenanian financial bourgeoisie, a banker based in Cologne. His father was a tobacco and oil merchant. Camphausen was married to the daughter of an industrialist, the owner of a spinning mill in Rheydt. The bank owned by him and his brother—the *Merchant and Banking House ("Handels- und Bankhaus") August and Ludolf Camphausen*—was the fourth largest bank in Cologne, the city that must be considered as the most important commercial and industrial center of the Prussian Rhine Province at the time. And the Rhine Province, to boot, was the most advanced province of Prussia in many respects, certainly with regard to industry. Politically, Camphausen was a so-called "moderate" (in actual fact, conservative) bourgeois Liberal.
138 Ludwig Gustav von Thile had been chief minister of Prussia from 1841 until March 19, 1848. Count Adolf Heinrich von Arnim-Boitzenburg had served under von Thile as Interior Minister from 1842 until 1845. In these years, his policy could be characterized as "bureaucratic-absolutist" according to Heinz Gollwitzer. (Gollwitzer, ibid, p.368) Nevertheless, Count Arnim gained a reputation as a "liberal" because he advocated a constitution when this issue was on the table during the deliberations that took place from April to June 1847 in the temporarily convocated United Diet. The issue was a simmering one as a constitution had long been promised by Frederick William III, the predecessor of the present king. On the other hand, Count Arnim's well-known utterance that Heinrich Heine's work "The Silesian Weavers" (Die schlesischen Weber) was an "address to the poor among the people" that was characterized by its "seditious tone" and that included "criminal utterances" (eine in aufrührerischem Ton gehaltene und mit verbrecherischen Äußerungen angefüllte Ansprache an die Armen im Volke) led to the interdiction of this work by the supreme Prussian court (the Kammergericht) and to a jail term pronounced for a reciter of the text. This unmasked Adolf Heinrich von Arnim in the eyes of many. Count Arnim resigned as Interior Minister in 1845 because he disagreed with the naively romantic reactionary position of the king regarding his absolutist "divine right" as monarch. When he was named chief minister on March 19, the king may have hoped to profit from Count Arnim's "liberal" reputation. During his term as chief-minister, the king promised a constitution and a "popular" electoral law, a declaration that was countersigned by von Arnim. On March 29, von Arnim had to step down because the king had reached an agreement with Rhenish capitalists and named the entrepreneur Gottfried Ludolf Camphausen (a commoner) Prime Minister of Prussia. Adolf Heinrich von Arnim was later a deputy elected at the end of December, 1848 to the second chamber of the Prussian Diet (the lower house, Zweite Kammer) and still later, until 1868, elected to the Lord's Chamber (Herrenhaus) of this new Prussian "parliament" that replaced Prussia's Constituent Assembly (Verfassungsgebende Versammlung), also known as Prussian National Assembly, after this assembly was factually barred from meeting on November 5, 1848 and permanently dissolved by royal decree of December 5 of the same year. In the new Prussian parliament, created on the basis of a royally imposed, anti-liberal constitution, Adolf Heinrich von Arnim was a conservative representative of the interests of big rural landowners, according to Gollwitzer. His basically conservative stance is also noted by G. Ritter. (See

Gerhard Ritter, *Die preußischen Konservativen und Bismarcks deutsche Politik 1858 bis 1876.* Heidelberg: Winter, 1913, XIV, 390 pp.)

139 The author of the article went on to say that "it was unfortunate, however, that he was thus deprived of the effects"—that is to say, the psychological and ideological impact and direct influence that could have occurred had he been in the immediate presence of the new government. Instead, "he returned to the very opposite, old-established influences" of people like von Radowitz, von Gerlach, etc. (N.N., "Friedrich Wilhelm IV., König von Preußen," in: *Unsere Zeit. Jahrbuch zum Conversations-Lexikon.* Sechster Band [Our Time; Yearbook attached to the Conversation Lexicon, Vol. 6]. Leipzig: F.A. Brockhaus, 1862, pp. 1-26, here: p.18)

140 We can safely assume that it is this stratum of petty-bourgeois moderates who had not been amused when "a crowd" appeared on the Palace Square on March 19, immediately after the victory of the revolution, demanding decisive action against the King's brother, the Prince of Prussia, and calling for a republic. Brass downplayed it, giving no further details regarding the social composition, the size, and the known spokespersons of this "crowd," when he refers to the "excited crowd which moved once more to the palace door, *demanding* to see the King. The resignation of the Prince of Prussia was *demanded*. Some people shouted even: A Republic! But they received no attention." But August Brass' conclusive remark, "Still, this was a moment of dangerous excitement," reveals his political distance and his fearful apprehension vis-à-vis the subaltern masses that did not devotedly petition but dared to demand. Certainly such "crowds" of workers and other poor people of Berlin (the "mob," the "majority") received "no attention" except one, and this particular attention was a negative and apprehensive attention on the part of even the very modestly propertied classes, let alone the rich bourgeoisie and the aristocracy (which included the King and his family). In such situations, the limitations of many truly democratic petty-bourgeois intellectuals became apparent. But also the lack of self-organization of the proletarianized masses who had not sufficiently found a way to speak and to make themselves heard. Curses and brief oral "explosions" of ire, and formulations of demands that consist of just a few words—sometimes perhaps merely two words, like "A Republic!"—are hardly enough.

141 On June 13–14, 1848, Engels wrote that due to the March Revolution in Berlin, "direct control passed into the hands of the big bourgeoisie"; what happened on March 29, was the formation of "the Camphausen-Hansemann Ministry, that is a Government representing the big bourgeoisie." (Frederick Engels, "The Berlin Debate on the Revolution," Neue Rheinische Zeitung, No. 14, June 14, 1848) And one or two days later he wrote that this "brought about the exclusive rule of the big bourgeoisie." (Neue Rheinische Zeitung, No. 15, June 15, 1848) Also online: http://www.marxists.org/archive/marx/works/1848/06/14a.htm. Accessed Feb.12, 2013, 8:35 PM. – This can be contested. It is clear that a government of the haute bourgeoisie was in office when Camphausen was appointed Prime Minister by the king, and Engels is right when he describes this as an alliance that both parties wanted, the king in a temporary position of utter weakness, and the big bourgeoisie because it was haunted by fears, dreading radical mass action, and desiring continuity as much as Count Arnim and other royalists who were briefly advising the king during the decisive days of March. But the very fact that Camphausen was not elected by the people but appointed by the king (and could be dismissed by him) says a lot. If we read the correspondence between Frederick William IV and Prime Minister Camphausen, we find clear directives given by

the king, expressed in unmistakable terms that order rather than beg, such as "ich verlange" (I demand) or, more politely, "ich bitte Sie dringend" (I urgently request you). The urgency expressed left the prime minister with no choice but to comply, even though he had some scope for maneuvering and attempting to postpone or reinterpret things. When the King expressed the wish that the Camphausen government support the return of his brother William (the Prince of Prussia), Camphausen complied basically but advised the King that the Prince of Prussia should slow things a bit. (See Erich Brandenburg (ed.), *König Friedrich Wilhelms IV. Briefwechsel mit Ludolf Camphausen*. Berlin: Gebr. Paetel, 1906.) Camphausen knew that the "people" resented William; most Berliners saw in him an utter reactionary. And Camphausen wanted to avoid trouble in the streets because he knew that the reactionaries in Prussia would blame him, saying that he was unable to maintain law and order with stern determination. If the king's position was still vulnerable, Camphausen's was, too, and the fact that he depended on the king, the bureaucracy and the army, rather than controlling it, as a government of the people should have done, reveals a situation that was all but comfortable. He was doubtlessly *in office*, but he and the class faction he represented were not *in power*.

142   David Hansemann (b. 1790, d. 1864) was a Rhenanian banker. Actively engaged in Aachen as an entrepreneur since 1817, he subsequently became active in lucrative property speculation in Aachen. He was also an important shareholder of the *Rheinische Eisenbahn Gesellschaft* (Rhenanian Railway Company) and pushed for the fast construction of the Cologne-Minden rail connection. He served as Minister of Finance (Secretary of commerce) in the cabinet led by Camphausen, and also under Camphausen's successor, Prime Minister Rudolf von Auerswald, a man of the lower aristocracy and a "moderate" (in fact, conservative) liberal. Hansemann resigned on September 8, 1848 simultaneously with von Auerswald's resignation.

143   David Hansemann was not only actively involved in railway companies, he was also a key actor in the speculative production of the new "Eisenbahn-Quartier" in Aachen—a town expansion, comprising five streets, a large, park-like square, that was laid out between the old urban center and the new railroad station. See: P. Willemsen, *Die Rhein-Provinz unter Preußen*, Elberfeld: Büschler, 1842, p. 145. (See also: http://reader.digitale-sammlungen.de/resolve/display/bsb10014452.html)

144   Jacques Lafitte (b. 1767, d. 1844) was president of Louis Philippe's Council of Ministers and simultaneously Minister of Finance in 1830–1831. A conservative "liberal" banker, he preceded the even more conservative banker Casimir-Pierre Perier in that position.

145   In fact, the leading figures in the early years of the American Republic—Washington, Jefferson, Hamilton, etc.—were (or in some cases, became) affluent members of the "propertied classes." This is why Thomas Paine was stigmatized and why the American farmers who asserted their traditional rights (e.g., to operate whiskey distilleries, and this without facing new taxation decided in the Massachusetts assembly by factual representatives of rich Boston merchants) faced repression, and likewise the farmers in New York or Pennsylvania threatened by foreclosure because they could not pay imposed taxes, and of course not only all those farmers but also all the employed artisans who clamored for the right to form associations and go on strike.

146   Entrepreneurs like the Crefeld-based merchant-manufacturer *von der Leyen* (an ancestor of the husband of a recent German minister of war) ran decentralized manufactories, relying on cottage industrial workers, and they centralized only the high-value-

added work processes in their mansion and adjacent workshops. By the 1750s, the von der Leyens "gave work" already to ca. 4,000 silk weavers. Apart from Marx, Otto Rühle also mentions the revolt of the silk weavers in Crefeld. See: Otto Rühle, Karl Marx: His Life and Works, New York: Viking Press, 1929. Also online: URL https://www.marxists.org/archive/ruhle/1928/marx/ - accessed Dec. 4, 2018, 8:00 PM.

147 We owe a good characterization of the political position of this liberal member of the Rhenish *grande bourgeoisie* and of his political companion, the wealthy Rhenish entrepreneur David Hansemann, to Thomas Nipperdey. Nipperdey writes about these "moderate liberals": "Liberty was supported, but with reservations; [...] there was a fear of the masses—'the uneducated and unpropertied rabble,' as Dahlmann called them." He adds that these liberals, especially in Southern Germany and in the Prussian Rhine Province, constituted a "new element representing bourgeois liberalism" [or liberalism of the grande bourgeoisie] typified by "entrepreneurs in the Rhineland, such as Beckerath, Camphausen, Hansemann and Mevissen [...] They had less time for theory [than the petty-bourgeois, far less moderate and far more democratic liberal intellectuals like Jung ...], but at the same time [they] were keenly power-conscious and self-confident; they were [...] fiercely opposed to bureaucratic strangulation of the economy and [...] aware of the class character of the emergent new society, and demanded that leadership ('the gravitational force of state,' to use Hansemann's words of 1830) should be ceded to their stratum. Suffrage was to be restricted, but parliament itself [dominated by their peers and partisans of their class] should be strong. A not insignificant [liberal-conservative] aristocratic element was also present among their ranks [...] [, thus] [s]ections of the East and West Prussian nobility ([e.g.] Rudolf von Auerswald) [...]. In this way the liberals were more than just a 'bourgeois' [tendency, group, or] party." (Thomas Nipperdey, *Germany from Napoleon to Bismarck: 1800-1866*. Transl. by Daniel Nolan. Princeton, NJ: Princeton Univ. Press, 2014, p.342.) G. Stedman Jones who notes how "Karl [Marx] argued [...] that from the very beginning we blamed Camphausen for not having [...] immediately smashed up and removed the remains of the old institutions," arrives at a conclusion not very different from Nipperdey's when he writes, "It was [...] true that because Camphausen's liberal ministry was fearful of the popular forces that had established it at the end of March, it did not press for major constitutional reforms at the moment when monarchical forces were at their weakest." Stedman Jones then adds, "But it was naïve of the *Neue Rheinische Zeitung* to imagine that a liberal ministry would not [...] [take] account of the danger of radicalism and the anger on the streets. For liberals were haunted by the memory of the French Revolution [...] For them, the threat represented by popular forces on the street was even more to be feared than [...] the Crown. If unchecked, it could lead to [...] violence and the rule of the [...] masses. That this belief was shared by the [...] [well-off parts of] the Berlin middle classes was apparent in a memorial procession in honor of the 'March fallen'. The event 'attracted well over 100,000 people, but these were virtually all labourers, working men and journeymen, or to put it more pointedly, people from the same social stratum as the dead barricade fighters themselves. Middle-class burghers of the kind who [now] predominated in the National Assembly [just elected on the basis of a flawed, undemocratically imposed electoral law that foresaw indirect election of assembly deputies] were conspicuous by their rarity [in the demonstration].(52) The aim of Camphausen, Hansemann and the liberal leadership of the [old] United Landtag [Vereinigter Landtag = United Diet] had

never been to establish a republic, but to achieve a constitutional monarchy. Their aim was to find an acceptable compromise between monarch and parliament supported by public opinion—the opinion of the propertied and educated [thus, a compromise between the monarch and their class]." Gareth Steadman Jones, *Karl Marx: Greatness and Illusion*. Cambridge, MA: Belknap Press of Harvard University Press, 2016; xvii, 750 pp., here: pp. 282f. – Deletions and additions (both in brackets) by me (AW).

148 The Memorandum of 1830 is reprinted in David Hansemann, *Das preußische und deutsche Verfassungswerk: mit Rücksicht auf mein politisches Wirken* [The Drafting of the Prussian and the German constitution: with regard to my political input]. Berlin: F. Schneider & Comp., 1850. The quoted passage is (in German): "[Zu] glauben, daß die Umgestaltung der politischen Verhältnisse Europa's ohne Einfluß auf Preußens Macht, wie diese durch die Verhältnisse im Innern und durch die zum Auslande bedingt ist, vor sich gehen könnem, wäre ge-|| fährliches Einwiegen in Täuschungen [...] Die erste Gefahr ist Aufstand der unteren Volksklassen. Unverkennbar sind diese jetzt vielfach von einem Geiste der Aufregung gegen gesetzliche Ordnung ergriffen [...]." (David Hansemann, "Denkschrift über Preußens Lage und Politik am Ende des Jahres 1830" [Memorandum on Prussia's Situation and Politics at the End of the Year 1830], in: Hansemann, *Das preußische und deutsche Verfassungswerk*, ibid, p.2f.) - Despite his "moderately liberal," in fact, bourgeois disgust for the German "virtue of subservience" (Tugend der Unterwürfigkeit) that he commented on sarcastically in his memorandum (Hansemann, "Denkschrift," ibid., p.2), noting that it was "wavering" or becoming uncertain, Hansemann was concerned about popular unrest in Germany because he was aware of the troubles in Krefeld where an "insurrection" of thousands of silk weavers had to be quelled by Prussian troops in 1828 and of the working class disturbances in Aachen in 1830. In his 1830 memorandum, he points out that the growth of the modern industrial sector has such effects as an increasing *division of labor* (which, he fails to add, devalues many old skills and tends to make them obsolete, thus sharpening the crisis of cottage industries such as weaving). He also notes the increasing number of those "deren Broterwerb nur auf den Verdienst des Tages angewiesen ist" ("whose earning only depends on the income of the day" –Hansemann, "Denkschrift," ibid, p.3), precariously situated workers who were not only depended on wage labor but on the necessity to find new work day by day, i.e. *Tagelöhner* (day laborers) who never knew whether they would find work the next morning.

149 Rudolf Boch maintains that "in 1848 the overthrow of Louis Philippe surprised Hansemann." ("Noch 1848 kam für Hansemann der Sturz Louis Philippes überraschend."(Boch, *Grenzenloses Wachstum?*, ibidem, footnote on p.357)

150 In German: "Der Dichter Lamartine, der Naturforscher Arago, der Sozialist Louis Blanc nebst mehreren anderen Schwärmern und Phantasten ergriffen die Zügel eines großen Staates, in welchem Freiheit, Ordnung und Wohlstand sich in den letzten 18 Jahren entwickelt hatten wie nie zuvor." (Hansemann, *Verfassungswerk*, ibid, p.77.) – Boch alerted me to this comment. It should be added here that even in 1848–1849, if not earlier, Hansemann repeatedly denounced the aspirations of liberal petty-bourgeois democrats and of democratic or republican workers and intellectuals as dangerous and irresponsible "Schwärmerei" [romantic illusions; enthusiastic but entirely unrealistic ideas]!

151 In German: "dass ein grosser Teil der Besitzenden aus den Pariser Ereignissen nicht die Lehre ziehen werde, dass man zeitig nachgeben müsse, sondern sich vielmehr

dem Absolutismus überantworte." See Konrad Repgen: *Märzbewegung und Maiwahlen des Revolutionsjahres 1848 im Rheinland*. Bonn 1955, p. 109.

152 "[…] 'Aristokratie in diesem Sinne genommen, daß die Vermögenderen und Angeseheneren des Staates den meisten Einfluß haben sollen, ist ganz mein System," formulierte Hansemann in Abgrenzung zu "überspannten demokratischen Ideen,' die er vor allem bei den Repräsentanten des Liberalismus in den deutschen Kleinstaaten zu entdecken glaubte." (Rudolf Boch, *Grenzenloses Wachstum?*, ibidem, p.121).

153 In this respect, Hansemann's position was typical of the bourgeoisie. Boch notes "since the early 1840s an increasingly sharp criticism of bureaucracy, focused principally on the incompetence of intransigent bureaucratic ways of wielding power" [In German: "seit Beginn der 1840er Jahre immer schärfer werdende Bürokratiekritik, in deren Mittelpunkt die Inkompetenz einer intransigenten Beamtenherrschaft [stand]." – Rudolf Boch, *Grenzenloses Wachstum?*, ibidem, pp.118f.) – The category "Wirtschaftsbürgertum" that Boch used is strange; literally translated, it would read "economic bourgeoisie" or "the stratum—or class?—of 'economic burghers.'" The terms reveals his determination to avoid the term bourgeoisie that is so typical of many West German historians. But he knows that the category of the "burghers" includes, massively, the backward, anti-industrialist stratum of small independent, petit-bourgeois artisans and small, impoverished as well as somewhat better-off shopkeepers. When using the term "Wirtschaftsbürgertum",Boch refers to wealthy bankers, owners of important merchant houses, new industrial entrepreneurs and wealthy merchant-manufacturers considering conversion of their decentralized manufactories into modern mechanized factories.)

154 Hansemann, "Denkschrift," ibid, p.2.

155 In the wake of the full-scale military occupation of Berlin, the commander in charge of the occupying troops, general Frederick von Wrangel, immediately outlawed *every political activity* on Nov. 12, 1848.

156 The source is: Anonymous [i.e. Mr. Petersen?], *Personen und Zustände Berlins…*, ibidem, pp. 22-23. Translation by me (AW). The text in German is as follows: Nachdem der Wunsch, wieder Truppen in die Hauptstadt zu ziehen, vielseitig ausgesprochen worden ist, haben des Königs Majestät genehmigt, daß das 4te Linien-Infanterie-Regiment, 2 Bataillons des 9ten Infanterie, das 3te Uhlanen-Regiment und die Lehr-Escadron am 30.d.M. und in den nächstfolgenden Tagen hier einrücken sollen, um den Wachdienst in Gemeinschaft mit der Bürgerwehr zu übernehmen und dadurch die schweren mit der rühmlichsten Hingebung geleisteten Pflichten der Bürger zu erleichtern. Es versteht sich von selbst, daß die Aufrechterhaltung der öffentlichen Ordnung lediglich der Bürgerwehr überlassen bleibt und die mögliche Hülfeleistung des Militairs nur für den äußersten Nothfall, und auch dann nur auf ausdrückliche Aufforderung der städtischen und Civil-Behörden erfolgen wird.

Berlin den 29ten März 1848.
Dittfurth. Minutoli.

157 We must not forget that—in the immediate aftermath of the armed struggle, at the moment when, euphorically, the decision to form a Civil Guard had been greeted by jubilation—there had been an immediate effort to collect all weapons that were in the hands of the insurgents. Almost simultaneously, Nobiling and Minutoli, in close contact with Count Arnim and thus with the court, took pains to create a truly bourgeois Civil Guard. (See the account provided by Prittwitz, in this respect!) Loyal civil servants of the government were prodded to join this force

of bourgeois "law and order." The selection of Civil Guard officers was steered carefully in a way that would exclude suspect radicals and discontent journeymen or factory workers; the cost of the uniform and the weapon that members of the guard had to buy was an additional obstacle. As a result, members of the bourgeoisie, the well-off parts of the petty-bourgeoisie and civil servants swelled the ranks of the Civil Guard, selecting notables as officers, mainly employers. Soon workers, many of whom had previously handed in weapons obtained from armories and gun stores on March 18–19, complained that they would have to buy the expensive Civil Guard uniform and the rifle if they wanted to join. It kept almost all of them from joining, because they could not afford it.

158 On April 13, 1848, an "Election Committee of the People" (or "Popular Election Committee," in German "Volkswahlkomitee"), apparently elected by a people's assembly (Volksversammlung) of politically awake Berliners that was organized by the "Volksverein unter den Zelten" (People's Association "Under the Marquees"), went to see the new Prime Minister of Prussia, Camphausen, in order to plead for an uncomplicated, normal definition of the already promised general suffrage. They were told quite frankly by Camphausen that he would not allow direct elections because it would empower the subaltern classes and result in "republican" conditions. An article by Marx, published in the Neue Rheinische Zeitung (New Rhenanian Gazette) indicates that the law prescribing indirect elections was passes (or entered into force) on April 8, 1848. – See Karl Marx, "Die Berliner 'National-Zeitung an die Urwähler", in: Neue Rheinische Zeitung, January 26, 1849; reprinted in: Karl Marx/Friedrich Engels, Werke (MEW), Vol. 6, p. 199, where he underlines the difference of the new "oktroyierte sogenannte allgemeine Wahlrecht" (of 1849) and the "Wahlrecht .... vom 8. April".) The Camphausen government had drawn up the bill concerning indirect elections and had presented it to the pre-revolutionary, "feudally" structured United Diet for ratification in order to be able to argue that it was bound by respect for legality and could not convert the indirect election process anymore by ordering in "dictatorial" fashion direct elections.

159 In German: "Hohe Versammlung! Se. Majestät der König haben mir den Befehl erteilt, den zweiten Vereinigten Landtag in Allerhöchstihrem Namen zu eröffnen." Adolph Carl (= Adolph Streckfuß), *Das freie Preußen! Geschichte des Berliner Freiheits-Kampfes und seiner Folgen*, Erster Band, *Geschichte Berlins vom 18. März bis 22. Mai* [The Free Prussia! History of the Berlin Freedom Battle and its Consequences, Vol. 1, History of Berlin from March 18 to May 22]. Berlin: A. Hüdenthal und Comp., 1848, p.160. (2nd edition).

160 See Adolph Carl (= Adolph Streckfuß), *Das freie Preußen!* Ibidem, pp.160ff.

161 Streckfuß, ibid, p.161.

162 In German, this was the "Entwurf eines Wahlgesetzes für die zur Vereinbarung der Preußischen Staatsverfassung zu berufende Versammlung" (Draft of an Electoral Law for the Election of the Assembly that is to reach an Agreement [sc. with the King] on the Prussian State-Constitution). The complete name of the bill is rarely used. This bill regarding the election of the Berlin constituent assembly as well as the bill concerning the election of the delegates to the German National Assembly in Frankfurt was presented to the United Diet in the form of a "Proposition Decree" issued by the king. The decree included these words of Frederick William IV: "We have therefore occasioned steps due to which a provisional electoral law has been drawn up." In German: "Wir haben deshalb ein vorläufiges Wahlgesetz entwerfen lassen, wonach diese Versammlung

[...] zu wählen und zu bilden sein wird." Here the king also noted that the United Diet would meet for the last time in April, after having passed the laws, for the decree ended with the words: "Indem Wir diesen Entwurf dem in der bisherigen Gestaltung zum letzten Male vereinigten Landtage vorlegen lassen, ec." A new representative body would be formed, based on what the future constitution would foresee in this respect. (The name of the bill and the king's words are quoted by Ludwig von Rönne, *Das Staats-Recht der Preußischen Monarchie*, ibid., p. 32, footnote 1.)

163 Receiving not only a monetary wage but also room and board was not untypical during the first half of the 19th century in the case of both journeymen and apprentices: it permitted the employer to slash the wage. It also occasioned many complaints about the quality of the food. Even so-called "artists" (better-paid artisans, like the porcelain painters of chinaware manufactories) and the master craftsmen of other proto-industrial manufactories were usually housed by the employer—either in his large house that included both dwelling rooms for his family and "dependents," his office, and perhaps even workshops, or in workers' houses especially produced by him for his skilled workers. Living in a shabby room in the attic or having only a hammock under the stairs for the short nightly period of rest was the rule in the case of servants. Even around 1900, bourgeois families often had only a small room in the attic for their "maid": the water in the portable basin, the "wash bowl," would freeze in winter, and many got pneumonia under such conditions. During the hot nights of summer, this chamber was also uncomfortable.

164 See Otto Brunner, "Das 'ganze Haus' und die alteuropäische 'Ökonomik,'" in: Familie und Gesellschaft [Familie and Society] (1966), pp.23-56 with respect to the early modern roots of the paternalistic system of dependency which had workers housed by the employer in his mansion, in the case of rich merchant-manufacturers, or his modest, perhaps even poor "burgher house" (Bürgerhaus)—if he was a master craftsman. It was the take-off of "modern industry" since the mid-1830s, the increase of modern factory work, the swelling number of industrial workers and the increasing number of other, usually unskilled and impoverished workers, 'set free' and condemned to search frequently for new employment by the transformation of the old paternalistic and clientelist, largely guild-regulated economy, that created a proletarian rental housing market, and new, no longer largely socially mixed, but quite genuinely proletarian neighborhoods like those outside the Rosenthal Gate in Berlin.

165 The fact that the Rhine Province set the legal age at 21 was a consequence of the period when it had formed part of Napoleonic France, adopting its *Code civil*.

166 The words used by Schilfert are: "das Übergewicht der arbeitenden Klassen in der künftigen 'preußischen Versammlung zur Vereinbarung der Verfassung' zu verhindern." (Gerhard Schilfert, Sieg und Niederlage des demokratischen Wahlrechts in der deutschen Revolution,, Berlin: Rütten & Loening, 1952, p. 59.) David Hansemann had desired such limitations much earlier, as Boch notes: "Already in 1830 Hansemann demanded a constitutionally secured participation of "the actual strength of the nation," the "middle class," in the Prussian state as a whole. He saw this "middle class" very narrowly as comprising the "higher segment of the burghers," as the central part of which he saw the "respected merchants and manufacturers." He demanded on the one hand general citizenship rights for "all state members" and a repeal of censorship, on the other hand, however, a clear political privilege of the propertied class. [...] His role model

was the high barrier introduced by the census suffrage of the French bourgeois monarchy that had just come to power." ["Hansemann verlangte bereits 1830 eine verfassungsmäßig abgesicherte Partizipation "der eigentlichen Kraft der Nation," der "Mittelstandes," im preußischen Gesamtstaat. Diesen "Mittelstand" faßte er sozial sehr eng als "höheren Bürgerstand" (16), als dessen zentralen Bestandteil er die "angesehenen Kaufleute und Fabrikanten" (17) sah. Er forderte einerseits allgemeine Staatsbürgerrechte für "alle Staatsmitglieder" und eine Aufhebung der Zensur, andererseits aber eine klare politische Bevorrechtigung des Besitzes. (…) Sein Vorbild was das hohe Zensuswahlrecht des gerade zur Macht gelangten französischen Bürgerkönigtums.] (Boch, *Grenzenloses Wachstum?*, ibid, pp.120f.)

167 In German: "aus directen Urwahlen hervorgehende Vertretung zur Republik führen werde und daß der Bestand der gegenwärtigen Regierung auf engste mit dem erlassenen Wahlrecht verknüpft sei." (Rüdiger Hachtmann, *Berlin 1848: eine Politik- und Gesellschaftsgeschichte der Revolution*. Bonn: Dietz, 1997, p. 298).

168 See Ludwig von Rönne, *Das Staats-Recht der Preußischen Monarchie*, ibid., p. 32, footnote 3.

169 Rönne, Ludwig von Rönne, *Das Staats-Recht der Preußischen Monarchie*, ibid., p. 32.

170 In German: "[der] Grundsatz [war] […], daß unter den Umständen, in denen ich das Ministerium führte, es rathsam und notwendig gewesen sei, lieber einen Schritt vor den Ereignissen zu bleiben, als sich von ihnen drängen zu lassen […] Was den Grundsatz selbst betrifft, so halte ich ihn für einen ganz richtigen, zu seiner Zeit." (Quoted by Streckfuß, ibid, p.184)

171 Engels saw this quite clearly. He wrote, "Not only the state, its citizens too had to be revolutionized. Their submissiveness could only be shed in a sanguinary liberation struggle." (Frederick Engels, "The Berlin Debate on the Revolution," in: Neue Rheinische Zeitung (New Rhenanian Gazette), June 14, 1848. Also online: URL https://www.marxists.org/archive/marx/works/1848/06/14a.htm. – Accessed May 2, 2018, 11:30 PM) This is the same dialectics that Fanon noted in the context of the Algerian revolution, and that Sartre was also aware of. The practice of resistance against injustice and oppression can not only change the situation (die gesellschaftlichen *Verhältnisse*: to translate this term as *social conditions* would be wrong, for it would be superficial, due to the lack of awareness that these conditions are structurally marked by social *relations*, e.g. class relations and relations of production); it also changes those actively engage in the act of resistance.

172 The king pronounced herewith that the future Constituent Assembly "is destined to come to an agreement with us regarding the content and form of the Free Constitution promised to Our people. But we want to announce already now some basics of this constitution and have therefore had an appropriate decree drafted, about which we look forward to the report of Our faithful estates [assembled in the United Diet]." The text of the Proposition Decree is reprinted in Gerhard Schilfer, Sieg und Niederlage des demokratischen Wahlrechts in der deutschen Revolution 1848/49. Rütten & Loening, 1952, p. 344.

173 See Marina Valensise (ed.), *François Guizot et la culture politique de son temps*. Paris: Gallimard, 1991.

174 Thus the interior ministers Camille Bachasson, comte de Montalivet [1830]; Casimir-Pierre Perier; Adolphe Thiers [1832]; Antoine Maurice Apollinaire, comte d'Argoult; Hughes Bernard Maret, duc de Bassanot [1834]; Adrien Etienne Pierre, comte de Gasparin [1836]; and Charles Marie Tanneguy, comte de Duchâtel. This

remarkable number of interior ministers used up in about 17 years bears witness to the restless Parisian subaltern classes that they tried to cope with.

175 These were no fortified walls any more. Berlin in the 1840s was surrounded by a simple customs wall: the "excise tax wall" (Akzisemauer). Guards at the gates collected an excise tax from farmers and merchants bringing vegetables, potatoes, meat or other goods into the city. Many utterly poor Berliners preferred to rent accommodation "outside the walls," thus, for instance, in the Rosenthal suburb (Rosenthaler Vorstadt), because living expenses were not as high as in the city.

176 See Adolph Wolff, *Berliner Revolutions-Chronik: Darstellung der Berliner Bewegungen im Jahre 1848 nach politischen, socialen und literarischen Beziehungen* [Chronicle of the Berlin revolution: An account of the Berlin movements in 1848 in political, social and literary respect], Vol. 3. Berlin: Gustav Hempel, 1854, pp.130-131.

177 See Gerd Fischer, "Die Lüfte der Zeit ließen sich nicht mehr absperren: Anfänge des politisch organisierten Liberalismus in Berlin" [The Atmosphere of the Time Could No Longer Be Locked Out: The beginnings of politically organized liberalism in Berlin], in: Probleme/Projekte/Prozesse: Liberalismus in Berlin 1848. Berlin Edition Luisenstadt, 1997, pp.12-19; here: p.14.

178 See the poster of the Volks-Verein that is reproduced in this book, see also Gerd Fischer, ibid, p.15.

179 See Wilhelm Blos, *Die Deutsche Revolution*, ibid, p.311.
180 See Wilhelm Blos, *Die Deutsche Revolution*, ibid, p.311.
181 See Gerd Fischer, ibid, p. 14.
182 See Gerd Fischer, ibid, p. 15.
183 See Gerd Fischer, ibid, p. 15.
184 See Rüdiger Hachtmann, *Berlin 1848: eine Politik- und Gesellschaftsgeschichte...*, Ibid, p.527, footnote 10.
185 See Rüdiger Hachtmann, *Berlin 1848: eine Politik- und Gesellschaftsgeschichte der Revolution*. Berlin: Dietz Verlag, 1997, p.527, footnote 10.
186 Quoted in W.Blos, ibid., p.227: "ein Volksverein, in dem alle Klassen vertreten sind, besonders aber Diejenigen, die den markigen Kern des Volkes bilden, die besitzlosen Arbeiter."
187 In German: "keine weiteren sozialen Programmpunkte" (Blos, ibid, p.227).
188 See Gerd Fischer, ibid, p.15.
189 See Gerd Fischer, ibid, p.14.
190 The Supreme Court in Berlin (Kammergericht zu Berlin) was not only the highest court in matters dealt with according to civil law; it had, as such, a reputation of independence, honesty and impartiality, ever since King Frederick II intervened in 1779 and had judges arrested who bent the law in favor of socially and economically powerful aristocrats, at the expense of a commoner (as the widely publicized and famous case of a watermill owner, Mr. Arnold, is supposed to prove). It also dealt with cases decided on the basis of criminal law, and was directly in charge in cases that fell under subsections of criminal law, thus political "crimes" and cases of "high treason." During the so-called Pre-March (Vormärz) Period of the 1830s and 1840s, it was in charge of political trials in all cases not only in Prussia, but in all of the German Confederation, after initial investigations of the accused had already occurred in the respective German state or Prussian Province. In the late 1840s, the Prussian spy network, that had informers in all of Germany and that sent spies even to Brussels and Paris in order to write reports on the political activities of German exiles, was overseen by the Chief of Police of the

Prussian capital, the "liberal" aristocrat von Minutoli, who reported in turn to the Prussian minister of the Interior. Julius von Minutoli regularly received reports on suspicious, potentially "subversive" democratic activities in Germany and abroad, and he was enough of a spy master to personally investigate democratic people's assemblies, such as those at the Zelten in Berlin, in early and mid-March,1848. When the student Gustav Adolph Schlöffel, a radical democrat who had already been politically active in South West Germany, arrived in Berlin soon after the days of street combats, von Minutoli had already been informed of his impending arrival and asked him immediately upon his arrival to appear in his office for the purpose of police questioning.

191 See Gerd Fischer, ibid, p.16.
192 With respect to German "True Socialism," Frederick Engels noted in 1847, "The most common kind of ['true'] socialist self-complacent reflection is to say that all would be well if only it were not for the poor on the other side. This argument may be developed with any conceivable subject-matter. At the heart of this argument lies the philanthropic petty-bourgeois hypocrisy which is perfectly happy with the positive aspects of existing society and laments only that the negative aspect of poverty exists alongside them, inseparably bound up with present society, and only wishes that this society may continue to exist without the conditions of its existence." (*Deutsche-Brüsseler-Zeitung* No. 74, September 16, 1847) As for Auguste Cornu, he wrote, "The 'true' socialism which arose in Germany between 1843 and 1847 was the specific form which utopian socialism took in that country. It came into being when modern capitalism was taking shape in Germany and was closely related to French socialism, which has arisen half a century previously, at the time of the bourgeoisie's coming to power in France. Like French socialism it has the earmarks of utopianism. Utopianism did not perceive the internal contradictions of capitalism, […] nor was it able, in view of the weakness of the proletariat, to envisage the class struggle as a means of emancipation." (Auguste Cornu, "German Utopianism: 'True' Socialism", in: *Science & Society*, Vol. 12, No. 1 (Winter, 1948), pp. 97-112, here: p.97.) See also another article by Engels, namely Frederick Engels, "The True Socialists," in Karl Marx and Frederick Engels, *Collected Works* (MECW), Vol. 5: Marx and Engels 1845–1847. London: Lawrence & Wishart, 1975, p.540. Here Engels noted for instance the "good-natured" (soft) way many "true" socialists critiqued German society. Mr. J. Beck was typical perhaps: "After […] [his] criticism of existing society […], let us see what his pia desideria [pious wishes] are with regard to the social aspects. At the end we find […] "Reconciliation", [a poem] written in a chopped-up prose […]." During much of 1848, reconciliation (with the king, the army, between burghers and workers, etc.) was obviously a key notion reoccurring *ad nauseam* in Berlin's liberal and much too often even in democratic discourse.
193 The quotation is taken here from Jacques Ranciere, *The Philospher and His Poor*. Durham: Duke Univ. Press, 1994, pp.71f. The quoted passage in German is: "Bei einem lokalisierten Berliner Schulmeister oder Schriftsteller dagegen, dessen Tätigkeit sich auf saure Arbeit einerseits und Denkgenuß andererseits beschränkt, dessen Welt von Moabit bis Köpenick geht und hinter dem Hamburger Tor mit Brettern zugenagelt ist…" etc. (Karl Marx / Friedrich Engels, Die deutsche Ideologie, in: MEW, Vol. 3, Berlin: Dietz, 1958, p.245. Reprint: Berlin: Hofenberg, 2016, p. 200.) When Ranciere comments on the passage, he is wrong in one respect: he took the idiomatic German phrase that refers to a "world" ("Welt") that is "nailed shut" (i.e., boarded up) "with boards" ("mit Brettern zugenagelt")

literally, whereas it is clearly an idiomatic expression that metaphorically indicates a limited view of the world. The gates of Berlin, though not as impressive as those of Paris, where not of the kind suggested by Jacques Rancière.

194 Gustav Julius, in: Extrablatt der Berliner Zeitungs-Halle [Special issue of BZH], Friday, March 24, 1848, morning edition, p.1.

195 See Rüdiger Hachtmann, *Berlin 1848: eine Politik- und Gesellschaftsgeschichte der Revolution*, ibidem, p. 160, Footnote 25.

196 See Rüdiger Hachtmann, ibidem, p. 271.

197 See Kurt Wernicke, "Die Spuren eines Revolutionärs: Gustav Adolph Schlöffel (1828-1849)" [The Traces of A Revolutionary: G.A. Schlöffel], in: *Berlinische Monatsschrift*, No.6 (1999), p.54.

198 In German: *Bürgertum*, in 1848 spelled Bürgerthum. This is the stratum of *burghers*, not in the political sense, in this case, but in the socio-economic sense. The term is often rendered as *middle class* in English; this is the part of the bourgeoisie that is sandwiched between the "big" (or high, in French: *haute*) *bourgeoisie* and the impoverished *petite bourgeoisie* or "small" bourgeoisie that is threatened by proletarization, but also eager to be upward mobile. Though *Bürgertum*, as used here, refers to "class" as a politico-economic category, their socio-economic situation and their economic interests obviously imply political perspectives and goals. In the legal, and thus *narrowly defined* political sense, the "burghers" (die Bürger) are *enfranchised* inhabitants of the towns. This group of enfranchised inhabitants included strata above and below the *Bürgertum* or modestly affluent bourgeoisie, thus the big bourgeoisie above them, and the tax-paying, house-owning but otherwise impoverished petty-bourgeoisie (Spießbürger, Pfahlbürger, Kleinbürger) below them. The poorest section of the petty-bourgeoisie, almost all workers, and the so-called Lumpenproletariat were not enfranchised, but especially in the larger cities they constituted the vast majority of the inhabitants in the 1840s.

199 This refers to the democratic *burschenschaften* (student associations) of the "Vormärz" (Pre-March) Period, i.e. mainly to the 1830s.

200 Gustav Adolph Schlöffel, *Dokumente der Revolutionen der Gegenwart: Kampf der jungen Pressfreiheit mit dem alten Beantenthum. Schlöffels des jüngeren Preßprocess verhandelt vor dem Kammergericht in Berlin. Vollständig aus den Akten, mitgetheilt von ihm selbst* [Documents of the revolutions of the present: fight of the young press freedom with the old bureaucracy. Schlöffel's recent press trial before the Berlin Supreme Court. Complete & from the files, communicated by himself. Berlin: Reuter & Stargardt, 1848, pp.3-5.

201 Such public work projects were undertaken by the government in order to expand the network of barge canals and of railroads. Berlin's unemployed could apply for work, and in so far these projects also served the purpose of alleviating unemployment in Berlin. The Berlin-Spandau ship canal, then known as the Spandau Canal (in German: Spandauer Canal) was built in 1848–1859 based on plans by Lenné. Another big public works project in 1848 was the *Ostbahn* (Eastern Railway).

202 The topographical term "Rehberge" (Deer Mountains) refers to hills of modest height north of Berlin's "town wall" and south of what is today the town quarter known as Reinickendorf. Like the topographical term "Rehberge," the name "Reineckendorf" suggests an animal: the animal *Reineke Fuchs* (Reineke Fuchs) is a mythical protagonist of an epic that first appeared in printed form in Northern

Germany as *Reynke de vos* (published in Lübeck in 1498). The hero is a typical underdog who slyly prevails in a world of superficially respectable adversaries. The epic was very popular. It was loved by the common people. Writers created literary versions, most notably Goethe who changed the name to Reinecke. Quite obviously, "Reinickendorf" can be read as "Fox Village" or Reinecke's village. The name "Hasenheide" (Hare's heath) is another topographical name in this area that alludes to animals. The Hasenheide is situated in the town quarter of New Cölln (Neukölln) in the Kreuzberg (Cross Mountain) neighborhood. "Rehberger" are people from the Rehberge, presumably a place where the down and out lived in the 1840s. "Rehberger" and other people from the Northern periphery (outside the walls) had been strongly present among the fighters on March 18–19. Now many were probably excluded from participating in even indirect elections because they received public assistance (and perhaps also if they worked on the Spandau Canal, if this counted as a form of public assistance, which it was in effect).

203 In German: "Schlöffels »Volksfreund« erschien wöchentlich zweimal in einer Auflage von 2 000, die der Herausgeber, Chefredakteur und Leitartikler offenbar aus seiner Tasche finanzierte. Ein Teil der Auflage wurde von ihm unentgeltlich an die Erdarbeiter verteilt, die bei Notstandsarbeiten beschäftigt waren und als »Rehberger« wegen ihres verwegenen Aussehens von Konservativen wie ruhebedürftigen gutbürgerlichen Liberalen als beliebter Bürgerschreck gehandelt wurden. Schlöffel verkündete im »Volksfreund« sein Programm für die Weiterführung der Revolution in zwei Hauptrichtungen: in die der Abschaffung des alten Machtapparates und die der Aufhebung der Ausbeutung der Arbeitskraft durch das Kapital. Diese radikale Position machte ihm sofort Feinde en masse, selbst bei Linksliberalen [...]" (Kurt Wernicke, "Die Spuren eines Revolutionärs: Gustav Adolph Schlöffel (1828-1849)" [The Traces of A Revolutionary: G.A. Schloeffel (b. 1828, d. 1849)], in: *Berlinische Monatsschrift* [Berlin Monthly Review], No.6 (1999), p.55.)

204 This refers to the French revolution that began in 1789. The text does not use the German term "Revolution" that existed already. The author—probably the editor of the 'Volksfreund', Schlöffel—prefers to use a by now antiquated term: "overturning of the state" or "revolution of the state": *Staatsumwälzung*.

205 The German term *geächtet* can be translated as *outlawed* or *ostracized*.

206 In German: geistige Schildwachen.

207 In German: Grundlagen (base; foundations).

208 The author uses the term *Gesinnung*, which can also be rendered "[basic] convictions."

209 The secretary and thus key figure of the People's Association was the young, very progressive, thus democratic merchant and *Cand. Phil.* Louis Levissohn. (The name is also spelled Levison and Loewinson. *Cand. phil.* means that he had completed his university studies and was about to receive his Ph.D., i.e., the degree of a *Doktor*.) The poster reproduced here says, "Workers! A malicious rumor has been spread in town [...] They say that the main reason why we meet is to deliberate how to undertake the pillage of shops and other such things. [...]" Calumny was a frequently employed weapon of many foes of democratization and social change. It is still today in the political sphere. In the 1950s, the West German Christian Democratic head of government, Mr. Adenauer, even denounced the reformist, law-and-order loving, anti-communist Social Democratic Party as "Moscow's Fifth Column." Fake news are nothing new. Willy Brandt was called as a "traitor of the Fatherland" by the Christian Democrats because he was in exile during World

War II. When Adenauer had to correct himself and retract a particularly blatant lie that had helped him to win the election, he apologized, slyly adding: "Aber es hat doch genützt." (But it helped [us] greatly.) Rüdiger Hachtmann discusses the role of rumors in the political context of 1848. See: Rüdiger Hachtmann, *Die Macht des Gerüchts in der Revolution von 1848 – Das Berliner Beispiel* [The Power of Rumors in the Revolution of 1848 – The Berlin Example], in: *Geschichte und Emanzipation*. Festschrift für Reinhard Rürup [History and Emancipation. Festschrift for R. Ruerup], ed. by Michael Grüttner, Rüdiger Hachtmann and Heinz Gerhard Haupt. Frankfurt am Main: Campus Verlag, 1999, pp. 189-216.

210 April 10 was the day when the United Diet was dissolved for good.
211 See W.Blos, ibid., p.226; see also G. Fischer, ibid.
212 See G.Fischer, ibid., pp.16f.
213 See W.Blos, ibid., p.226.
214 See W.Blos, ibid., pp.226f.
215 Blos, ibid, p. 227.
216 Blos, ibid, p. 227.
217 Blos, ibid, p. 227.
218 Blos, ibid, p. 227.
219 The commander at the time was Major von Aschoff.
220 The letter was reprinted in: *Kgl. Privilegirte Berlinische Zeitung*, No. 94, Thursday, April 20, 1848, p.1. (The newspaper is published by the Vossische Zeitungs-Expedition, 8, Breite Strasse, in Berlin).
221 The argument of the Magistrat glossed over the fact that the constitutional ("verfassungsmäßige") process of debating and adopting the new election law was based on an absolutist "constitution" that had already been recognized as antiquated in 1815, when the first decisive calls asking for a replacement by a more progressive constitution were heard. The Magistrat thus reveals the same penchant for an empty, purely formal "legalism" that the powers that be still cling to in many cases, today.
222 In German: "Wir sind amtlich benachrichtigt, daß in Folge eines Beschlusses einer vor den Zelten abgehaltenen Volksversammlung morgen [an] dem 20sten d.M. in einem zahlreichen Aufzuge dem Staats-Ministerium eine Petition überreicht werden soll, welche die Abänderung des verfassungsmäßig erlassenen Wahlgesetzes bezweckt. [...] Das Staats-Ministerium hat erklärt, wie es jederzeit bereit sei, Petitionen [...] anzunehmen [...]. Es hat es aber nicht für zulässig erachtet, daß das Petitionsrecht in einer Weise ausgeübt werde, welche dazu führen kann, die öffentliche Ordnung und den Stadtfrieden zu stören. Berufen, diese ersten Erfordernisse bürgerlicher Freiheit und Wohlfahrt zu schützen, wenden wir uns zunächst mit vollstem Vertrauen an die Vorstände, Meister, und Gesellschaften aller hiesigen Gewerke mit der dringenden Aufforderung, sich diesem ungesetzlichen Vorhaben nicht anzuschließen. Die beabsichtigte Petition kann, welche Ansichten man auch über den derselben zum Grunde liegenden Gedanken eines direkten Wahlsystems haben mag, keinen Erfolg haben, weil das Ministerium das verfassungsmäßige Wahlgesetz nicht eigenmächtig abändern darf; weil, wenn es eine solche Abänderung vornehmen könnte, die Interessen Preußens und Deutschlands durch die eintretende Unmöglichkeit, daß preußische Volk auf dem deutschen Reichstage rechtzeitig vertreten zu lassen, auf das Empfindlichste verletzt werden würden; und weil endlich eine solche Maaßregel nur getroffen werden könnte, wenn die Stimme des ganzen Landes darüber gehört wäre u. sich dafür entschieden hätte. Wir erwarten daher von allen unseren Mitbürgern,

auch von denen, welche nach ihrer politischen Ueberzeugung direkte Wahlen für die richtigeren halten, daß sie bei der Art und Weise ihre Ansichten geltend zu machen, sich von Demonstrationen fernhalten werden, die als Partei-Ansicht von der entgegenstehenden Meinung eines großen Theiles des Landes als eine gegen dieses geübte Anmaßung keine Billigung finden können.

    Berlin, den 19. April 1848. Der Magistrat." (*Kgl. Privilegirte Berlinische Zeitung*, No. 94, Thursday, April 20, 1848, p.2.)

223 In German: "Das Kgl. Staats-Ministerium hat den auf heute verabredeten, die Abänderung des Wahlgesetzes bezweckenden Volksaufzug untersagt." Of course, Minutoli was expressing also his hope that the "sensible," "law-abiding" Berliners would understand this measure and would support him. (*Kgl. Privilegirte Berlinische Zeitung*, No. 94, Thursday, April 20, 1848, p.2.)

224 When Martin Luther King initiated the March on Washington and when—wasn't it perhaps hundreds of thousands?—at least a vast mass of people followed him, this was an occasion that lets us decipher the turning point where a symbolic act that the dominant people can stomach becomes an act that they consider truly dangerous. Did they fear more such marches, an avalanche? Did they fear—and do they still, that "black, brown, and beige" can unite: the Afro-American movement for civil and socio-economic rights, Latino activists, the class-conscious part of the "Anglo"-American working class? Was this fear the reason, deep down in their "state apparatus," why Martin Luther King had to die? And are similar reasons responsible for the fact that the New York Times attempts a "demontage" of Bernie Sanders, depicting this brave man as "too old?"

225 Wilhelm Blos, *Die deutsche Revolution von 1848 und 1849*. Stuttgart: Dietz, 1891; new edition, 1893; also: Berlin; Bonn: Dietz, 1978; also: Paderborn: Europäischer Geschichtsverlag, 2015. [Reprint]

226 Both of them, Nauwerk and Berends, were singled out as especially progressive, in August Brass's book. And in fact, Karl Marx is known to have had discussions with Berends, but also with Carl d'Ester and Georg Jung when he visited Berlin in August, 1848.

227 Hans Herzfeld speaks of a complicated indirect system with electors ("einem komplizierten indirekten System mit Wahlmännern") and notes that "the remarkable number of 60,000 'Urwähler' [original voters in Berlin who were to elect the "Wahlmänner" (electors) in a complicated way, who would then, in turn, determine the delegates to the Prussian national assembly in a complicated way] took part in the national assembly election on May 1 [, 1848]." (Hans Herzfeld, ibidem, p. 60) Herzfeld speaks of the "lack of a popular basis" of the elected assembly, noting with regret that, in comparison with prior representation in the United Prussian Diet (Vereinigte Landtag) in 1847, the percentage of big landowners (Rittergutsbesitzer) of aristocratic descent had shrunk from 50 percent to 20 percent whereas the [partially conservative, partially "moderately" liberal (that is to say, "conservative liberal"] state bureaucracy was now represented strongly (with civil servants forming 36 % of the elected delegates). Herzfeld gives absolute figures for other groups: he refers to 50 parsons (and priests) and 50 merchants and industrialists (the bourgeoisie, described by him as "members of free professions"). He regretfully notes that only 17 lawyers were elected, and notes 15 physicians. Last and in fact least noted by him are 15 elected craftsmen (either self-employed master artisans or employed journeymen), 6 "clerks" (Angestellte), and 5 workers. (Hans Herzfeld, ibidem, p. 61) Thus the vast majority of Prussia's population was represented by perhaps eleven to maximally 27 delegates with a

working-class background—perhaps only by 5, as clerks and self-employed artisan would most likely belong to the lower petty bourgeoisie. Apparently, Herzfeld assumes that the traditional ways of representing "strata" or "ranks" (estates) were popular ("volkstümlich") and that breaking with such patterns had to cause resistance by the "Prussian powers."

228 "Die Bürgerwehr erwies sich dabei als eine reaktionäre Institution; sie kam dem eingeschüchterten Ministerium zu Hülfe und hielt der friedlichen [...] Volksdemonstration für direktes Wahlrecht die Spitzen ihrer Bayonnette entgegen." (Wilhelm Blos, Die deutsche Revolution 1848 und 1849, Paderborn 2015, p.235.)

229 See: *Preußische Parlamentszeitung* [Prussian Parlamentary Gazette], No. 1, May 22, 1848. See also Bärbel Holtz, Rainer Paetau, Hartwin Spenkuch, Reinhold Zilich (compilers), *Acta Borussica: Die Protokolle des Preußischen Staatsministeriums 1817-1934/38* [Minutes of the Prussian Government],Vol. 4-10 (1848–1918), edited by the Berlin-Brandenburgische Akademie der Wissenschaften. Hildesheim: Georg Olms Verlag, 1999–2003.

230 The text here quoted that is the key part of Camphausen's speech in the Prussian National Assembly on May 30, 1848, was included in an article by Karl Marx that appeared in the New Rhenanian Gazette on June 3. See: Karl Marx, "Camphausen's Statement at the Session of May 30," in: *Neue Rheinische Zeitung*, No.3, June 3, 1848. Reprinted in Karl Marx and Frederick Engels, *Collected Works* (MECW), Vol. 7, ibidem, p. 30.

231 The text here quoted that is the key part of Camphausen's speech in the Prussian National Assembly on May 30, 1848. It forms part of an already mentioned article by Karl Marx that appeared in the New Rhenanian Gazette on June 3. See: Karl Marx, "Camphausen's Statement at the Session of May 30," in: *Neue Rheinische Zeitung*, No.3, June 3, 1848. Reprinted in Karl Marx and Frederick Engels, *Collected Works* (MECW), Vol. 7, ibidem, p. 30.

232 According to Herzfeld, "the young Schlöffel" (i.e. Gustav Adolph Schlöffel, b. 1828 in Silesia, killed in action on June 21, 1849 during the days of republican resistance in Baden) belonged "to the most radical figures of the March Revolution"; as we know due to other sources, he sided with the workers when they staged a demonstration against the "indirect vote" soon after the fight on the barricades. Herzfeld, an objective and neutral historian by the standards of the discipline, with much sympathy or empathy for the king, the conservative "liberals," and the bourgeoisie and very little for the "mob," is aware of the role the proletarian, pauperized masses that Schlöffel sided with, played during the March Revolution; he confirms that from the very beginning when one shot resounded on the Palace Square (perhaps fired by a person among the crowd, something Brass hinted at), or two "unfortunate shots" were fired (more obviously by soldiers, according to official sources Herzfeld leans on), the "masses" ["die Masse"] were the key protagonists of the revolution. Herzfeld adds, "It cannot be put in doubt today anymore that it was … an insurgency of the Berlin population, and that the main heroes were Kleinbürger, Handwerker and Arbeiter [petty bourgeois guys (members of the petty bourgeoisie), craftsmen, and workers] who were making the biggest sacrifice and who often were very young. The participation of university students was relatively limited in quantitative terms. Of those 2,000 students enrolled at the university of Berlin, no more than 100 took part in the armed struggle, and even among them, Schlöffel remained an exception." (Hans Herzfeld, ibidem, p.57f.)

233 In German: "Auf dem grünen Donnerstag wollen wir mit dem Ministerium Kamphausen das Abendmahl feiern, auf das es gekreuzigt werde. Einst haben die Juden Barabam freigegeben, um einen großen Volksaufwiegeler und Revolutionär, der Jahrtausende lang als 'Gott' verehrt wurde, zu hängen. Morgen wollen wir den Barnabas Kamphausen nicht freigeben, und unsere Freiheit, die wir augenblicklich in den Volkswahlen verkörpert sehen, für immer retten. Darum trauet nicht jenen Schriftgelehrten und Pharisäern im konstitutionellen Club und jenen königlichen Kriegsknechten in den Wachtstuben der Bürgerwehr, und dem Pontius Pilatus Minutoli, die ||auch alle erzählen, wie gut und vortrefflich der Barnabas ist, und wie gefährlich jener politische 'Christus,' das demokratische Wahlgesetz (denn es führt ja zur Republik), sondern laßt Euch nicht davon abwendig machen, in Masse mit nach Golgatha vor das königliche Schloß zu ziehen, wo jener barbarische Friedrich Wilhelm Titus Euch vor 4 Wochen zusammenschießen ließ [...]. Wir wollen nicht [...] zu stillschweigenden Mördern unserer eigenen Freiheit werden und es zugeben, wie durch das schlechte Wahlgesetz [...] die reichen und ordnungsliebenden Kameele durch das Nadelöhr der landräthlichen Wahlcontrole gehen." (G. A. Schlöffel, "Die große Wahldemostration," in: *Der Volksfreund*, No. 3, April 1, 1848, reprinted in: Gustav Adolph Schlöffel, *Dokumente der Revolutionen der Gegenwart*, ibid., pp.6f.).

234 Radical republicans like Schlöffel (who joined the Republican insurgence in Baden after serving his prison term in Prussia, and who lost his life in battle in 1849) and Stefan Born (who was the most notable member of the Federation of Communists in Berlin during the events of 1848) clearly saw that the electoral process prescribed by the Prussian government turned the supposedly "general suffrage" that had been "granted" by the King into nothing but an instrument of "duperie" whereas it was clear that they already desired to turn this "moyen de duperie ... en instrument d'emancipation" by mobilizing also those parts of the working class who were still too passive. (See also the respective, very relevant remarks of Lucio Coletti, in his introduction that discusses the "Political Legacy [or: Testament] of Engels," in: Eduard Bernstein, *Socialismo e Socialdemocrazia*, Bari: Laterza, 1968.)

235 This refers to the Body of Laws known as "Allgemeines Preußisches Landrecht" or General State Laws of the Prussian State, promulgated in 1794.

236 In German: "Mitten in dieser Lage [...] greift die ängstliche Hoffnungslosigkeit 6 Wochen nach Erringung der Preßfreiheit zu dem Mittel des Preßprocesses und glaubt sich gerettet, wenn sie einige Literaten einsperrt. Die konstitutionelle Bourgeoisie bettelt bei dem absoluten Landrechte um Schutz gegen das Volk. [...] Es weiß nicht was thun mit dem Volksfreunde, der trotz der allgemeinen Niedergeschlagenheit den Muth nicht verliert. (Schlöffel, *Dokumente...*, pp. 5f.)

237 In the *Yearbook for the Year 1845*, an anonymous author mentions the Tumult Law which would be remembered in 1848 and which seems to have been replaced with a new version a year later. At least, a new bill—submitted by the government —was debated in the summer of 1848 by the press and in the Prussian National Assembly. The author writing in the Yearbook states, that on September 30, 1836, the Tumult Law that had been submitted on August 17, 1835, was promulgated. He adds, "See Hansemann's motion." (In German: Unter dem 30. September 1836 wurde das Tumultgesetz vom 17ten August 1835 deklarirt. (Siehe Hansemanns Antrag [...]) - N.N., "Die Sicherung der Unabhängigkeit des Richteramtes und der persönlichen Freiheit in der preußischen Rheinprovinz. Nebst Verhandlungen darüber in der 30. Sitzung des rheinischen Landtages (1. April 1845.)" [Securing the independence of the magistracy and personal freedom

in the Prussian Rhine Province. In addition to negotiations about it in the 30th session of the Rhenish Provincial Diet], in: *Konstitutionelle Jahrbücher*, Dritter Band (1845), [Constitutional Yearbooks, Yearbook for the Year 1845, Vol. 3], edited by Dr. Karl Weyl, Stuttgart: Adolph Krabbe, 1845, pp. 71-172, here p.89.

238 In German: "Der Prozeß war—von den wenigsten Zeitgenossen in seiner tiefen Bedeutung so eingeschätzt—ein Meilenstein in der Blockierung des mit dem 18./19. März im Barrikadenkampf eingeleiteten Prozesses hin zu einem demokratischen preußischen Staat. Erstmals wurde von einer tragenden Stütze des Staates vorgeführt, daß die stattgehabten revolutionären Ereignisse keineswegs revolutionäres Recht geschaffen hatten, sondern das seit 1794 geltende Recht unverdrossen weitergalt—wenn man den Aufruhrparagraphen nicht noch nachträglich gegen die Barrikadenkämpfer anwandte, war das allenfalls königlicher Gnade zuzuschreiben! Die Anklage des Staatsanwalts Julius von Kirchmann (1802–1884) warf Schlöffel nämlich neben »Verleitung zu persönlicher Mißhandlung des Staatsministers Camphausen« auch »versuchte Verleitung zum Aufruhr« vor." Kurt Wernicke, *Die Spuren eines Revolutionärs: Gustav Adolph Schlöffel (1828–1849)* [The Traces of A Revolutionary: G.A. Schlöffel (1828-1849)], in: Berlinische Monatsschrift [Berlin Monthly Review], No.6 (1999), p.55.

239 See the commentary that appears under the heading "Vereinigtes Deutschand" in the Kgl. Privilegierte Berlinische Zeitung of May 25, 1848, p.1.

240 James M. Brophy, Capitalism, Politics, and Railroads in Prussia, 1830–1870, ibidem, p.12.

241 See See Rüdiger Hachtmann, *Berlin 1848: eine Politik- und Gesellschaftsgeschichte der Revolution*, ibidem, p.160, footnote 25.

242 Willibald Steinmetz, "'Speaking is a Deed for You': Words and Action in the Revolution of 1848," in: Dieter Dowe, Heinz-Gerhard Haupt, et al. (eds.), *Europe in 1848 Revolution and Reform*. New York and Oxford: Berghahn, 2001, pp. 830-868, here: p.853, footnote 94)

243 In German, the words spoken by Camphausen were these, "daß wir keine aus dem Interesse des Landes hervorgehende Veranlassung gehabt haben, früher auf die Zurückberufung anzutragen. Ich nehme aber keinen Anstand, hinzuzufügen, daß wir nicht glauben, zu einem Schritte rathen zu müssen, der eine bedenkliche Aufregung zu ungeeigneter Zeit erzeugt haben würde. Wenn uns dieserhalb ein Vorwurf trifft, so müssen wir uns demselben unterwerfen. Als aber der Zeitpunkt der Einberufung einer Versammlung, mit welcher die künftige Verfassung des Landes begründet werden soll, herannahte, da haben wir es als unerläßlich erachtet, daß der Thronfolger im Lande anwesend sei, da haben wir es für unsere Pflicht erachtet, unsererseits auf die Rückkehr anzutragen." (Adolph Wolff, *Berliner Revolutions-Chronik: Darstellung der Berliner Bewegungen im Jahre 1848*, Vol.3, ibidem, 1854, p.149.)

244 See Adolph Wolff, *Berliner Revolutions-Chronik*, Vol.3, ibidem, 1854, p.156.

245 From the *Staatsanzeiger* [State Gazette] of June 4, 1848. The entire letter of Prince William, dated May 30, 1848, is reprinted in: Adolph Wolff, *Berliner Revolutions-Chronik*, Vol.3, ibidem, p.154. The part quoted now reads in German: "[...] Ich halte diesen Zeitpunkt für den passendsten, um meine Eurer Majestät schon bekannten Gesinnungen [...] nochmals offen auszusprechen. Ich gebe mich der Hoffnung hin, daß die freien Institutionen, zu deren festerer Begründung Ew. Majestät jetzt die Vertreter des Volkes berufen haben, [...] sich zum Heile Preußens mehr und mehr entwickeln werden. Ich werde dieser Entwicklung mit Zuversicht und Treue alle meine Kräfte widmen und sehe dem Augenblick entgegen, wo

ich der Verfassung, welche Ew. Majestät mit Ihrem Volke nach gewissenhafter Berathung zu vereinbaren im Begriffe stehen, die Anerkennung ertheilen werde, welche die Verfassungs-Urkunde für den Thronfolger festsetzen wird. Brüssel, 30, Mai 1848 – Prinz von Preußen."

246 In German: "Bürger seid wachsam! Seht, welche Schwierigkeiten man erhebt, um Euch die einzige und volle Garantie in die Hände zu geben, welche die unveräußerlichen Rechte des Volkes sichert! Wie hartnäckig man verhindern will, daß die Volksbewaffnung eine Wahrheit werde."

247 In German: "daß die Vereins-Mitglieder einstimmig dem Antrag beigetreten seien, der hierauf am 4. [sc. Juni] dem in jenem Bezirk gewählten Abgeordneten Jung zu [r] schleunigsten Vorlage an die National-Versammlung übergeben und in vielen hundert Exemplaren verbreitet worden. Warum den Antrag aber Hr. Berends und nicht Hr. Jung zum Vortrag gebracht (habe), darüber—sagt Hr. Benda—"mögen diese Herren sich aussprechen." (Adolph Wolff, *Berliner Revolutions-Chronik*, Vol.3, ibidem, p.159.

248 In German: "Einige Reactionäre wiegeln die Provinzen gegen Berlin auf. Bedrohen das Vaterland mit Bürgerkrieg und Untergang, nennen die glorreiche Revolution des März "Verbrechen" und die unsterblichen Helden dieser Tage "Verbrecher." Das geschieht nur zwei Monate nach der mit dem edelsten Blute errungenen Freiheit. Aber jene Reactionäre werden zu ihrem verderblichen Treiben ermuthigt, weil das aus der März-Revolution unmittelbar hervorgegangene Ministerium ängstlich vermeidet: diese Revolution und das Verdienst derer, die dafür gekämpft anzuerkennen, wodurch es alle wahren Vaterlandsfreunde mit Unruhe, Mißtrauen und Besorgnis gegen die unklaren Absichten der Regierung erfüllt und die Rückkehr zu Ruhe und Ordnung verhindert. Um so schmerzlicher werden jene reactionären Aufwiegelungen empfunden, zumal sie vorzugsweise durch Intrigen und Machinationen von Regierungs-Beamten hervorgerufen scheinen, die nicht nur die Errungenschaften der Revolution, sondern selbst die Sicherheit und den Bestand des Vaterlandes in Frage stellen." (Adolph Wolff, *Berliner Revolutions-Chronik*, Vol.3, ibidem, p.138.)

249 Adolph Wolff, *Berliner Revolutions-Chronik*, Vol.3, ibidem, pp. 138f.

250 Adoph Wolff speaks of "more than 100,000"! Adolph Wolff, *Berliner Revolutions-Chronik*, Vol.3, ibidem, p.136.

251 Adolph Wolff sums up the content of several speakers. The main tendency is this: emphasis on harmony, and unity of burghers and workers. A strange united front when it works only at the graveside, and in "real life" the burghers were for indirect elections at the expense of the working class, and when their burgher guard shot at protesting workers. Stephan Born was the only one of the well-known speakers who did not get much applause. He had been too critical and it spoiled the atmosphere of harmony and reconciliation. Regarding Born's speech, see Adolph Wolff, *Berliner Revolutions-Chronik*, Vol.3, ibidem, p.130 and p. 134.

252 The attack lead to a brief occupation of the "Zeughaus," accompanied by the seizure of weapons and destructive acts directed against symbols of Prussian militarism. This spontaneous mass action failed in the end, also due to lack of further strategy and determined leadership.

253 Kgl. privilegirte Berlinische Zeitung, No. 162, 1. Beilage [1st supplement], July 15, 1848, pp.2f.

254 In German: Bekanntmachung:
Es ist heute zur Kenntniß der Staats-Anwaltschaft gekommen, daß bei dem Angriff auf das hiesige Zeughaus in der vergangenen Nacht aus demselben eine

bedeutende Anzahl von Gewehren, mehrere werthvolle Waffen und andere zur Ausrüstung des Heeres gehörige Gegenstände gewaltsam fortgenommen sind. Ich fordere einen Jeden, der hierüber durch Angaben bestimmter Thatsachen gegen einzelne Personen nähere Aufklärung zu geben vermag, auf, dieselben mir mitzutheilen. (…)

Berlin, den 15. Juni 1848,
Staatsanwalt beim Königl. Kriminalgericht. Temme.
Source: Kgl. Priv. Berl. Ztg. No. 138, Saturday, June 17, 1848.

255 See Alexander Bergengrün, David Hansemann, Berlin: J. Guttentag, 1901, p.488.
256 In German: "Dem Vernehmen nach haben die Minister von Arnim, Graf Schwerin und von Kanitz um ihre Entlassung nachgesucht." (*Kgl. Privilegierte Berlinische Zeitung*, No. 138, Sunday, June 17, 1848, p.2)
257 In German: "Gestern Nachmittag um 5 Uhr wurde an die Stelle des plötzlich zurückgetretenen Major Blesson der Major Rimpler fast einstimmig zum interimistischen Kommandeur der Bürgerwehr durch die im Marstall versammelten Hauptleute und Zugführer gewählt." (*Kgl. Privilegierte Berlinische Zeitung*, No. 138, Sunday, June 17, 1848, p.2)
258 The successor of von Minutoli was Moritz von Bardeleben, the son of a General of the Infantery. Von Bardeleben had studied law at the university in Bonn, and then served in a minor function at the supreme court in Berlin. Since 1846 he was county president (Landrat) of Bernkastel county, in the Mosel valley region of the Rhine Province, something that may have contributed to a liberal image. It is likely that he was picked by Hansemann or Auerswald, and not by the king. Von Bardeleben remained in office as chief of police until November, 1848, when the reaction in Berlin and Prussia openly triumphed.
259 See Bergengrün, ibidem, p. 488.
260 Sessions of the National Assembly had been adjourned for a few days because of the government crisis, and then, when it was convened again "on the 20th of June, […] the message of Camphausen was read in the Prussian National Assembly that he had asked [the king] for his dismissal because he had failed to form a new cabinet, as he had been asked to do." (Alexander Bergengrün, ibidem, p. 488)
261 See James M. Brophy, *Capitalism, politics, and railroads in Prussia, 1830–1870*. Columbus, Ohio : Ohio State Univ. Press, 1998, p.50.
262 Schreckenstein might be read as *Horrible Stone* or Frightening Stone, but also as "Frightens even stones."
263 *Berliner Krakehler*, no. 11, July 4, 1848, p. 2.
264 *Kgl. Privilegirte Berlinische Zeitung*, no. 169, Sunday, July 23, 1848, p.4.
265 These are the exact words that report the problem faced by the authorities: "In dem hier garnisonirenden 24. Regiment sind in letzter Zeit mehrfache Vergehen wieder die Subordination vorgekommen. Durch ruhiges und festes Einschreiten hat sich indeß der rege gewordene üble Geist wieder gelegt […]" (*Kgl. Privilegirte Berlinische Zeitung*, no. 169, July 23, 1848, p. 4.)
266 "The Downfall of the Camphausen Government," in *Neue Rheinische Zeitung*, No. 22, June 22, 1848, in English in: Karl Marx and Frederick Engels, *Collected Works* (MECW), Vol. 7, ibidem, p. 106)
267 "The Downfall of the Camphausen Government," in *Neue Rheinische Zeitung*, No. 22, June 22, 1848; in English in: Karl Marx and Frederick Engels, *Collected Works* (MECW), Vol. 7, ibidem, p. 106.
268 See Gerd Heinrich, Introduction, in: Karl Ludwig Prittwitz, *Berlin 1848: das Erinnerungswerk des Generalleutnants Karl Ludwig von Prittwitz und andere Quellen*

zur Berliner Märzrevolution und zur Geschichte Preußens um die Mitte des 19. Jahrhunderts. Bearbeitet und eingeleitet von Gerd Heinrich. Berlin; New York: de Gruyter, 1985, pp.xliii-xliv.

269 "The Downfall of the Camphausen Government," in: *Neue Rheinische Zeitung*, No. 23, June 23, 1848. Reprinted in English in: Karl Marx and Friedrich Engels, Collected Works (MECW), Volume 7, ibidem, p. 107.

270 "The Hansemann Government," in: *Neue Rheinische Zeitung*, No. 24, June 24, 1848. Reprinted in English in: Karl Marx and Friedrich Engels, Collected Works (MECW), Volume 7, ibidem, p.111.

271 "Threat of the Gervinus Zeitung," in: Neue *Rheinische Zeitung*, No. 25, June 25, 1848. Reprinted in English in: Karl Marx and Friedrich Engels, Collected Works (MECW), Volume 7, ibidem, p. 115.

272 See: Christian Gottfried Daniel Nees von Esenbeck, *Die demokratische Monarchie. Ein Gesetz-Vorschlag, der National-Versammlung zu Berlin vorgelegt den 1. Juli 1848* [The Democratic Monarchy. Proposal of a bill; submitted to the Berlin National Assembly on July 1, 1848]. Berlin: J. Springer, 1848; 26pp.

273 See: C. G. D. Nees von Esenbeck, *Die Demokratische Monarchie. Ein Gesetz-Vorschlag, der National-Versammlung in Berlin vorgelegt den 1.Juli 1848* [The Democratic Monarchy. A law proposal (i.e., a bill) submitted to the National Assembly in Berlin on July 1, 1848]. Berlin: Springer, 1848, 26pp.

274 *Berliner Krakehler*, No. 154, July 22, 1848, p.1. – The publisher and editor of the journal was Ernst Litfaß.

275 Frederick Engels, "The Frankfurt Assembly Debates the Polish Question," in: *Neue Rheinische Zeitung*, No. 93, September 3, 1848. Published in English as a part of a series of articles that supported the cause of Polish fighters for national independence, in: Marx and Engels: *Articles from the Neue Rheinische Zeitung*, Moscow 1972, pp. 83–102.

276 Frederick Engels, "The Frankfurt Assembly Debates the Polish Question" (several articles without title in the Neue Rheinische Zeitung (New Rhenanian Gazette) since August 7, 1848. The quoted passage is from Neue Rheinische Zeitung, No. 93, September 3, 1848. http://hiaw.org/defcon6/works/1848/08/09.html.

277 Like Camphausen and Hansemann, Beckerath belonged to those big bourgeois "Liberals" who certainly would not refrain from an armed crackdown on the Democrats, if necessary. The experience of the riots in Frankfurt between September 16 and 18 made Beckerath turn even further to the right. He was aghast when protests erupted after news of the ceasefire that the Prussian government had concluded with Denmark reached the city.

278 Beckerath was also a railroad entrepreneur, like Camphausen and Hansemann. See James M. Brophy, *Capitalism, Politics, and Railroads in Prussia, 1830–1870*, ibidem, p.49.

279 See James M. Brophy, *Capitalism, Politics, and Railroads in Prussia, 1830-1870*, ibidem, p. 203, footnote 11. See also Jonathan Sperber, *Rhineland Radicals: The Democratic Movement and the Revolution of 1848–49*. Princeton: Princeton University Press, 1991, p. 329.

280 See also Ernest Mandel, La formation de la pensée économique de Karl Marx : De 1843 jusqu'à la rédaction du "Capital" : Étude génétique. Paris : Maspero, 1967.

281 Marx critiqued the limited scope of the petty-bourgeois democratic demands in his article entitled "On the Jewish Question" (Karl Marx, "Zur Judenfrage," in: *Deutsch-Französische Jahrbücher*, Feb. 1844). He wrote, "What kind of emancipation do they desire? Civic, political emancipation." It was not enough

for him. Critiquing Bruno Bauer's approach, he said very clearly that the decisive thing was to achieve clarity as to what kind of emancipation should be demanded. Only emancipation of Jews? And if not, if everyone's emancipation, then only political emancipation? "What kind of emancipation is in question? What conditions follow from the very nature of the emancipation that is demanded? Only the criticism of political emancipation itself would have been the conclusive criticism of the Jewish question and its real merging in the 'general question of time'"—the social question which had a political and social, a politico-economic dimension, and which, if solved, would aim nothing less than the full emancipation of all women and men as human beings. (The text is republished in: Karl Marx, *Frühe Schriften*. Darmstadt : wbg Academic, n.d. – Electronic resource. In English see Marx and Frederick Engels, Collected Works (MECW), Vol. 3. London: Lawrence & Wishart, 1975, p.149.

282 "Mais il n'y avait ni programme, ni revendication, ni organisation." (But there was no program, no demands, no organization.) Marc Reynebeau, *Histoire belge* : 1830–2005. Bruxelles : Éditions Racine, 2005, p.62.

283 Friedrich Engels, "Neueste Nachrichten vom 23. Juni 1848" [The Latest News of June 23, 1848], in: Neue Rheinische Zeitung [New Rhenanian Gazette], No. 26, June 26, 1848. Reprinted in: Karl Marx, Friedrich Engels, *Gesamtausgabe* (MEGA), I, 7, Berlin: Dietz, 2016, p.184. The passage referred to says (in German): "Eine Frau vom Volke beklagte sich so eben bei mir, daß die Nationalgarde, deren Uniform ich trage, zuerst auf das Volk geschossen habe. Ich warf ihr ein, daß wir unsere Pflicht erfüllen, indem wir die Emeutiers auseinanderjagen. Was soll das? Antwortete sie, man muß nicht auf das Volk schießen: es ist so unglücklich!"

284 Yes, it is true: in Berlin, too, the blouses *bleues des travailleurs* could be seen, worn by men of all ages who manned the barricades. They were a frequent sight, far more so than the feathered hats and green coats of the Rifleman's Association—expensive clothes that a worker could not afford. The blue blouse was typical: in Paris, in Brussels, in Berlin, for it was relatively cheap yet sturdy, and those who wore it were massively present in the fight, outnumbering the men of the Rifleman Association in their expensive clothes by far. Working people like Gus Hesse and the young apprentices (Ernst Zinna and Heinrich Glasewaldt) who still braved the assault of the troops when others were already running, deserting their barricade, became famous in Berlin. The list of the dead fighters also proves that people from the "laboring classes" paid the biggest prize. Not commanded, not forced to risk their life, by an officer or a government, but because they had chosen to fight.

285 This appears as factual and true to me even though workers in France knew and would say they were French, and workers in Germany would say they were German, and that Germany mattered to them. There exists a feeling of belonging to a place even in those who are no "nationalists." Nationalism was a very bourgeois and petty-bourgeois sentiment at the outset—and soon enough, an ideology with bourgeois meanings.

286 It could be interesting to compare the dress, posture, and visible attitude apparent in facial expression—thus, the expressed habitus—of these gentlemen with those traits we might decipher in a painting or engraving depicting a group of key American leaders in the 1790s or during the first decade of the 19th century. Let us remember why Bourdieu noted the significance of "habitus."

287 This is also what Georg Büchner (as a dramatist, the author of the most advanced plays written in the German language during the 19th century and also a revolutionary activist who had to flee his native Germany) had recognized. He expressed this insight in a letter to Gutzkow: "Das Verhältnis zwischen Armen und Reichen ist

das einzige revolutionäre Element in der Welt." [The rapport (relationship) between the poor and the rich is the only revolutionary element in the world.] See: Werner Meyer, ibidem, p.116.

288 Karl Marx, "Die Junirevolution" [The Revolution in June 1848], in: *Neue Rheinische Zeitung* [New Rhenanian Gazette], No. 28, June 1848, reprinted in: Karl Marx/ Friedrich Engels, *Werke* [MEW], Vol. 5, Berlin: Dietz Verlag, 1871, p. 133. Also online: http://www.mlwerke.de/me/me05/me05_133.htm.

289 See Ernest Mandel; George Novack, *The Revolutionary Potential of the Working Class*. New York (N.Y.) : Pathfinder press, 1974.

EPILOGUE

by ANDREAS WEILAND

1848 is so far back in time, almost forgotten—just like the Forty-Niners who left Europe after the defeat they had suffered—and with them, the countries they came from. The March Revolution in Prussia's capital, Berlin, in 1848 wasn't the only uprising in those two years of revolutionary turbulence, 1848–1849, and by no means the first one. But in the German context, it was tragic, I think, that it failed: it prefigured German history, in a decisive way, for years to come. There might never have been a German Empire, dominated at least initially—and to some extent also later—by an aristocratic stratum (or class?) of very big and also, for the most part, extremely conservative landowners[1] and all their sons and other relatives serving in key positions of the army and the bureaucracy.[2] These were people who soon found themselves coveted as precious political allies by emerging dynasties of industrialists, and by a commercial bourgeoisie coveting a "place in the sun"—most notably in parts of the African continent. And it was obviously this group that constituted the second important pillar of the dominant classes, soon even more important than the old landowning aristocracy, though coveting the "von" of the gentry.[3] Quite a few of them were in fact nobilitated, and the closeness of tycoons of heavy industry to German admirals and generals and bureaucrats proved both profitable and, in the end, disastrous.[4]

Whether a republic, in the hands of these same social forces, would have been less dangerous, less imperialist and less colonialist, is another matter. France, a bourgeois republic, certainly had its own imperialist stakes in Africa, South East Asia and the Pacific, and even the United States found its own imperialist role in the late 19th century when it attacked Spain, in order to possess Cuba and the Philippines and a few smaller islands.[5]

1848, as a turning point in German history, is a thing of the past. The class relations that had an impact on the outcome of the democratic revolution are not a matter of a bygone era, however—though it is clear that they evolved. The financial bourgeoisie that placed one of its own at the head of the Prussian government in the immediate wake of the armed struggle in Berlin found its worthy successors: firms stronger than ever today, in Germany,[6] despite the shabby and criminal role that the OMGUS files (OMGUS, Office of the Military Government—U.S. zone—in Germany) documents with regard to their role in the final years of the Weimar Republic when they furthered the ascent of Hitler's chauvinist, pseudo-socialist party, the National Socialist Party of Germany,[7] while Mr. Thyssen, the steel baron, boasted publicly in an American newspaper, that he was the man who bankrolled Hitler.[8] The steel barons, Krupp,[9] Thyssen, and Roechling,[10] had to face charges as war criminals for good reason in Nuremberg in 1946,[11] almost a hundred years after the March Revolution in Berlin. Those who were not condemned (and Mr. Thyssen was not condemned), did not stay in jail for long.[12] The Cold War prompted American authorities to let them off the hook, and these steel corporations that had not been nationalized, despite the fact that they had employed slave labor during the war, played a significant role in the restoration period of 1947–1965/66 in West Germany, a period that saw top personnel of the Third Reich in key functions in the Foreign Ministry, the armed forces, the foreign secret service, the inland secret service, the police, and the legal system, from the upper to the most local courts.[13]

In other words, the same social forces are still around that played a dubious role in 1848, when the democratic gains attained were quickly lost, due in large part to their ambivalence, and when those more comprehensive gains hoped for by many—gains that seemed close at hand—were not attained even briefly, because they were feared by the "liberal" bourgeoisie,

The question that 1848 poses for us, and that we must answer, and actually do answer, one way or another, by the way we relate to it, is quite clear. Was 1848, the revolution in March in Berlin, really a cul de sac, in historical terms? A mere waste of energy, senselessly spilled blood, all due to a "misunderstanding"—as the King of Prussia, Frederick William IV, claimed in one of his messages shortly after he suffered defeat during the days of battle in March, and as the rather conservative "moderate liberals" of the time, the Camphausens, Hansemanns, and their followers,[14] were gladly ready to believe?[15]

Their argument was quite clear: before the fighting erupted in the city, on March 18, the King had already promised what they—the conservative, propertied commoners[16] of Berlin (and of Prussia)—wanted: modest reforms; a convocation of the United Diet;[17] deliberations that would lead to a constitution; freedom of the press. That the majority of the population of Berlin and of Prussia might not obtain the right to vote, did not matter at all to most of these "moderate liberals." That the questions of extreme underemployment and unemployment, the food question, the housing question, the enormous misery that existed in the countryside and among the working people in the cities were not answered did not matter. "Progress is slow, incremental; believe in reforms, in evolution; all revolutions lead only to another hell." This was the implicit message. And it still is today.[18]

"We have to keep moving [...]," Sibylle Plogstedt, a fairly progressive[19] civil rights activist who can look back to a bad experience with post-Stalin East European étatisme in the defunct ČSSR in 1968, wrote quite recently in the

German journal Erziehung & Wissenschaft. "I believe we are capable of it, especially because 1968 was no revolution [she actually uses the term "Umsturz" that refers to an act of overthrowing the established order] but the beginning of slow change. For it is so that revolutions [literally, acts of overthrowing things; Umstürze] give raise to anxieties and resistance. Changes, occurring thanks to the self-organization of those concerned, are careful and much more effective. They pervade society in a sustainable way."[20]

Let me ask questions. Who are those who fear change, and why? Who are those who keep the ball rolling, and in what direction, and why? Is history the way many think it is—thus, evolutionary? Do we proceed and progress continually, perhaps held up only temporarily, perhaps slowed down at times, but still…? Is it thus as the evolutionists and reformers tell us—all those believers in inescapable progress, in advancement towards perfection? Surely, Sibylle Ploogstedt doesn't see it as something automatic; she thinks we have to work for it, and should get organized in an autonomous, self-determined way. But she shares the evolutionary concept with all those admirers of supposedly inescapable technical, social, and moral progress who follow in the footsteps of 19th century Social Darwinists who were so popular at the time—the 1880s, 1890s, and around 1900—in North America, in Europe, even in Japan and China.[21]

But is it a fact that we have to reckon with the incremental advance of humanity and thus society (or society, and thus humanity)? Was that the case up to now, and is it happening still, even now? Is it thus confirmed by history?

Or is progress a matter of "jumps," followed more often than not, by backlashes, by regression, and not just retardation?[22] In other words, a "dance of sorts—two steps ahead and one step back," as some maintain. And sometimes, a thousand steps back, into the hells of Auschwitz and Hiroshima?[23]

Marx, as far as I see, was aware of continuities; it was he who wrote, in *The 18th Brumaire of Louis Bonaparte*, on the occasion of the French events in 1852, that "[t]he tradition of all dead generations weighs like a nightmare on the brains of the living." History has been a matter of developments produced by man that brought advances in various fields, transforming social relations and affecting the forces of production. But belief systems, ideologies, traditions and institutions could reveal a strange inertia, an enduring stability for a long time, in fact for so long that they became anachronistic. Feudal relations in the Polish countryside were recognized by him as anachronistic in the late 1840s, and the remnants of feudal rights—and privileged political representation in the United Diet!—enjoyed by the Junker class in Prussia were no less anachronistic, as was the "Christian-Germanic" ideology of Frederick William IV and his refusal to accept a constitution.[24] And, in Marx's view, it was this overdue change that had to lead to radical, and often, quite sudden ruptures. He clearly was no evolutionist in that regard. Though he saw the necessity of radical change, he did not assume that change was a matter of some automatism. It had to be brought about by men who got actively involved in this project, a project that had to embrace, in its immediate perspective, the realization of democracy (and in the German context, also national unity in the form of a German republic).

Perhaps contrary to Marx, both liberal thinkers and Marxists shared, for a long time, the belief in human progress that must and will happen almost by itself.[25] It is the experience of unimagined catastrophes produced by man in the 20th century that has dampened many hopes and contributed to a more careful assessment of mankind's future. And this entails doubts. Thus, the doubt that there is only one way, one direction that is possible: forward! Forward became the name of the Social-Democratic party newspaper in 1876, and this not by chance. It revealed an optimism that is almost "North American." But is such optimism really justified?

There can be no question that the least we must say, if we shy away from utter pessimism, is this: that the future is open-ended. We may well continue to embrace projects of justice, equality, and comprehensive human emancipation—thus the goal of Menschwerdung des Menschen, the humanization of mankind, the vision that man, not yet humane enough, can become fully human if the effort is made, if social conditions become more apt to support his/her humanization. It is a vision—a humane vision, no more and no less. And there are no guarantees, and there exists no prefigured path, no security, no road map. We can only hope, and work in a direction which will lead us into unknown, uncharted territory.

Endnotes

[1] As Eichholtz shows, this stratum or "class" formed links to the evolving financial bourgeoisie quite early, despite their conservatism. Bent on grain exports from East Elbian regions of Prussia, they were in need of traffic connections by rail and steamboat. See Dietrich Eichholtz, *Junker und Bourgeoisie vor 1848 in der preussischen Eisenbahngeschichte*: Über das Verhältnis zwischen Junkern und Bourgeoisie vor 1848 in der preussischen Eisenbahngeschichte. Berlin: Akademie-Verlag, 1962. Often in need of credit due to intended "ameliorations," the landed aristocracy also formed commercial links to mortgage lenders; but these links as well as those to international grain merchants must rather be interpreted in terms of their dependence on them, whereas railroad speculators and exporting *junkers* had a similar political agenda with respect to proposed railroad lines that required consent of the government.

[2] See Hans Rosenberg, *Bureaucracy and Aristocracy: The Prussian Experience, 1660-1815*. Cambridge, Mass.: Harvard University Press, 1958 ; see also J.R. Gillis. *The Prussian Bureaucracy in Crisis, 1840-1860 : Origins of an Administrative Ethos*. Stanford : Stanford University Press, 1971.

[3] The term gentry, in this book, is always used for the German term "niederer Adel" (lower aristocracy, or lower nobility). It is of course a very British term, but more comfortable to use than "lower nobility" or "lower ranks of the nobility."

[4] See François-Emmanuel Brézet, *Le plan Tirpitz (1897-1914) : une flotte de combat allemande contre l'Angleterre*. Paris : Librairie de l'Inde Ed., 1993. ISBN 2-905455-21-7; see also Rolf Hobson, *Imperialism at Sea : Naval Strategic Thought, the Ideology of Sea Power, and the Tirpitz Plan, 1875 - 1914*. Boston: Brill, 2002. Also relevant in this regard: Eckart Kehr, *Economic Interest, Militarism, and Foreign Policy : essays on German history*. Edited and with an introduction by Gordon A. Craig ; translated by Grete Heinz. Berkeley: University of California Press, 1977.

[5] See Richard H. Collin, *Theodore Roosevelt, Culture, Diplomacy, and Expansion: A New View of American Imperialism*. Baton Rouge: Louisiana State Univ. Press 1985; see Jeffrey H. Wallenfeldt, *U.S. Imperialism and Progressivism: 1896 to 1920*. New York : Britannica Educational Publ. in association with Rosen Educational Services, 2013. See also Matthew McCullough, *The Cross of War: Christian Nationalism and US Expansion in the Spanish American War*. Madison, Wisc.: University of Wisconsin Press, 2014; and see Frank R. Villafaña, *Expansionism : Its Effects on Cuba's Independence*. London : Routledge, 2017.

[6] The biggest of these inheritors of the financial capitalist past that produced Rhineland-based bankers like David Hansemann in the 1830s and 1840s, is *Deutsche Bank*, the bank accused of shady practices in the context of the U.S. subprime mortgage lending crisis by the city of Cleveland. See Karen Pierog, "Cleveland Sues 21 Banks Over Mortgage Foreclosures" (Reuters, Jan 14m 2008), https://www.reuters.com/article/sppage012-n11294432-oisbn-idUSN1129443220080114 See also Steve Schifferes, "Foreclosure Wave Sweeps America," BBC NEWS, Nov. 5, 2007. URL http://news.bbc.co.uk/2/hi/business/7070935.st . – With regard to Deutsche Bank, see also the files of the U.S. Military Government in Germany (OMGUS files) on Hermann Joseph Abs, a key figure of Deutsche Bank during the Nazi's Third Reich. The files were published in German by Greno Publishers: O.M.G.U.S.: *H[ermann] J. Abs im Dritten Reich : Mitglied des Vorstands der Deutschen Bank. Mitglied des Aufsichtsrats der I.G. Farben. [Mitglied des Aufsichtsrats der Dresdner Bank.]*. Nördlingen: Greno,

1985. After the war, Hermann Joseph Abs became the key advisor of Konrad Adenauer, the first prime minister of West Germany. Mr. Globke, a key Nazi, also became an important adviser, and Mr. Gehlen, another key Nazi, continued as a secret service man (as before, under Hitler) when he was entrusted by Adenauer (or the American government) with the constructed of a German secret service which he headed for many years. The secret service and the police, also staffed largely by former Nazis, began to arrest Leftist concentration camp survivors in the 1950s and they were usually condemned to prison terms by judges who had already faithfully served the Nazi regime. At the same time, the State's district attorneys, police, and judges looked the other way for decades when they could have arrested key figures involved in the genocide and war crimes committed by the regime, even though the whereabouts of these persons were known to public authorities.

[7] See IMSF (ed.), *Bericht über die Ermittlungen in bezug auf die Deutsche Bank* [Report on the Investigations Regarding Deutsche Bank, Nov. 1946. German translation of the report of the U.S. Military Government issued in Nov. 1946.] / [ed. by the Institut für Marxistische Studien und Forschungen e. V. (IMSF), Frankfurt on Main, 1971 (=The OMGUS files; OMGUS = Office of the Military Government (U.S. zone) in Germany); see also *Ermittlungen gegen die Deutsche Bank : 1946/1947 / Militärregierung d. Vereinigten Staaten für Deutschland, Finanzabt., Sekt. für Finanzielle Nachforschungen.* [Übersetzt und bearbeitet von der Dokumentationsstelle zur NS-Politik, Hamburg]. Nördlingen: Greno, 1985. ISBN 3-921568-66-8; and see: Christopher Simpson (ed.), *War crimes of the Deutsche Bank and the Dresdner Bank : Office of Military Government (US) reports.* Ed. and with an introd. by Christopher Simpson. New York ; London : Holmes and Meier, 2001. ISBN 0-8419-1407-9. - See also Christoph Weisz, *OMGUS-Handbuch, die amerikanische Militärregierung in Deutschland 1945–1949.* München: Oldenbourg, 1994. – Abs was not the only one who claimed to be innocent and kind of neutral, preserving 'clean hands' due to occasional "good deeds." We may say that the Swiss bankers who financed Nazi aggression against the Soviet Union when Hitler Germany was bankrupt, were also no Nazis; they simply preferred good business opportunities and probably liked the idea that an anti-Bolshevik bulwark existed in Germany. An attack on the Soviet Union was desired by many who were no Nazis. See: Adam LeBor, *Hitler's Secret Bankers : the Myth of Swiss Neutrality during the Holocaust.* Secaucus NJ: Carol Publ. Group, 1997. See also: Adam LeBor, *Hitler's Secret Bankers : How Switzerland Profited from Nazi Genocide.* New York: Pocket 1999. ISBN 0-671-03395-6. (Paperback edition of the book originally published in 1997). And also: Jean Ziegler, *The Swiss, the Gold, and the Dead.* New York: Harcourt Brace 1998. And: Isabel Vincent, *Hitler's Silent Partners: Swiss Banks, Nazi Gold, and the Pursuit of Justice.* New York: Morrow 1997. ISBN 0-688-15425-5. See also: Bettina Zeugin and Thomas Sandkühler, *Die Schweiz und die deutschen Lösegelderpressungen in den besetzten Niederlanden: Vermögensentziehung, Freikauf, Austausch 1940-1945 : Beitrag zur Forschung.* Zürich : Chronos, 2001. ISBN 3-0340-0624-1. (Veröffentlichungen der Unabhängigen Expertenkommission Schweiz, Zweiter Weltkrieg / Commission indépendante d'experts Suisse-Seconde guerre mondiale; Vol. 24)

[8] See Henry Ashby Turner, "Fritz Thyssen und 'I Paid Hitler,'" in: Vierteljahrshefte für Zeitgeschichte, Vol. 19, No. 3 (1971), pp. 225-244. See also: Fritz Thyssen, *I paid Hitler.* Translated from the original manuscript by César Saerchinger. London: Hodder and Stoughton, 1941.

9   In 1950, a baron (in German, Freiherr), the Freiherr von Wilmowsky, referred to the condemnation of the German steel industry's most important tycoon, Mr. Krupp, in the Nuremberg trial of major Nazi war criminals as an error based on legends and as a "miscarriage of justice" (Justizirrtum). The old affinities and the correspondence of interests that developed in the course of the antidemocratic and anti-republican coalition of aristocrats and members of the *haute bourgeoisie* since the 1840s still seemed to come into play, despite the horrendous defeat these supporters of Hitler's ascent to power had suffered in 1945. See Tilo, Freiherr von Wilmowsky, *Warum wurde Krupp verurteilt?* [Why was Krupp condemned?] Stuttgart : Vorwerk, 1950. Of course, Stuttgart, the capital of Baden-Württemberg, was the best place to publish the book. It was the region that produced Kurt Georg Kiesinger, the German "Christian Democratic" Prime Minister (Chancellor or Bundeskanzler) of West Germany who was slapped in public by Beate Klarsfeld in 1968 because of his Nazi past (he was not only a Nazi party member in 1933 but had joined the Nazi Foreign Ministry in 1940), and it was the home of Filbinger, the "Christian Democratic" Prime Minister of Baden Württemberg, who had condemned four members of the Nazi-German navy to death (and had three of them executed) as a military judge and condemned at least one other soldier in his capacity as a superior in Norway while he and the soldier he condemned were already British prisoners of war in the Oslo region. The reason the soldier was condemned was that he had called him a "Nazi dog."

10 See for instance the Röchling biography of the German aristocrat Wolfgang von Hippel, *Hermann Röchling 1872–1955: Ein deutscher Großindustrieller zwischen Wirtschaft und Politik: Facetten eines Lebens in bewegter Zeit* [Herman Roechling, 1872–1955 – A Big German Industrialist Involved in Business and Politics: Facets of a Life in Turbulent Times]. Göttingen: Vandenhoek & Ruprecht, 2018 (1,100 pages!) – It is certainly a euphemism to refer to the period of Nazi aggression and genocide as "turbulent times!"

11 See Annette Wieviorka (ed.), *Les procès de Nuremberg et de Tokyo* / [organisé par le Mémorial de Caen et le CNRS, CRHQ]. Sous la dir. de Annette Wieviorka. Textes de Kentaro Awaya et al. Bruxelles: Versaile Ed. 2010. ISBN 2-87495-121-8.

12 See Donald McKale, *Nazis after Hitler : How Perpetrators of the Holocaust Cheated Justice and Truth.* Lanham, Md. ; Boulder, Colo. ; New York, NY ; Toronto ; Plymouth, UK : Rowman & Littlefield 2014. ISBN 978-1-4422-1317-3. – Klaus Barbie, the slaughterer who tortured and murdered the hero of the French resistance, Jean Moulin, when he was Gestapo boss in Lyon, was released from a French prison shortly after the war, due to U.S. pressure, and worked for the American military occupation government in Southern Germany as a "hunter of communists." Adolf Eichmann, a key figure in the genocidal murder of six million human beings labeled "Jews" (an undertaking that relied, largely, on files that traced their Jewish descent, targeting people bureaucratically and extremely effectively, by using IBM punch cards, and this regardless of whether they considered themselves to be Jewish) was aided in his escape to Argentine and became a key sales representative of Mercedes-Benz in Buenos Aires after the war. His whereabout must have been known to the German embassy in that city and to the Israeli government. It was only due to the activity of a courageous Argentinian citizen of Jewish descent that the Israeli government saw itself finally compelled to abduct Eichmann and put him on trial in Jerusalem. It is not clear why they hesitated for so long. That Eichmann and Barbie, but also industrialists charged with war crimes like Krupp, Thyssen, and Röchling were left off the hook soon

after the end of World War II, lets us see no more than the tip of the iceberg. There are far more outrageous examples that could be added.

13 See Rolf Badstübner and Siegfried Thomas, Restauration und Spaltung: Entstehung und Entwicklung der BRD 1945-1955. Köln : Pahl-Rugenstein 1975, 512 pp.; see also Gilbert Krebs (ed.), *L'Allemagne de Konrad Adenauer : rénovation et restauration en République Fédérale d'Allemagne entre 1949 et 1966* ; études / réunis et publiées par Gilbert Krebs. Centre de Recherches sur la Société Allemande aux XIX. et XX. Siècles. Asnières : Institut d'Allemand Université de la Sorbonne Nouvelle 1982, and see Eckart Spoo, in cooperation with Arno Klönne (eds.), *Tabus der bundesdeutschen Geschichte*. Hannover : Ossietzky 2006. ISBN 3-9808137-4-6.

14 To critical minds, it was apparent that Conservative Liberals like Camphausen and David Hansemann were intent on using the constitution they desired—and constitutional government—as a shield against the masses exposed to misery. And misery had many faces, at the time: it entailed a long work day of 14 to 16 hours, starving wages, high food prices, inadequate housing conditions, job insecurity, frequent underemployment and joblessness, denial of the right to vote, paternalistic relations between bosses and the employed, police arrogance and brutality, and surveillance. It mattered to the bourgeoisie to protect existing property relations against those denounced in dominant discourse as "plunderers," "thieves" and the likes—in other words, as "the mob," or if we want to express it more soberly, the subaltern classes, should they put existing property relations in question. See also Part III of the book *Constitutionalism, legitimacy, and power*, dedicated to the use of constitutions as stabilizing factors serving the preservation of existing property relations. Here, the article of Olivier Beaud matters very much [Olivier Beaud, "Constitution, Ownership, and Human Rights", in: Kelly L. Grotke and Markus J. Prutsch (eds.), *Constitutionalism, legitimacy, and power*. Oxford, UK: Oxford University Press, 2014, pp.127-142]. Olivier Beaud focuses on the interest of "owners" to see "property" constitutionally protected. In other words, it is necessary to see that in revolutionary and immediate post-revolutionary contexts, the constitution becomes the ideological expression and thus "justification" of the maintenance of "law and order" by the armed might of the constitutional monarchy (or bourgeois republic, as in Paris on June 23–26, 1848)—by its army, national guard, or police who will know how to deal with violations of legality. The *socio-economic and thus, civil rights* of hungry and dispossessed masses remain outside the scope of constitutional order and legality, whereas the State protects the "human rights" of "owners" to own property, to engage in business, to accumulate capital and to exploit wage labor in the context of a mode of production that subsumes use value to value of exchange and the real needs of people to the necessity of producing for the sake of maximizing profit.

15 Not only Camphausen, Hansemann, Auerswald, and von Pfuel but all of the "liberal" constitutional monarchists believed in legitimacy and embraced the project of a constitution for this very reason. And for them, the king was legitimate, the center of legitimacy they did not want to break with. In other words, they did not believe in revolution and that the "people" are the sovereign and the center and source of all legitimacy. Marx critiqued this anti-people stance already in 1848, whereas August Brass—like many progressive liberal democrats—was wishy-washy. He did not want to disown the revolution he had fought in; but neither did he want to break with the legitimacy that was rooted in the King and the Prussian monarchic political system. A liberal republican approach to these questions is

discussed in Paul W. Kahn, Legitimacy and History: Self-Government in American Constitutional Theory. New Haven: Yale University Press, 1992. Here, as in the U.S. constitution and French constitutions adopted ever since the revolution of 1789, the basic premise is the sovereignty of the people. This was well-recognized by King Frederick William IV and his key advisers, like Radowitz. As Dirk Blasius writes, it was already the German historian Leopold von Ranke, who identified "resistance against changes of the form of the State and society [...] [as] 'the constant feature of the politics of the king'." (Dirk Blasius, Friedrich Wilhelm IV. 1795-1861: Psychopathologie und Geschichte [Frederick William IV, 1795-1861: Psychopathology and History]. Göttingen: Vandenhoeck & Ruprecht, 1992; the quotation used by Blasius is from Leopold von Ranke, "Friedrich Wilhelm IV, König von Preußen," in: Allgemeine Deutsche Biographie [General German Biography], Vol. 7. Leipzig 1878, pp. 729-776; the historian L. von Ranke belonged to the (inner?) circle of the king.) This is why they rejected every type of constitution and constitutionalism so vehemently. But then, under pressure by the "force des choses," they were compelled to adopt the ploy of imposing a constitution they could no longer avoid, writing it in a way that would protect the power of the king and of the hitherto dominant social forces as much as possible while trying to minimize the role that "ordinary commoners" could play in politics. See Felix Rachfahl, Deutschland, König Friedrich Wilhelm IV. und die Berliner Märzrevolution [Germany, King Fredrick William IV and the Berlin March Revolution]. Bremen: DOGMA in Europäischer Hochschulverlag 2013, especially pp.52-53 (with respect to the decidedly anti-constitutionalist position of the king and Radowitz). See also Volker Sellin, "Restorations and Constitutions," in: Kelly L. Grotke and Markus J. Prutsch (eds.), Constitutionalism, Legitimacy, and Power: Nineteenth-Century Experiences. Oxford: Oxford University Press 2014, pp. 84-103. In Part II, the book edited by Grotke and Prutsch discusses "Constitutions as Anti-Revolutionary Devices"—thus also in an article by Anna Gianna Manca on the Italian experience ("State Building by Means of Constitution in the Italian Constitutional Monarchy"), and especially in the very relevant article by Volker Sellin ("Restorations and Constitutions"). It is pointed out that, quite obviously, constitutions can be used after revolutionary upheavals by the powers that be in an attempt to consolidate the relations of

16 The use of "the "commoners" did not mean, at the time, that the very rich, the rich, and the fairly well-off commoners (in other words, members of the bourgeoisie) were part of "the common people": it meant, in this period, that they—as members of the bourgeoisie—were second class citizens in comparison with the aristocracy. They shared this quality with members of the petty-bourgeoisie, and with the wage-earners in the towns. Most peasants who were not even fully free to move and settle elsewhere, because they owed the lord of the manor certain services, can be considered as even less emancipated than the types of commoners referred to. A "serf" or someone who had hardly escaped that status, or had not fully succeeded to shake it off, was not even a commoner.

17 Commoners and perhaps aristocrats, as well, had for long hoped that a representative body would be convocated by the King. It was in 1847 that the United Diet (a joint meeting of the delegates of the eight Diets or "parliaments" of all provinces of Prussia) had been finally convocated for the first time, and this in order to consent to new taxes in view of the government's (and the King's) financial problems. Nothing was attained, and the King dissolved the United Diet,

showing little interest in convening it again, even though such popular demands were voiced. For the bourgeoisie, tax questions were significant, but it also desired to deliberate—and be heard—with regard to other questions.

18 With regard to the discursive positions featuring images of evolution and evolutionism in antagonistic political debates, and the modes of using these images, see: "Le imagerie de l'evolutionnisme", in: Pierre Bourdieu and Luc Boltanski, "La production de l'idéologie dominante," In : Actes de la Recherche en Sciences Sociales, Vol. 2, no. 2-3 (1976), pp. 3-73, here : pp.40f.

19 It matters of course to understand that the term progressive is a wishy-washy, extremely ideological term. Technocrats, capitalists—even fascists—all believe in "progress." On the left, the term "progress" is also considered to be appropriate, and "progressive" is used as an antonym of reactionary. It is in this sense that the term is used here, implying that S. Ploogstedt is by no means a reactionary, even if the author of this text disagrees with her.

20 Sibylle Ploogstedt, in "Wir müssen am Ball bleiben [We must keep the ball rolling]," Interview with Sibylle Ploogstedt, interviewer: Anja Dilk, in Erziehung und Wissenschaft, Zeitschrift der Bildungsgewerkschaft GEW, May, 2018, subsection *Dialogue*,2/2018, p.4.

21 The works of thinkers like Herbert Spencer, John Burgess, W. G. Sumner and John Fiske were widely read and uncritically received at the time. The most cynical and most dangerous branch of this ideology was constituted by fascism since the 1920s, and the war of aggression of Hitler Germany, the Nazi death camps as sites of genocide, and also Japanese militarism and its acts of aggression, particularly against China and against the United States, were a direct consequence. Social Darwinist thought is still implicitly at work in North American society with its widely shared believe in endless advance and progression, and there are even those who see man becoming "godlike," which is a particularly interesting aspect of this *basically secular* technological and progressist ideology. Another aspect of the Social Darwinist current is of course the modern North American version of the assumption that the population of the U.S.A., or at least its more WASPish segment, constitutes from the very beginning god's chosen people and that it has every right to pillage the world and use up about 60 per cent of the planet's resources (according to, admittedly, not very recent, but at any rate post WWII statistics).

22 See Rossana Rossanda, Über die Dialektik von Kontinuität und Bruch: Zur Kritik revolutionärer Erfahrungen—*Italien, Frankreich, Sowjetunion, Polen, China, Chile*. [On the Dialectics of Continuity and Rupture: Critique of Revolutionary Experiences—Italy, France, Soviet Union, Poland, China, Chile.] Frankfurt : Suhrkamp, 1975. Habermas refers to the concept of a dialectics of continuity and rupture ("dialettica di continuita e rottura"), too. See Jürgen Habermas, *La rivoluzione in corso*. Milano : Feltrinelli, 1990, p. 53. (German edition: Jürgen Habermas, *Die nachholende Revolution*. Frankfurt : Suhrkamp, 1990.)

23 See Günter Anders, *Die Antiquiertheit des Menschen. Part 2: Über die Zerstörung des Lebens im Zeitalter der dritten industriellen Revolution*. [The Antiquatedness (or Obsolescence) of Man: About the Destruction of Life in the Age of the Third Industrial Revolution], 3rd edition. Munich: C.H. Beck, 2002. And see John Christoph Müller. *Prometheanism: Technology, Digital Culture and Human Obsolescence*. [With a translation of the essay "On Promethean Shame", by Günther Anders.] London: Rowman & Littlefield, 2016. See likewise: Konrad Paul Liessmann, "Reflexión después de Auschwitz e Hiroshima: Günther Anders

y Hannah Arendt [Thought after Auschwitz and Hiroshima: Günther Anders and Hannah Arendt]", in: Enrahonar: Quadernos de Filosofía (Universitat Autónoma de Barcelona), no. 46 (2011), pp.123-135. See also Harold Marcuse, "Günther Anders. Journalist, Philosopher, Essayist" (a page by Harold Marcuse, Professor at UC Santa Barbara). URL http://www.history.ucsb.edu/faculty/marcuse/anders.htm . Accessed May 21, 2018 2:44 PM. – Theodor W. Adorno was likewise convinced that Auschwitz constituted a watershed in human history, a deep fall into an unfathomable abyss. According to him, poetry was no longer possible "after Auschwitz." – Mariuccia Salvati has referred to "the modernity [that was] 'realized'" or achieved by Auschwitz, and to the fact that Auschwitz also constituted a "preannouncement of the past." In doing so, she refers us specifically to Walter Benjamin and Benjamin's *Geschichtsphilosophische Thesen* (Tesi di filosofia della storia), commenting: "Si tratta di un punto di vista in cui la dialettica tra continuità e rottura con il passato, implicita nell'evento Auschwitz, sembra scalzare alla base quella che nel Novecento è stata la più seria risposta storiografica alla crisi dello storicismo positivista e cioè la prospettiva della 'lunga durata': come è stato osservato, essa sembra particolarmente impotente a coglierne il carattere di rottura improvvisa e irreversibile dello sterminio ebraico [...]." [This is a point of view according to which the dialectics between continuity and rupture with the past, implicit in the event of Auschwitz, seems to fundamentally undermine what was the most serious historiographical response to the crisis of positivist historicism, and that is the *longue durée* perspective: as has been observed, it seems particularly incapable of grasping the sudden and irreversible character of the extermination of Jews.] Mariuccia Salvati, "Il Novecento," in: Claudio Pavone (ed.), *Novecento: I tempi della storia.* [The 20th century: The tempos of history], Roma: Donzelli Editore (Universale Donzelli) 1997, pp.40f. See also: Walter Benjamin, *Geschichtsphilosophische Thesen.* [Schulbuchausgabe für Japan aus Walter Benjamin : Schriften, 1955 (Documenta nova, 5)]. - Osaka, 1967, and Walter Benjamin, *Werke und Nachlaß: kritische Gesamtausgabe*; Vol 19: Über den Begriff der Geschichte [On the Concept of History]. Berlin : Suhrkamp, 2017.

[24] In fact, it is possible to speak of a contradiction between a fairly advanced early-capitalist development that was affecting Germany in the towns and in the countryside by 1848, and political forms that reflected the anachronistically preserved privileges of once feudal social forces, namely, the aristocracy. In the towns, small-scale production was still constituting the most important sector, but it was subject to qualitative change, due to the parallel existence of "manufakturen" (pre-industrial centralized as well as decentralized manufactories) and a small, but fast expanding modern industrial sector that developed especially in the larger cities like Berlin and Cologne. To the impact of the latter on small-scale production and thus on profits and wages in this sector—and the livelihood of all those active in small-scale workshop-based "industry"—must be added such other factors as the growth of a modern financial sector, the transportation revolution thanks to steamboats on major rivers and to railway construction (financed by speculating financial capitalists), and the modernization that was undoubtedly occurring in a largely export-oriented agricultural sector—the wheat-producing large estates of East Elbian *junkers*, a stratum that succeeded to produce, despite its political conservatism, the beginnings of socially disturbing and uprooting agrarian capitalist change in the countryside. It was exactly the ongoing dissolution of feudal remnants (and the concomitant payments and forfeiture of part of the land they owned, but could not consider as modern "property"), that resulted in

increased pauperization and misery in the countryside and occasioned a stream of vagrants and beggars that added to those seeking work in the cities, especially in the context of the economic crisis of the late 1840s that was aggravated by crop failures and steeply rising food prices.

25 The concept of *progress* figures among the concepts singled out by Bourdieu and Boltanski because of their ideological significance or ideological character. See Pierre Bourdieu and Luc Boltanski, "La production de l'idéologie dominante," In : *Actes de la Recherche en Sciences Sociales*, Vol. 2, no. 2-3 (1976), pp. 3-73, here : p.28.

LAST WORDS

by PETER LIGHT

I started my Foreword by telling how I had grown up hearing the bare-bones about my great-grandfather August Brass. Now, after many years of being involved with this book and with Andreas Weiland—so much more than my translator—I feel that Brass has grown up for me, from those bare-bones into a somewhat fleshed out human being.

Both merits and flaws emerged.

I have become very impressed with him as a writer; with the courage of his convictions; with the risks he took and the observations he made. I was also impressed, but surprised, by his constant attempts at fairness—by granting to the soldiers their humanness, by being able to feel compassion for them and their suffering; even by trying to see things from the point of view of the king. Shades of Gandhi, despite the guns!

I was disappointed, however, to see him so obsequious towards the king, so fooled by him, so convinced of his honesty. I was also disappointed to see how history has finally judged him, because of his relationship with Bismarck. I think it may be a shallow treatment of a whole human being, and a superficial understanding of that part of his life.

But I never met the man.

I've never met Andreas, either, but as with Brass, I have met his writing. To a remarkable degree, [we] share an activist background, many of the same thoughts, a similar radical analysis, the same deeply felt sorrows for the pain felt by so many around the world. He clings to hope more than I do, and is still attached to the idea of successful revolutionary change, so suffers more than I do at the insanity of the words and actions we both tune into daily. So we have some divergences in our thinking. I had come to know of them through our personal correspondence; they were made evident again as I read his brilliant Introduction and Epilogue for this book. The rest of this "Afterword" is comprised of some of my ideas on the same subjects that concern him, to do with the state of the world, and the possibilities of positive change—thoughts that I articulate to suggest other less gloomy and oppressive ways to view these matters.

As Andreas Weiland has indicated, the fact that the 1848 German Revolution failed needs to be put into the context of the failure of all of the other uprisings that swept across Europe one after another that year—affecting 56 countries—and of all the uprisings that came before and after. The earlier French Revolution produced a bloodbath and Napoleon;

the earlier American Revolution was a phony one if ever there was one, fought *for* the rich elite, *by* the hoodwinked poor that those elites had been oppressing, and *against* British rule for narrow economic self-interests; and which elites, once victorious, thanks to the spilled blood of those hapless downtrodden, returned immediately to oppressing them again (see A People's History of America by Howard Zinn); the 1918–1919 German revolution was accompanied by a litany of compromises and sellouts; the Russian and Chinese revolutionaries betrayed their principles and the people, and were responsible for some of the most inhuman crimes against humanity ever committed; the Cuban revolution, though in many ways a successful revolution, fell short of the full ideals of freedom, equality, and democracy; and, in somewhat of a stark contrast, the recent Arab Spring soon collapsed into an Arab winter.

Even Gandhi's revolution failed, producing a nonviolent Nehru who, as free India's first Prime Minister, armed his country with nuclear weapons. Nothing could better illustrate the maxim "power tends to corrupt and absolute power corrupts absolutely," and the fact that ideological politics and Realpolitik are two very different things.

Becoming aware of, examining, and then analyzing these examples, and no doubt many others, however, may not necessarily mean that if we peer closely enough at them we might come to understand the causes of their failures in enough detail to increase the chances "next time" of successfully bringing about the humanitarian world we wish for. It may lead, instead, to the perhaps simpler and more obvious conclusion: that revolutions in the streets almost never bring about the radical changes espoused and hoped for; that the leaders of these uprisings always tend to become corrupted by power; and that the constant failures are indications [changed order] that doing something over and over again that hasn't worked is called insanity.

Coming back to the focus of our book, recalling the ideals fought for, and cognizant of all the failures of that year in Europe—the betrayals and re-entrenchment of reactionary forces—might also jar us to the surprising realization that despite those 1848 failures, many of the changes demanded and fought for—civil rights, more social and economic freedom—in jurisdiction after jurisdiction, *relative to what came before*, and allowing for the inevitable ups and downs of social change, *nevertheless came to pass*: borders shifted; ruling monarchies became a thing of the past; independent states were created; economies were liberalized; greater democracy began to flourish, as did free speech, free press, and freedom of religion; the emancipation of the peasant began, as did the improvement of the condition of the workers; famine and disease became less common and were mostly held in check; and in many places, socialist policies were adopted.

Even in modern China and Russia, despite what the propaganda of Western media would lead us to believe, many of these betterments, albeit within clear limits, are enjoyed by the citizens of these two countries.

We might then ask ourselves, "How can this be?"

Steven Pinker, in his magnum opus *The Better Angels of Our Nature, A History of Violence and Humanity*, has exhaustively and, I think, convincingly shown that the movement *towards* civilization, stable nation-states, and present day modernity—and *from* prehistoric times, hunter-gatherers, and hunter-agriculturalist and other tribal groups—has been inexorably accompanied by a reduction of violence of all kinds, whether on the scale of millennia, centuries, decades, or years; and whether speaking of wars, torture, terrorism, homicides, assaults, rapes, spanking children, cruelty to animals, the treatment of women, or intolerance and violence directed at gays and people of color. After documenting this decline in the first 579 pages, he then, first, discusses what he refers to as the "inner demons" that propel us to act cruelly and violently; and then "the better angels of our nature: the psychological faculties that steer us away from violence, and whose increased engagement over time can be credited for declines in violence." The exploration of these faculties, says Pinker, "must show not only how they steer us away from violence, but why they so often fail to do so; not just how they have been increasingly engaged, but why history had to wait so long to engage them fully."

The "inner demons" he enumerates are predation, dominance, revenge, sadism, and ideology; the "better angels" he discusses are empathy, self-control, morality and taboo, and reason.

In the final chapter, "On Angels' Wings," he first notes some important but inconsistent forces that one might have thought *would* be important—important to the processes ("the Pacification Process," "the Civilizing Process"); the "peaces," ("the Long Peace," "the New Peace") and revolutions ("the Humanitarian Revolution," "the Rights Revolutions")—but turn out to not have been. Those forces, he says, are not minor, but have not *consistently* worked to reduce violence. Those forces are weaponry and disarmament; resources and power; affluence; and religion.

(Notably, nowhere does Pinker link the humanization trend—the overall reduction of violence in human history—to citizen campaigns, nonviolent actions, mass uprisings, planned revolutions, or armed insurgencies. That may be due to an oversight, his biases, or an absence of any such links, but I admit to being puzzled by the lack of any discussion in this regard.)

Then, in light of the history and psychology he has covered, Pinker identifies five developments that he contends "*have* [emphasis mine] pushed the world in a peaceful direction" and have allowed our better angels to start winning the upper hand, developments he has titled: The Leviathan; Gentle Commerce; Feminization; The Expanding Circle (of sympathy); and The Escalator of Reason. The first two refer to, one, the move towards states that use a monopoly of force to protect its citizens from each other; and, two, the move towards the growing profitability of mutual cooperation. The meaning of the other three are obvious.

I think, Andreas, that it is these four angels, riding the turbulent thermal winds of five historical developments, that "up to now" have been propelling the, yes, *evolution* of the aspect of history we are talking about here. I think Pinker shows that it *is*, as you asked, "confirmed by history," that we *have*, as you wonder, been proceeding and progressing continually, "incrementally... slowed down at times," and *also* in "jumps...backlashes...regressions...two steps ahead and one step back...even a thousand steps back." Yes, the indicator lines are often zig-zags—but the overall trend in all cases is down.

Perhaps the importance of revolutionary uprisings or any other manifestation of citizen concern— large or small, violent or nonviolent, left or right—is not that they immediately succeed, *but that they simply occur*. Their principal value may be as signals of the sentiments of sections of the population, markers on a movement towards a different world, reflections of the degree to which changes in people's and societies' attitudes have *already* occurred.

Demands for "change now" are always resisted by rulers and bosses. Nobody likes to be told they *have to* do something; everybody resents being ordered around. Why would we think that people in positions of authority would react any differently? Why wouldn't we think that they might dig in their heels? Chogyam Trumpa once said that he thought that the anti-Vietnam war protests may have *prolonged* the war.

While *no* human enjoys being forced to do anything, whether it is someone living on a street corner or in a castle, the higher you are, the further you fall. Street people may look at the cop sullenly, but they have little power and little to lose, so they move on to another corner. There are fewer castles for a King to move to, much more to lose, and greater danger and change to fear. The poor sullen soul wishes he had the power to say no; the rich and powerful do. And do!

Andreas asks, "Who are those who fear change, and why?" Most of us, I would reply, though less so as young adults first defining ourselves, who haven't lived long enough to have embedded ourselves in our own matrixes, to have wrapped ourselves in our own lifestyles and cloaks of conformity. Once we have, most of us who feel comfortable and secure with our beliefs, our behaviors, our jobs, our lifestyles, are going to feel uncomfortable if told we might have to alter any of them.

Yet changes do occur, of course, and over the course of the last 17,000 years; furthermore, they have shown, no matter the ups and downs, an inexorable movement towards humans treating all other sentient beings better and better—progress, that Pinker argues, has, relatively speaking, resulted in us living in the best time in human history.

He emphasizes rates—numbers per 100,000—showing, correctly, how they are much more important than absolute numbers. Knowing that his findings and scholarship would produce incredulity, not to mention defensiveness and anger, he says that he has had to take over a 1000 pages to prove his point and convince the reader. I think that it is an important book. It is a healthy correction for all of us who have been fueled by a belief that the world is getting worse and worse. Yet it is possible to accept and even embrace and celebrate his presentation of the facts of the matter, and his conclusions, while at the same time continuing to be appalled by the amount of violence and injustice that still exists. Instead of being motivated by the belief that everything is going to hell in a handbasket, we can be encouraged to continue the good fight with some degree of optimism because of the gains we have made, and despite the distance still to go.

(I think, on the other hand, that the broader modernity that Pinker extols brings with it unique problems that threaten humans in unprecedented ways and numbers, but here is not the place for that discussion.)

Perhaps "freedom for, and freedom from," then, comes down to intrinsic human traits and major historical stages and developments that are then manifested through individual expression of values, sentiments, and behaviors rooted in our "better angels," and that it is this that shifts us, measure by measure, towards the development of—and on behalf of "the people," I reclaim the phrase—a kinder and gentler world.

Today, most barricades are those erected by governments—to keep people in or out, whether walls to bar refugees, or police lines to kettle demonstrators.

Today, the only revolution that at times has shown a significant degree of success has been, ironically, the one conducted by ISIS in the Middle East!

Today, no uprising of *any* sort can or will bring about the critical improvements that are absolutely necessary because there is no movement, no NGO, certainly no government, and, indeed, virtually no voice that comes close to articulating and campaigning for the most radical, fundamental changes necessary to solve, or even make inroads into solving, humanity's many problems: an end to, and reversal of, economic growth; and an end to, and reversal of, population growth. These are the two elephants in the global room. And there may even be only one, because it seems as though capitalist expansion, at least from the Industrial Revolution onwards, demands always more people, needed as workers and consumers. I have come to think that perhaps that is why over-population, once very much on the table, isn't anymore.

Even more particularly, it seems clear to me that the biggest driver of the capitalist beast is the shareholder, demanding a good, steady return on his buck. It may be simplistic in the extreme to suggest that all of the world's problems are predicated on him, but it certainly is true that almost all are at least *exacerbated* by the two elephants and their masters. But often size alone, in many cases—perhaps all—*is* the problem. Ecosystems might be able to handle the industrial impact of one billion people, but certainly not eight billion. The first number took 200,000 thousand years to reach; the second, 200, thanks to the most dramatic and successful revolution of them all, unleashed between 1780 and 1830: the Industrial Revolution.

Today, as well, *no* revolution will bring about the changes necessary to stop global warming, even if the world slammed on the brakes, because the damage has already been done: scientific estimates for the length of time it takes for the effects of CO2 production to manifest range from 10 years to centuries; added CO2 in the atmosphere can continue to affect climate for thousands of years; and dozens of positive feed-back loops have either already started, or are about to.

As well, we couldn't *afford* this revolution: Where would the hundreds of *trillions* of dollars that would be needed to even make the sincere attempt come from?

And, finally, no plan has been presented or is in place for a radically new and different way to live, *anyway*!

Personally, I'm the most pessimistic of people. I think we don't stand a chance. We're not just toast: we're burnt toast. However, although fixing the world may be hopeless, we are not helpless. There is a tried and tested way to live a radically different way.

There was a revolution that has so far not been touched on within these pages, one that I have been a part of, and observing, for 52 years.

The so-called hippy revolution, synonymous with the psychedelic revolution, in one sense has followed the same course as most other revolutions—it seemed to come and go, supposedly ended, in this case, by the announced "death of hippy"—media-manufactured by a controlled press, made up out of the whole cloth of Hell's Angels and Rolling Stones. But in many senses, it never went away. The dominant culture was infused—partly by the teeny-bopper second wave that dropped back in—by color and psychedelics; by children's festivals and folk festivals; by healthy foods and yoga; by free children and free thought; and by other sparks of light uncountable.

It never went away in another sense. The "old originals," the first hippy wave, settled down everywhere, and are mostly still around, because the hippy revolution spawned, and was inspired by, what I consider to be the most important, profound, and timeless teaching of the sixties: "Turn on, tune in, drop out." A revolution with this at its core, along with the mandate to "create your own reality," to "do your own thing" as long as that doesn't hurt someone else—"bum someone out"—and, of course, "love and peace" at least holds a better chance of succeeding than any revolution fueled by anger and violence, and demanding that *others* should change.

Most immediately, Timothy Leary, with this phrase, was reflecting, and putting words to, what was already beginning to happen: a personal, political and public withdrawal of support for, and participation in, the institutions of the dominate culture—a rejection of church and state; school, factory, and office; legal marriage; corrupt cops enforcing crazy laws; wasting our power by getting and spending—the listings of the ship jumped goes on.

To live this revolution—to demonstrate and be the changes one wishes to see, to embrace principles and practices that hold to higher priorities than does consumer society and the military industrial complex, principles and practices which, when simply lived by, start to change the world, start to inspire others to begin solving those stresses of their lives brought on by participation in the mainstream by adopting simple, radical, alternative ways of living, and thus, almost incidentally, to begin to "build a new society within the shell of the old"—to live thise revolution may do neither more nor less than does overt campaigning and confronting, but it has the distinct advantage of allowing one to live a better life—one wished for the whole world—here and now, rather than spending our whole lives living without what we want while we meanwhile demand that others provide it for us.

Of course, it may be that the two approaches reinforce each other. I long thought that I had left three years of full-time demonstrating far behind when I morphed from a peace worker into a hippy, until, decades later, I articulated for myself my most important life goal: demonstrating permaculture, which I call hippy homesteading. Suddenly, I saw with wonder that they were the same word!

Dropping out also solved a major social embarrassment and ethical dilemma for me. No longer could my ideas so easily be challenged, belittled, and dismissed by the accusation that I was not practicing what I preached. I felt that there was less blood on my hands than full collusion and cooperation with capitalism's amorality and immorality brings. Nothing is perfect, but small is beautiful, and voluntary poverty possible without deprivation. It is much better to climb carefully down through the cracks now than to fall through them later. It is better to be prepared for worsening times than to be caught with one's pants down. I felt no greater sense of security than when I realized that my whole lifestyle was my survival kit.

There is a third sense in which this alternate culture revolution did not go away: generation after generation has continued to be influenced by it, through parents and grandparents, through its history and legends, and through cannabis and psychedelics; and to live it, by seeing the dominant paradigm through eyes unpeeled.

* * *

In 1967, my third drop-out took me, with my wife and one-month-old daughter, up an inlet fifteen miles beyond roads and electricity, last dime flipped into the wake behind us.

Within a short time, we had built a simple sauna—of plastic, blankets, sleeping bags, and cedar boughs—at the mouth of the creek, just in behind the trees; made a little dam of rocks to back up some water into a little pool; and put an after-sauna bathtub out in the open a few feet onto the estuary, above the high tide mark, warming the water with a little fire underneath. I vividly remember one time in the tub, warm and languid, dusk deepening, the line of dark blue hills and higher ridges drawn through a Venus sky, dead calm water showing double, the photo-moment utter breath-held peace made sudden movie by silent glide and pterodactyl croak of cousin heron—and, anchored in our little bay, across the way, a yacht, peaceful too: the privileged, on vacation. Yet here *we* were—*washed* hippies, thank you very much!—poor as crash-pad mice, living in this idyllic place all year 'round. The enormity of it swept through me almost like a rush of fear—that I might wake from dream or delusion, be busted for possession of forbidden magic secrets. The moment was a heady realization and a powerful confirmation that we really must have embraced some significant formulas to be able to live simply in "beautiful British Columbia." We were actually doing it, actually living the dream.

Before my move out of the city I had had a romantic vision of what our family lifestyle would look like. All during those years in our Garden of Eden it felt as though I was living in the midst of that romantic vision.

My daughter describes those first ten years of her life as "utopian." My grand-daughter described my current, [deleted] rustic lifestyle as "paradise."

We left the inlet in 1978, but I brought the lifestyle with me, into the city and into the country, and have been living it ever since.

So take heart, dear reader, and radical change artists everywhere. Despite all appearances, maybe a revolution *is* possible, after all!

Spread the word!

Peter Light
Roberts Creek, B.C., Canada
December, 2018

August Heinrich Brass

August Heinrich Brass (1818 to 1876) was born in Berlin, the son of a court councilor who had been an "educated, high-ranking military officer" in Germany's 1813 war with France and Napoleon. He attended the *Friedrichsstädter Gymnasium*—a high school of the old type that was the normal type in those days; kids attended it starting at age ten, and were taught Latin (for 9 years) in addition to Classic Greek (for 6 years), reading the old Classical authors from Greek antiquity—Herodotus, Xenophon, Plato respectively Socrates, Euripides, Aeschylus, Sophocles, etc., and many Latin authors (typically, Caesar, Sallust, Virgil, Ovid, Catullus, and others) in the original. He went on to study philosophy and history at the Friedrich Wilhelm University in Berlin, where the influence of Hegel was still strong, and obtained a doctoral degree. As a student, he was probably influenced by the "Young Hegelians" and may have joined the "Doktorsclub." If so, this is where he probably met Marx, who encountered him again in September 1848 when he came to Berlin to talk with a number of revolutionaries, after having been in Vienna and Dresden for the same purpose

August Brass was married twice, and had ten children, one in Switzerland, nine in Berlin.

Some of Brass's contemporaries were Friedrich Engels, Johann Wolfgang von Goethe, Ludwig van Beethoven, Niccolò Paganini, Felix Mendelssohn, Robert Schumann, Richard Wagner, Johannes Brahms, and—as indicated already—Karl Marx, the latter born the same year as Brass, and who became a personal friend.

Brass was a German "man of letters," known variously as a Liberal, Socialist, socio-political activist, "red democrat," "bourgeois democrat," "red republican," "old revolutionary," "freelance journalist," "publisher," "publicist," and, late in life, also as a "Gutsbesitzer" (owner of a large agricultural estate). He was the author of historical novels and biographies, mysteries, histories, and political songs and tracts, both before and after the March Revolution. He was the founder and editor-in chief of four newspapers, two in Switzerland, the *"Neue Schweizer Zeitung"* and the *"Grenzpost,"* and two in Germany, the *"Norddeutsche Allgemeine Zeitung"* (1862) and *"Die Post"* (1871).

As a convinced democrat, he actively participated in the March Revolution of 1848 in Berlin, fighting on March 18 and 19 on the barricade at Alexander Square (Alexanderplatz). A monument there honours the successful resistance against the government troops under the command of Johann Carl von Möllendorff by the leaders at two barricades at that location: "the *Landwehrmann* (i.e., member of the territorial army) August Brass and the veterinarian Friedrich

Ludwig Urban," who were in command of revolutionaries manning different barricades at the heavily contested square.

Having already played this active and significant role in the 1848 March Revolution in Berlin, Brass became a soldier in the *Badische Volksheer* (Baden Peoples Army), and an active participant in the final revolutionary struggle, in Baden in 1849, fighting against the anti-revolutionary forces during the so-called imperial constitutional campaign, after which, along with many others, he was forced to flee to Switzerland to avoid execution or a long prison sentence. In 1861, as part of a general amnesty, he returned to Berlin, where he bought or founded (it is not clear which) the democratically-minded *Norddeutsche Allgemeine Zeitung*.

With bribes, and assurances that Brass would be free to publish socialist articles and commentary daily, Bismarck ensured that this *"North German General Newspaper"* would increasingly report government policy, and Brass gradually began to change the political direction of the paper, supporting more and more Bismarck's interests. The socialist colleagues he had hired quit the paper, and Brass, too, eventually proved too self-willed to follow all of Bismarck's instructions. It came to a break. In 1871 he sold the paper and started his own, the independent *Die Post*. With the money from the sale, he bought property and lived at Lake Wochowsee, where he died at 1:45 a.m. on December 8, 1876.

History, in the end, may have judged Brass too harshly, by condemning him for a flawed judgment call and a poor decision; and by neglecting to acknowledge the details of his rupture with Bismarck, and his founding of an independent newspaper. But his downfall may have been sealed by the duplicitous wiles of Bismarck, the old revolutionary's personal hubris, and the disapprobation of his former left-wing colleagues. This notwithstanding, he leaves behind a remarkable record of accomplishments.

- Peter Light

For the democratic tradition and revolutionary spirit

1848 March Revolution 1998

Here on the Alexanderplatz the barricades' defenders under the militiaman August Brass and the veterinarian Friedrich Ludwig Urban successfully fought and stood their ground from March 18th to 19th against the forces of General Johann Karl von Möllendorff.

Despite everything, it will come to pass that all about, man shall extend the hand of brotherhood to mankind, despite everything.

Ferdinand Freiligrath (1843), after Robert Burns (1795)

Also available from Black Rose Books

THE FORGOTTEN REVOLUTION
THE 1919 HUNGARIAN REPUBLIC OF COUNCILS
Edited by András B. Göllner

Paper ISBN: 978-1-55164-715-9
Cloth ISBN: 978-1-55164-717-3
Ebook ISBN: 978-1-55164-719-1

Also available from Black Rose Books

Paper ISBN: 978-1-55164-645-9
Cloth ISBN: 978-1-55164-647-3
Ebook ISBN: 978-1-55164-649-7

Also available from Black Rose Books

1917
Revolution in Russia and its Aftermath

GOLDMAN
BERKMAN
BOOKCHIN
METT

Paper ISBN: 978-1-55164-662-6
Cloth ISBN: 978-1-55164-664-0
Ebook ISBN: 978-1-55164-666-4

Also available from Black Rose Books

Cloth ISBN: 978-1-55164-213-0
Paper ISBN: 978-1-55164-612-3

www.ingramcontent.com/pod-product-compliance
Lightning Source LLC
Chambersburg PA
CBHW070307230426
43664CB00015B/2660